TODAY'S TOP HOME DESIGNS

325 New House Plans

Updated Classics for Today's Homeowner

FOR 2007

325 New House Plans for 2007

Published by Hanley Wood
One Thomas Circle, NW, Suite 600
Washington, DC 20005

Distribution Center
PBD
Hanley Wood Consumer Group
3280 Summit Ridge Parkway
Duluth, Georgia 30096

Vice President, Home Plans, Andrew Schultz
Associate Publisher, Editorial Development, Jennifer Pearce
Managing Editor, Hannah McCann
Editor, Simon Hyoun
Assistant Editor, Kimberly Johnson
Publications Manager, Brian Haefs
Production Manager, Melissa Curry
Director, Plans Marketing, Mark Wilkin
Senior Plan Merchandiser, Nicole Phipps
Plan Merchandiser, Hillary Huff
Graphic Artist, Joong Min
Plan Data Team Leader, Susan Jasmin
Marketing Director, Holly Miller
Marketing Manager, Brett Bryant

Most Hanley Wood titles are available at quantity discounts with bulk purchases for educational, business, or sales promotional use. For information, please contact Andrew Schultz at aschultz@hanleywood.com.

VC Graphics, Inc.
Creative Director, Veronica Vannoy
Graphic Designer, Jennifer Gerstein
Graphic Designer, Denise Reiffenstein

Photo Credits
Front Cover Main: Design HPK2600017 by Alan Mascord.
For details, see page 26. Photo by Bob Greenspan.

Front Cover Inset Left: Design HPK2600324 by Studer Residential Design.
For details, see page 244. Photo by Ron Kolb, Exposures Unlimited;
digital editing by Joseph Bove, Cincinnati Aerial Photography.

Front Cover Inset Right: Design HPK2600249 by Sater Design Collection.
For details, see page 191. Photo by Kim Sargent.

Back Cover: Design HPK2600022 by Larry E. Belk Designs.
For details, see page 31. Photo by Larry E. Belk Designs.

Back Cover Inset: Design HPK2600021 by Alan Mascord.
For details, see page 30. Photo by Bob Greenspan.

10 9 8 7 6 5 4 3 2 1

All floor plans and elevations copyright by the individual designers and may not be reproduced by any means without permission. All text, designs, and illustrative material copyright ©2006 by Home Planners, LLC, wholly owned by Hanley Wood, LLC. All rights reserved. No part of this publication may be reproduced in any form or by any means — electronic, mechanical, photomechanical, recorded, or otherwise — without the prior written permission of the publisher.

Printed in the United States of America

Library of Congress Control Number: 2006925827

ISBN-13: 978-1-931131-65-0
ISBN-10: 1-931131-65-1

325 New House Plans for 2007

- **4** INTRODUCTION
- **8** NATURE'S THEME
- **12** EDITOR'S PICKS
- **33** CRAFTSMAN & RANCH HOMES
- **84** COUNTRY HOMES
- **131** COLONIAL HOMES
- **166** EUROPEAN & MEDITERRANEAN HOMES
- **211** NEW AMERICAN HOMES
- **248** HOW TO ORDER
- **WEB** www.hanleywoodbooks.com/newhouseplans2007

For access to bonus home plans, articles, online ordering, and more.

Introduction

The Total Package

New designs emphasize a home's inner and outer beauty

What do you see when you imagine your ideal home? Is it a robust stone castle or a tall brick beauty? Do you venture inside to find soaring two-story ceilings with exposed beams and trusses or do low-pitched rooflines bring a cozy sense of comfort? Likely, every room is clean and ready to accept company, with a place for everything and everything in its place. This dream home—the blend of an attractive exterior with a functional interior—is possible, and it's what the designers featured in *325 New House Plans for 2007* achieved. These house plans have exquisite interiors and exteriors, innovative use of design and materials, and the latest trends and amenities.

INSIDE

Elaborate baths are standard with the master suites of high-end homes, but they're no longer reserved for the upscale lifestyle. Designers have found ways to bring that extra luxury to mid-sized and smaller homes, too, with standing showers, garden tubs, double vanities, and separate water closets. Nearly every master suite also includes at least one walk-in closet, or perhaps it's warmed by fireplace; and now convenience takes priority with master-suite laundry rooms and built-in ironing boards in the wardrobes. With so many amenities, you don't need a lot of square footage to live in your very own mansion.

Don't think that the master suite gets all the attention; specialty rooms (namely, game and media rooms) make frequent appearances. These rooms are designed to hold the family brood for cartoon-watching or the guys on football Sundays, reserving family and great rooms for more quiet and intimate gatherings. Include a built-in entertainment center to house electronic equipment and DVDs,

This home attractively combines brick, shingles, and white-painted timbers for excellent curb appeal. Order plan HPK2600206 on page 163.

ORDER BLUEPRINTS 24 HOURS, 7 DAYS A WEEK, AT 1-800-521-6797 OR EPLANS.COM

or convert the space to a saloon, complete with wet bar and pool table. There are possibilities in every price range for these increasingly popular spaces.

AND OUT
Some of the most exciting rooms of these houses aren't inside—they're out. Outdoor living spaces have quickly become some of the most utilized areas, akin to a second family room. Designers took note of this growing trend and included an abundance of porches, decks, and patios on their brand new plans, ready to accommodate any occasion. More than just spots with a good view, these extensions of the home can be equipped with the ultimate comforts: roofs, screens, fireplaces, bars, built-in grills, even televisions and sound systems, just to name a few.

While amenities and appliances can make a house fun and functional, building materials can make it look bold and beautiful. Having trouble deciding between the look of brick and the affordability of siding? Why not have a little of both? A continuing trend, seen often in this plan selection, blends materials to achieve the desired result in cost and visual appeal. Mix stucco with timber, shingle with stone, brick with siding, or creatively combine any other pairing of materials to make your house into a dream home.

Above: A walk-in shower hides behind the center wall against the center whirlpool tub. HPK2600007 is an Editor's Pick on page 16.

Right: Grand master suites put everything at your fingertips. The bedroom of HPK2600325 on page 245 has a breakfast/coffee bar and entertainment center, and includes a large bath, several walk-in closets, and a laundry room conveniently nearby.

Make a finished basement your entertainment hub like HPK2600271, with a full bar, fireplace, and media center. For more information, turn to page 208.

Glass and stone accents throughout this home bring continuity, flow, and artistic interest to a contemporary design

Nature's Theme

The kitchen island separates the workspace from the great room and includes a stovetop, sink, and snack bar. Its orientation in the room makes for easy interaction between cook and guests.

Square pillars supporting the entryway introduce the stone used for the home's interior columns, walls, and three fireplaces.

This home encompasses everything this book has to offer in new home design. The contemporary hillside plan combines stone and wood siding for an exterior that adds style to its appearance. Glass and stone themes draw the interior and exterior together, with window walls encompassing much of the home and decorative stone pillars in the common rooms mimicking the structural stone of the entryway. The foyer incorporates these columns with a bench and a niche. This home has an open stairway beside a wall of muntin picture windows that leads to the lower level, but a similar home on page 30 embraces single-story living. An artistic glass floor characterizes the overlook.

The rooms are as comfortable as they are stylish. A wet bar connects the vaulted dining room to the professional-style kitchen and nearby walk-in pantry. An adjoining vaulted nook provides sliding doors to a rear deck, adding to the many seamless connections between the home and the outdoors. Step down into the vaulted, sunken great room that opens to the patio and outdoor kitchen, complete with built-in grill and fireplace; this comfortable outdoor space is ideal for entertaining. Nearby, the master suite stays in stride with 2007 trends by including such comforts as a double vanity, compartmented toilet, garden tub, walk-in shower, and two large walk-in closets (one with a washer and dryer). Downstairs there are three family bedrooms, a game room with a built-in entertainment center, another laundry room, and a snack bar. The lower-level patio is accessible from the left-side family bedroom or the game room.

A vaulted niche with picture windows provides the perfect alcove for the master bath garden tub.

Above: The rear deck houses a summer kitchen equipped with a grill, hearth, and comfortable seating. For more incredible outdoor spaces, see "European & Mediterranean Homes" on page 166.

Right: Light streams down into the game room through the glass floor overhead. Windows near the stairs and along the patio keep this lower-level room well lit.

A partial wall with shelf and inset mirror divides the master bedroom from the bath. Amenities include a fireplace, access to the upper patio, a garden tub, and His and Hers walk-in closets.

A mural on a wall in the right corner bedroom creates a fun environment for a child's play-room.

Plan:
HPK2600002

Style:
PRAIRIE

Main Level:
2,624 SQ. FT.

Lower Level:
1,976 SQ. FT.

Total:
4,600 SQ. FT.

Bedrooms:
4

Bathrooms:
3 1/2

Width:
76' - 6"

Depth:
65' - 0"

Foundation:
FINISHED WALKOUT BASEMENT

Main Level

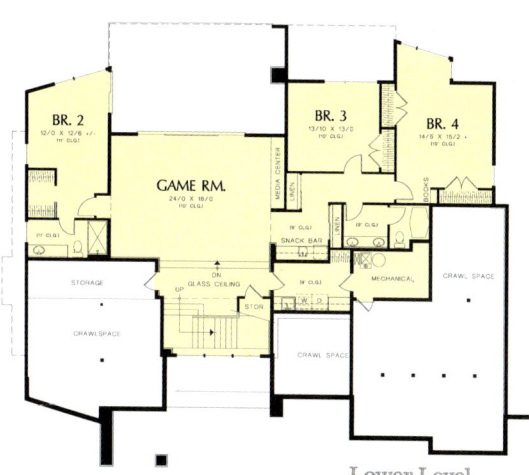

Lower Level

ORDER BLUEPRINTS 24 HOURS, 7 DAYS A WEEK, AT 1-800-521-6797 OR EPLANS.COM

325 New House Plans — Editor's Picks

Plan:
HPK2600003

Style:
COUNTRY

Square Footage:
1,752

Bedrooms:
3

Bathrooms:
2

Width:
64' - 0"

Depth:
45' - 10"

Foundation:
SLAB

Behold this classic traditional with a European touch. A vaulted ceiling in the master bedroom and a tray ceiling in the great room creates the illusion of additonal space in each area. The open floor plan features a split bedroom arrangement. A porch in the rear means summer grilling is just steps away. Don't miss the raised island bar in the kitchen, great for casual meals.

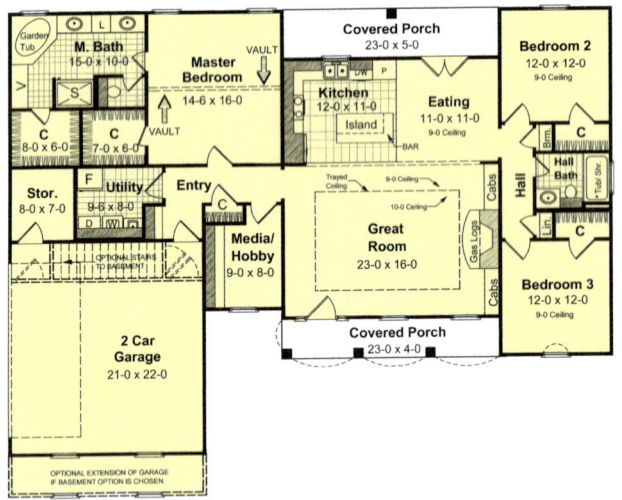

ORDER BLUEPRINTS 24 HOURS, 7 DAYS A WEEK, AT 1-800-521-6797 OR EPLANS.COM

Editor's Picks

© William E Poole Designs, Inc.

Plan:
HPK2600004

Style:
FARMHOUSE

Square Footage:
1,942

Bonus Space:
1,040 SQ. FT.

Bedrooms:
3

Bathrooms:
2 1/2

Width:
64' - 10"

Depth:
58' - 2"

Foundation:
CRAWLSPACE, UNFINISHED BASEMENT

Welcome to the perfect starter home: one you'll never want to leave. Classical elements lend an air of formality so you'll always feel comfortable welcoming visitors to this tidy cottage; a wealth of bonus space on the second floor invites expansion as your family grows and matures. All the basic elements are here: a formal dining room, a spacious great room, an open kitchen and nook, and a master suite with all the amenities. Elegant touches include paired columns supporting a pedimented porch roof, oculus windows in the great room and master suite, and a built-in bookcase beside the great room's fireplace. Two family bedrooms share a full bath on the first floor, but there is room for more upstairs; or, if you prefer, you can transform your extra space into a home office, an exercise room, or a game room.

ORDER BLUEPRINTS 24 HOURS, 7 DAYS A WEEK, AT 1-800-521-6797 OR EPLANS.COM

325 New House Plans — Editor's Picks

Plan:
HPK2600005

Style:
CRAFTSMAN

Square Footage:
2,019

Bedrooms:
3

Bathrooms:
2

Width:
57' - 0"

Depth:
65' - 8"

© 2004 Donald A. Gardner, Inc.

Stone and siding join a hipped roof and gables to give this home a European ambiance. A single dormer highlights the courtyard-entry garage, and the dramatic entry features columns, an arch, and circle-head transom. Double-doors lead from the foyer into the study/bedroom, which features a second entrance near the bonus room stairs. Built-in cabinetry flanks the fireplace, while columns and a tray ceiling define the dining room.

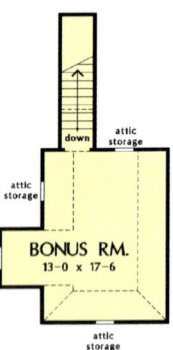

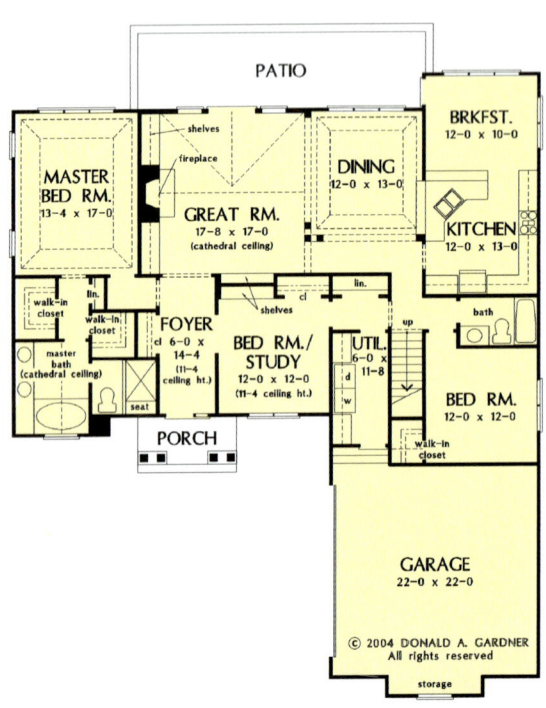

ORDER BLUEPRINTS 24 HOURS, 7 DAYS A WEEK, AT 1-800-521-6797 OR EPLANS.COM

Editor's Picks

325 New House Plans

Plan
HPK2600006

Style:
COTTAGE
First Floor:
1,305 SQ. FT.
Second Floor:
1,116 SQ. FT.
Total:
2,421 SQ. FT.
Bedrooms:
4
Bathrooms:
2 ½
Width:
62' - 0"
Depth:
45' - 0"
Foundation:
UNFINISHED BASEMENT

A blend of Traditional and European influences present an appealing exterior for this two-story home. Inside, the floor plan centers around the spacious great room and flows to the adjoining common areas. The enclosed den doubles as a secluded home office space. Upstairs, the second-floor master suite boasts great views of the backyard and beyond. Three additional family bedrooms share a hall bath.

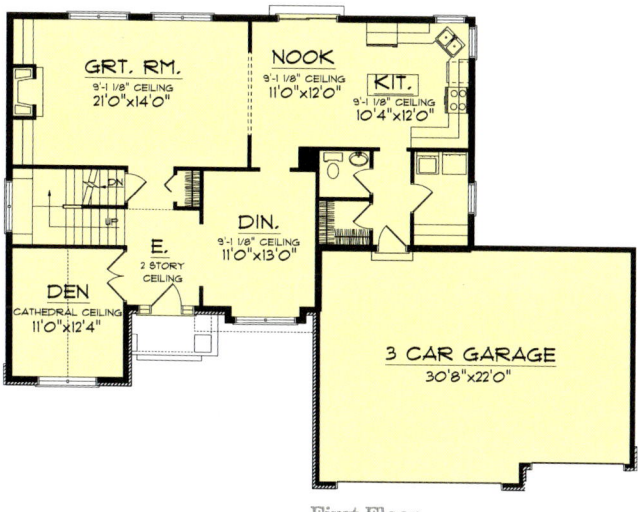

First Floor

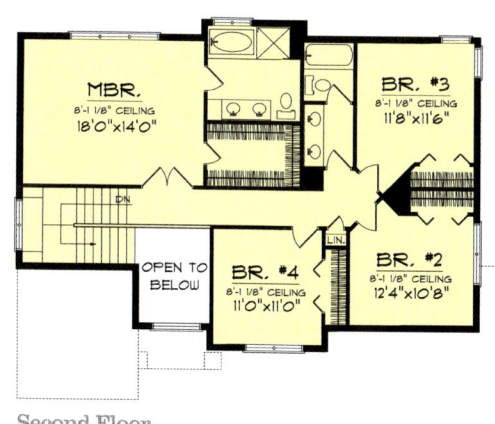

Second Floor

ORDER BLUEPRINTS 24 HOURS, 7 DAYS A WEEK, AT 1-800-521-6797 OR EPLANS.COM

325 New House Plans
Editor's Picks

Plan:
HPK2600007

Style:
FARMHOUSE

Square Footage:
3,553

Bedrooms:
3

Bathrooms:
3 1/2

Width:
75' - 0"

Depth:
111' - 4"

Foundation:
SLAB

A stately cupola atop the entry portico keeps watch over the sprawling lawn and colorful gardens of the front elevation, while creating a lofty focal point for the facade of this Revival-style home. Formal yet friendly, the lovely living room offers a warm welcome to those who enter. A trio of floor-to-ceiling glass invites the outdoors in, treating guests to scenic panoramas of the exterior landscape. After dark, the covered lanai glows and glitters, reflected lights dancing on the surface of the tranquil turquoise pool. The leisure room, breakfast nook, and gourmet kitchen flow into one another, creating an expansive family area that is both fashionable and functional. The fabulous gourmet kitchen is a chef's dream; everything comes in pairs such as double ovens, double sinks, double center island counters, and double windows. A starry sky appears through the bay windows of the formal dining room, serving dinner guests a breathtaking view along with their dinner. A master foyer connects the suite to spacious "His" and "Her" walk-in closets and then to a lavish master bath. Double doors open from the master suite onto a breezy lanai.

Photo by: CJ Walker.
This home, as shown in photographs, may differ from the actual blueprints.
For more detailed information, please check the floor plans carefully.

ORDER BLUEPRINTS 24 HOURS, 7 DAYS A WEEK, AT 1-800-521-6797 OR EPLANS.COM

Editor's Picks

325
New House Plans

Plan:
HPK2600008

Style:
NEW AMERICAN

First Floor:
1,349 SQ. FT.

Second Floor:
1,368 SQ. FT.

Total:
2,717 SQ. FT.

Bedrooms:
5

Bathrooms:
3

Width:
51' - 0"

Depth:
45' - 0"

Foundation:
CRAWLSPACE, SLAB, UNFINISHED WALKOUT BASEMENT

Here is the perfect home for a family that seeks both a traditional layout and the openness of modern design. The foyer is flanked by formal living and dining rooms, but its two-story height prevents it from feeling enclosed. It leads to a similarly lofty family room, whose grand fireplace will likely become the focal point of family gatherings. An informal breakfast room adjoins an up-to-date island kitchen. The first floor includes an additional room with a closet and nearby full bath, perfect for a guest suite, study, or exercise room. The master bedroom and bath are upstairs, conveniently adjacent to the laundry room. Three family bedrooms share a bath.

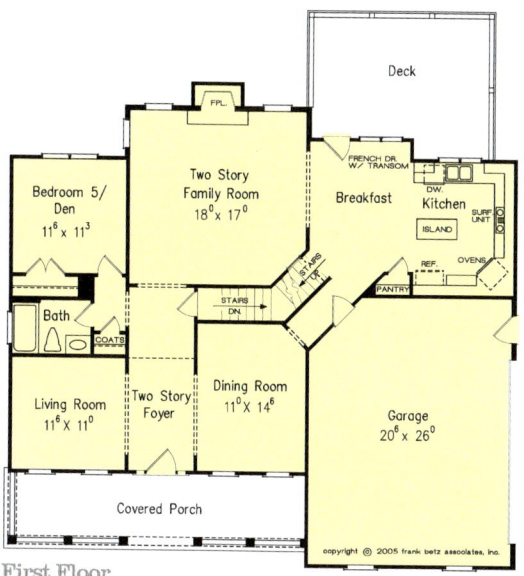

First Floor

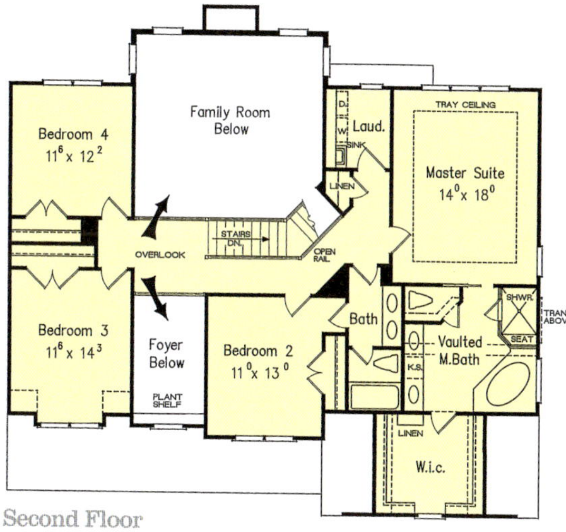

Second Floor

ORDER BLUEPRINTS 24 HOURS, 7 DAYS A WEEK, AT 1-800-521-6797 OR EPLANS.COM   17

325 New House Plans

Editor's Picks

Plan:
HPK2600009

Style:
FRENCH COUNTRY

First Floor:
2,084 SQ. FT.

Second Floor:
671 SQ. FT.

Total:
2,755 SQ. FT.

Bedrooms:
4

Bathrooms:
3

Width:
57' - 4"

Depth:
55' - 10"

Foundation:
CRAWLSPACE, SLAB

A creative blend of exterior materials gives this home a stunning facade. The generous great room will provide the perfect setting for family gatherings. Preparing and serving meals will be a breeze in this kitchen with adjoining breakfast and dining rooms. A spacious grilling porch also lends outdoor options. The master suite is nestled in the rear of this home on the main level. A trip to the upper floor offers beautiful balcony views of the great room and the foyer, as well as two more bedrooms and a media room option.

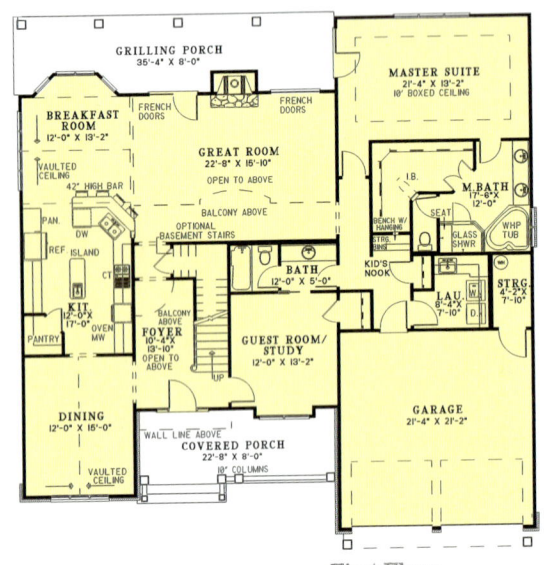

First Floor

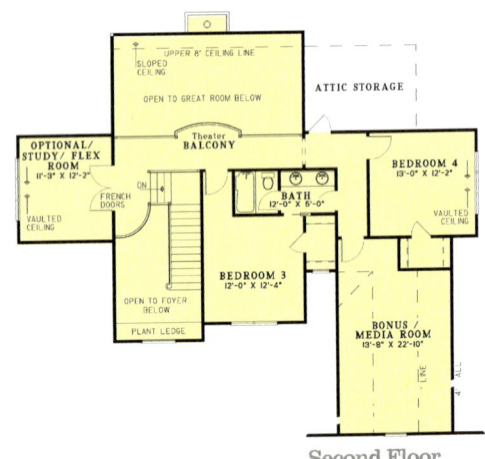

Second Floor

18 ORDER BLUEPRINTS 24 HOURS, 7 DAYS A WEEK, AT 1-800-521-6797 OR EPLANS.COM

Editor's Picks

325 New House Plans

Plan:
HPK2600010

Style:
FRENCH COUNTRY

Square Footage:
2,758

Bedrooms:
4

Bathrooms:
3 ½

Width:
66' - 4"

Depth:
57' - 8"

Foundation:
UNFINISHED BASEMENT

The combination of brick, stone, shakes and a covered porch showcase this home in a spectacular fashion. The luxurious master suite features a sitting area with raised ceiling, and a bath with double bowl vanity, whirlpool tub, and shower enclosure. A wood burning fireplace and a view to the rear yard decorate the great room. Informal dining can be enjoyed in the spacious breakfast area and a formal dining room provides space for special occasions. Angled stairs lead to the second floor where three additional bedrooms, each with private bath access, complete this wonderful family-friendly home.

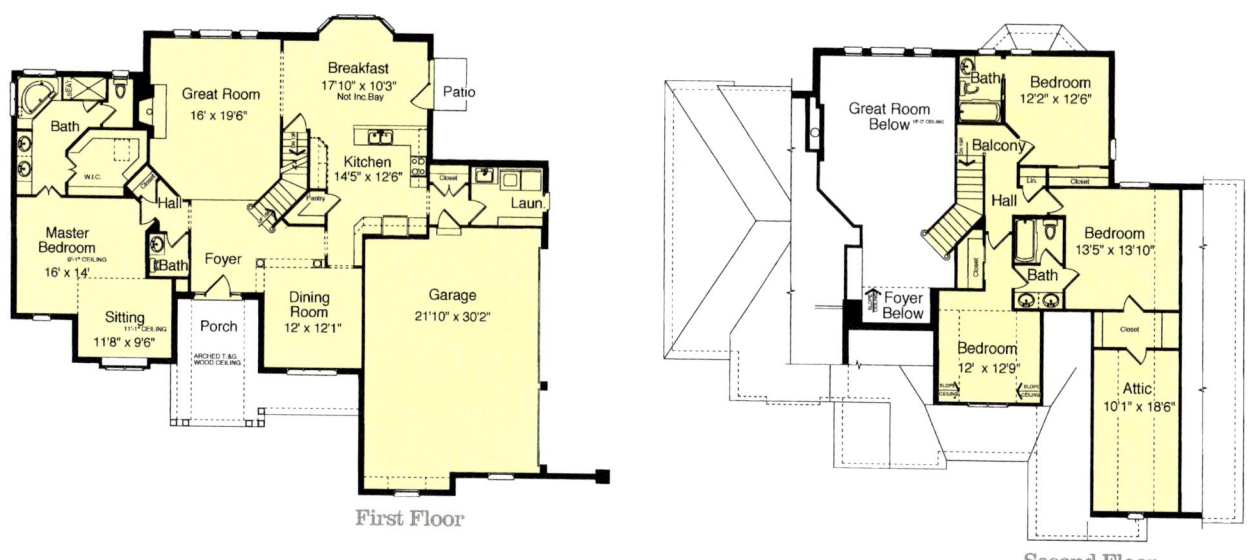

ORDER BLUEPRINTS 24 HOURS, 7 DAYS A WEEK, AT 1-800-521-6797 OR EPLANS.COM

325 New House Plans
Editor's Picks

Plan:
HPK2600011

Style:
COTTAGE

First Floor:
2,399 SQ. FT.

Second Floor:
726 SQ. FT.

Total:
3,125 SQ. FT.

Bonus Space:
425 SQ. FT.

Bedrooms:
4

Bathrooms:
4

Width:
58' - 4"

Depth:
72' - 0"

Foundation:
CRAWLSPACE, UNFINISHED WALKOUT BASEMENT

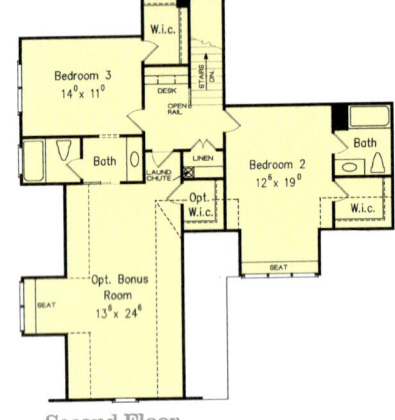
Second Floor

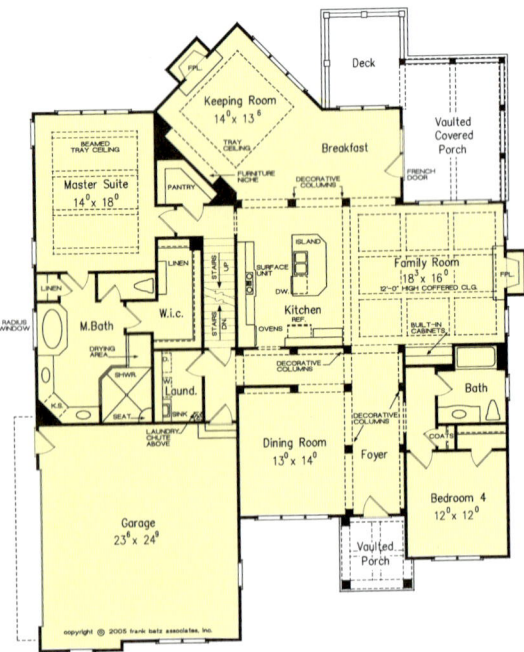
First Floor

A white picket gate that opens to a home of brick, siding, and shingles—it doesn't get more American than that! This design borrows from the best-loved traditions, along with today's modern trends, and forms them into a wonderful family home. Coffered and vaulted ceilings throughout add architectural interest while the open layout maintains a fresh, airy, sunlit environment. Fireplaces in the family room and keeping room keep the first floor cozy; a master bath with corner shower, garden tub, and walk-in closet keeps homeowners happy. Upstairs, an optional bonus room will make a perfect game or rec room, and each of the two bedrooms has its own full bath and walk-in closet.

20   ORDER BLUEPRINTS 24 HOURS, 7 DAYS A WEEK, AT 1-800-521-6797 OR EPLANS.COM

Editor's Picks

325 New House Plans

Plan:
HPK2600012

Style:
CRAFTSMAN
First Floor:
2,063 SQ. FT.
Second Floor:
1,170 SQ. FT.
Total:
3,233 SQ. FT.
Bonus Space:
370 SQ. FT.
Bedrooms:
3
Bathrooms:
3 1/2
Width:
40' - 0"
Depth:
63' - 0"
Foundation:
UNFINISHED WALKOUT BASEMENT

This Craftsman is at home in any location. Notice how the contrasting light and dark tones blend with the surroundings, while vertical siding and columns create height. The entry leads to the great room, with the dining room on the right and stairs on the left. Counters and cabinets border the kitchen walls and surround the working island. A pass-through divides the adjacent keeping room, which—along with the great room—accesses the deck with fireplace and built-in grill. The master suite offers its own deck access and amenities: the bath includes twin vanity sinks and separate shower and spa tub, the walk-in closet stores clothes for every season. Venture upstairs from the foyer, where each of two bedrooms directly accesses a full bath; one shares with the study. Go downstairs near the laundry room, cross the breezeway, and use the exterior stairs to reach the private suite above the garage.

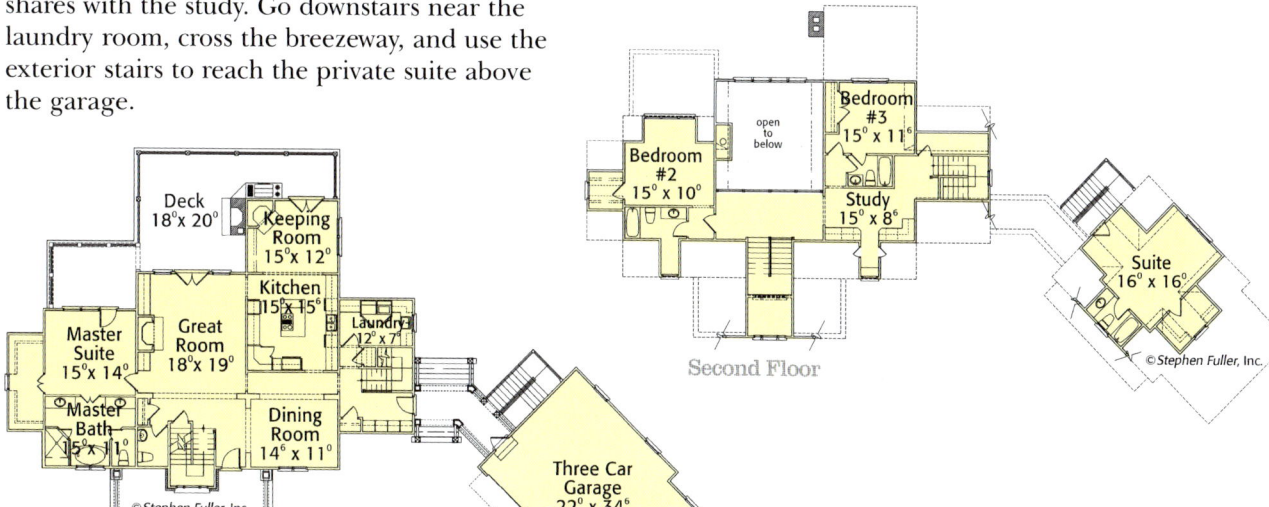

ORDER BLUEPRINTS 24 HOURS, 7 DAYS A WEEK, AT 1-800-521-6797 OR EPLANS.COM

325 New House Plans

Editor's Picks

Plan:
HPK2600013

Style:
FRENCH COUNTRY

Square Footage:
3,385

Bedrooms:
4

Bathrooms:
3 ½

Width:
66' - 4"

Depth:
54' - 0"

Foundation:
UNFINISHED WALKOUT BASEMENT

This spectacular home showcases exterior features such as brick, stone, cedar shakes, multiple gables, and a covered porch. An equally exciting interior with formal and informal spaces creates a luxurious showplace. The master suite enjoys a sitting area with 11-foot ceilings and a bath with double bowl vanity and whirlpool tub. Two gas fireplaces warm the entertainment areas and the kitchen offers a counter with seating and a large bay window by the breakfast area. The hearth room provides a quiet, cozy space for family relaxation. Three additional bedrooms, each with private access to a bath and large closets and a multipurpose bonus room, complete this magnificent home.

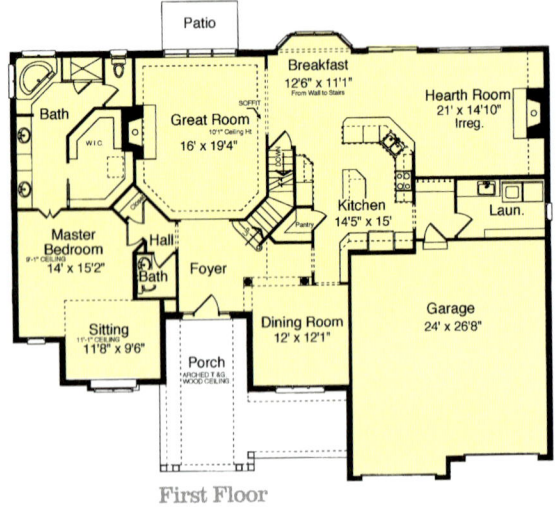

First Floor

Second Floor

ORDER BLUEPRINTS 24 HOURS, 7 DAYS A WEEK, AT 1-800-521-6797 OR EPLANS.COM

Editor's Picks

325 New House Plans

Plan:
HPK2600014

Style:
COUNTRY
First Floor:
1,737 SQ. FT.
Second Floor:
1,837 SQ. FT.
Total:
3,574 SQ. FT.
Bedrooms:
5
Bathrooms:
4
Width:
55' - 0"
Depth:
50' - 6"
Foundation:
CRAWLSPACE, UNFINISHED WALKOUT BASEMENT

Greet friends from the porch of this traditional beauty, then step through the two-story foyer into a large family room with coffered ceiling and fireplace, perfect for entertaining. The left side of this plan is filled with amenities and perfect spots to retreat. The central kitchen with serving bar is surrounded by a keeping room, breakfast nook, computer area, laundry room, and dining room. Step onto the screened porch for some fresh air, or get a better view of the yard from the rear deck. In addition to one bedroom on the first floor, four bedrooms reside upstairs and all have walk-in-closets. Relax in the lap of luxury with an expansive master suite complete with his and her closets and tray ceiling. An added bonus is a large children's retreat, perfect for playing on rainy days.

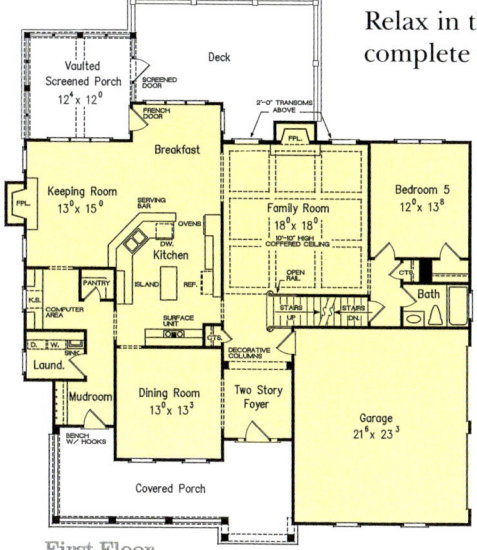

First Floor

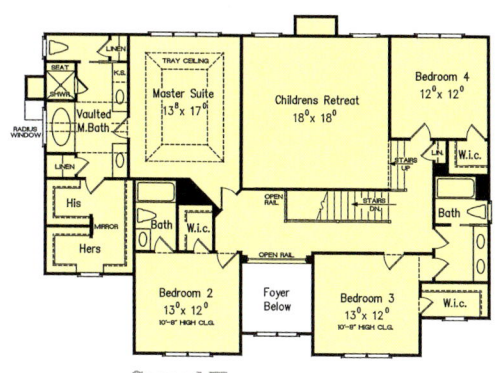

Second Floor

ORDER BLUEPRINTS 24 HOURS, 7 DAYS A WEEK, AT 1-800-521-6797 OR EPLANS.COM

325 New House Plans
Editor's Picks

Plan:
HPK2600015

Style:
CRAFTSMAN

First Floor:
2,745 SQ. FT.

Second Floor:
1,133 SQ. FT.

Total:
3,878 SQ. FT.

Bonus Space:
649 SQ. FT.

Bedrooms:
4

Bathrooms:
4 1/2

Width:
69' - 0"

Depth:
85' - 6"

Foundation:
CRAWLSPACE, UNFINISHED WALKOUT BASEMENT

Spacious, luxury living is the hallmark of this Craftsman home. The exterior is immediately appealing but the real treat awaits inside. A coffered ceiling in the family room adds an elegant touch. The bayed breakfast nook overlooks the rear deck, beckoning for outdoor meals. The master suite extends the entire length of the plan and features a private sitting room complete with deck access. The second floor houses three additional bedrooms, each with a full bath. An optional bonus room above the garage encourages future expansion.

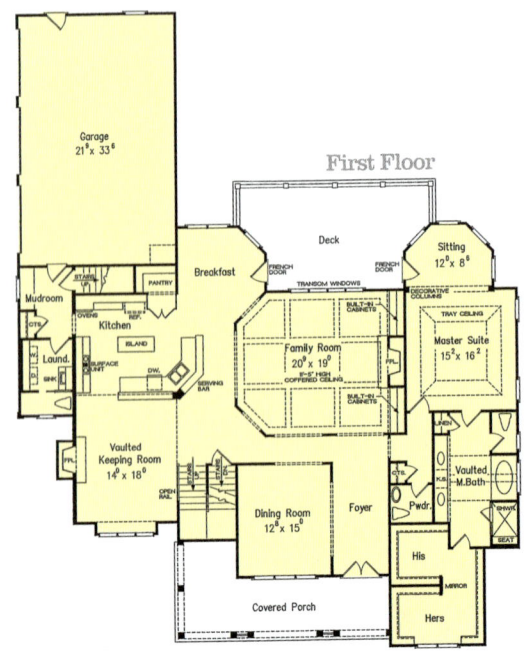
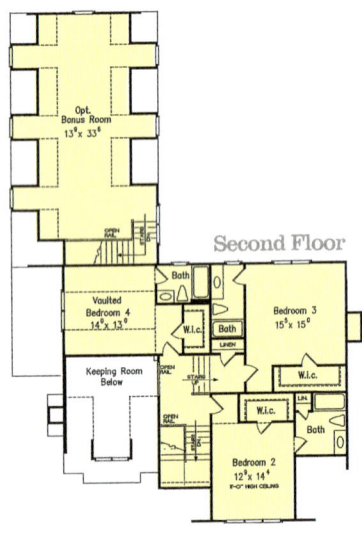

24 ORDER BLUEPRINTS 24 HOURS, 7 DAYS A WEEK, AT 1-800-521-6797 OR EPLANS.COM

Editor's Picks

325 New House Plans

Rear Exterior

Plan:
HPK2600016

Style:
CRAFTSMAN
Main Level:
2,487 SQ. FT.
Lower Level:
1,817 SQ. FT.
Total:
4,304 SQ. FT.
Bonus Space:
686 SQ. FT.
Bedrooms:
4
Bathrooms:
3 1/2
Width:
67' - 2"
Depth:
104' - 2"
Foundation:
FINISHED WALKOUT BASEMENT

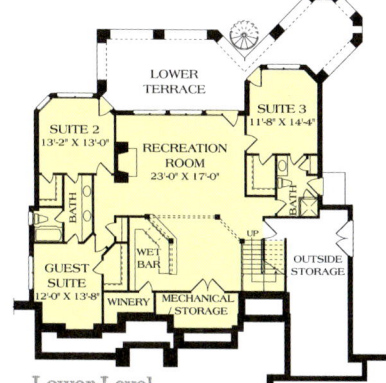

Main Level

Lower Level

Purely rustic with resplendent details, this Craftsman home welcomes with comfort and elegance. Wood shingles, stone accents, and a sizeable porch punctuate the exterior, while the interior awaits family living. The entire left side of the main level holds the master suite with tray ceilings and two walk-in closets. The family room has plenty of windows looking out toward the expansive covered deck and rear yard. The kitchen is open to a breakfast area and sunroom, which also accesses the deck. The lower level is ideal for both solemn retreat and lively entertaining. In addition to three bedrooms, a wet bar/winery, recreation room, and lower terrace complete the package.

Photo Courtesy of Living Concepts. This home, as shown in photographs, may differ from the actual blueprints. For more detailed information, please check the floor plans carefully.

ORDER BLUEPRINTS 24 HOURS, 7 DAYS A WEEK, AT 1-800-521-6797 OR EPLANS.COM

325 New House Plans
Editor's Picks

Plan:
HPK2600017

Style:
SHINGLE

First Floor:
3,800 SQ. FT.

Second Floor:
990 SQ. FT.

Total:
4,790 SQ. FT.

Bedrooms:
4

Bathrooms:
5 1/2

Width:
116' - 0"

Depth:
88' - 0"

Foundation:
CRAWLSPACE

Rear Exterior

First Floor

Second Floor

Entertaining is easy in this spacious four-bedroom home with an expansive U-shaped interior. From the foyer, an office with built-ins and a pass-through bar to the great room sits on the left; to the right is a formal dining room with a built-in hutch and a butler's pantry with wine closet. The kitchen includes counter space on three walls plus a center island with a sink and space for casual eating. The right wing consists of a four-bay garage, workshop area, and inset barbecue porch. In the opposite wing lies a guest room, pool bath, and master suite with His and Hers amenities. A convenient bonus is the pre-installed ironing board in the larger walk-in closet. Joining the home's two wings is the great room. Here, a built-in media center and access to the bar and the veranda make it an excellent room for entertaining or spending time with the family. Upstairs, two bedroom suites with built-in desks, walk-in closets, and private baths flank a flexible media/playroom area.

Photo by Bob Greenspan. This home, as shown in photographs, may differ from the actual blueprints. For more detailed information, please check the floor plans carefully.

Editor's Picks

325 New House Plans

Plan:
HPK2600018

Style:
FRENCH COUNTRY

Main Level:
3,012 SQ. FT.

Lower Level:
2,067 SQ. FT.

Total:
5,079 SQ. FT.

Bedrooms:
5

Bathrooms:
4 ½

Width:
88' - 0"

Depth:
77' - 4"

Foundation:
FINISHED WALKOUT BASEMENT

Impressive amenities delight in this lovely hillside home. Inventive room shapes add a contemporary feel. The kitchen boasts abundant counter space, an island snack bar, a walk-in pantry, and access to the rear covered deck. A fireplace in the master suite adds ambiance and warmth. The study is a potential home office or an ideal guest suite, complete with an adjacent full bath. On the lower level, enjoy the family room equipped with a wet bar for casual entertaining. The exercise room is an added bonus.

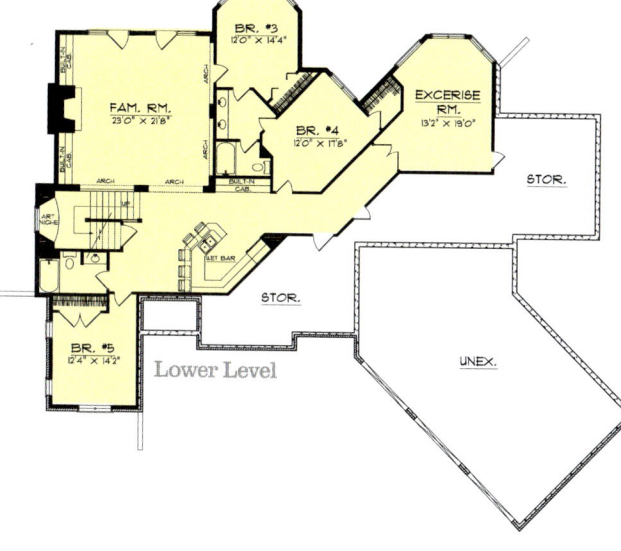

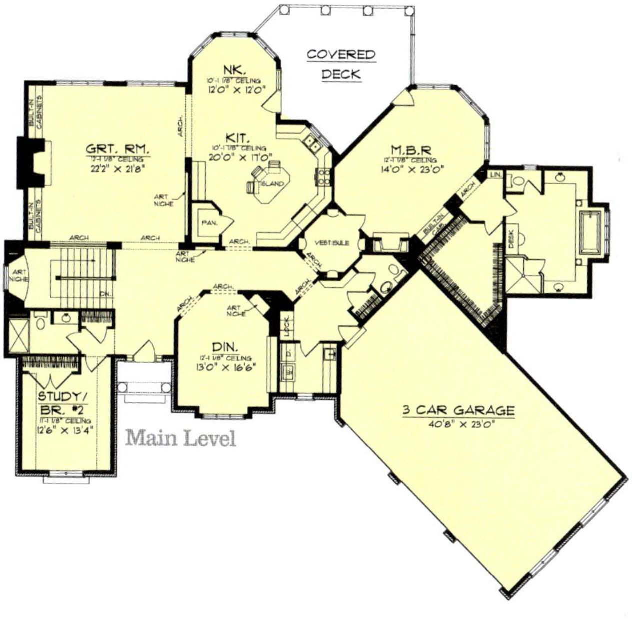

ORDER BLUEPRINTS 24 HOURS, 7 DAYS A WEEK, AT 1-800-521-6797 OR EPLANS.COM

325 New House Plans
Editor's Picks

Plan:
HPK2600019

Style:
MEDITERRANEAN

Square Footage:
5,109

Bedrooms:
4

Bathrooms:
4 1/2

Width:
100' - 0"

Depth:
138' - 10"

Foundation:
SLAB

Rear Exterior

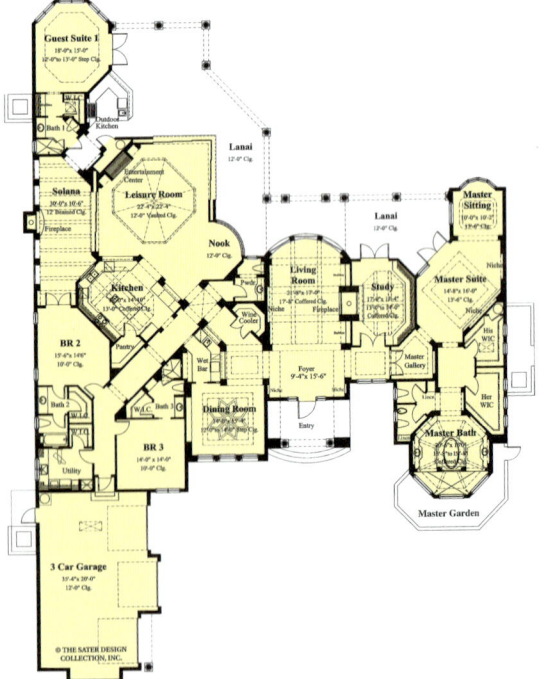

This Mediterranean palace is the home of your dreams! Whether you've been fantasizing about impressive spaces in which to entertain your friends or luxurious privacy to while away your leisure time, this home has it all. An outdoor barbecue may take place on the exotic lanai, which spans the back of the home with access from the leisure room, the master suite, and the guest room. A more intimate solana to the side of the home provides a place to retreat by the fire as the night air settles in. In cooler weather, entertain in the formal living and dining rooms, complete with convenient wet bar and wine cooler. When the party is over, retreat to the master suite, which occupies an entire wing of the home. Don't miss the master spa, where you can bathe in a private garden!

Photo by Joseph Lapeyra.
This home, as shown in photographs, may differ from the actual blueprints. For more detailed information, please check the floor plans carefully.

Editor's Picks

325 New House Plans

Plan:
HPK2600020

Style:
CRAFTSMAN
Main Level:
2,481 SQ. FT.
Upper Level:
1,598 SQ. FT.
Lower Level:
1,381 SQ. FT.
Total:
5,460 SQ. FT.
Bedrooms:
5
Bathrooms:
5 1/2
Width:
73' - 0"
Depth:
78' - 4"
Foundation:
UNFINISHED WALKOUT BASEMENT

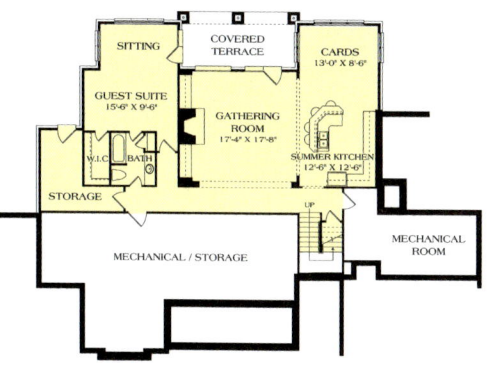

Lower Level

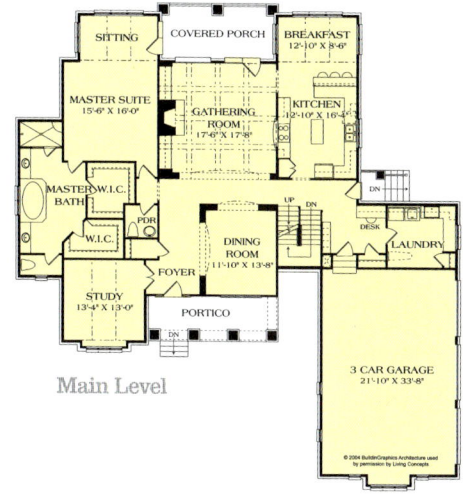

Main Level

Craftsman details such as stone and casement windows, as well as a cozy columned porch, will immediately welcome visitors. Enter the foyer where a dining room sits to the right and a large gathering room with coffered ceiling and fireplace is straight ahead. The master suite and private study are resplendent with amenities such as a sitting room that opens to a covered porch, and a master bath with two walk-in closets. The kitchen with eating bar and center island is open to a breakfast room that also accesses the porch. The second floor holds a large recreation room in the center, as well as three bedrooms, each with a private bath.

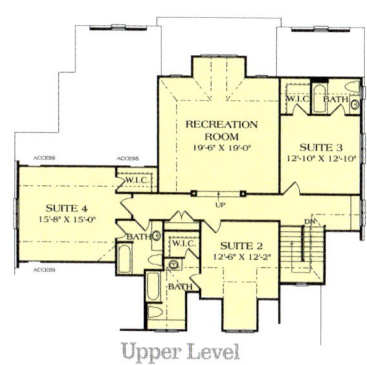

Upper Level

ORDER BLUEPRINTS 24 HOURS, 7 DAYS A WEEK, AT 1-800-521-6797 OR EPLANS.COM

325 New House Plans

Editor's Picks

Plan:
HPK2600021

Style:
PRAIRIE

Square Footage:
5,628

Bedrooms:
5

Bathrooms:
5 1/2

Width:
165' - 0"

Depth:
115' - 8"

Foundation:
SLAB

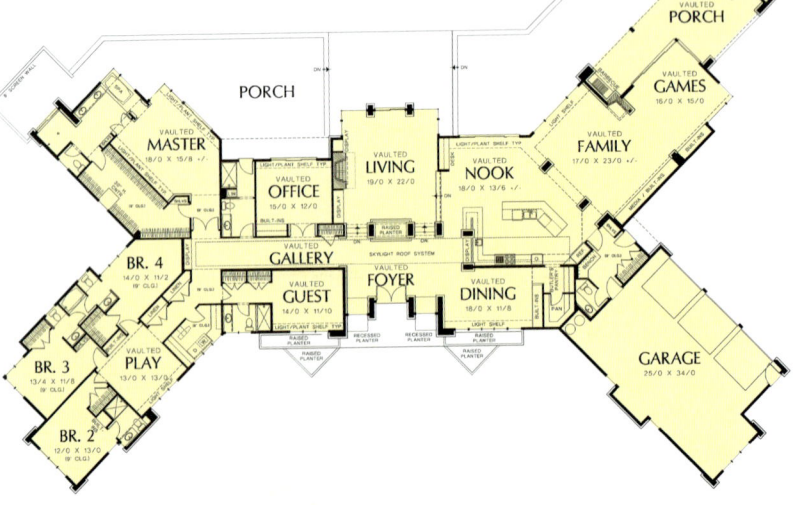
Rear Exterior

A unique X-shaped floor plan manages to accomodate over 5,000 square feet of living space and amenities on one level. Raised and recessed planters greet visitors at the entryway and along the exterior, and a raised planter subtly and elegantly separates the great room from the foyer. Clever design brings the outdoors in through plant shelves in most rooms and stacked stone in columns and fireplaces inside and out. Stone floors in the common areas create seamless flow from room to room. Custom-style built-ins in nearly every room personalize the space and provide display areas for books, art, and entertainment.

Editor's Picks

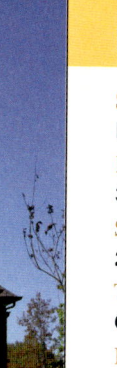

325
New House Plans

Plan:
HPK2600022

Style:
FRENCH COUNTRY
First Floor:
3,623 SQ. FT.
Second Floor:
2,507 SQ. FT.
Total:
6,130 SQ. FT.
Bedrooms:
5
Bathrooms:
5 1/2
Width:
105' - 10"
Depth:
96' - 8"
Foundation:
SLAB

This thoroughly modern plan works hard to meet the needs of busy families. To start, two studies—on the first floor, near the entry; on the second floor, above the garage—serve homeowners who require a dedicated office space for business or a library for literary leisure. Shared spaces are plentiful, beginning with the large great room, where built-in bookcases and a fireplace structure the layout and allow easy flow from the foyer and breakfast nook. Dual two-car garages form a courtyard "friend's" entry at the left of the home. The oversized utility area will prove to be a must-have room, working as a mudroom, laundry room, locker, and storage space.

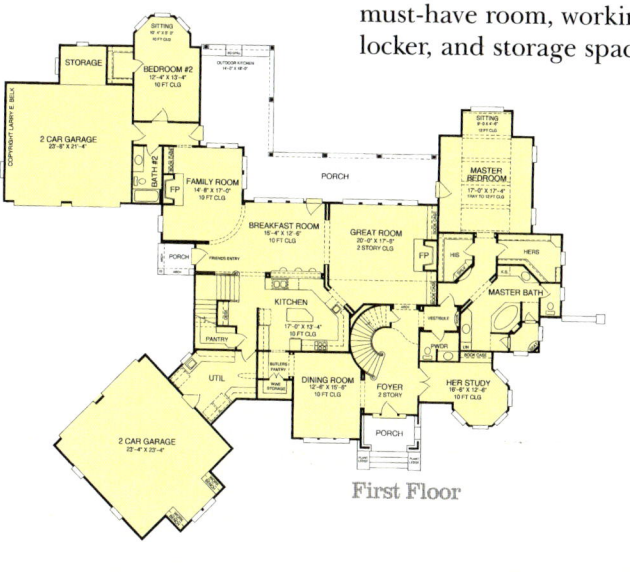

First Floor

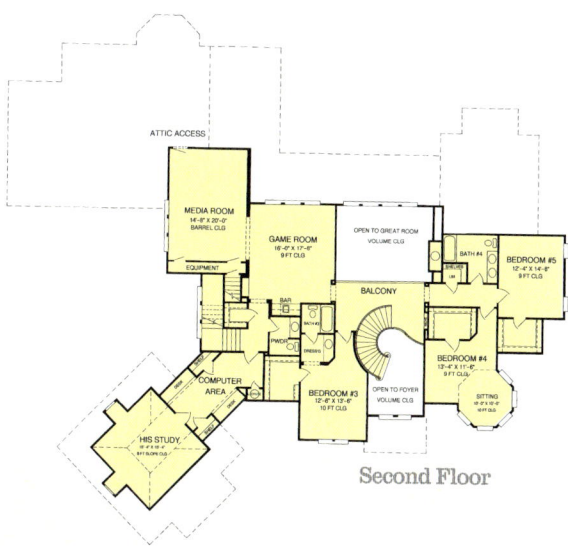

Second Floor

ORDER BLUEPRINTS 24 HOURS, 7 DAYS A WEEK, AT 1-800-521-6797 OR EPLANS.COM

325 New House Plans — Editor's Picks

Plan:
HPK2600023

Style:
MISSION

First Floor:
4,747 SQ. FT.

Second Floor:
1,737 SQ. FT.

Total:
6,484 SQ. FT.

Bedrooms:
5

Bathrooms:
4 ½ + ½

Width:
161' - 9"

Depth:
60' - 7"

Foundation:
CRAWLSPACE

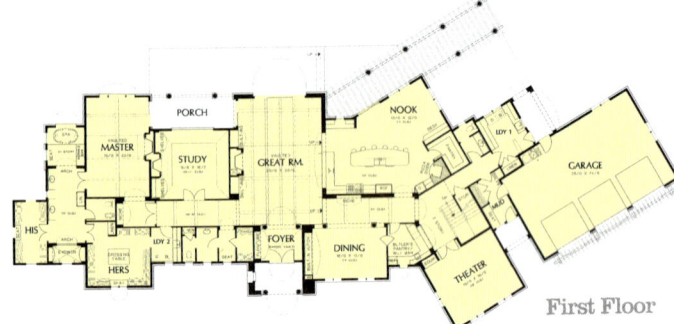

First Floor

Second Floor

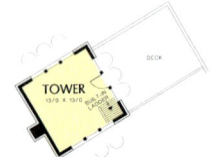

Rear Exterior

The facade is a mix of California Mission style and Italianate with stone siding, stucco accents, and a tile roof. The thoroughly modern interior is nearly mansion-sized and designed for luxury living. Some of the many elements you'll love about this design include: four family bedrooms (two with private baths), a master suite with His and Hers walk-in closets and dressing areas, two laundry areas, a home theater room, a vaulted playroom, and a unique tower room with attached deck. Choose formal or casual dining spaces—they flank the island kitchen, which also boasts a pizza oven and walk-in pantry. A butler's pantry and a wet bar add convenience to entertaining. Enjoy the outdoor spaces with three trellised porches at the rear of the plan. A three-car garage accesses the main part of the house via a handy mudroom.

ORDER BLUEPRINTS 24 HOURS, 7 DAYS A WEEK, AT 1-800-521-6797 OR EPLANS.COM

Craftsman & Ranch Homes

325 New House Plans

Plan:
HPK2600024

Style:
BUNGALOW

Square Footage:
1,100

Bedrooms:
3

Bathrooms:
2

Width:
44' - 0"

Depth:
50' - 0"

Foundation:
CRAWLSPACE, SLAB

Plan:
HPK2600025

Style:
RANCH

Square Footage:
1,400

Bedrooms:
3

Bathrooms:
2

Width:
54' - 0"

Depth:
47' - 0"

Foundation:
SLAB

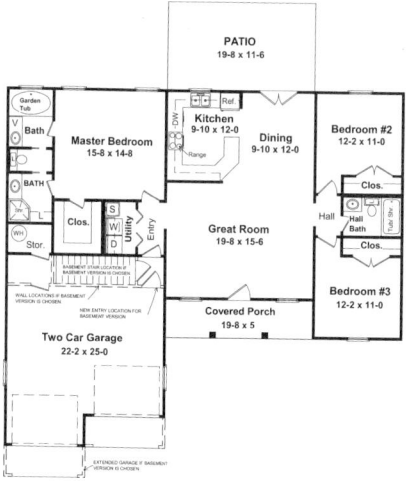

ORDER BLUEPRINTS 24 HOURS, 7 DAYS A WEEK, AT 1-800-521-6797 OR EPLANS.COM

325 Craftsman & Ranch Homes
New House Plans

Plan:
HPK2600026

Style:
BUNGALOW

Square Footage:
2,194

Bedrooms:
3

Bathrooms:
2

Width:
66' - 0"

Depth:
62' - 0"

Foundation:
SLAB

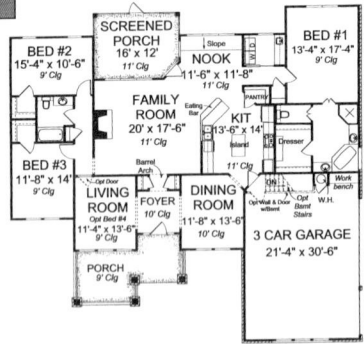

Plan:
HPK2600027

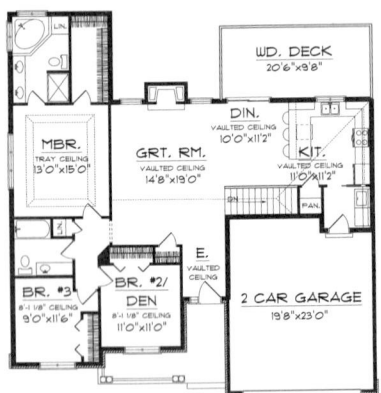

Style:
RANCH

Square Footage:
1,495

Bedrooms:
3

Bathrooms:
2

Width:
50' - 0"

Depth:
51' - 8"

Foundation:
UNFINISHED BASEMENT

ORDER BLUEPRINTS 24 HOURS, 7 DAYS A WEEK, AT 1-800-521-6797 OR EPLANS.COM

Craftsman & Ranch Homes

325 New House Plans

Plan:
HPK2600028

Style:
COTTAGE

Square Footage:
1,502

Bedrooms:
3

Bathrooms:
2

Width:
51' - 8"

Depth:
51' - 2"

Foundation
CRAWLSPACE, SLAB

Plan:
HPK2600029

Style:	Bathrooms:	Depth:
COTTAGE	**2**	**51' - 2"**
Square Footage:	Width:	Foundation:
1,504	**51' - 8"**	**CRAWLSPACE, SLAB**
Bedrooms:		
3		

ORDER BLUEPRINTS 24 HOURS, 7 DAYS A WEEK, AT 1-800-521-6797 OR EPLANS.COM   35

325 Craftsman & Ranch Homes
New House Plans

Plan:
HPK2600030

Style:
RANCH

Square Footage:
1,564

Bedrooms:
3

Bathrooms:
2

Width:
54' - 0"

Depth:
46' - 0"

Foundation:
CRAWLSPACE

Plan:
HPK2600031

Style:
RANCH

Square Footage:
1,600

Bedrooms:
3

Bathrooms:
2

Width:
51' - 8"

Depth:
59' - 0"

Foundation:
UNFINISHED BASEMENT

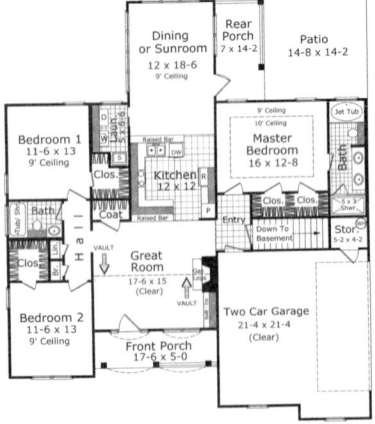

ORDER BLUEPRINTS 24 HOURS, 7 DAYS A WEEK, AT 1-800-521-6797 OR EPLANS.COM

Craftsman & Ranch Homes

325 New House Plans

First Floor

Second Floor

Plan:
HPK2600032

Style:
CRAFTSMAN

First Floor:
1,078 SQ. FT.

Second Floor:
594 SQ. FT.

Total:
1,672 SQ. FT.

Bedrooms:
4

Bathrooms:
2 1/2

Width:
40' - 0"

Depth:
52' - 0"

Foundation:
CRAWLSPACE

Plan:
HPK2600033

Style:
RANCH

Square Footage:
1,777

Bedrooms:
3

Bathrooms:
2

Width:
67' - 2"

Depth:
50' - 0"

Foundation:
CRAWLSPACE, SLAB

ORDER BLUEPRINTS 24 HOURS, 7 DAYS A WEEK, AT 1-800-521-6797 OR EPLANS.COM   37

325 New House Plans

Craftsman & Ranch Homes

Plan:
HPK2600034

Style:
COTTAGE

Square Footage:
1,808

Bedrooms:
3

Bathrooms:
2

Width:
55' - 4"

Depth:
58' - 0"

Foundation:
UNFINISHED BASEMENT

The layout for this home is well-suited to empty-nesters and first-time home builders. The master suite is a spacious, private retreat for the homeowner. Two secondary bedrooms—one easily converted to a home office—sit at the front of the home and share a full bath. The family room, adjacent to the sleeping quarters, is a central gathering place for family and friends. A snack bar in the nearby kitchen is great for informal meals.

Craftsman & Ranch Homes

325 New House Plans

Plan:
HPK2600035

Style:
BUNGALOW

Square Footage:
1,820

Bonus Space:
470 SQ. FT.

Bedrooms:
3

Bathrooms:
2

Width:
53' - 0"

Depth:
62' - 0"

This efficient design would suit a family just starting out as well as an empty-nester couple, providing all of the necessities, a few of the luxuries, and the opportunity to expand as needed. The principal living areas are arranged around the great room, where a cathedral ceiling and transom-topped windows visually expand the space. Built-in media cabinets and bookshelves flanking the fireplace lend a sense of formality and reduce furniture needs. The spacious island kitchen includes a computer center for conducting household business without leaving the hub of the home. In the front corner of the home, two bedrooms and a bath are perfect for children (or grandchildren). The master suite includes all the practical luxuries: dual sinks, compartmented bath, and large shower. If finished, the optional lower level provides over 1,000 square feet of recreational space for growing children or visiting family.

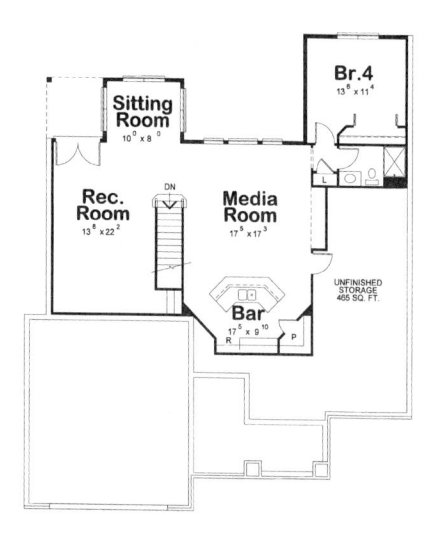

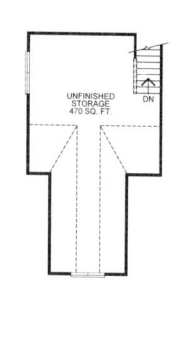

ORDER BLUEPRINTS 24 HOURS, 7 DAYS A WEEK, AT 1-800-521-6797 OR EPLANS.COM

325 New House Plans
Craftsman & Ranch Homes

Plan:
HPK2600036

Style:
BUNGALOW

Square Footage:
1,828

Bedrooms:
3

Bathrooms:
2

Width:
47' - 0"

Depth:
53' - 4"

Foundation:
UNFINISHED BASEMENT

This home befits an empty-nester or first-time home builder interested in bungalow living. The exterior is appealing and the interior features three bedrooms and two full baths. One of the bedrooms can easily be converted to a home office. The family room sits at the rear of the home with a scenic view of the backyard. A fireplace here adds warmth and ambiance. A two-car garage completes this plan.

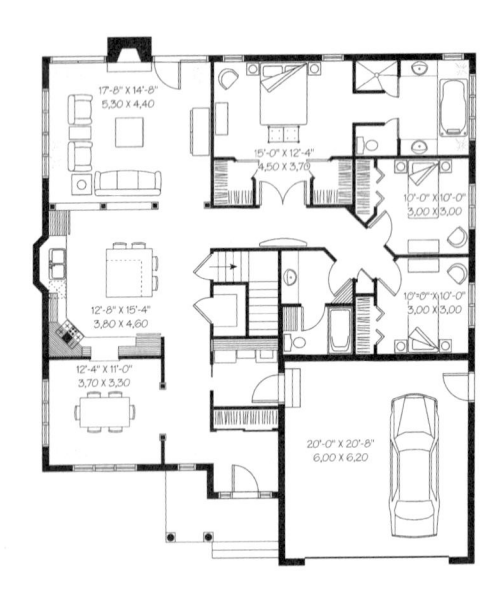

Craftsman & Ranch Homes

325 New House Plans

Plan:
HPK2600037

Style:
RANCH

Square Footage:
1,830

Bedrooms:
3

Bathrooms:
2

Width:
54' - 4"

Depth:
61' - 4"

© 2004 Donald A. Gardner, Inc.

Stone and siding provide a beautiful low-maintenance facade. Gables and decorative dormers accentuate the hipped-roof, while a box-bay window de-emphasizes the garage. Room positioning plays an important role in this floor plan. The kitchen is somewhat hidden from the foyer, yet it remains connected to the dining room and open to the great room/breakfast area. Great for entertaining, the screened porch can be accessed from the versatile study/bedroom and the great room. Other special features include a bonus room, reach-in pantry, and built-in cabinetry. An art niche and spacious closet enhance the foyer, and the master bath is quite the retreat.

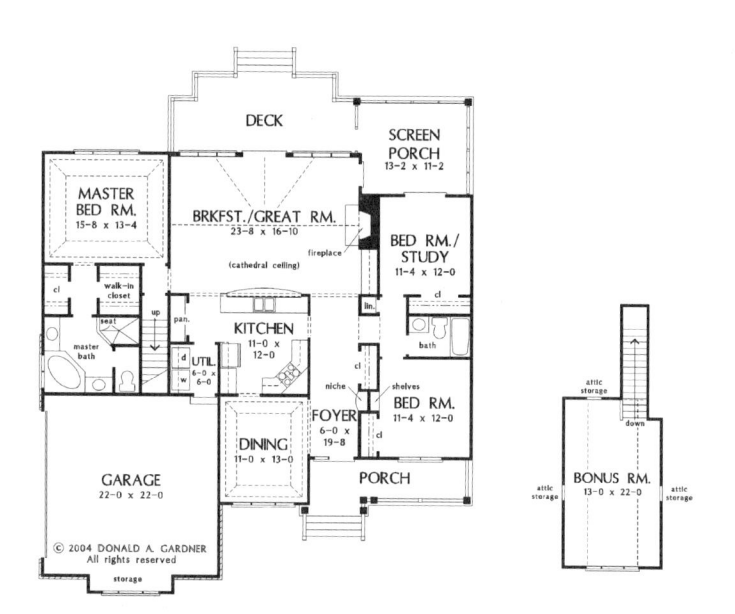

ORDER BLUEPRINTS 24 HOURS, 7 DAYS A WEEK, AT 1-800-521-6797 OR EPLANS.COM

325 New House Plans
Craftsman & Ranch Homes

Plan:
HPK2600038

Style:
COTTAGE

Square Footage:
1,837

Bonus Space:
357 SQ. FT.

Bedrooms:
3

Bathrooms:
2

Width:
56' - 4"

Depth:
61' - 4"

© 2004 Donald A. Gardner, Inc.

A bay window adorns the side-loading garage, adding interest to the facade of this efficient home. An attractive columned porch, topped with a bracketed gable and keystone motif, further enhances the design's curbside presence. Inside, the dine-in kitchen benefits from the at-hand pantry and utility area. The breakfast nook and great room interact easily for casual gatherings, leaving the dining room to handle more formal occasions. A tray ceiling in the dining room, as in the master bedroom, helps refine and distinguish the space. Larger families could consider converting the above-garage bonus space into a fourth bedroom.

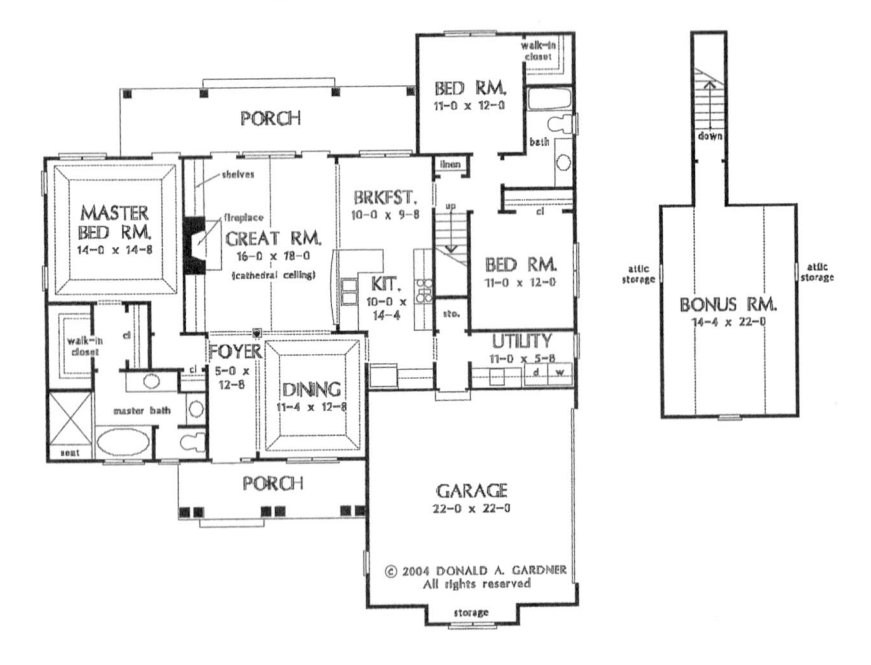

42   ORDER BLUEPRINTS 24 HOURS, 7 DAYS A WEEK, AT 1-800-521-6797 OR EPLANS.COM

Craftsman & Ranch Homes

325 New House Plans

Plan:
HPK2600039

Style:
COTTAGE

Square Footage:
1,854

Bonus Space:
343 SQ. FT.

Bedrooms:
3

Bathrooms:
2

Width:
45' - 8"

Depth:
63' - 4"

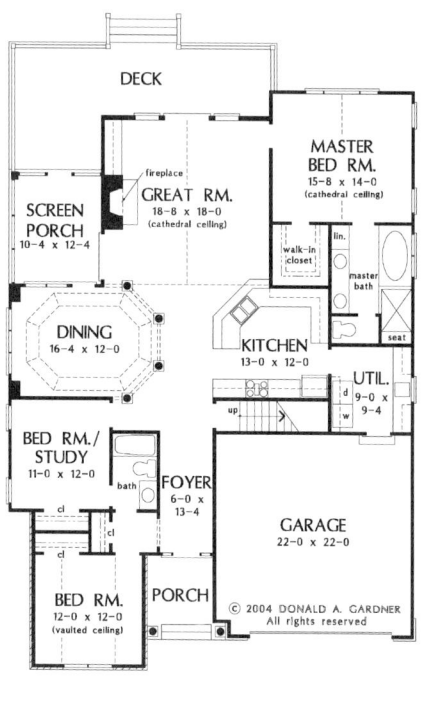

© 2004 Donald A. Gardner, Inc.

Combining the layout strategies of a row house, shotgun house, and mill house, this bungalow offers an efficient balance of living spaces. Upon entry, the impression for visitors is of modest elegance. An unobstructed view extends from the front door to French doors and the deck. At the center of the home, decorative ceilings and columns enhance the dining room, and an angled counter in the kitchen provides space for preparing and sharing meals. French doors lead from the great room and dining room into the screened porch—ideal for larger gatherings. The bonus room provides space for expansion, and the bedroom/study offers flexibility. The front-entry garage helps conserve space on a smaller lot.

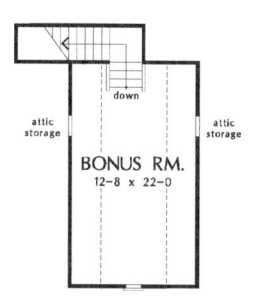

325 New House Plans
Craftsman & Ranch Homes

Plan:
HPK2600040

Style:
CRAFTSMAN

First Floor:
1,300 SQ. FT.

Second Floor:
560 SQ. FT.

Total:
1,860 SQ. FT.

Bedrooms:
3

Bathrooms:
2 1/2

Width:
82' - 0"

Depth:
42' - 0"

Foundation:
CRAWLSPACE, SLAB

First Floor

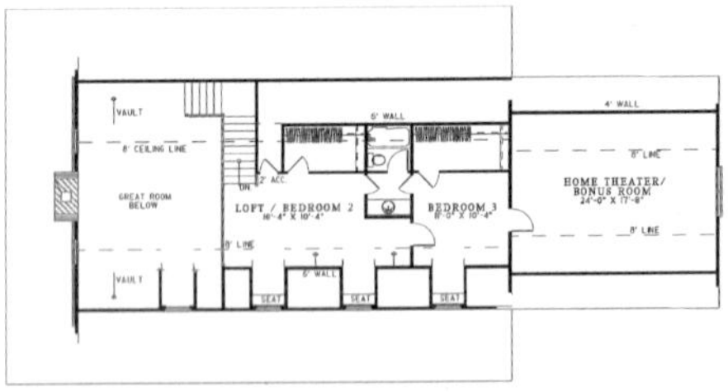

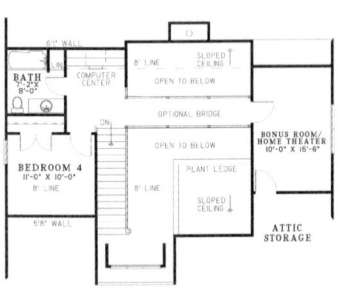

Second Floor

Plan:
HPK2600041

Style:
BUNGALOW

First Floor:
1,588 SQ. FT.

Second Floor:
287 SQ. FT.

Total:
1,875 SQ. FT.

Bedrooms:
4

Bathrooms:
3

Width:
42' - 0"

Depth:
68' - 6"

Foundation:
CRAWLSPACE, SLAB

First Floor

Second Floor

44 ORDER BLUEPRINTS 24 HOURS, 7 DAYS A WEEK, AT 1-800-521-6797 OR EPLANS.COM

Craftsman & Ranch Homes

325 New House Plans

Plan:
HPK2600042

Style:
BUNGALOW

Square Footage:
1,883

Bedrooms:
3

Bathrooms:
2

Width:
68' - 8"

Depth:
41' - 8"

Foundation:
UNFINISHED BASEMENT

An appealing plan to passers-by, this design makes a practical starter home for first-time builders. With a great use of space, the designer aptly fit three bedrooms and two full baths on one floor, using less than 1,900 square feet. A home office near the front door easily converts to a fourth bedroom if needed.

ORDER BLUEPRINTS 24 HOURS, 7 DAYS A WEEK, AT 1-800-521-6797 OR EPLANS.COM

325 New House Plans

Craftsman & Ranch Homes

Plan:
HPK2600043

Style:
CRAFTSMAN

Square Footage:
1,884

Bedrooms:
3

Bathrooms:
2

Width:
60' - 0"

Depth:
50' - 0"

Foundation:
CRAWLSPACE

Slender columns on brick veneer bases immediately catch the eye. Other Craftsman accents on this contemporary home include multi-paned windows and textured shake siding filling the apexes of both front gables. The foyer passes a traditional living room and dining room. With a full view of everything going on in the family room, nook, patio, and rear yard, the family chef can converse with people in all of those inner areas from the built-in range. An arched hallway at the juncture of the kitchen and nook leads to the master suite and utility room that connects with the two-car garage. Master suite amenities include a deep walk-in closet, double vanity, walk-in shower, and private toilet. A pass-through in the family room leads to two more bedrooms, where they share use of a central bathroom.

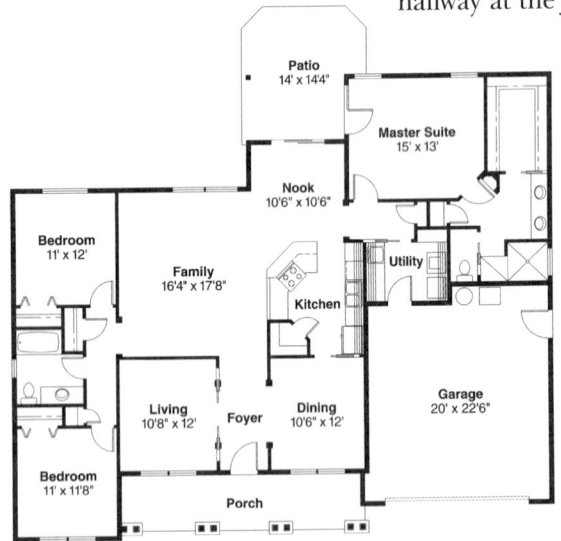

Craftsman & Ranch Homes

325 New House Plans

Plan:
HPK2600044

Style:
CRAFTSMAN

First Floor:
995 SQ. FT.

Second Floor:
902 SQ. FT.

Total:
1,897 SQ. FT.

Bedrooms:
4

Bathrooms:
3

Width:
34' - 4"

Depth:
40' - 4"

Foundation:
SLAB

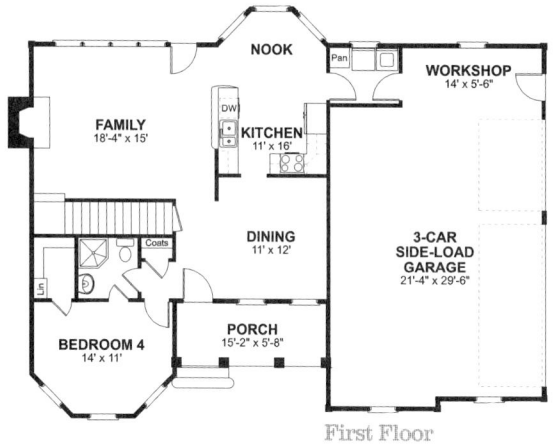

This timeless two-story has touches of Craftsman style. The exterior is accented with Craftsman details and "fish scale" siding. The front porch provides an inviting entry. The efficient design provides four spacious bedrooms and three baths using less than 2,000 square feet. Downstairs, Bedroom 4 serves as a perfect guest room with direct access to the bath. The three-car garage satisfies the increasing demand for multiple vehicle storage. There's even a workshop for those weekend projects. Upstairs, the luxurious master suite includes a sitting area and an enormous walk-in closet. The bonus area above the garage is perfect for a playroom, home theater, or just a large storage area. The basement provides plenty of space for future area needs.

ORDER BLUEPRINTS 24 HOURS, 7 DAYS A WEEK, AT 1-800-521-6797 OR EPLANS.COM

325 New House Plans
Craftsman & Ranch Homes

Plan:
HPK2600045

Style:
CRAFTSMAN

First Floor:
1,254 SQ. FT.

Second Floor:
655 SQ. FT.

Total:
1,909 SQ. FT.

Bedrooms:
3

Bathrooms:
2 1/2

Width:
54' - 0"

Depth:
38' - 0"

Foundation:
UNFINISHED BASEMENT

First Floor

Second Floor

Plan:
HPK2600046

Style:
RANCH

First Floor:
1,427 SQ. FT.

Second Floor:
489 SQ. FT.

Total:
1,916 SQ. FT.

Bedrooms:
3

Bathrooms:
2 1/2

Width:
42' - 0"

Depth:
54' - 0"

Foundation:
CRAWLSPACE

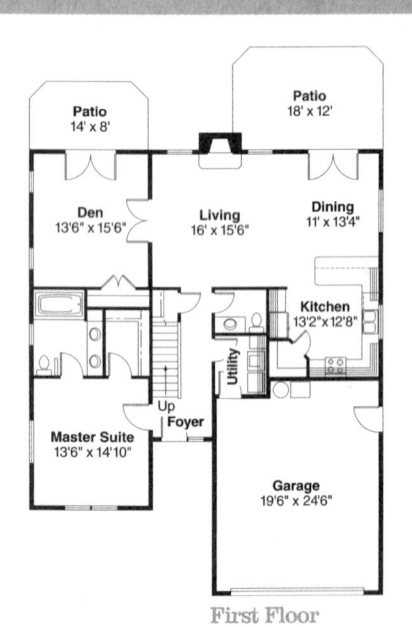

First Floor

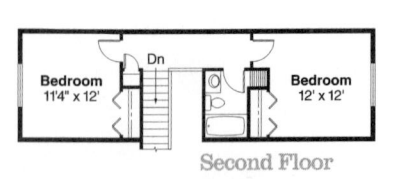

Second Floor

ORDER BLUEPRINTS 24 HOURS, 7 DAYS A WEEK, AT 1-800-521-6797 OR EPLANS.COM

Craftsman & Ranch Homes

325 New House Plans

Plan:
HPK2600047

Style:
RANCH

Square Footage:
1,921

Bonus Space:
812 SQ. FT.

Bedrooms:
3

Bathrooms:
2

Width:
84' - 0"

Depth:
55' - 6"

Foundation:
CRAWLSPACE, SLAB, UNFINISHED BASEMENT

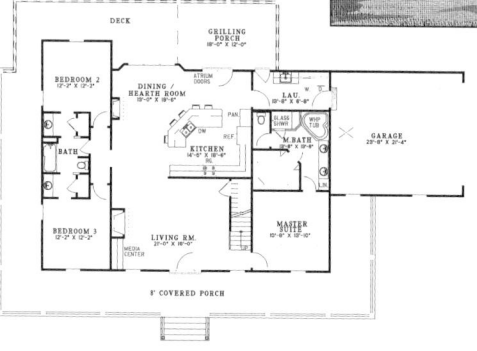

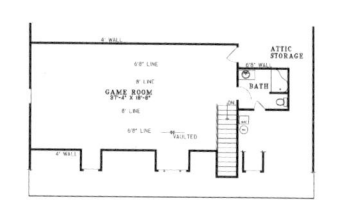

Plan:
HPK2600048

Style:
COTTAGE

First Floor:
968 SQ. FT.

Second Floor:
953 SQ. FT.

Total:
1,921 SQ. FT.

Bedrooms:
4

Bathrooms:
2 ½

Width:
45' - 0"

Depth:
42' - 2"

Foundation:
UNFINISHED BASEMENT

First Floor

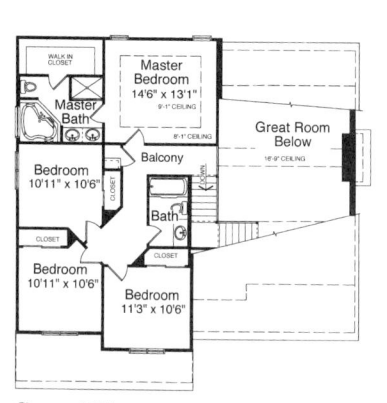

Second Floor

ORDER BLUEPRINTS 24 HOURS, 7 DAYS A WEEK, AT 1-800-521-6797 OR EPLANS.COM

325 New House Plans
Craftsman & Ranch Homes

Plan:
HPK2600049

Style:
CRAFTSMAN

First Floor:
1,012 SQ. FT.

Second Floor:
920 SQ. FT.

Total:
1,932 SQ. FT.

Bedrooms:
4

Bathrooms:
3

Width:
52' - 0"

Depth:
40' - 4"

Foundation:
UNFINISHED BASEMENT

The ever popular brick exterior is assurance of long lasting beauty and low maintenance. A columned porch conveniently invites guests into the dining room. The clever and efficient design provides the second floor with two family bedrooms and a master suite, which includes a sitting area and an enormous walk-in closet. Downstairs, a fourth bedroom has direct access to the bath, making it an ideal guest room. Store the family fleet and more in the three-bay garage. DIYers will appreciate the dedicated workshop. The bonus area above the garage is available for future expansion, or simply use it for storage.

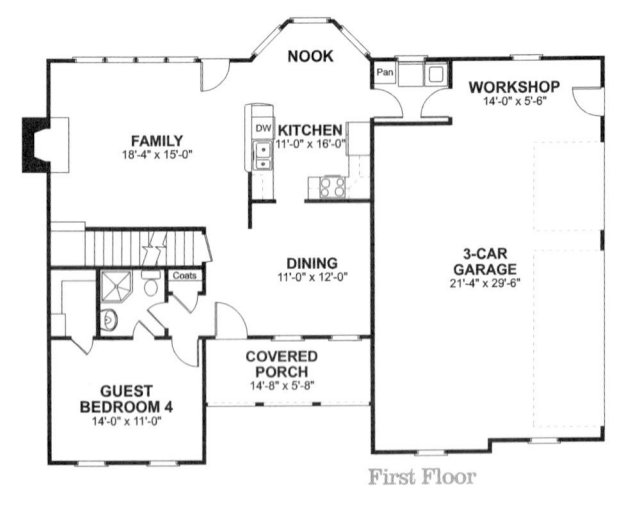

Craftsman & Ranch Homes

325 New House Plans

Plan:
HPK2600050

Style:
COTTAGE

Square Footage:
1,956

Bonus Space:
358 SQ. FT.

Bedrooms:
3

Bathrooms:
2

Width:
57' - 0"

Depth:
66' - 8"

© 2004 Donald A. Gardner, Inc.

Columns, arched openings, and stone accents provide an abundance of curb appeal. Siding provides a low-maintenance exterior, freeing up time for family and fun. A courtyard entrance to the garage helps make the most of a smaller lot. Inside, the gathering rooms are open to each other, creating a natural traffic flow. A cathedral ceiling, fireplace, and built-in cabinetry highlight the great room, while a counter separates the kitchen from the breakfast nook. At the end of a private hallway, a niche featuring favorite art announces the entrance to an elegant master suite. Secondary bedrooms are found at the opposite end of the house, along with a stair to the bonus room above the garage.

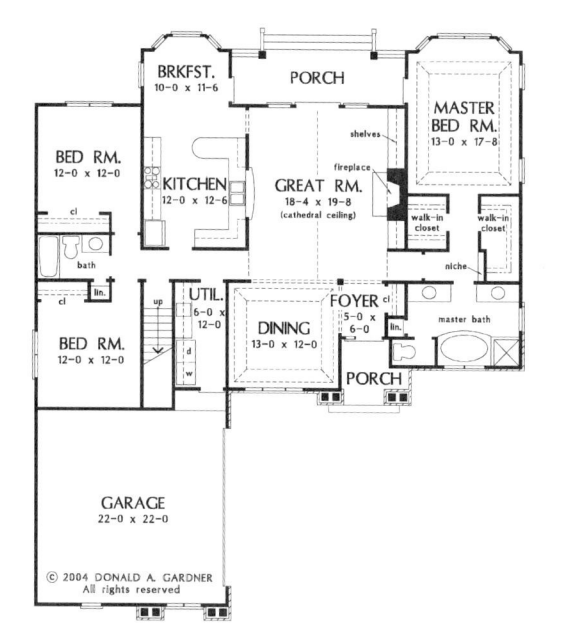

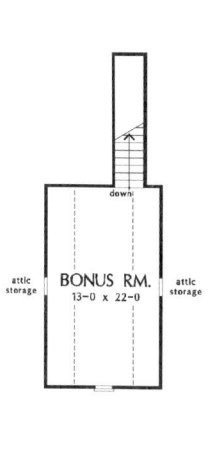

ORDER BLUEPRINTS 24 HOURS, 7 DAYS A WEEK, AT 1-800-521-6797 OR EPLANS.COM

325 New House Plans
Craftsman & Ranch Homes

Plan:
HPK2600051

Style:
COTTAGE

Square Footage:
1,963

Bedrooms:
3

Bathrooms:
2

Width:
37' - 8"

Depth:
37' - 6"

Foundation:
SLAB

This striking and distinctive ranch includes all the frills. From the inviting front porch to the screen porch and deck, this home provides dramatic rooms, luxurious appointments, and spacious living areas. The bonus room and basement provide plenty of space for expansion, so this home is one that won't soon be outgrown. Just beyond the porch is an entry with an 11-foot-high ceiling. To the left is the dining room open to the entry and family room, also with an 11-foot-high ceiling. Stairs to the bonus room are directly off the family room. The U-shaped kitchen is open and includes a breakfast bar. The master suite has access to the screen porch, a sitting room, deluxe bath, and His and Hers walk-in closet. The comfortably-sized secondary bedrooms are connected by a Jack-and-Jill bath arrangement.

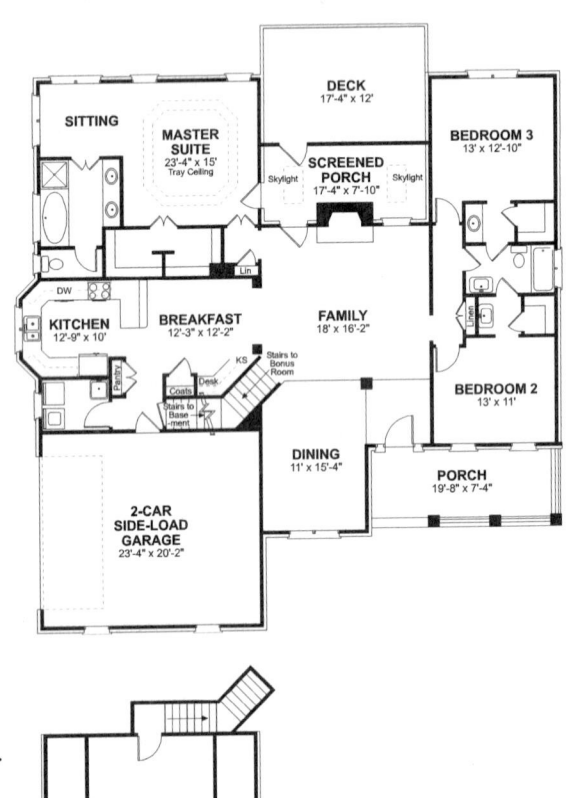

ORDER BLUEPRINTS 24 HOURS, 7 DAYS A WEEK, AT 1-800-521-6797 OR EPLANS.COM

Craftsman & Ranch Homes

325 New House Plans

Plan:
HPK2600052

Style:
CRAFTSMAN

Square Footage:
1,965

Bedrooms:
3

Bathrooms:
2

Width:
54' - 4"

Depth:
59' - 0"

© 2004 Donald A. Gardner, Inc.

Gables accented with cedar shakes join with a shed dormer to create a charming cottage exterior. Arts and Crafts columns highlight arches on the front porch, and the front-entry garage provides convenience. Over the front door, a transom floods the foyer with natural light, and the absence of two walls in the dining room give the feeling of airiness to the common rooms. An angled counter, built-in cabinetry, and French doors add a custom-styled touch to the interior, providing both beauty and function. A rear porch encourages outdoor living, while a bonus room offers flexible space above the garage. The utility room/mudroom provides additional built-in shelving for storage.

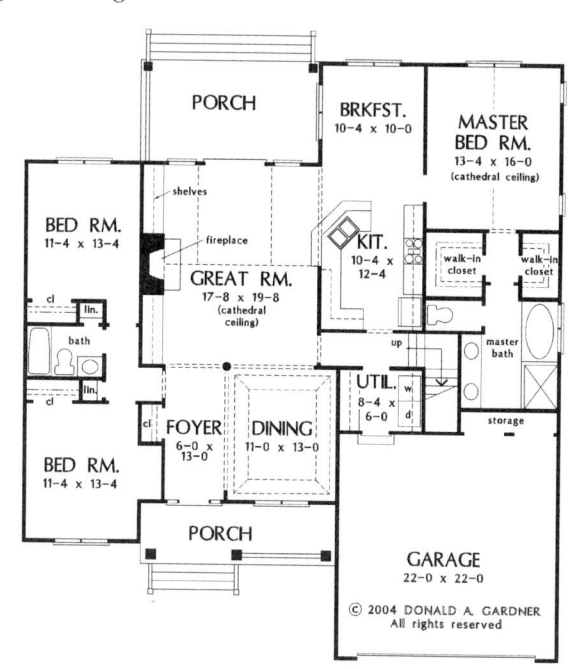

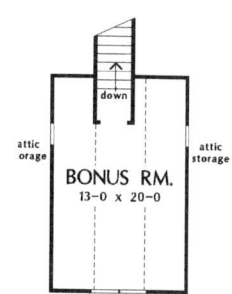

325 New House Plans
Craftsman & Ranch Homes

Plan:
HPK2600053

Style:
COTTAGE

Square Footage:
1,986

Bonus Space:
376 SQ. FT.

Bedrooms:
3

Bathrooms:
2

Width:
67' - 4"

Depth:
57' - 8"

© 2004 Donald A. Gardner, Inc.

Cedar shakes and stone add Old World character to this European cottage. The dramatic portico towers above the entrance and the positioning of the garage doesn't take away from the intimacy of the design. Remarkably open, the floor plan allows every common room to take advantage of rear views. Columns define the dining room, and the tray ceiling expands it. A cathedral ceiling extends from the fireplace to the serving bar. The utility room is conveniently located next to the kitchen and a bathroom, reducing the amount of plumbing needed. Other special features include built-in cabinetry, a bonus room, and French doors.

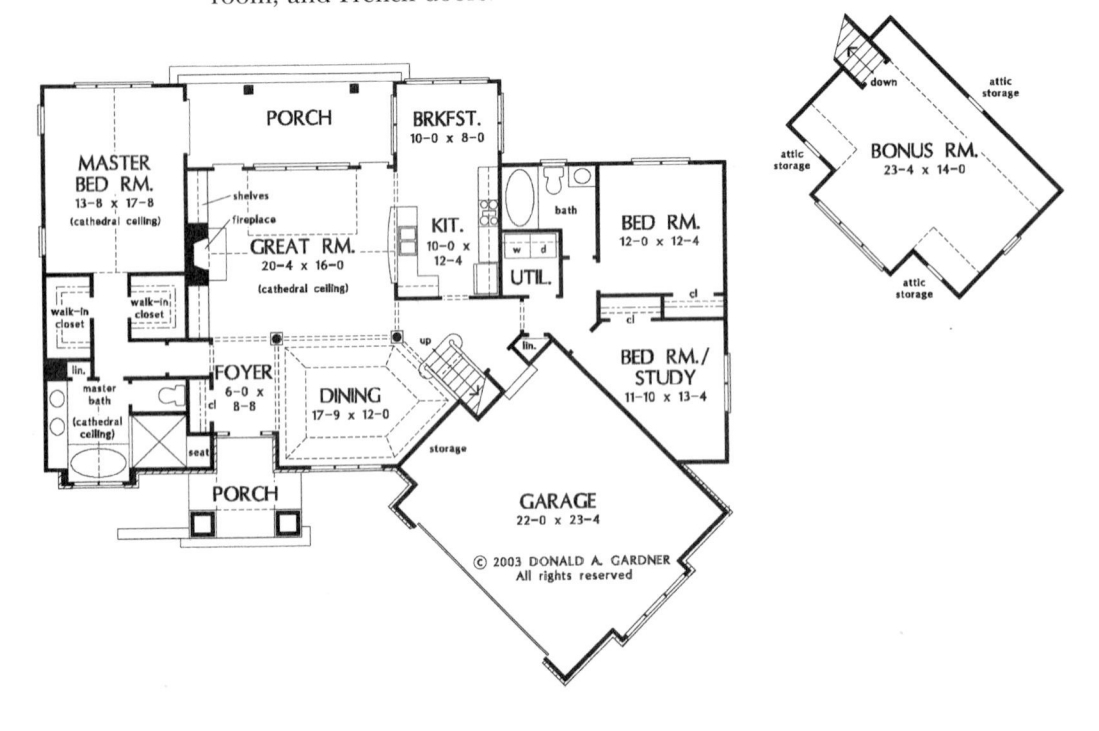

ORDER BLUEPRINTS 24 HOURS, 7 DAYS A WEEK, AT 1-800-521-6797 OR EPLANS.COM

Craftsman & Ranch Homes

325
New House Plans

Plan:
HPK2600054

Style:
CRAFTSMAN

Square Footage:
2,009

Bonus Space:
489 SQ. FT.

Bedrooms:
3

Bathrooms:
2

Width:
60' - 0"

Depth:
54' - 0"

Foundation:
CRAWLSPACE

The appearance of this plan is at once solid, warm, and comfortably unpretentious. Two wide banks of gridded windows sparkle across the recessed front porch, creating a sense of openness. Inside, the living room and dining room are located to the left and right of the foyer, and a spacious family room lies directly ahead. A gas fireplace nestles into one rear corner, at the end of a long wall of windows. In the opposite corner, a raised eating bar offers a natural area for family and friends to settle in for a chat with the chef. The master suite boasts a deep soaking tub, plus a separately enclosed shower and toilet. Secondary bedrooms and a bathroom are on the other side of the plan. Upstairs, bonus space offers possibility and flexibility.

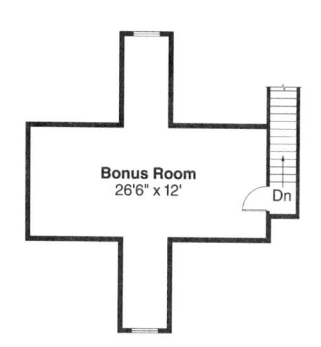

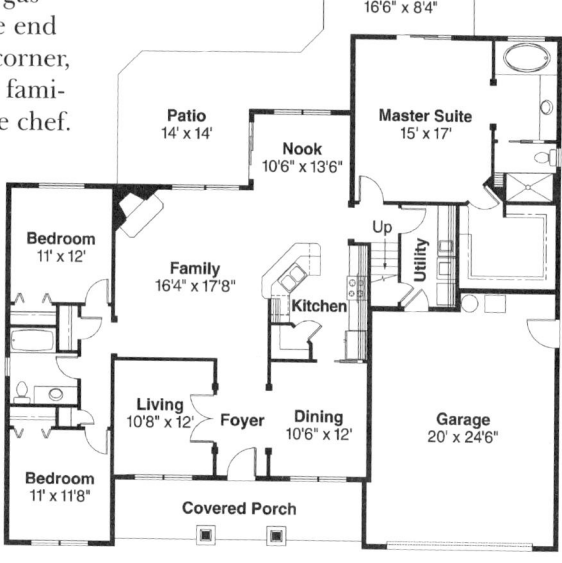

ORDER BLUEPRINTS 24 HOURS, 7 DAYS A WEEK, AT 1-800-521-6797 OR EPLANS.COM

325 New House Plans

Craftsman & Ranch Homes

Plan:
HPK2600055

Style:
RANCH

Square Footage:
2,011

Bonus Space:
288 SQ. FT.

Bedrooms:
3

Bathrooms:
2

Width:
65' - 11"

Depth:
53' - 5"

© 2004 Donald A. Gardner, Inc.

Red brick, gables, and bold columns give this home a handsome exterior. Inside, an open floor plan facilitates natural traffic flow, and special features like tray ceilings, built-in cabinetry, and a walk-in pantry accomodate the needs and wishes of today's family. A cathedral ceiling and a fireplace enhance the warm atmosphere in the great room, where an angled breakfast bar enables interaction among family members in the kitchen and nook. At bedtime, however, homeowners can enjoy the privacy of the secluded master suite, shielded from street noise by the side-entry garage. Laundry facilities are nearby, with direct access from a covered service porch for active kids and pets. Bonus space above the garage allows the plan to be customized according to the family's needs.

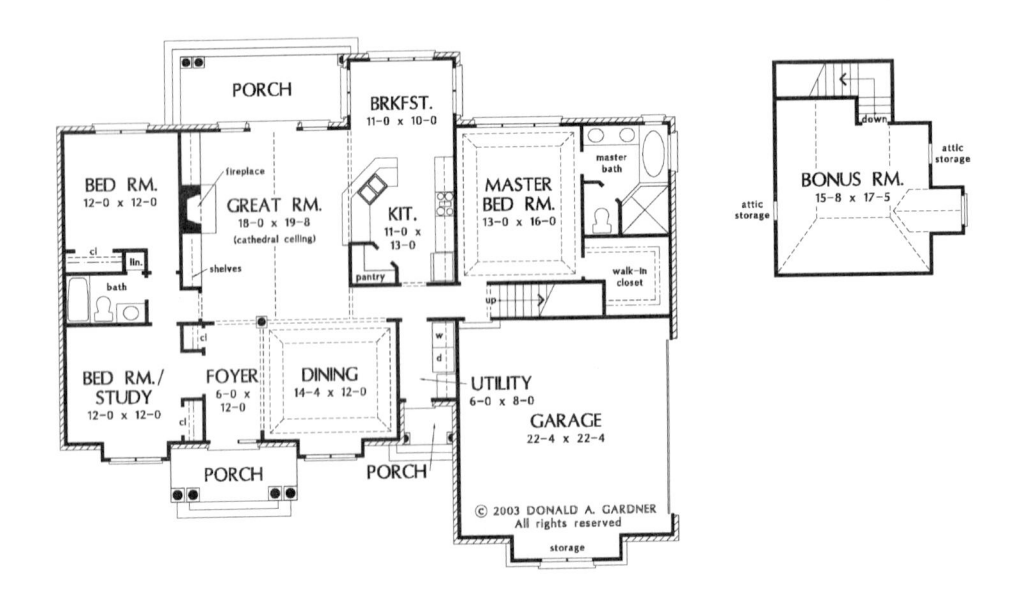

ORDER BLUEPRINTS 24 HOURS, 7 DAYS A WEEK, AT 1-800-521-6797 OR EPLANS.COM

Craftsman & Ranch Homes

325 New House Plans

Plan:
HPK2600056

Style:
RANCH

Sqaure Footage:
2,019

Bedrooms:
3

Bathrooms:
2 1/2

Width:
64' - 0"

Depth:
58' - 10"

Foundation:
UNFINISHED BASEMENT

Welcome home to this great house with large spaces and plenty of the features that homeowners adore. The functional split-floor plan layout separates the master suite from the secondary bedrooms. Amenities include an expansive master suite with His and Hers walk-in closets, a jet tub, and a walk-in shower. A large sunroom/breakfast area is ideal for those lazy weekend mornings. The spacious great room is accentuated by built-in cabinets and a gas log fireplace. Abundant storage space is an added bonus. Don't miss the large utility room. Home office space with an optional half-bath completes this plan.

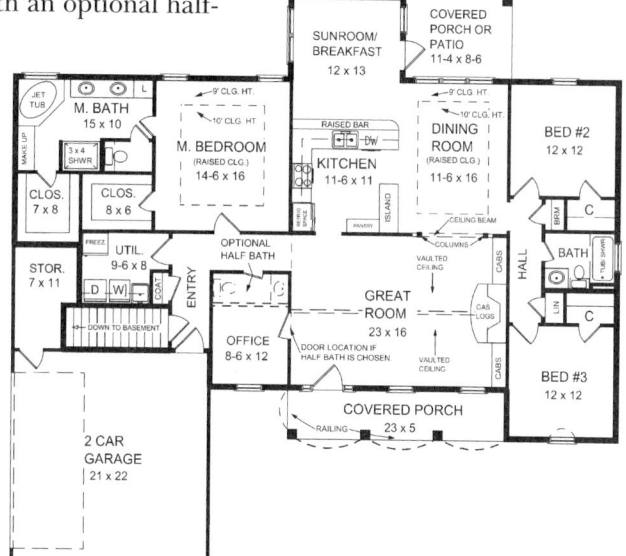

ORDER BLUEPRINTS 24 HOURS, 7 DAYS A WEEK, AT 1-800-521-6797 OR EPLANS.COM

325 New House Plans

Craftsman & Ranch Homes

Plan:
HPK2600057

Style:
BUNGALOW

Square Footage:
2,103

Bonus Space:
414 SQ. FT.

Bedrooms:
3

Bathrooms:
2

Width:
66' – 0"

Depth:
64' – 0"

Foundation:
CRAWLSPACE

This contemporary Craftsman-style bungalow fits right in beside an ocean or lake, and is equally adaptable for year-round living in a suburban neighborhood. Plenty of natural light beams into the vaulted foyer through sidelights and a wide transom. Double doors on the left access a vaulted room that could be a den or home office. The foyer opens to the spacious, vaulted living room, where windows fill most of the rear wall. A gas fireplace nestles into the far corner at the window's edge. Opposite the fireplace, two openings lead to the kitchen and dinette. A long, raised eating bar is great for snacking, chatting, and homework supervision. In the kitchen there's plenty of counter and cupboard space, built-in appliances, and a walk-in pantry. Laundry appliances are located in a utility room that connects to the three-car garage. In the far corner of the home, the master suite features a luxury bath and patio access. Two secondary bedrooms and a bath open from a small hallway off the foyer.

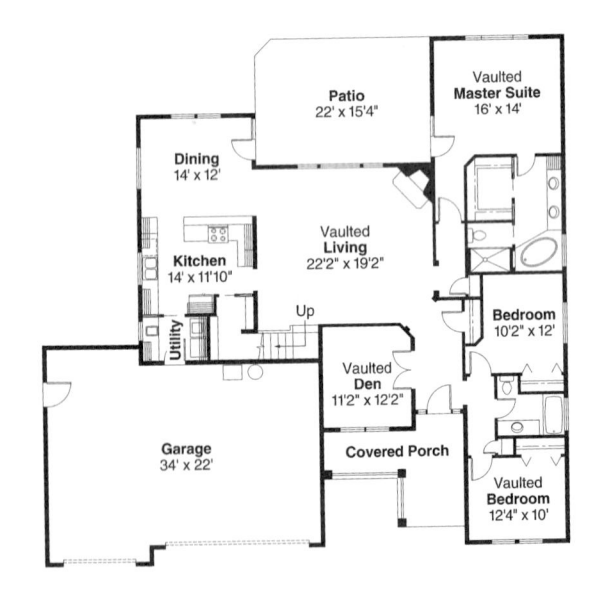

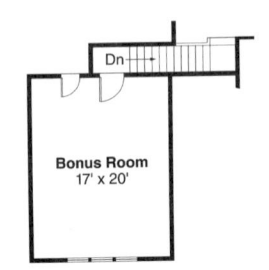

Craftsman & Ranch Homes

325 New House Plans

Plan:
HPK2600058

Style:
CRAFTSMAN

Square Footage:
2,129

Bedrooms:
3

Bathrooms:
2 ½

Width:
60' - 0"

Depth:
74' - 8"

Foundation:
CRAWLSPACE, SLAB

Charming columns on the front covered porch of this Craftsman-style plan complement the exterior. This split-bedroom design allows privacy for all family members and guests. Entertaining is made easy with the openness of the great and dining rooms and with the addition of the grilling porch at the rear of this home. The master suite and two additional bedrooms are comfortably located on the main floor of this home. The upper floor provides bonus space that will put your imagination to work, including options for future home theater enjoyment and another bedroom for guests or an addition to your family.

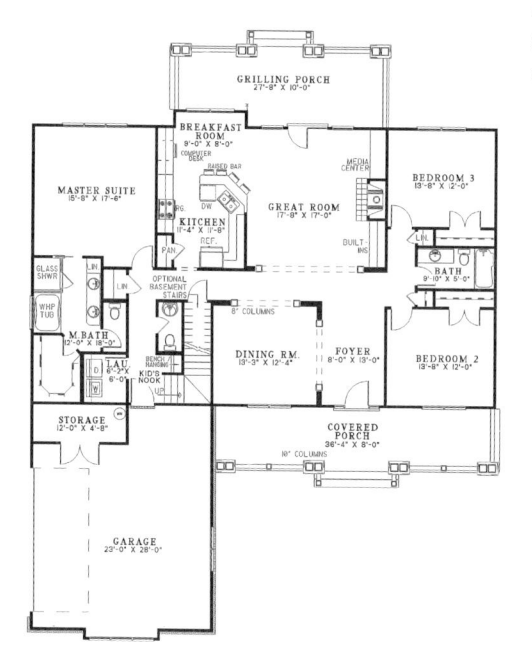

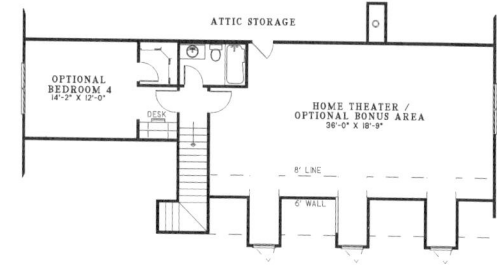

ORDER BLUEPRINTS 24 HOURS, 7 DAYS A WEEK, AT 1-800-521-6797 OR EPLANS.COM

325 New House Plans
Craftsman & Ranch Homes

Plan:
HPK2600059

Style:
CRAFTSMAN

First Floor:
1,635 SQ. FT.

Second Floor:
538 SQ. FT.

Total:
2,173 SQ. FT.

Bonus Space:
239 SQ. FT.

Bedrooms:
3

Bathrooms:
2 ½

Width:
61' - 10"

Depth:
44' - 0"

Foundation:
CRAWLSPACE

Shingle and stone accents settle this home firmly in the Craftsman idiom, rendering it equally harmonious in a mature neighborhood as it would be in a rural setting. From the lofty foyer, double doors lead to a parlor, which could also be furnished as a study or formal dining room. The latter would be well-served by the wet bar under the stairs. In the two-story living room, wide windows flank a gas fireplace. The kitchen and nook are cleverly designed to bring in maximum light without sacrificing counter space or cabinetry. There is even room for a built-in desk! The master suite enjoys private access to the side garden, plus a luxurious bath including a spa tub and oversized shower. Upstairs, two spacious bedrooms share a split bath, while a bonus room provides options for future expansion.

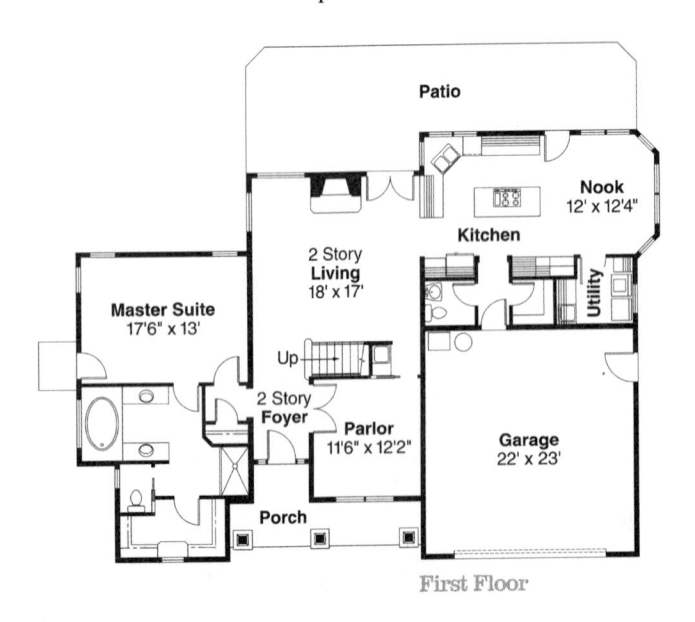

First Floor

Second Floor

ORDER BLUEPRINTS 24 HOURS, 7 DAYS A WEEK, AT 1-800-521-6797 OR EPLANS.COM

Craftsman & Ranch Homes

325 New House Plans

Plan:
HPK2600060

Style:
CRAFTSMAN

Square Footage:
2,174

Bedrooms:
3

Bathrooms:
2

Width:
78' - 0"

Depth:
65' - 0"

Foundation:
CRAWLSPACE

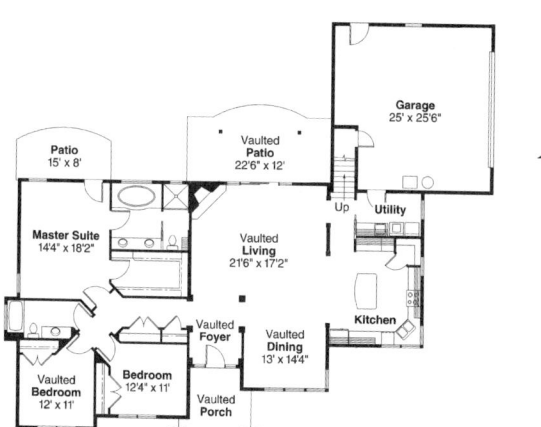

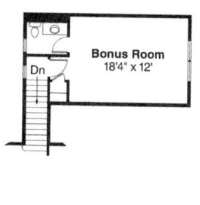

Plan:
HPK2600061

Style:
RANCH

Square Footage:
1,869

Bonus Space:
306 SQ. FT.

Bedrooms:
3

Bathrooms:
2

Width:
58' - 0"

Depth:
62' - 0"

Foundation:
CRAWLSPACE

ORDER BLUEPRINTS 24 HOURS, 7 DAYS A WEEK, AT 1-800-521-6797 OR EPLANS.COM

325 New House Plans

Craftsman & Ranch Homes

Plan:
HPK2600062

Style:
CRAFTSMAN

Square Footage:
2,193

Bedrooms:
3

Bathrooms:
2

Width:
56' - 4"

Depth:
73' - 0"

© 2005 Donald A. Gardner, Inc.

An Arts and Crafts facade boasts elegant curb appeal as double dormers echo the dual-arched portico. Twin sets of tapered columns provide architectural detail in this lavish exterior. Vaulted ceilings in the great room offer generous height throughout the open living spaces. Ceiling treatments enhance the dining room and foyer, creating splendid vertical volume. The master bedroom is flanked by a large rear porch that creates additional space to entertain guests or enjoy Mother Nature. A vaulted ceiling, dual sinks, and walk-in closets give the master suite additional flair. Secondary bedrooms run parallel to one another and share a common bathroom, making this home live easier.

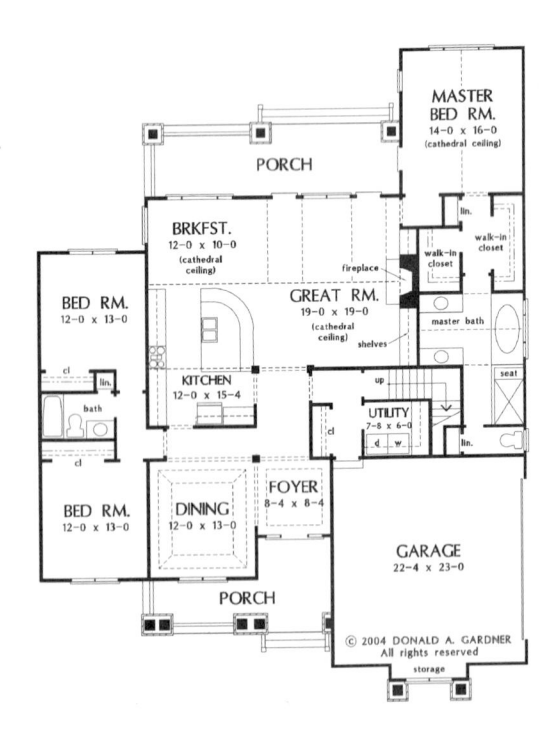

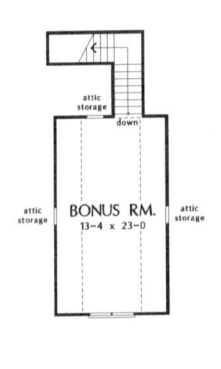

Craftsman & Ranch Homes

Plan:
HPK2600063

Style:
CRAFTSMAN

First Floor:
1,599 SQ. FT.

Second Floor:
611 SQ. FT.

Total:
2,210 SQ. FT.

Bonus Space:
230 SQ. FT.

Bedrooms:
3

Bathrooms:
2 1/2

Width:
55' - 0"

Depth:
52' - 0"

Foundation:
CRAWLSPACE

This Craftsman-style cottage offers fine vistas from all rear rooms on the main floor. In the great room, a gas fireplace flanked by wide, tall windows creates a focal point. This lofty space is totally open to the nook and kitchen. Glass doors in the nook slide open to let in summer breezes and provide easy access to a partially covered patio. Counters and cupboards wrap around three sides of the spacious kitchen. A central island creates additional storage and work space, and a walk-in pantry fills one entire corner. The built-in desk is perfect for keeping on top of household bills. Laundry appliances and a powder room are close by. The master suite, which fills the left wing, boasts a huge walk-in closet and roomy bathroom. Two more bedrooms share a split bath upstairs.

ORDER BLUEPRINTS 24 HOURS, 7 DAYS A WEEK, AT 1-800-521-6797 OR EPLANS.COM

325 New House Plans

Craftsman & Ranch Homes

Plan:
HPK2600064

Style:
COTTAGE

Square Footage:
2,225

Bonus Space:
302 SQ. FT.

Bedrooms:
4

Bathrooms:
2

Width:
60' - 10"

Depth:
63' - 0"

Foundation:
CRAWLSPACE, SLAB

A traditional country exterior hides a thoroughly modern open floor plan within. Nothing but a single column marking the corner of the dining room and an angled breakfast bar interrupt the flow of traffic and sightlines throughout the public areas of this home. Bedrooms are secluded in either wing; to the left, the master suite features a tall sloped ceiling and luxury bath. The right wing houses two secondary bedrooms and a high-ceilinged study, whose large closet and proximity to the hall bath could accommodate a fourth bedroom. Bonus space above the garage may be finished now or later, as needed.

ORDER BLUEPRINTS 24 HOURS, 7 DAYS A WEEK, AT 1-800-521-6797 OR EPLANS.COM

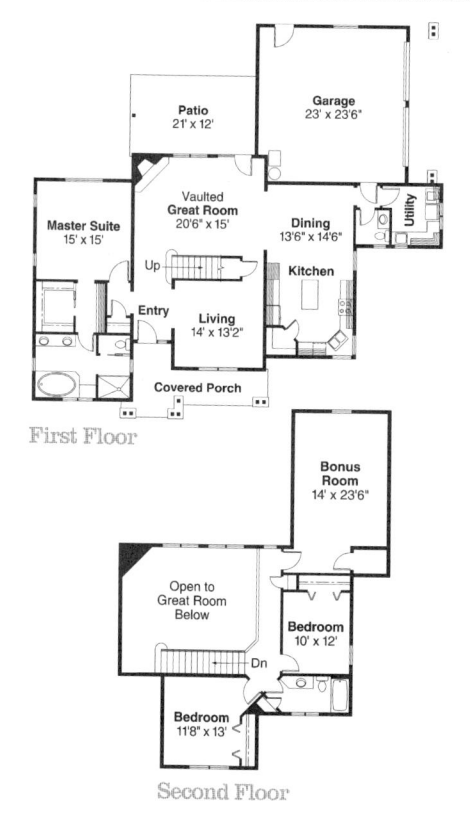

Craftsman & Ranch Homes

325 New House Plans

Plan:
HPK2600065

Style:
RANCH

Square Footage:
2,260

Bedrooms:
3

Bathrooms:
3

Width:
62' - 0"

Depth:
69' - 2"

Foundation:
UNFINISHED BASEMENT

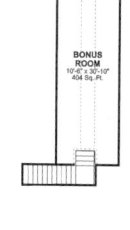

Plan:
HPK2600066

Style:
CRAFTSMAN

First Floor:
1,728 SQ. FT.

Second Floor:
534 SQ. FT.

Total:
2,262 SQ. FT.

Bedrooms:
3

Bathrooms:
2 ½

Width:
64' - 6"

Depth:
60' - 0"

Foundation:
CRAWLSPACE

First Floor

Second Floor

ORDER BLUEPRINTS 24 HOURS, 7 DAYS A WEEK, AT 1-800-521-6797 OR EPLANS.COM

325 New House Plans
Craftsman & Ranch Homes

Plan:
HPK2600067

Style:
COTTAGE

Square Footage:
2,278

Bonus Space:
306 SQ. FT.

Bedrooms:
3

Bathrooms:
2

Width:
61' - 7"

Depth:
80' - 1"

© 2004 Donald A. Gardner, Inc.

Striking architectural details enhance an orderly design in which public and private rooms occupy opposite wings of the home. Beyond the foyer, a hallway to the right leads to the sleeping quarters. The two front rooms share a box-bay window and a bath. The large walk-in closet and luxury bath of the master suite create a buffer between the family bedrooms. The suite's cathedral ceiling and many windows will make it a welcome retreat for the homeowners. The family will come together in front of the great room's fireplace, or gather at the snack counter to chat about the days' events as dinner is prepared. A spacious island makes the kitchen a great place for multiple cooks. A bay window highlights the breakfast room. Out back, both screened and open porches offer options for outdoor living.

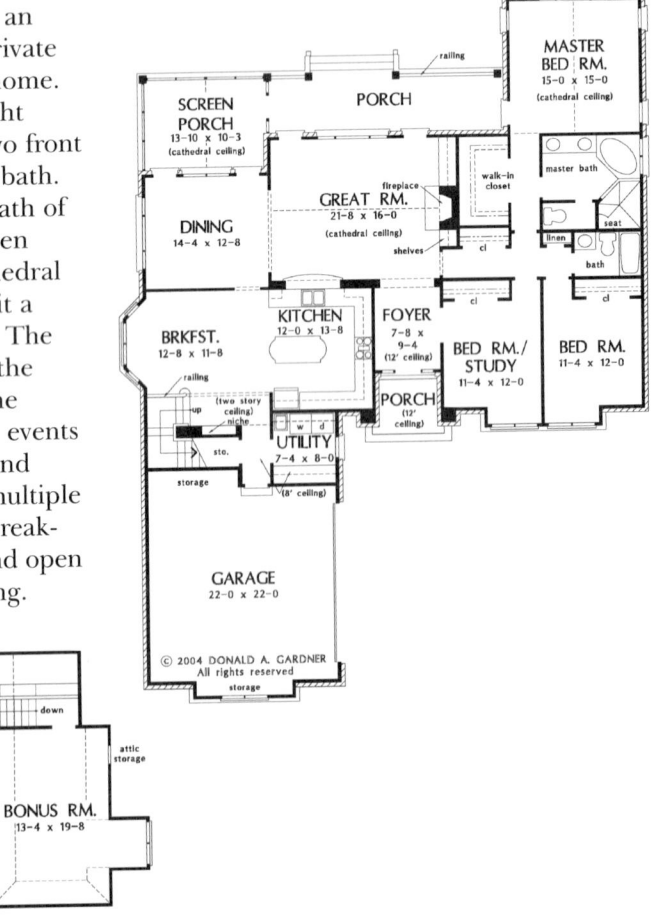

Craftsman & Ranch Homes

Plan:
HPK2600068

Style:
CRAFTSMAN

First Floor:
1,323 SQ. FT.

Second Floor:
985 SQ. FT.

Total:
2,308 SQ. FT.

Bonus Space:
636 SQ. FT.

Bedrooms:
3

Bathrooms:
3

Width:
38' - 0"

Depth:
49' - 0"

Foundation:
CRAWLSPACE

It's easy to picture this home nestled in a grove of tall oak trees, but it would blend into a suburban neighborhood just as nicely. One of its most notable features is an old-fashioned covered porch that wraps around three sides of the home. Outdoor lovers will appreciate this feature, whether the sky is filled with sunshine, clouds, rain, or snow. Two large rooms occupy the front of the plan, linked by French double doors. One could be outfitted as a home office, parlor, or guest room. It has a closet and direct access to a full bath. Beyond that, the spacious kitchen opens to a bayed dining area and a skylit, vaulted living room. A woodstove sits beside the stairs in the gathering room. The master suite is upstairs, along with two family bedrooms that share a bath.

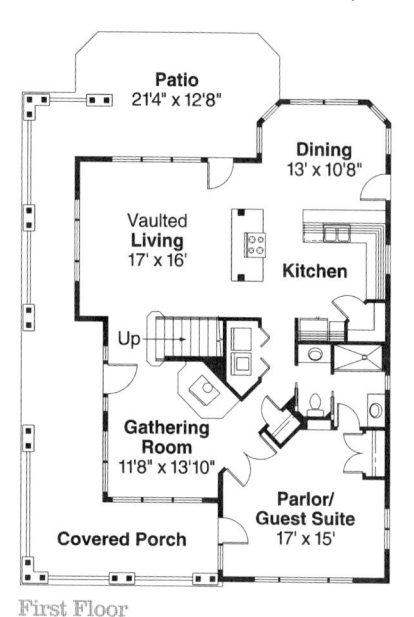

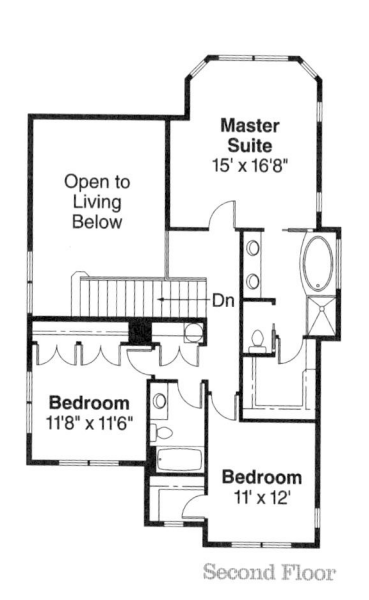

First Floor

Second Floor

ORDER BLUEPRINTS 24 HOURS, 7 DAYS A WEEK, AT 1-800-521-6797 OR EPLANS.COM

325 New House Plans
Craftsman & Ranch Homes

Plan:
HPK2600069

Style:
RANCH

Square Footage:
2,315

Bedrooms:
3

Bathrooms:
2

Width:
71' - 0"

Depth:
57' - 2"

© 2005 Donald A. Gardner, Inc.

This traditional home features a low-maintenance exterior of brick and siding, along with arched keystones and dual columns on the porch that spark instant curb appeal. The rear of the home includes a porch off the great room that is perfect for outdoor entertaining. A second porch off the utility room provides a convenient place for dirty shoes or washing pets before coming indoors. The spacious master suite includes a ceiling treatment and His and Hers walk-in closets. In the master bath, twin vanities and a separate shower and bathtub ensure convenience. Secondary bedrooms are positioned in the front of the house and share a full bath. The rest of the home is entirely open as only columns separate the great and dining rooms. Flowing into the kitchen and breakfast room, the great room features a cathedral ceiling, rear porch access, fireplace, and built-in shelves.

68 ORDER BLUEPRINTS 24 HOURS, 7 DAYS A WEEK, AT 1-800-521-6797 OR EPLANS.COM

Craftsman & Ranch Homes

325 New House Plans

Plan:
HPK2600070

Style:
CRAFTSMAN

First Floor:
1,916 SQ. FT.

Second Floor:
554 SQ. FT.

Total:
2,470 SQ. FT.

Bedrooms:
4

Bathrooms:
4

Width:
57' - 0"

Depth:
62' - 0"

Foundation:
UNFINISHED BASEMENT

This spectacular "master-down" blends a luxurious and flexible floor plan with an unforgettable facade to create a simply exquisite home design. An inviting front porch welcomes all to the dramatic two-story entry adorned by a lovely radius glass window above. To the right is an elegant dining room. Beyond the stairs is a dramatic family room with a sloped ceiling, fireplace, and built-in cabinets. The magnificent master suite includes a tray ceiling, bowed rear window wall, His and Hers closets, a fitness area, and a bath with a six-foot round spa and sit-down shower. Bedroom 2 will be a perfect guest room with direct access to a full bath. The large screened porch is the perfect place to relax after a long day at the office. The basement provides plenty of space for storage and future expansion. The second floor houses two spacious bedrooms each with direct access to a full bath. The bonus room provides additional flexible space to suit the family's needs.

First Floor

Second Floor

ORDER BLUEPRINTS 24 HOURS, 7 DAYS A WEEK, AT 1-800-521-6797 OR EPLANS.COM

325 Craftsman & Ranch Homes
New House Plans

Plan:
HPK2600071

Style:
CRAFTSMAN

First Floor:
1,875 SQ. FT.

Second Floor:
622 SQ. FT.

Total:
2,497 SQ. FT.

Bonus Space:
374 SQ. FT.

Bedrooms:
3

Bathrooms:
2 ½

Width:
53' - 0"

Depth:
66' - 0"

Foundation:
CRAWLSPACE

This Craftsman-flavored Cape Cod is thoroughly modern on the inside. Vaulted ceilings span the open floor plan, anchored by a spacious great room with corner fireplace. Family activities will gravitate toward this space and its satellites: an airy breakfast nook and storage-rich kitchen. Pocket doors separate the kitchen from the formal dining room, where walls of windows bring in natural light. The master suite boasts a deep soaking tub, over-sized cultured marble shower, and twin vanities. Two upstairs bedrooms share a compartmented bath, and a huge bonus room may be finished off as a fourth bedroom, rec room, or exercise room.

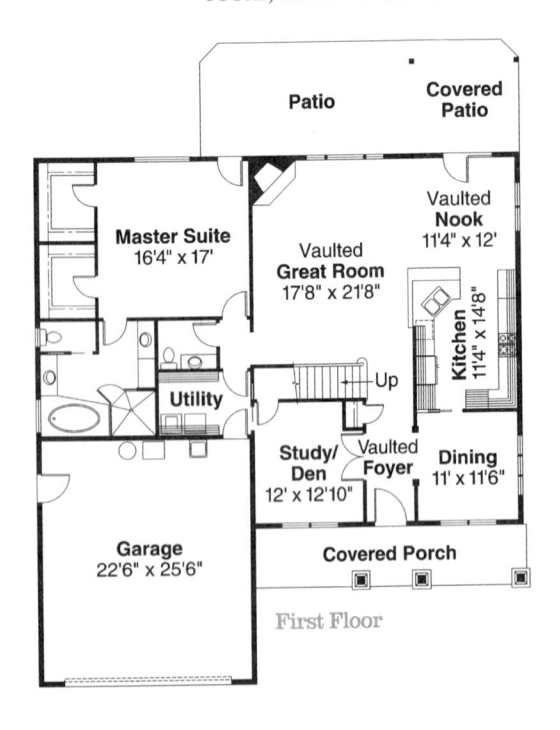

ORDER BLUEPRINTS 24 HOURS, 7 DAYS A WEEK, AT 1-800-521-6797 OR EPLANS.COM

Craftsman & Ranch Homes

325 New House Plans

Plan:
HPK2600072

Style:
RANCH

First Floor:
2,100 SQ. FT.

Second Floor:
405 SQ. FT.

Total:
2,505 SQ. FT.

Bedrooms:
4

Bathrooms:
3

Width:
79' - 4"

Depth:
53' - 6"

Foundation:
SLAB

Plan:
HPK2600073

Style:	Bedrooms:	Width:
RANCH	**3**	**59' - 4"**
Square Footage:	Bathrooms:	Depth:
2,506	**2 ½**	**88' - 0"**

Optional Layout

ORDER BLUEPRINTS 24 HOURS, 7 DAYS A WEEK, AT 1-800-521-6797 OR EPLANS.COM

325 Craftsman & Ranch Homes
New House Plans

Plan:
HPK2600074

Style:
RANCH

Square Footage:
2,522

Bedrooms:
2

Bathrooms:
2

Width:
70' - 0"

Depth:
61' - 0"

Foundation:
CRAWLSPACE

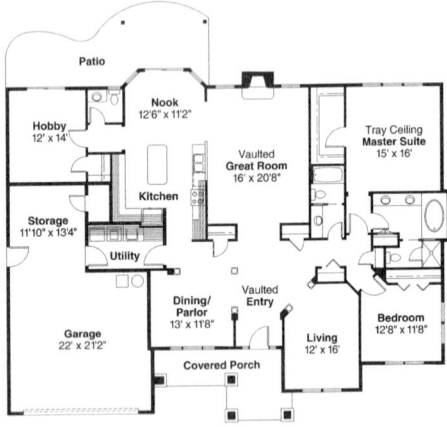

Plan:
HPK2600075

Style:
CRAFTSMAN

First Floor:
1,310 SQ. FT.

Second Floor:
1,249 SQ. FT.

Total:
2,559 SQ. FT.

Bedrooms:
4

Bathrooms:
2 ½

Width:
45' - 0"

Depth:
47' - 0"

Foundation:
UNFINISHED BASEMENT

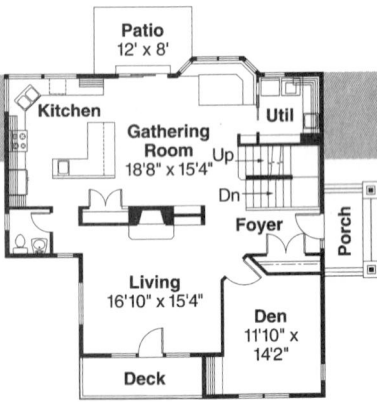

ORDER BLUEPRINTS 24 HOURS, 7 DAYS A WEEK, AT 1-800-521-6797 OR EPLANS.COM

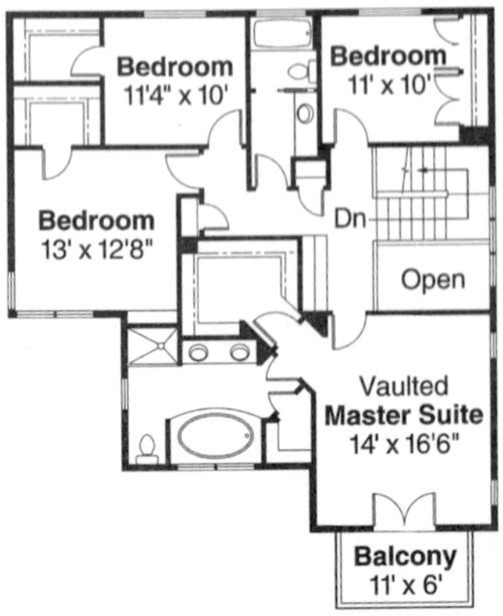

Craftsman & Ranch Homes

325 New House Plans

Plan:
HPK2600076

Style:
RANCH

Square Footage:
1,506

Bedrooms:
3

Bathrooms:
2

Width:
71' - 0"

Depth:
42' - 4"

© 1989 Donald A. Gardner Architects, Inc.

This unusual compact house maximizes its use of living areas and offers features usually found only in larger house plans. A lovely facade, adorned with multi-pane windows, shutters, dormers, bay windows and a covered porch, gives way to a truly livable floor plan. The living room, with a cathedral ceiling, fireplace, paddle fan, built-in cabinets and bookshelves, directly accesses the sun room through two sliding glass doors. Decorative columns between the foyer and great room create a dramatic entrance. Sleeping accommodations include a master suite with ample closet space and two family bedrooms. Note the split-bedroom plan configuration—providing utmost privacy.

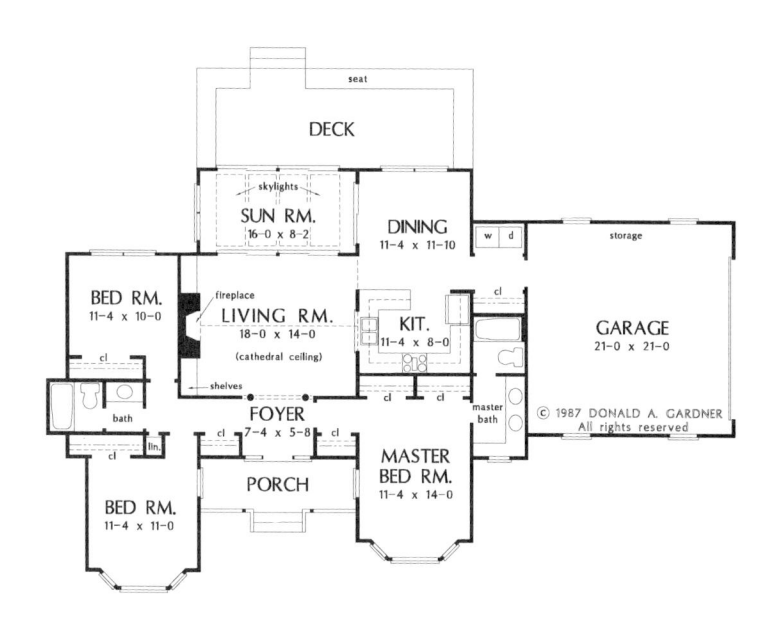

ORDER BLUEPRINTS 24 HOURS, 7 DAYS A WEEK, AT 1-800-521-6797 OR EPLANS.COM

325 New House Plans
Craftsman & Ranch Homes

Plan:
HPK2600077

Style:
BUNGALOW

First Floor:
2,372 SQ. FT.

Second Floor:
263 SQ. FT.

Total:
2,635 SQ. FT.

Bedrooms:
3

Bathrooms:
2

Width:
83' - 0"

Depth:
75' - 0"

Foundation:
UNFINISHED WALKOUT BASEMENT

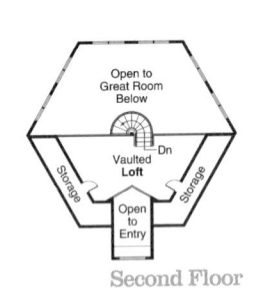

Second Floor

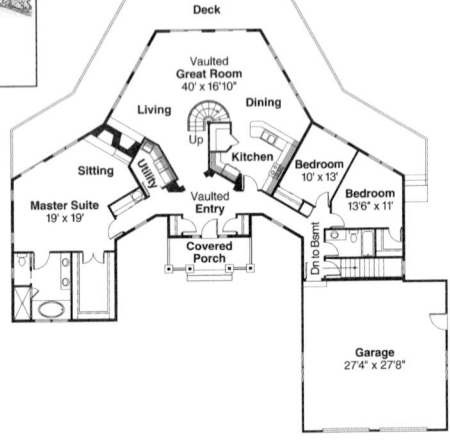

First Floor

Plan:
HPK2600078

Style:
RANCH

Square Footage:
2,653

Bedrooms:
3

Bathrooms:
2 1/2

Width:
84' - 0"

Depth:
66' - 0"

Foundation:
CRAWLSPACE

ORDER BLUEPRINTS 24 HOURS, 7 DAYS A WEEK, AT 1-800-521-6797 OR EPLANS.COM

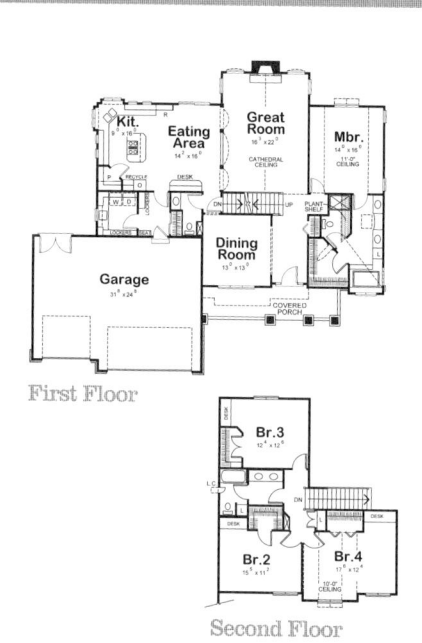

Craftsman & Ranch Homes

325 New House Plans

Plan:
HPK2600079

Style:
CRAFTSMAN
First Floor:
1,792 SQ. FT.
Second Floor:
898 SQ. FT.
Total:
2,690 SQ. FT.
Bedrooms:
4
Bathrooms:
2 1/2
Width:
67' - 0"
Depth:
56' - 0"

First Floor
Second Floor

Plan:
HPK2600080

Style:
CRAFTSMAN
First Floor:
1,849 SQ. FT.
Second Floor:
855 SQ. FT.
Total:
2,704 SQ. FT.
Bedrooms:
4
Bathrooms:
3 1/2
Width:
69' - 0"
Depth:
55' - 8"

First Floor 
Second Floor
Optional Layout

ORDER BLUEPRINTS 24 HOURS, 7 DAYS A WEEK, AT 1-800-521-6797 OR EPLANS.COM

325 New House Plans
Craftsman & Ranch Homes

Plan:
HPK2600081

Style:
CRAFTSMAN

Square Footage:
2,711

Bedrooms:
3

Bathrooms:
2 ½

Width:
130' - 4"

Depth:
70' - 6"

Foundation:
SLAB

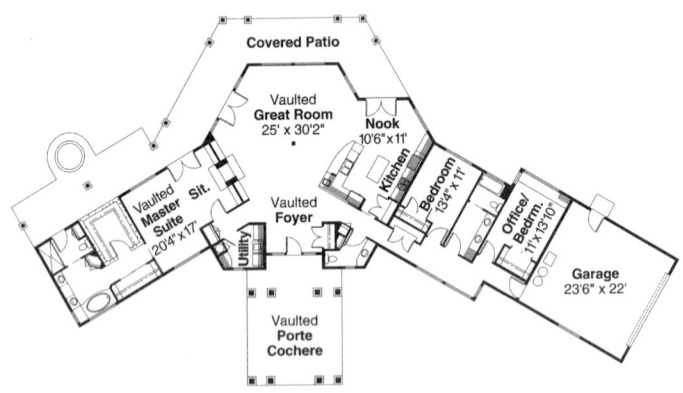

Plan:
HPK2600082

Style:
RANCH

Square Footage:
2,804

Bedrooms:
4

Bathrooms:
2 ½

Width:
87' - 10"

Depth:
54' - 6"

Foundation:
CRAWLSPACE, SLAB

ORDER BLUEPRINTS 24 HOURS, 7 DAYS A WEEK, AT 1-800-521-6797 OR EPLANS.COM

Craftsman & Ranch Homes

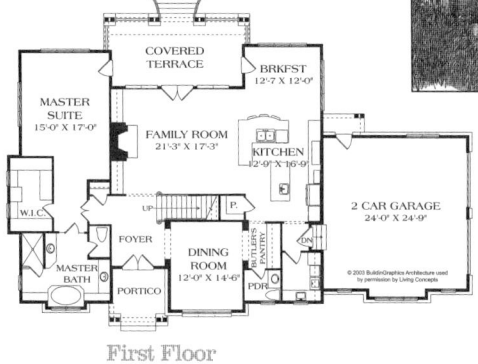

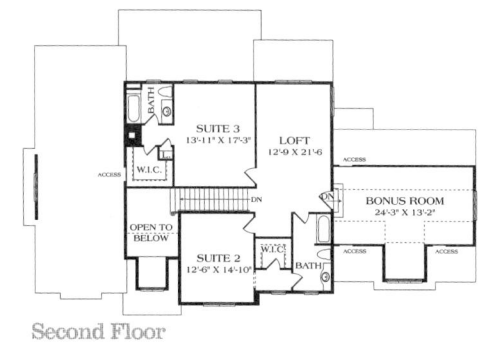

325 New House Plans

Plan:
HPK2600083

Style:
CRAFTSMAN

First Floor:
2,012 SQ. FT.

Second Floor:
1,149 SQ. FT.

Total:
3,161 SQ. FT.

Bonus Space:
379 SQ. FT.

Bedrooms:
3

Bathrooms:
3 1/2

Width:
53' - 4"

Depth:
51' - 4"

Foundation:
CRAWLSPACE

First Floor

Second Floor

Plan:
HPK2600084

Style:
CRAFTSMAN

Main Level:
1,993 SQ. FT.

Lower Level:
1,251 SQ. FT.

Total:
3,244 SQ. FT.

Bedrooms:
3

Bathrooms:
3 1/2

Width:
66' - 0"

Depth:
57' - 6"

Foundation:
FINISHED WALKOUT BASEMENT

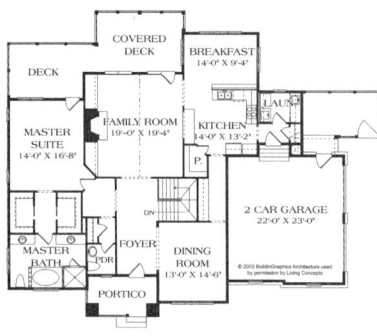

Main Level

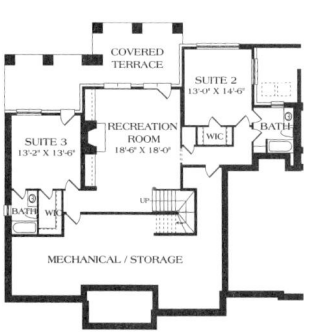

Lower Level

ORDER BLUEPRINTS 24 HOURS, 7 DAYS A WEEK, AT 1-800-521-6797 OR EPLANS.COM

325 New House Plans
Craftsman & Ranch Homes

Plan:
HPK2600085

Style:
CRAFTSMAN

Main Level:
1,604 SQ. FT.

Upper Level:
655 SQ. FT.

Lower Level:
1,247 SQ. FT.

Total:
3,506 SQ. FT.

Bonus Space:
307 SQ. FT.

Bedrooms:
5

Bathrooms:
3 1/2

Width:
59' - 0"

Depth:
59' - 8"

Foundation:
FINISHED BASEMENT

Upper Level

Lower Level

Main Level

Plan:
HPK2600086

Style:
COTTAGE

First Floor:
2,308 SQ. FT.

Second Floor:
1,445 SQ. FT.

Total:
3,753 SQ. FT.

Bedrooms:
4

Bathrooms:
3 1/2

Width:
78' - 0"

Depth:
52' - 0"

Foundation:
CRAWLSPACE, SLAB, UNFINISHED WALKOUT BASEMENT

First Floor

Second Floor

ORDER BLUEPRINTS 24 HOURS, 7 DAYS A WEEK, AT 1-800-521-6797 OR EPLANS.COM

Craftsman & Ranch Homes

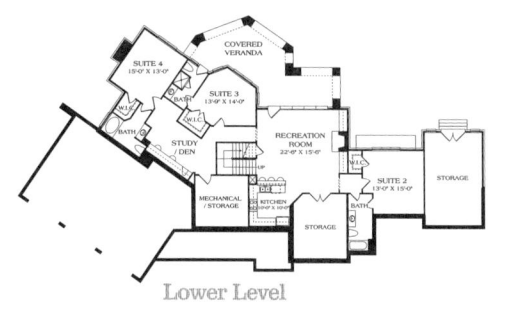

325 New House Plans

Plan:
HPK2600087

Style:
CRAFTSMAN

Main Level:
2,738 SQ. FT.

Lower Level:
1,960 SQ. FT.

Total:
4,698 SQ. FT.

Bedrooms:
5

Bathrooms:
5 1/2

Width:
117' - 6"

Depth:
65' - 8"

Foundation:
FINISHED WALKOUT BASEMENT

Plan:
HPK2600088

Style:
CRAFTSMAN

Main Level:
2,059 SQ. FT.

Upper Level:
1,621 SQ. FT.

Lower Level:
1,639 SQ. FT.

Total:
5,319 SQ. FT.

Bonus Space:
471 SQ. FT.

Bedrooms:
5

Bathrooms:
5 1/2

Width:
63' - 5"

Depth:
66' - 5"

Foundation:
FINISHED WALKOUT BASEMENT

ORDER BLUEPRINTS 24 HOURS, 7 DAYS A WEEK, AT 1-800-521-6797 OR EPLANS.COM

325 Craftsman & Ranch Homes
New House Plans

Plan:
HPK2600089

Style:
CRAFTSMAN

Main Level:
2,576 SQ. FT.

Upper Level:
1,139 SQ. FT.

Lower Level:
2,138 SQ. FT.

Total:
5,853 SQ. FT.

Bedrooms:
6

Bathrooms:
5 1/2

Width:
84' - 8"

Depth:
88' - 8"

Foundation:
FINISHED WALKOUT BASEMENT

This home blends the classic, rustic appeal of Craftsman stylings with modern innovations. The lower level is the destination for indoor and outdoor fun. Centered around the recreation room and flanked by a wet bar and the nearby hot tub, guests won't want to leave. Four bedrooms on this level offer ample accomodations. On the main level, the homeowner enjoys a private sunroom and library/study access. The upper level houses a guest apartment, complete with a second kitchen and a private porch.

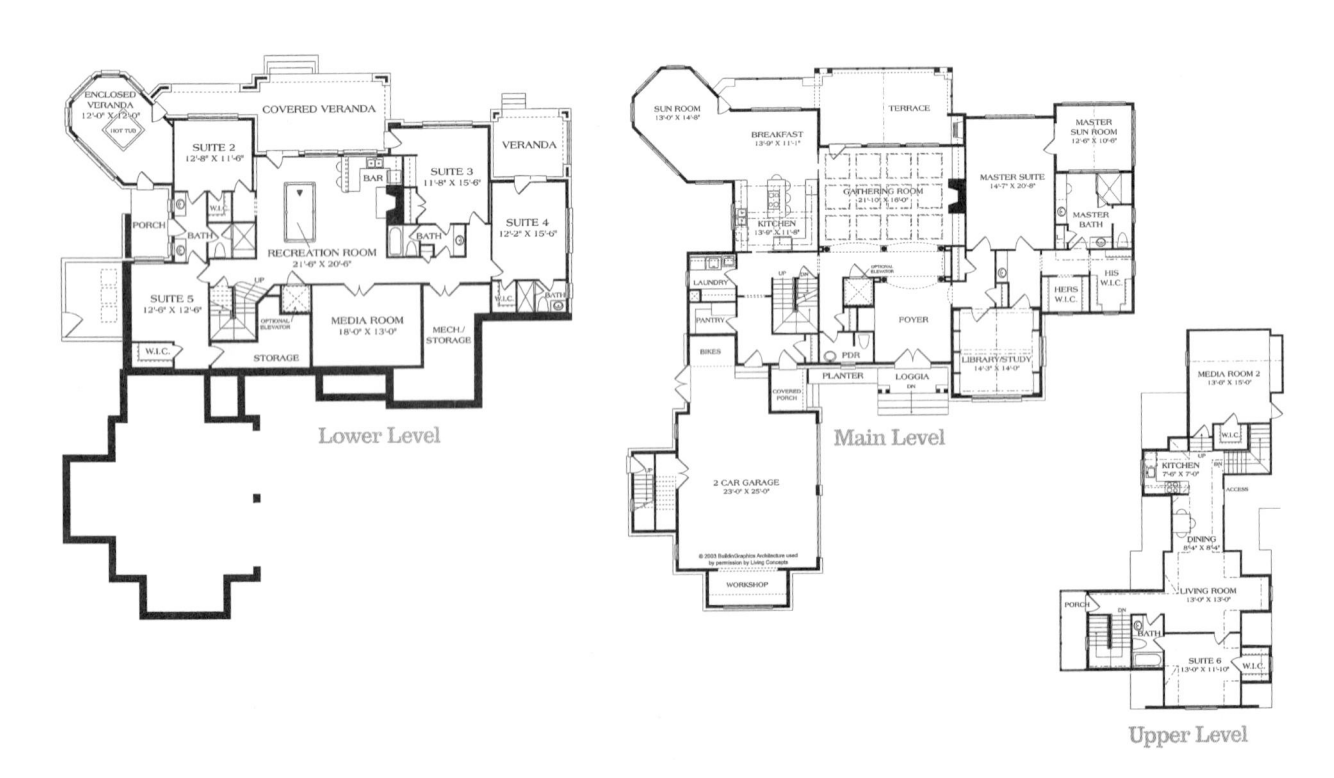

Lower Level

Main Level

Upper Level

80   ORDER BLUEPRINTS 24 HOURS, 7 DAYS A WEEK, AT 1-800-521-6797 OR EPLANS.COM

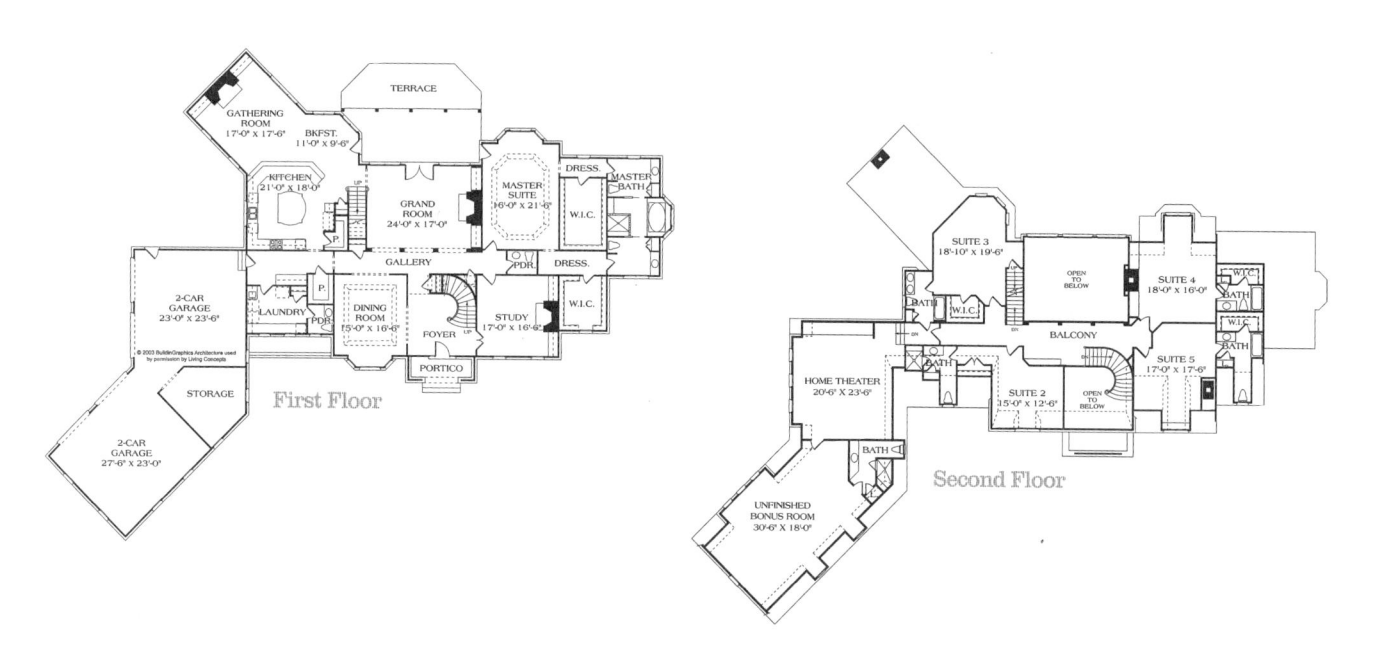

Craftsman & Ranch Homes

325 New House Plans

Plan:
HPK2600090

Style:
CRAFTSMAN

First Floor:
3,767 SQ. FT.

Second Floor:
2,665 SQ. FT.

Total:
6,432 SQ. FT.

Bonus Space:
780 SQ. FT.

Bedrooms:
5

Bathrooms:
5 1/2 + 1/2

Width:
133' - 10"

Depth:
102' - 8"

Foundation:
CRAWLSPACE

This inspiring design features the perfect master suite. Designed for elegance, convenience, and privacy, it is certain to delight and comfort the homeowners day after day. With 344 square feet of floor space under a 10-foot, octagonal tray ceiling, it will easily accomodate a grand old bed and several bureaus without feeling cramped. A window-lined bay with access to the terrace can hold a couple of comfortable chairs. The master bath provides each spouse with his or her own private space, approached through two separate dressing areas with adjoining walk-in closets. Each bath includes a sink, vanity, linen closet, and toilet. They are linked by a bayed space containing a huge soaking tub and a shower. Look closely at the floor plan to see that this home contains all the other conveniences and everyday luxuries demanded by today's homeowners.

First Floor

- GATHERING ROOM 17'-0" x 17'-6"
- BKFST. 11'-0" x 9'-6"
- TERRACE
- KITCHEN 21'-0" x 18'-0"
- GRAND ROOM 24'-0" x 17'-0"
- MASTER SUITE 16'-0" x 21'-0"
- DRESS.
- MASTER BATH
- W.I.C.
- 2-CAR GARAGE 23'-0" x 23'-6"
- LAUNDRY
- GALLERY
- DINING ROOM 15'-0" x 16'-0"
- PDR.
- DRESS.
- W.I.C.
- STUDY 17'-0" x 16'-0"
- FOYER
- PORTICO
- STORAGE
- 2-CAR GARAGE 27'-6" x 23'-0"

Second Floor

- SUITE 3 18'-10" x 19'-6"
- BATH
- W.I.C.
- OPEN TO BELOW
- SUITE 4 18'-0" x 16'-0"
- W.I.C.
- BATH
- BALCONY
- HOME THEATER 20'-6" x 23'-6"
- BATH
- SUITE 2 15'-0" x 12'-6"
- OPEN TO BELOW
- SUITE 5 17'-0" x 17'-6"
- BATH
- UNFINISHED BONUS ROOM 30'-6" x 18'-0"

325 New House Plans
Craftsman & Ranch Homes

Plan:
HPK2600091

Style:
CRAFTSMAN

Main Level:
3,211 SQ. FT.

Upper Level:
1,561 SQ. FT.

Lower Level:
1,850 SQ. FT.

Total:
6,622 SQ. FT.

Bedrooms:
5

Bathrooms:
5 1/2 + 2 HALF-BATHS

Width:
88' - 9"

Depth:
88' - 5"

Foundation:
UNFINISHED BASEMENT

Stone, siding, and a front porch give this home a traditional feel, but step inside and a modern layout is what you'll find. A sweeping staircase draws the eyes up as you enter the two-story foyer and between columns into the family room with fireplace and lanai access. A master suite with a sitting area and exercise room fills the left side of the plan, along with a study with fireplace and optional elevator. The right side of the house is where the family will gather, with a kitchen open to the breakfast and keeping rooms, made cozy with a fireplace. The second story holds three bedrooms, each with a private bath and walk-in closet. The two rear bedrooms have a sitting area inside a cupola with plenty of windows for expansive views.

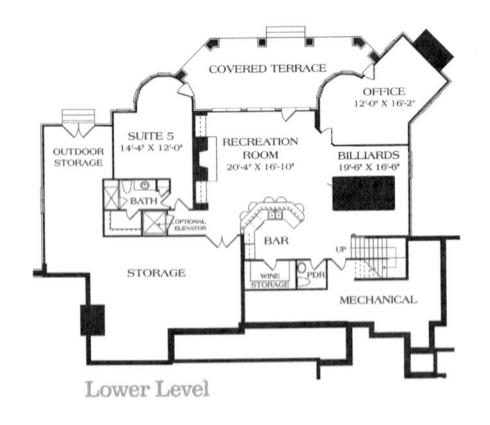

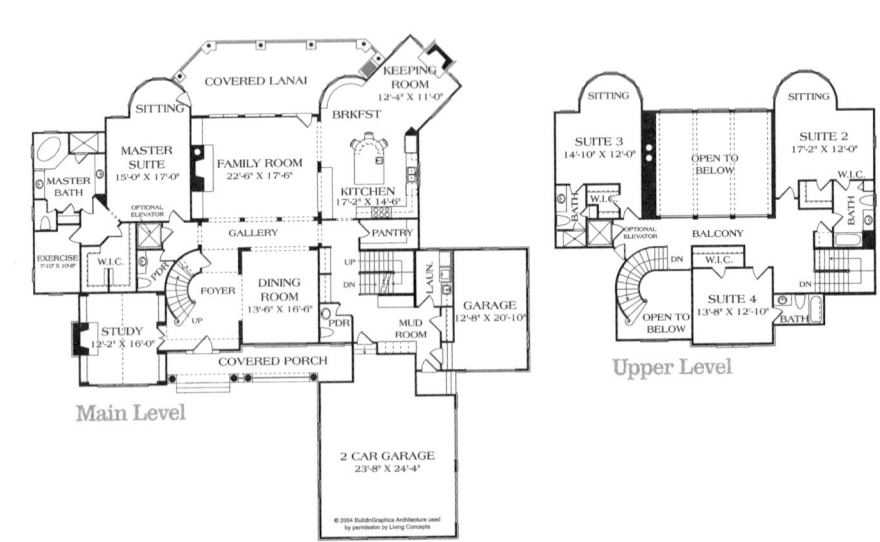

ORDER BLUEPRINTS 24 HOURS, 7 DAYS A WEEK, AT 1-800-521-6797 OR EPLANS.COM

Craftsman & Ranch Homes

325 New House Plans

Plan:
HPK2600092

Style:
CRAFTSMAN
Main Level:
3,320 SQ. FT.
Upper Level:
1,579 SQ. FT.
Lower Level:
1,936 SQ. FT.
Total:
6,835 SQ. FT.
Bedrooms:
5
Bathrooms:
5 1/2 + 2 HALF-BATHS
Width:
100' - 6"
Depth:
95' - 6"
Foundation:
FINISHED WALKOUT BASEMENT

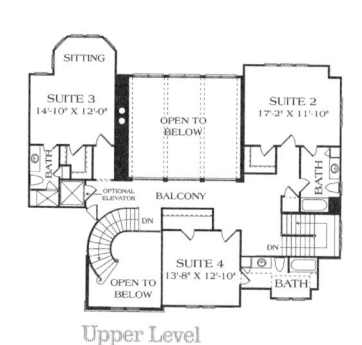

Upon first glance, this grand Craftsman home doesn't reveal the expansive floor plan that awaits inside. At nearly 7,000 square feet, it boasts every amenity imaginable, including an optional elevator. The lower level is a mix of business and pleasure housing the recreation room and bar plus a large home office. A secondary bedroom on this level is ideal for a teenager. The main level houses the master suite complete with an exercise room. The kitchen is a chef's dream, and the fireplace in the adjoining keeping room adds a cozy appeal. On the upper level, three additional secondary bedrooms each feature a full bath.

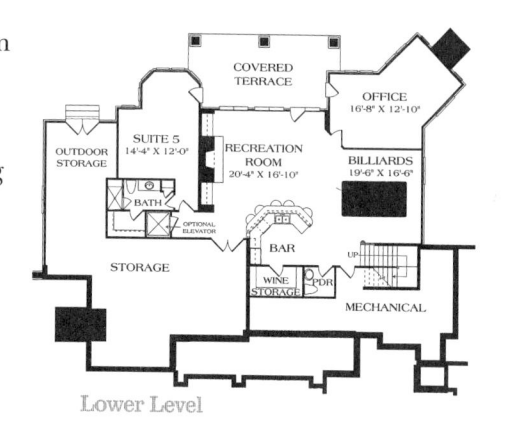

Lower Level

Main Level

Upper Level

ORDER BLUEPRINTS 24 HOURS, 7 DAYS A WEEK, AT 1-800-521-6797 OR EPLANS.COM

325 New House Plans

COUNTRY Homes

Plan:
HPK2600093

Style:
COUNTRY

Square Footage:
1,343

Bedrooms:
3

Bathrooms:
2

Width:
50' - 0"

Depth:
50' - 0"

Foundation:
UNFINISHED BASEMENT

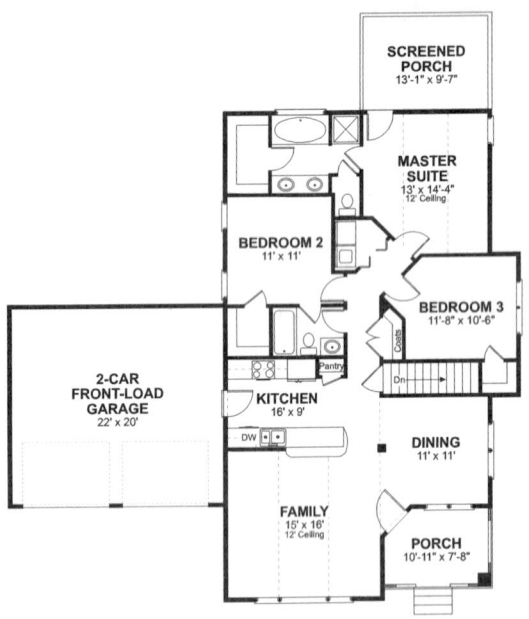

SCREENED PORCH
13'-1" x 9'-7"

MASTER SUITE
13' x 14'-4"
12' Ceiling

BEDROOM 2
11' x 11'

BEDROOM 3
11'-8" x 10'-6"

2-CAR FRONT-LOAD GARAGE
22' x 20'

KITCHEN
16' x 9'

DINING
11' x 11'

FAMILY
15' x 16'
12' Ceiling

PORCH
10'-11" x 7'-8"

This lovely 1,343-square-foot front porch design is as versatile as it is attractive. It makes a perfect starter home or vacation home and lends itself to narrow lots, with a garage that may easily be reduced in size or omitted entirely. The angled entry opens into a spacious open plan, including a dramatic vaulted family room lit by a large Palladian-style window. The master suite is also vaulted, and includes a luxurious bath, walk-in closet, and an inviting screened porch. The two remaining bedrooms share a hall bath and each features a walk-in closet. The washer and dryer are tucked conveniently in a laundry closet.

Country Homes

325 New House Plans

Plan:
HPK2600094

Style:
COUNTRY

Square Footage:
1,501

Bedrooms:
3

Bathrooms:
2

Width:
61' - 0"

Depth:
47' - 4"

Foundation:
SLAB

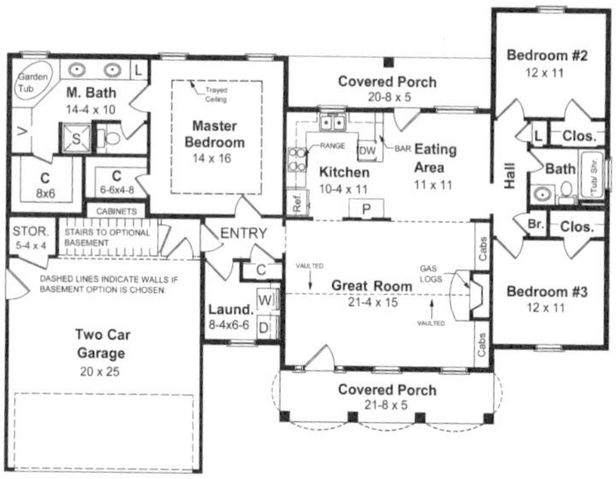

Plan:
HPK2600095

Style:
COUNTRY

Square Footage:
1,420

Bedrooms:
3

Bathrooms:
2

Width:
50' - 0"

Depth:
57' - 4"

Foundation:
UNFINISHED BASEMENT

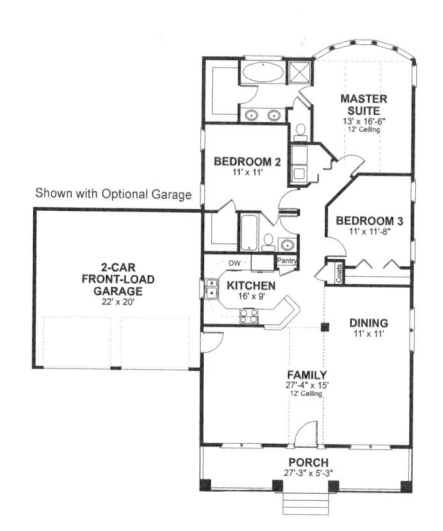

ORDER BLUEPRINTS 24 HOURS, 7 DAYS A WEEK, AT 1-800-521-6797 OR EPLANS.COM

85

325 Country Homes
New House Plans

Plan:
HPK2600096

Style:
COUNTRY

Square Footage:
1,536

Bedrooms:
3

Bathrooms:
2

Width:
55' - 4"

Depth:
51' - 0"

© 2005 Donald A. Gardner, Inc.

Twin dormers mirror a double-arched entryway in this convenient floor plan. Flanked by two gables, the front porch creates an inviting exterior. A low-maintenance facade and front-entry garage provide ultimate convenience, making this floor plan perfect for first-time homebuyers or those looking to downsize. French doors accent the great room, while a ceiling treatment expands vertical volume. A dining room rests just off the great room, enhancing the open layout. An optional bonus room above the garage becomes a perfect space for a child's playroom or media center. The privately located master bedroom features a walk-in closet, His and Hers sinks, and a separate garden tub.

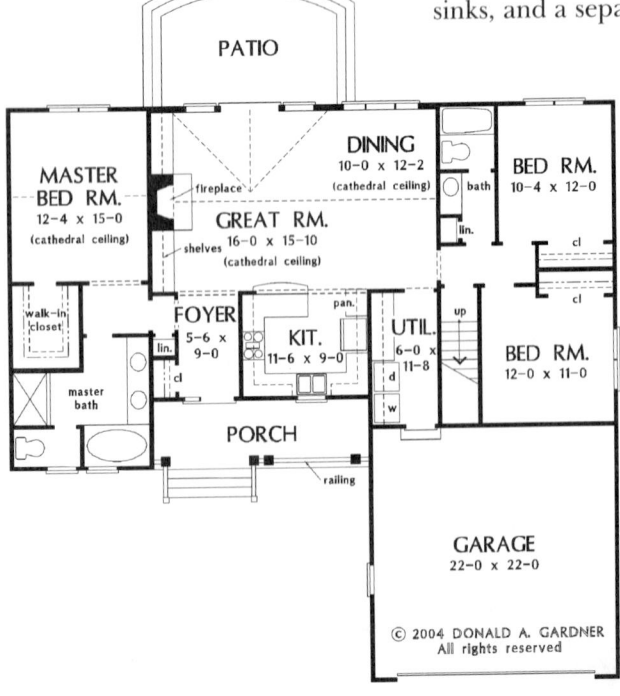

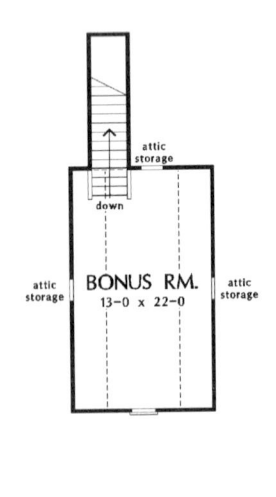

ORDER BLUEPRINTS 24 HOURS, 7 DAYS A WEEK, AT 1-800-521-6797 OR EPLANS.COM

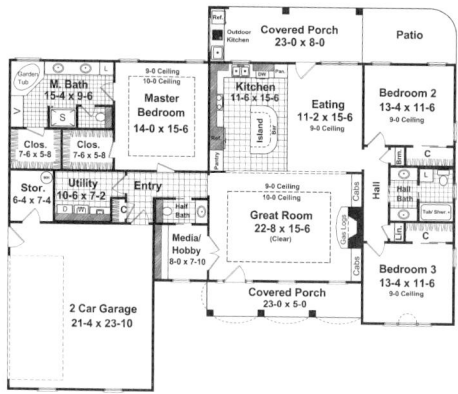

Country Homes

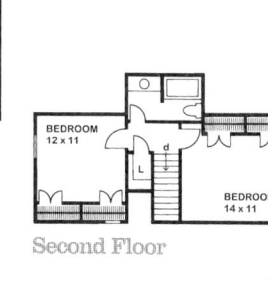

325 New House Plans

Plan:
HPK2600097

Style:
COTTAGE

First Floor:
1,075 SQ. FT.

Second Floor:
500 SQ. FT.

Total:
1,575 SQ. FT.

Bedrooms:
3

Bathrooms:
2

Width:
52' - 0"

Depth:
37' - 0"

Foundation:
CRAWLSPACE

Plan:
HPK2600098

Style:
COUNTRY

Square Footage:
2,000

Bedrooms:
3

Bathrooms:
2 1/2

Width:
67' - 0"

Depth:
56' - 0"

Foundation:
CRAWLSPACE, SLAB

ORDER BLUEPRINTS 24 HOURS, 7 DAYS A WEEK, AT 1-800-521-6797 OR EPLANS.COM

325 New House Plans

Country Homes

Plan:
HPK2600099

Style:
COTTAGE

First Floor:
1,010 SQ. FT.

Second Floor:
595 SQ. FT.

Total:
1,605 SQ. FT.

Bedrooms:
3

Bathrooms:
2

Width:
32' - 0"

Depth:
44' - 0"

Foundation:
UNFINISHED BASEMENT

This classic Craftsman-style bungalow features a full-width porch anchored by stone columns, a fieldstone chimney, and a gable dormer. Sidelights flank the front door and brighten the entryway. A large hearth fireplace helps make the living room cozy at the front. The kitchen services the screened-in porch as well as the breakfast nook and dining room. The first-floor master suite has a walk-in closet and French doors that open to the porch. Upstairs, a hallway separates two bedrooms, each of which has ample closet space and shares a full bath.

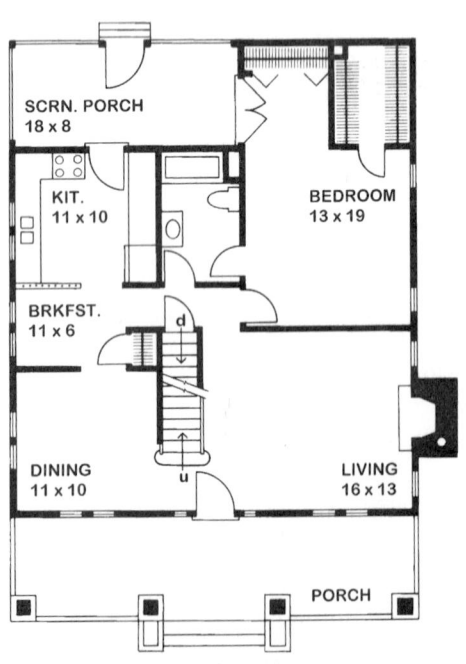

First Floor

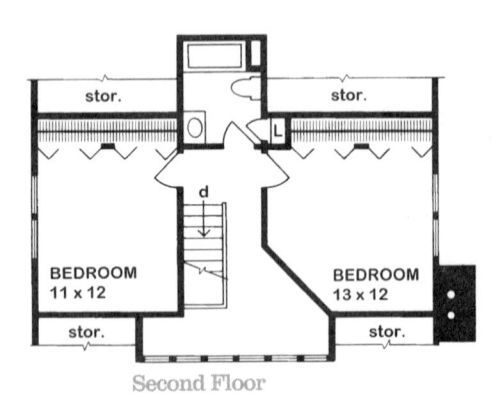

Second Floor

ORDER BLUEPRINTS 24 HOURS, 7 DAYS A WEEK, AT 1-800-521-6797 OR EPLANS.COM

Country Homes

325
New House Plans

Plan:
HPK2600100

Style:
COUNTRY

Square Footage:
1,685

Bedrooms:
3

Bathrooms:
2

Width:
36' - 4"

Depth:
88' - 8"

© 2004 Donald A. Gardner, Inc.

Perfect for long narrow lots, this plan combines simplistic needs with exciting extras. A welcoming front porch coupled with a large, single gable creates an inviting exterior. The porte cochere, defined by decorative columns, becomes a quick, covered spot for vehicles and can be accessed via the kitchen. A garage at the rear extends driveway space, perfect for a basketball or hopscotch court. Tray ceilings crown the dining room, master suite, and bedroom/study, increasing volume in each. Wraparound countertops expand meal preparation areas in the kitchen, as it gently flows into the great room, promoting open spaces. The master bedroom features His and Hers sinks, a garden tub, and a generous walk-in closet.

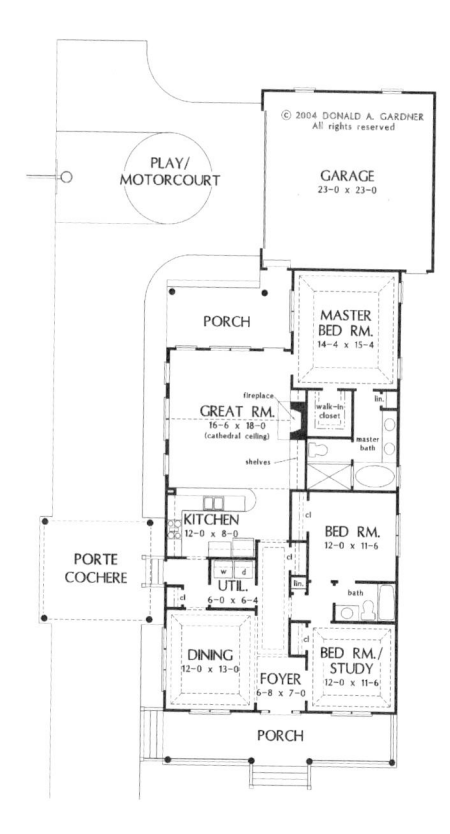

ORDER BLUEPRINTS 24 HOURS, 7 DAYS A WEEK, AT 1-800-521-6797 OR EPLANS.COM

325 New House Plans
Country Homes

Plan:
HPK2600101

Style:
COTTAGE

First Floor:
1,232 SQ. FT.

Second Floor:
987 SQ. FT.

Total:
2,219 SQ. FT.

Bedrooms:
3

Bathrooms:
3 ½

Width:
67' - 0"

Depth:
40' - 0"

Foundation:
UNFINISHED WALKOUT BASEMENT

First Floor

Second Floor

Plan:
HPK2600102

Style:
FARMHOUSE

Square Footage:
1,799

Bedrooms:
3

Bathrooms:
2 ½

Width:
78' - 0"

Depth:
46' - 0"

Foundation:
SLAB

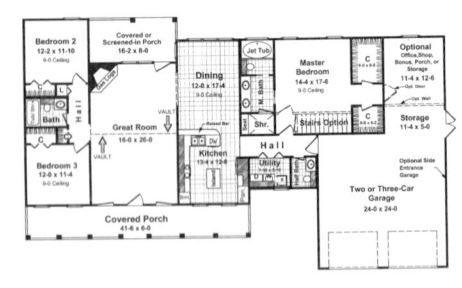

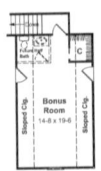

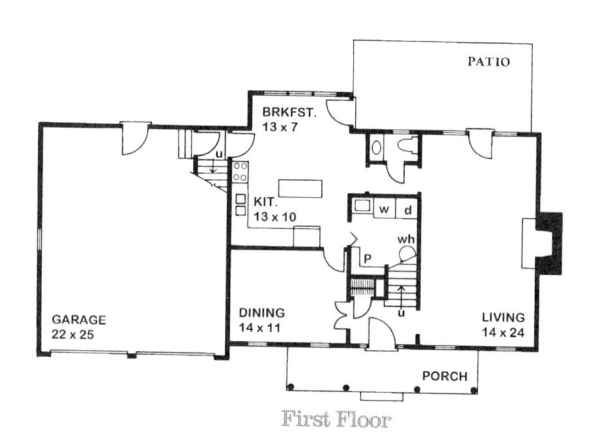

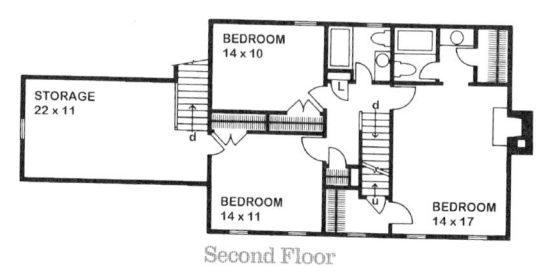

Country Homes

325 New House Plans

Plan:
HPK2600103

Style:
FARMHOUSE

First Floor:
925 SQ. FT.

Second Floor:
875 SQ. FT.

Total:
1,800 SQ. FT.

Bedrooms:
3

Bathrooms:
2 1/2

Width:
58' - 0"

Depth:
34' - 0"

Foundation:
CRAWLSPACE

Two fireplaces warm this timeless farmhouse. Classic features inspired by 18th-century American homes distinguish this three-bedroom dwelling. A center gable accentuates its symmetrical facade, and wooden shutters flank traditional double-hung windows. The covered front porch is large enough to accommodate outdoor furniture. Abundant storage space on the second floor is an added bonus.

ORDER BLUEPRINTS 24 HOURS, 7 DAYS A WEEK, AT 1-800-521-6797 OR EPLANS.COM

325 Country Homes
New House Plans

Plan:
HPK2600104

Style:
COTTAGE

Square Footage:
1,806

Bedrooms:
3

Bathrooms:
2

Width:
63' - 0"

Depth:
54' - 4"

Foundation:
CRAWLSPACE, SLAB

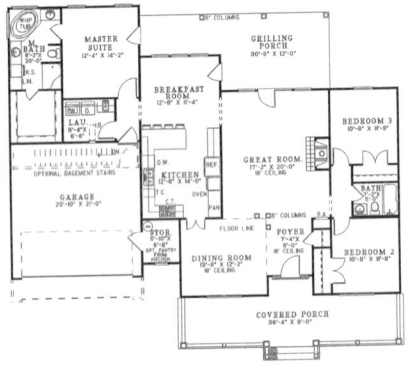

Plan:
HPK2600105

Style:
COUNTRY

Square Footage:
1,818

Bedrooms:
3

Bathrooms:
3

Width:
63' - 4"

Depth:
53' - 0"

Foundation:
UNFINISHED BASEMENT

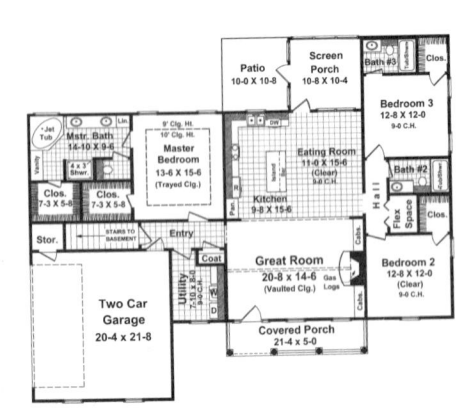

ORDER BLUEPRINTS 24 HOURS, 7 DAYS A WEEK, AT 1-800-521-6797 OR EPLANS.COM

Country Homes

325
New House Plans

Plan:
HPK2600106

Style:
FARMHOUSE

Square Footage:
1,838

Bonus Space:
362 SQ. FT.

Bedrooms:
3

Bathrooms:
2

Width:
70' - 8"

Depth:
70' - 10"

© 1996 Donald A. Gardner Architects, Inc.

This plan offers all the amenities for family living and formal entertaining on one convenient level. Off the generous wraparound porch, a columned foyer opens to the elegantly treated dining room and the lofty great room. Here a grand fireplace anchors a soaring clerestory window. An angled snack bar unites the great room, kitchen, and light-filled breakfast nook. The back porch bridges the house and the detached garage, with plenty of space for sitting beneath its sunny skylights. To the left of the living spaces, the master bedroom and bath occupy the back corner of the house, while two secondary bedrooms share a bath in the front corner. A bonus room above the garage offers additional space for a home office, guest suite, or rec room for the kids.

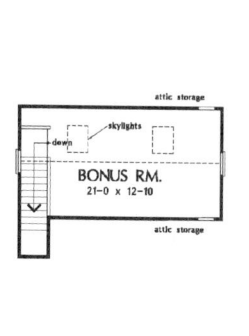

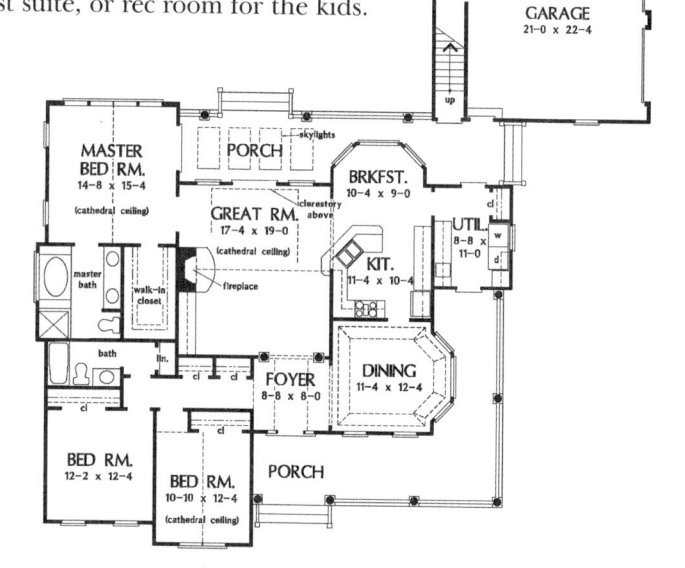

ORDER BLUEPRINTS 24 HOURS, 7 DAYS A WEEK, AT 1-800-521-6797 OR EPLANS.COM

325 New House Plans

Country Homes

Plan:
HPK2600107

Style:
COUNTRY

Square Footage:
1,852

Bedrooms:
3

Bathrooms:
2 1/2

Width:
78' - 0"

Depth:
49' - 6"

Foundation:
SLAB

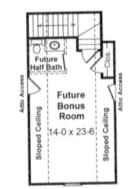

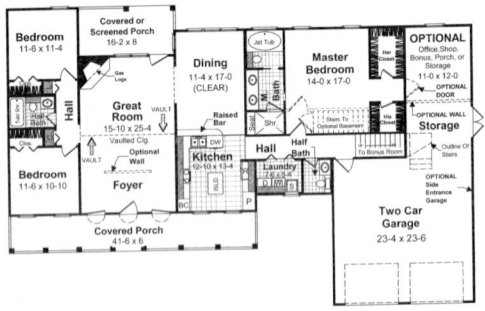

Plan:
HPK2600108

Style:
COUNTRY

Square Footage:
1,886

Bonus Space:
588 SQ. FT.

Bedrooms:
3

Bathrooms:
2

Width:
51' - 6"

Depth:
65' - 8"

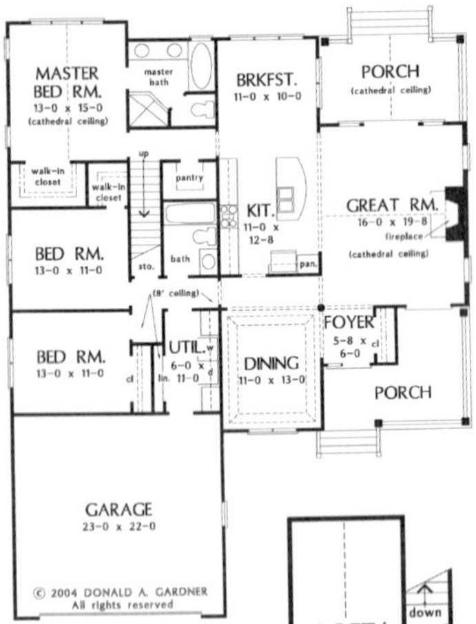

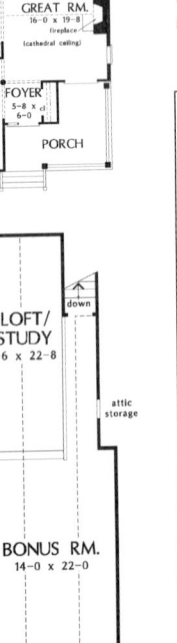

ORDER BLUEPRINTS 24 HOURS, 7 DAYS A WEEK, AT 1-800-521-6797 OR EPLANS.COM

Country Homes

325 New House Plans

Plan:
HPK2600109

Style:
COUNTRY

Square Footage:
1,921

Bonus Space:
449 SQ. FT.

Bedrooms:
3

Bathrooms:
2

Width:
62' - 6"

Depth:
49' - 8"

© 2004 Donald A. Gardner, Inc.

Brick and siding blend to form a classic facade for this elegant yet economical home. Two sets of twin columns accent the front door, while each set frames striking double-hung windows. The front-entry garage allows the home to fit on a small or narrow lot, cutting costs. Off the foyer, double doors lead to the flexible bedroom/study, and across the hall a tray ceiling highlights the dining room. A coffered ceiling adds architectural interest to the great room, while a cathedral ceiling tops the master bedroom. An open island kitchen has views of the breakfast area and great room, which also has built-in shelves flanking the fireplace. In the master bath, a privy and dual vanity sinks conveniently help coordinate morning routines. As a covered porch off the great room provides space for outdoor relaxation and entertaining, the bonus room above the garage offers expansion possibilities.

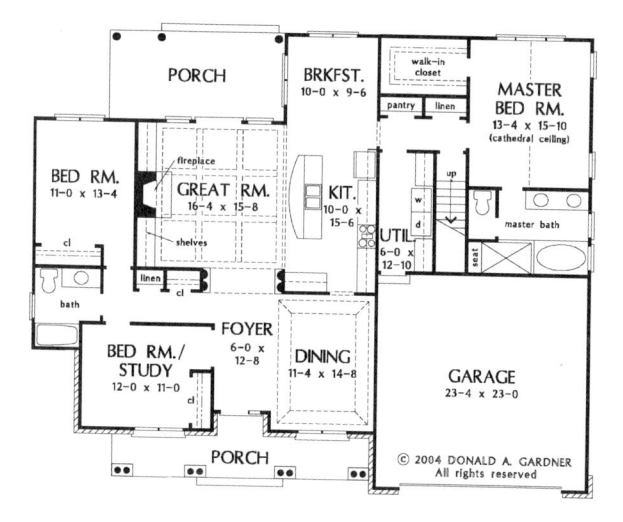

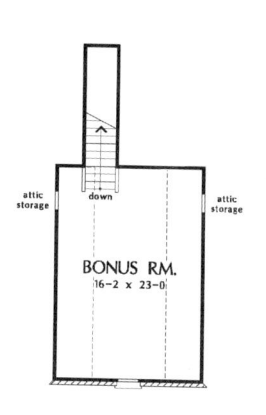

ORDER BLUEPRINTS 24 HOURS, 7 DAYS A WEEK, AT 1-800-521-6797 OR EPLANS.COM

325 Country Homes
New House Plans

Plan:
HPK2600110

Style:
COUNTRY

Square Footage:
1,939

Bedrooms:
3

Bathrooms:
2

Width:
56' - 6"

Depth:
62' - 0"

© 2004 Donald A. Gardner, Inc.

A charming front porch and box-bay window combine with twin dormers and two gables to create stunning curb appeal for this country home. Metal roofs accentuate the front porch and box-bay, while a screened porch creates a comfortable outdoor space in the back. Displaying more traditional room definition, the great room is separated from the other gathering areas, yet it's connected to the kitchen by the dining room and a hallway with columns. Creating quite a centerpiece for the common areas, the octagonal dining room is almost completely surrounded by windows and crowned with a tray ceiling. A cathedral ceiling highlights the great room, while a bonus room allows expansion. The kitchen provides space for a computer hub.

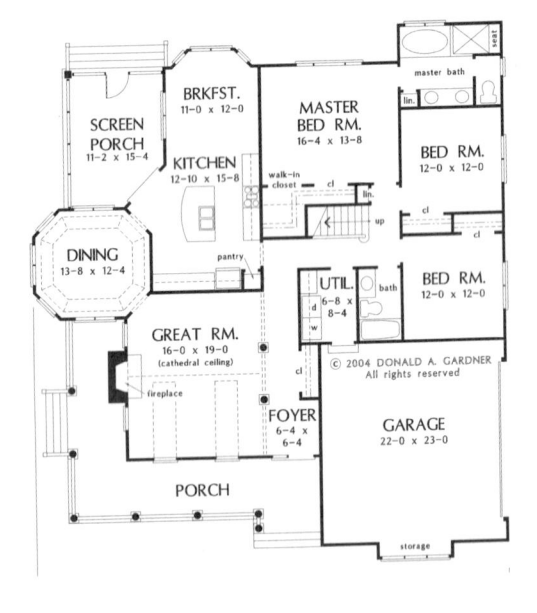

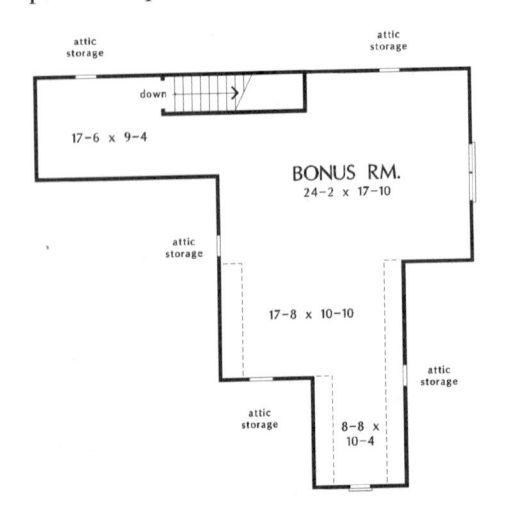

ORDER BLUEPRINTS 24 HOURS, 7 DAYS A WEEK, AT 1-800-521-6797 OR EPLANS.COM

Country Homes

325
New House Plans

Plan:
HPK2600111

Style:
COUNTRY

Square Footage:
1,965

Bedrooms:
4

Bathrooms:
2

Width:
74' - 4"

Depth:
56' - 6"

Foundation:
CRAWLSPACE

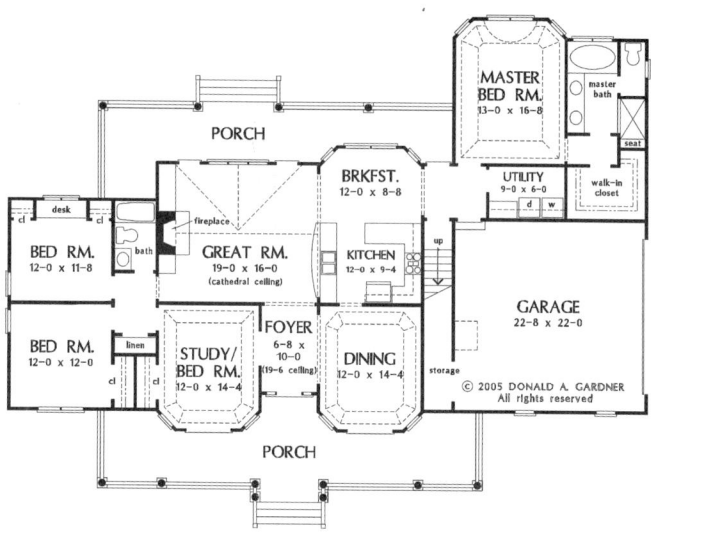

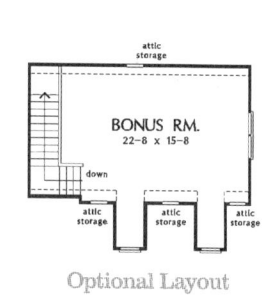

© 2005 Donald A. Gardner, Inc.

Optional Layout

© 2005 DONALD A. GARDNER
All rights reserved

Designed with a touch of farmhouse flair, this home combines a modern floor plan with the look of yesterday. The stunning exterior is made up of columns, several dormer windows, and porches that wrap almost entirely around the home. Inside, bay windows expand the versatile study/bedroom, dining room, and master bedroom. Each crowned with a tray ceiling, these rooms are nothing short of luxurious. The master bedroom also features a barrel vault, and the master bath includes a separate tub and shower with built-in seat. The breakfast room and kitchen are open to the great room and create a natural traffic flow between the rooms. A spacious rear porch completes the home and provides ample space for outdoor entertaining.

325 New House Plans

Country Homes

Plan:
HPK2600112

Style:
FARMHOUSE

Square Footage:
2,000

Bedrooms:
4

Bathrooms:
2

Width:
68' - 0"

Depth:
55' - 8"

Foundation:
SLAB

This four-bedroom beauty should fulfill the needs of many with the optional bedroom/game room/den, and the flex space (hobby/office). An open-plan, split-bedroom layout provides good use of space. The master suite is packed with features including a jet tub, dual lavatories, oversized shower, His and Hers walk-in closets, and a vaulted ceiling in the master bedroom. A great plan for socializing with friends and family, it includes a kitchen with raised bar, great room with gas-log fireplace, front porch, rear grilling porch, and screened porch. The oversized garage and unheated storage area are a plus. The exterior traditional styling with brick and contrasting trim provides an architectural presentation that looks great now and will look great for years to come.

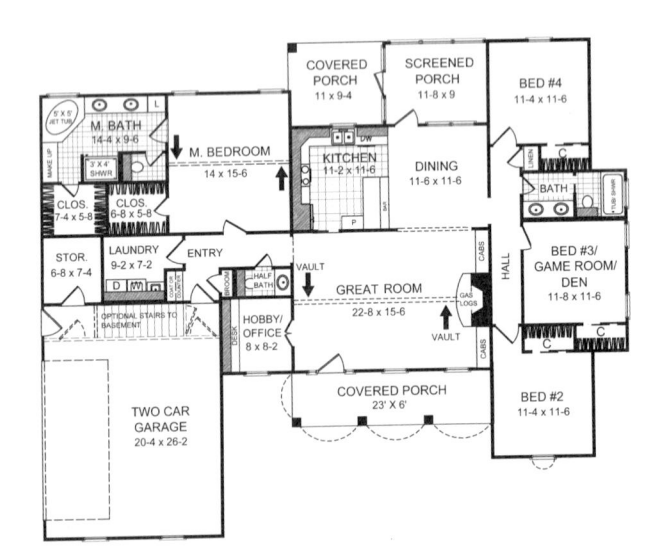

ORDER BLUEPRINTS 24 HOURS, 7 DAYS A WEEK, AT 1-800-521-6797 OR EPLANS.COM

Country Homes

325 New House Plans

Plan:
HPK2600113

Style:
COUNTRY

Square Footage:
2,001

Bedrooms:
3

Bathrooms:
2

Width:
64' - 0"

Depth:
54' - 4"

Foundation:
SLAB

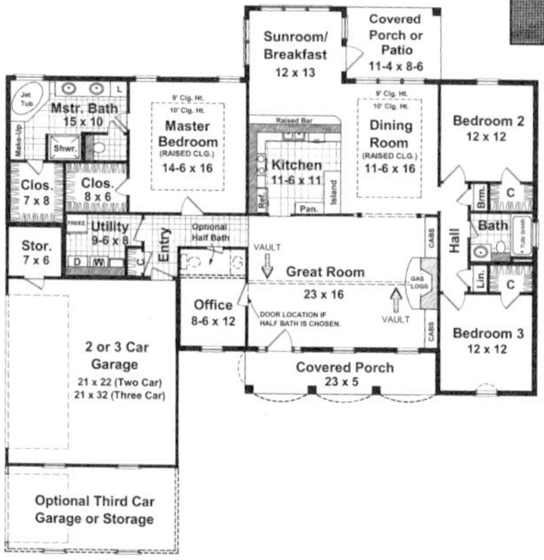

Plan:
HPK2600114

Style:
COUNTRY

Square Footage:
2,002

Bedrooms:
3

Bathrooms:
2

Width:
64' - 6"

Depth:
61' - 4"

Foundation:
UNFINISHED BASEMENT

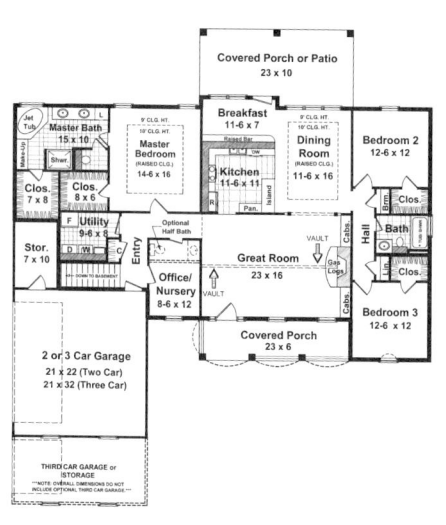

ORDER BLUEPRINTS 24 HOURS, 7 DAYS A WEEK, AT 1-800-521-6797 OR EPLANS.COM

325 New House Plans
Country Homes

Plan:
HPK2600115

Style:
FARMHOUSE

Square Footage:
2,008

Bonus Space:
354 SQ. FT.

Bedrooms:
3

Bathrooms:
2 ½

Width:
78' - 0"

Depth:
49' - 6"

Foundation:
CRAWLSPACE, SLAB

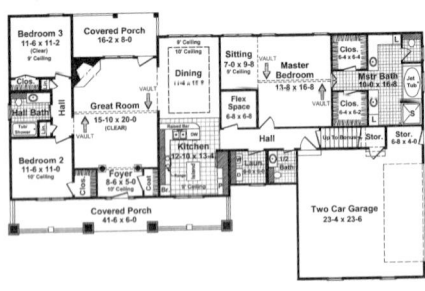

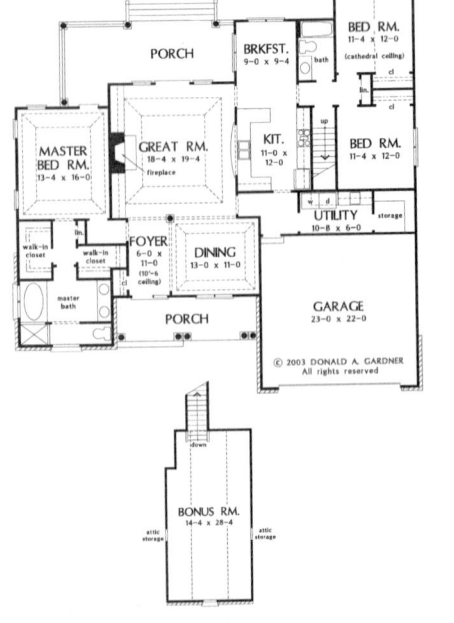

Plan:
HPK2600116

Style:
COUNTRY

Square Footage:
2,021

Bonus Space:
471 SQ. FT.

Bedrooms:
3

Bathrooms:
2

Width:
60' - 3"

Depth:
58' - 10"

ORDER BLUEPRINTS 24 HOURS, 7 DAYS A WEEK, AT 1-800-521-6797 OR EPLANS.COM

Country Homes

325 New House Plans

Plan:
HPK2600117

Style:
COUNTRY

Square Footage:
2,249

Bonus Space:
553 SQ. FT.

Bedrooms:
3

Bathrooms:
2 ½

Width:
72' - 6"

Depth:
55' - 4"

Foundation:
SLAB

A large covered porch beckons those warm evenings sitting in the rocker enjoying the surrounding neighborhood ambiance. Upon entry notice the vista view through the home, the covered patio, and the rear yard beyond. To the right is the formal dining room with trayed ceiling and large buffet niche. To the left is the study, easily converted to a living room. The family room has a fireplace and space for a built-in media center. The secondary bedrooms share a semi-private bath. The master suite enters off the vestibule next to the nook, which also provides access to the bonus room over the garage and the laundry area. Note the built-in niche. The master suite is large and has access to the covered patio as well as the well-appointed master bath with a large walk-in closet. The master bath includes a corner tub, walk-in shower, private toilet chamber, and dual vanities with a center make-up area.

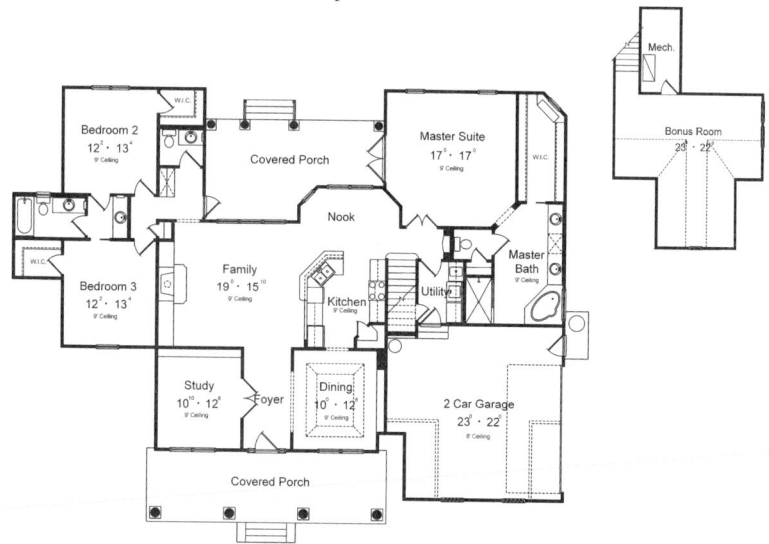

ORDER BLUEPRINTS 24 HOURS, 7 DAYS A WEEK, AT 1-800-521-6797 OR EPLANS.COM

325 New House Plans

Country Homes

Plan:
HPK2600118

Style:
VICTORIAN ECLECTIC

First Floor:
1,502 SQ. FT.

Second Floor:
549 SQ. FT.

Total:
2,051 SQ. FT.

Bonus Space:
285 SQ. FT.

Bedrooms:
3

Bathrooms:
2 ½

Width:
43' - 0"

Depth:
57' - 6"

© 2004 Donald A. Gardner, Inc.

A stone-and-siding exterior creates incredible curb appeal for this country cottage. Decorative brackets accent the gables and a metal roof tops columns on the front and rear porches. Inside, the floor plan opens common areas—kitchen, great room, and breakfast area—to each other, and uses a balcony to divide the two-story foyer from the great room. A dining room near the front entry provides a formal atmosphere for meals. Bay windows extend the floor space here as well as in the breakfast nook and master bedroom. A tray ceiling, also in the master bedroom, creates height, while a conventional closet paired with a walk-in provides space for clothes and other storage. A corner shower and corner tub give the master bath spa-like luxury. Above the garage, a bonus room provides space for a family's everchanging needs and a large linen closet adds space for storage.

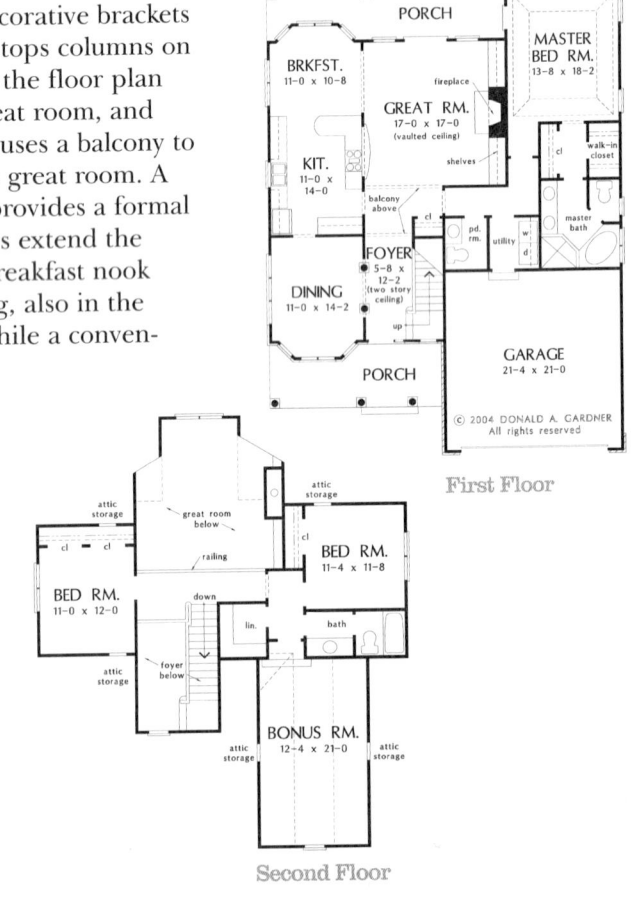

First Floor

Second Floor

102　ORDER BLUEPRINTS 24 HOURS, 7 DAYS A WEEK, AT 1-800-521-6797 OR EPLANS.COM

Country Homes

325 New House Plans

Plan:
HPK2600119

Style:
FARMHOUSE

Square Footage:
2,070

Bedrooms:
3

Bathrooms:
2 1/2

Width:
70' - 0"

Depth:
59' - 0"

Foundation:
CRAWLSPACE

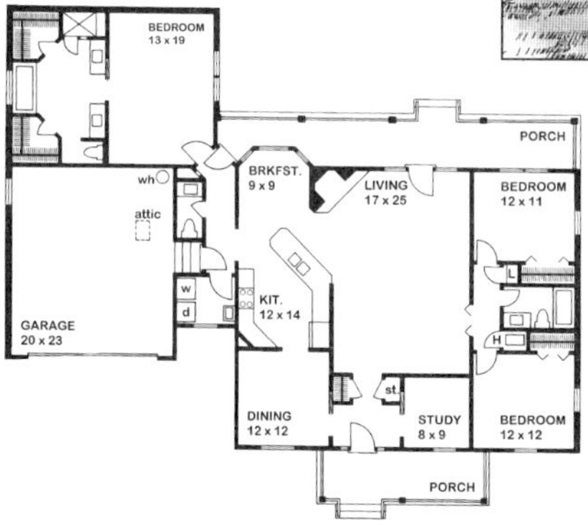

Plan:
HPK2600120

Style:
COTTAGE

First Floor:
1,550 SQ. FT.

Second Floor:
545 SQ. FT.

Total:
2,095 SQ. FT.

Bedrooms:
2

Bathrooms:
2

Width:
30' - 0"

Depth:
38' - 0"

Foundation:
UNFINISHED BASEMENT

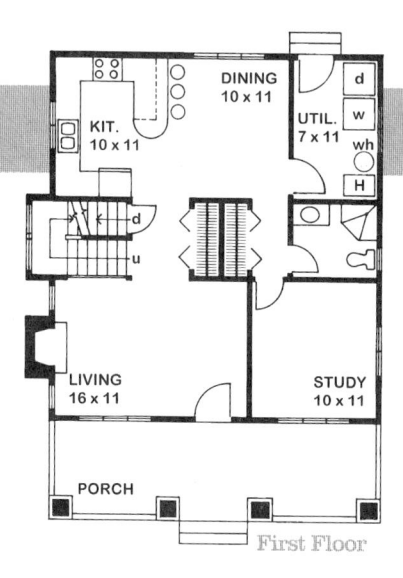

First Floor

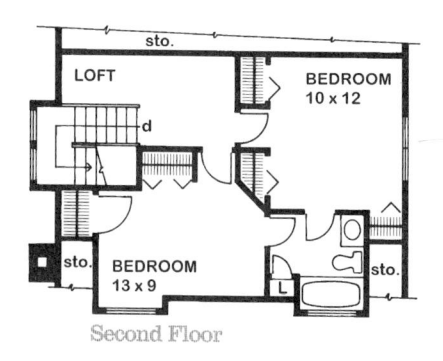

Second Floor

ORDER BLUEPRINTS 24 HOURS, 7 DAYS A WEEK, AT 1-800-521-6797 OR EPLANS.COM

325 New House Plans
Country Homes

Plan:
HPK2600121

Style:
FARMHOUSE

Square Footage:
2,100

Bedrooms:
3

Bathrooms:
3

Width:
79' - 4"

Depth:
53' - 6"

Foundation:
SLAB

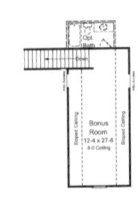

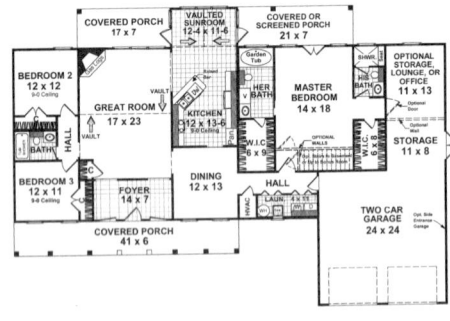

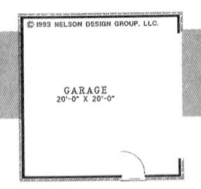

Plan:
HPK2600122

Style:
COTTAGE

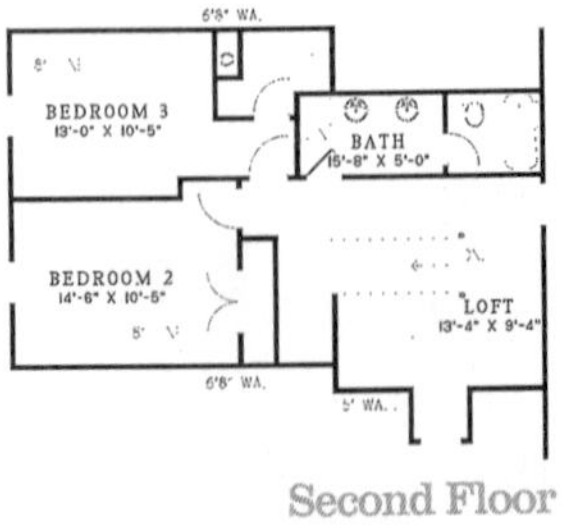

First Floor:
1,393 SQ. FT.

Second Floor:
742 SQ. FT.

Total:
2,135 SQ. FT.

Bedrooms:
3

Bathrooms:
2 1/2

Width:
35' - 10"

Depth:
77' - 4"

Foundation:
CRAWLSPACE, SLAB

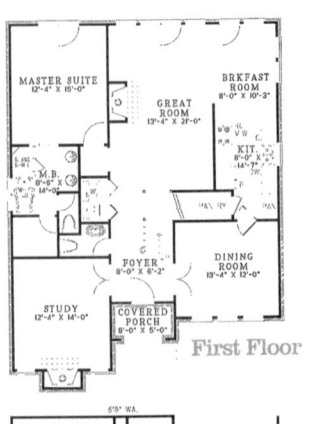

First Floor

Second Floor

104 ORDER BLUEPRINTS 24 HOURS, 7 DAYS A WEEK, AT 1-800-521-6797 OR EPLANS.COM

Country Homes

325
New House Plans

Plan:
HPK2600123

Style:
FARMHOUSE

First Floor:
1,529 SQ. FT.

Second Floor:
613 SQ. FT.

Total:
2,142 SQ. FT.

Bedrooms:
3

Bathrooms:
2 1/2

Width:
59' - 8"

Depth:
55' - 4"

Foundation:
CRAWLSPACE

© WILLIAM E POOLE DESIGNS, INC.

Imagine whiling away the long summer days on this glorious wraparound porch. Follow the sun or enjoy the shade; chat with neighbors out front or hide around back with a good book. Enveloping three sides of the home, this porch offers a space for every hour of the day and every mood. Inside, comfort rules with a hearth-warmed family room and a kitchen open to the breakfast area. The master suite offers a bath with a double vanity, shower, and whirlpool tub. There's plenty of room for family and guests upstairs with two bedrooms, a loft, full bath, and future rec room.

First Floor

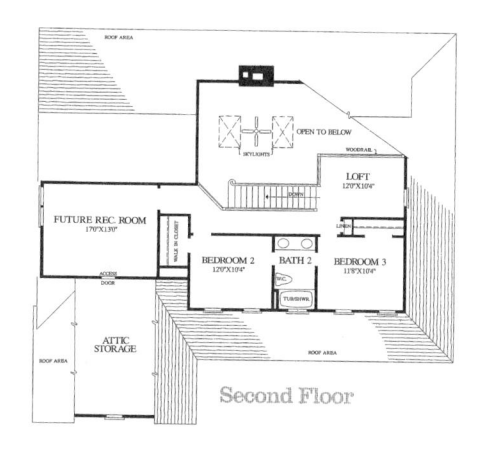

Second Floor

ORDER BLUEPRINTS 24 HOURS, 7 DAYS A WEEK, AT 1-800-521-6797 OR EPLANS.COM

325 New House Plans
Country Homes

Plan:
HPK2600124

Style:
COTTAGE

First Floor:
1,280 SQ. FT.

Second Floor:
878 SQ. FT.

Total:
2,158 SQ. FT.

Bedrooms:
3

Bathrooms:
3 1/2

Width:
43' - 6"

Depth:
55' - 8"

© 2005 Donald A. Gardner, Inc.

Great for rectangular lots, this home lives much larger than its cottage exterior appears. Immediately through the foyer is the formal dining and great room. A single column and tray ceiling grant architectural interest to the dining room, while the fireplace, rear porch entrance, and overhead balcony provide stunning details to the great room. Accessing the rear porch and gracefully flowing into the kitchen, the great room is the perfect entertaining space. The master suite is truly pampering. Located on the first floor, it is tucked away for privacy and includes an indulging bathroom with a garden tub, separate shower with seat, and twin vanities. The kitchen and utility room complete the first floor. The second level includes two secondary bedrooms, each with walk-in closet and private bath as well as a loft/study that overlooks the great room.

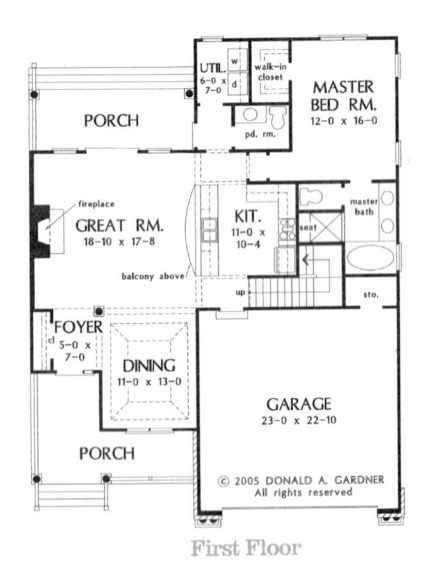

First Floor

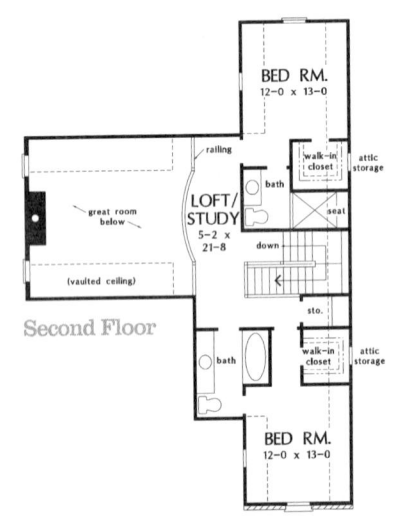

Second Floor

106   ORDER BLUEPRINTS 24 HOURS, 7 DAYS A WEEK, AT 1-800-521-6797 OR EPLANS.COM

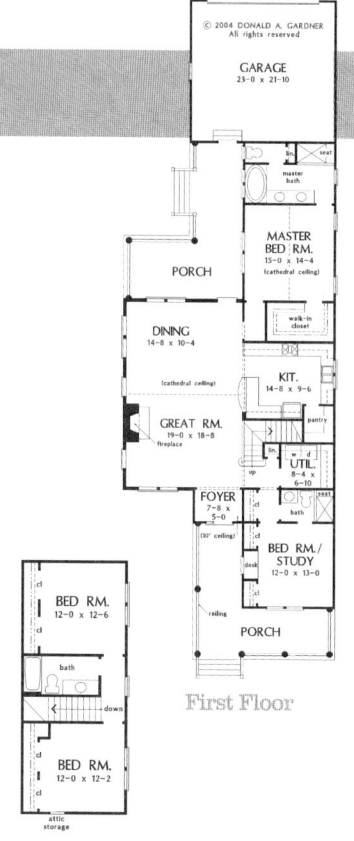

Country Homes

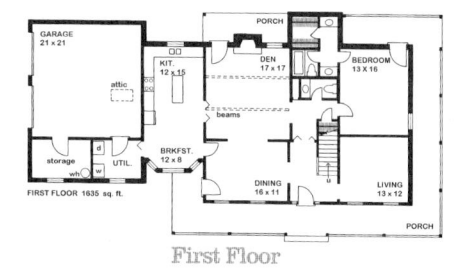

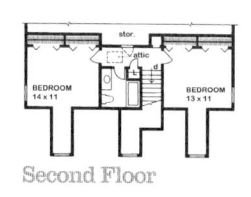

325
New House Plans

Plan:
HPK2600125

Style:
COTTAGE

First Floor:
1,635 SQ. FT.

Second Floor:
575 SQ. FT.

Total:
2,210 SQ. FT.

Bedrooms:
3

Bathrooms:
2 ½

Width:
80' - 0"

Depth:
42' - 0"

Foundation:
CRAWLSPACE

Plan:
HPK2600126

Style:
COUNTRY

First Floor:
1,726 SQ. FT.

Second Floor:
487 SQ. FT.

Total:
2,213 SQ. FT.

Bedrooms:
4

Bathrooms:
3

Width:
34' - 6"

Depth:
103' - 6"

ORDER BLUEPRINTS 24 HOURS, 7 DAYS A WEEK, AT 1-800-521-6797 OR EPLANS.COM

325 New House Plans

Country Homes

Plan:
HPK2600127

Style:
COUNTRY

First Floor:
1,699 SQ. FT.

Second Floor:
532 SQ. FT.

Total:
2,231 SQ. FT.

Bonus Space:
549 SQ. FT.

Bedrooms:
3

Bathrooms:
2 ½

Width:
48' - 10"

Depth:
73' - 2"

© 2004 Donald A. Gardner, Inc.

A great design for growing families, this plan features over 500 square feet of bonus space. An open floor plan, generously-sized living areas, and high ceilings in several rooms make the home feel spacious. The entry hall is a two-story space, with a light-filled stairwell to the right and dining room to the left. The great room lies beyond; a grand fireplace flanked by built-in shelves is the focal point of this room. In the kitchen, counter space and cabinetry surround a central island. Secluded in the left corner of the home, the master suite offers all the essential luxuries: His and Hers walk-in closets, dual vanities, soaking tub, spacious shower, and compartmented toilet. At the top of the stairs, a bridge leads to two bedrooms and a hall bath. The expansive bonus space may accommodate games, studying, hobbies, exercise, or all of the above.

First Floor

Second Floor

108 ORDER BLUEPRINTS 24 HOURS, 7 DAYS A WEEK, AT 1-800-521-6797 OR EPLANS.COM

Country Homes

325
New House Plans

Plan:
HPK2600128

Style:
FRENCH COUNTRY

Square Footage:
2,264

Bonus Space:
394 SQ. FT.

Bedrooms:
3

Bathrooms:
2

Width:
57' - 0"

Depth:
73' - 4"

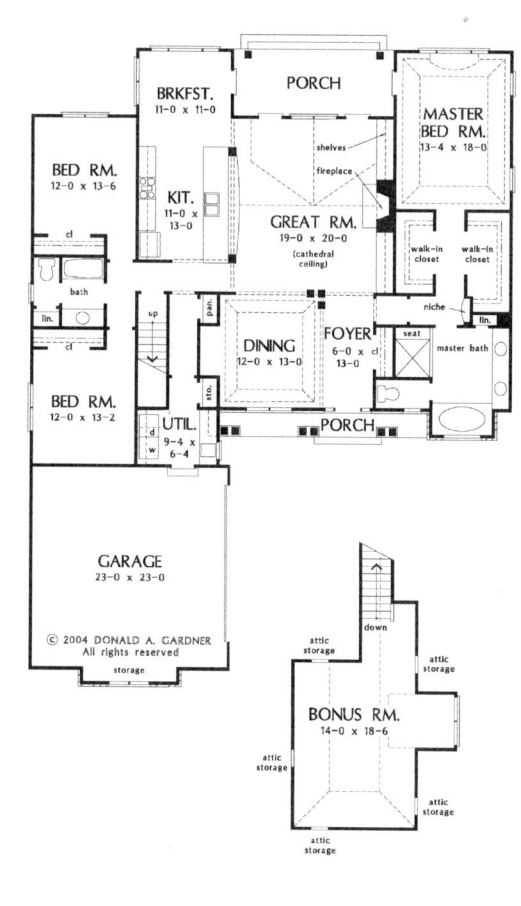

Stone and siding, plus a side-loading garage, form an attractive exterior for this cottage-like home. Double columns frame the front entry leading to the bright foyer and open floor plan. Decorative columns accent the interior and define the kitchen and formal dining room. Built-in cabinets embrace the fireplace, and French doors flank a prominent window in the great room. A closet between the kitchen and dining room could easily be used as a reach-in pantry. Tray ceilings enhance the dining room and master bedroom, while a cathedral ceiling highlights the great room. Designed to pamper, the master suite features a Palladian-style window in the bedroom, two walk-in closets, and a private master bath. The master bath includes a double vanity, shower with seat, garden tub, and separate privy. An art niche, a linen closet, and porch access complete the suite.

ORDER BLUEPRINTS 24 HOURS, 7 DAYS A WEEK, AT 1-800-521-6797 OR EPLANS.COM

325 New House Plans

Country Homes

Plan:
HPK2600129

Style:
COUNTRY

Square Footage:
2,304

Bonus Space:
361 SQ. FT.

Bedrooms:
4

Bathrooms:
3

Width:
58' - 4"

Depth:
69' - 8"

© 2004 Donald A. Gardner, Inc.

A judicious mix of board-and-batten siding and stone creates a distinguished facade. Small architectural details, such as the paired dormer windows, box-bay window, and rooftop turret, add more interest to the exterior. The layout poses an efficient strategy for balancing shared, flexible areas with well-defined retreat spaces. The multifunctional great room takes in natural light from the center of the plan. The breakfast nook serves doubly as a dining area and buffer for the bedrooms on the right side of the home. The bedroom/study at the bottom left of the plan serves also to shield the master suite from street-side noise. The extended foyer is a refining touch.

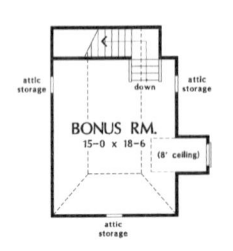

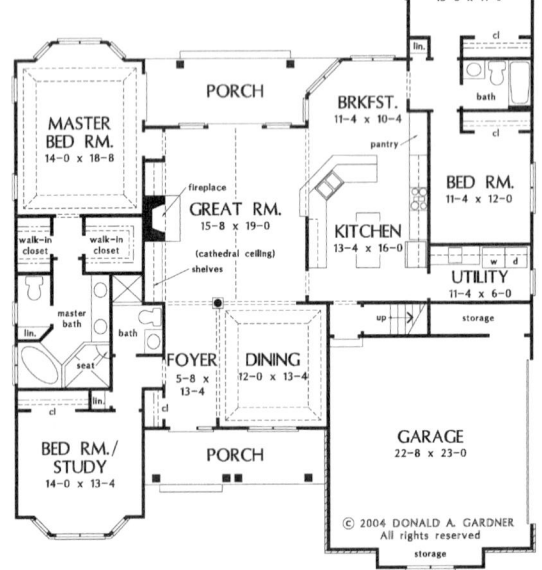

Country Homes
325 New House Plans

Plan:
HPK2600130

Style:
FARMHOUSE
First Floor:
1,352 SQ. FT.
Second Floor:
953 SQ. FT.
Total:
2,305 SQ. FT.
Bonus Space:
539 SQ. FT.
Bedrooms:
3
Bathrooms:
2 ½
Width:
66' - 0"
Depth:
38' - 0"
Foundation:
UNFINISHED BASEMENT

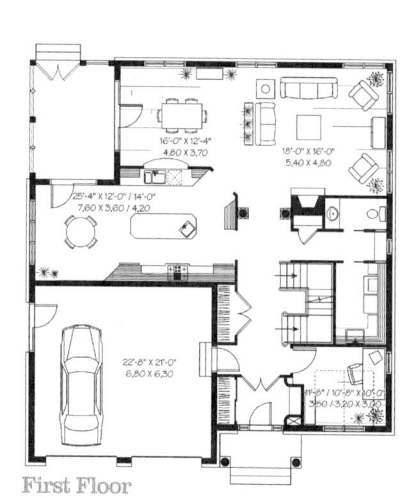

First Floor
Second Floor 

Plan:
HPK2600131

Style:
COTTAGE
First Floor:
1,325 SQ. FT.
Second Floor:
990 SQ. FT.
Total:
2,315 SQ. FT.
Bedrooms:
4
Bathrooms:
2 ½
Width:
63' - 0"
Depth:
42' - 0"
Foundation:
UNFINISHED BASEMENT

First Floor 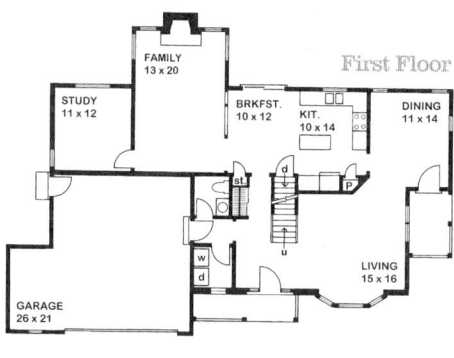
Second Floor

ORDER BLUEPRINTS 24 HOURS, 7 DAYS A WEEK, AT 1-800-521-6797 OR EPLANS.COM

325 New House Plans
COUNTRY Homes

Plan:
HPK2600132

Style:
COTTAGE

Square Footage:
2,325

Bedrooms:
3

Bathrooms:
2 1/2

Width:
66' - 3"

Depth:
74' - 0"

Foundation:
WALKOUT BASEMENT

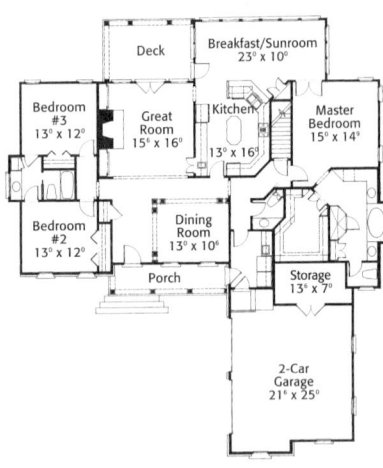

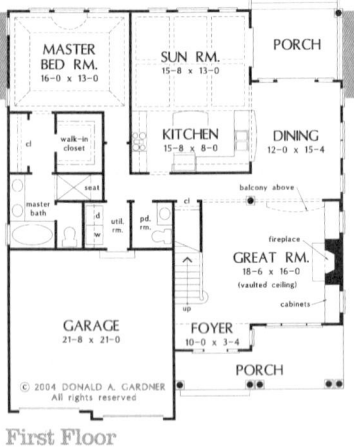

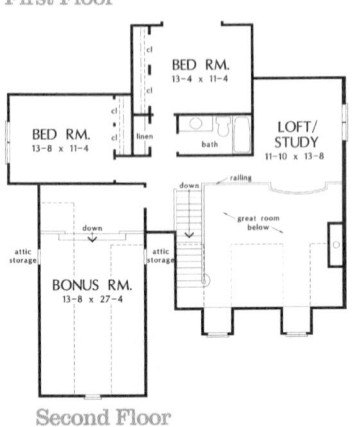

Plan:
HPK2600133

Style:
COUNTRY

First Floor:
1,575 SQ. FT.

Second Floor:
776 SQ. FT.

Total:
2,351 SQ. FT.

Bonus Space:
394 SQ. FT.

Bedrooms:
3

Bathrooms:
2 1/2

Width:
45' - 0"

Depth:
54' - 0"

112 ORDER BLUEPRINTS 24 HOURS, 7 DAYS A WEEK, AT 1-800-521-6797 OR EPLANS.COM

Country Homes

325
New House Plans

Plan:
HPK2600134

Style:
COUNTRY

Square Footage:
2,354

Bonus Space:
396 SQ. FT.

Bedrooms:
3

Bathrooms:
2

Width:
64' - 0"

Depth:
64' - 0"

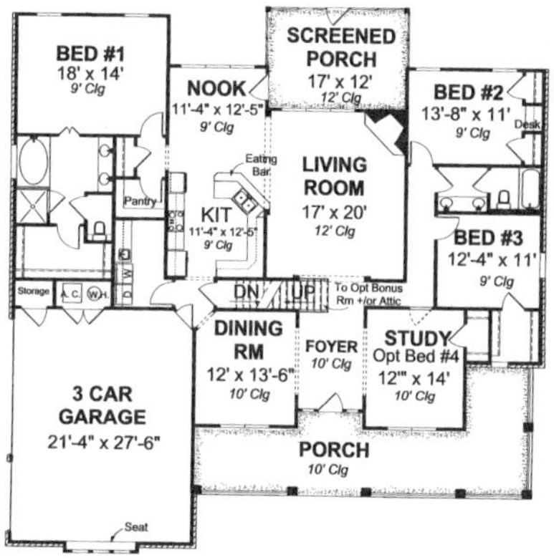

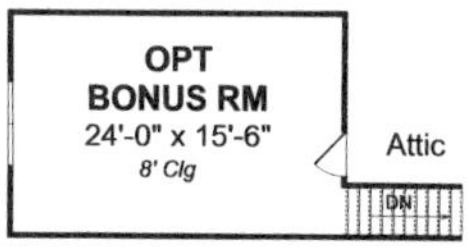

BED #1 18' x 14' 9' Clg
SCREENED PORCH 17' x 12' 12' Clg
NOOK 11'-4" x 12'-5" 9' Clg
BED #2 13'-8" x 11' 9' Clg
LIVING ROOM 17' x 20' 12' Clg
KIT 11'-4" x 12'-6" 9' Clg
BED #3 12'-4" x 11' 9' Clg
DINING RM 12' x 13'-6" 10' Clg
FOYER 10' Clg
STUDY Opt Bed #4 12'" x 14' 10' Clg
3 CAR GARAGE 21'-4" x 27'-6"
PORCH 10' Clg

OPT BONUS RM 24'-0" x 15'-6" 8' Clg
Attic

Plan:
HPK2600135

Style:
COUNTRY

First Floor:
1,619 SQ. FT.

Second Floor:
747 SQ. FT.

Total:
2,366 SQ. FT.

Bedrooms:
4

Bathrooms:
2 ½

Width:
59' - 4"

Depth:
57' - 0"

MASTER BED RM. 15-8 x 13-4 (cathedral ceiling)
BRKFST. 11-4 x 9-4
PORCH
UTIL. 8-4 x 6-4
KIT. 11-4 x 12-4
GREAT RM. 17-8 x 21-0
GARAGE 21-10 x 22-0
DINING 11-4 x 15-0 (two story ceiling)
FOYER 8-8 x 4-0
PORCH

© 2004 Donald A. Gardner All rights reserved

First Floor

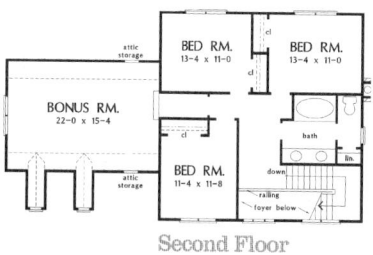

BED RM. 13-4 x 11-0
BED RM. 13-4 x 11-0
BONUS RM. 22-0 x 15-4
BED RM. 11-4 x 11-8
bath

Second Floor

© 2004 Donald A. Gardner, Inc.

ORDER BLUEPRINTS 24 HOURS, 7 DAYS A WEEK, AT 1-800-521-6797 OR EPLANS.COM

113

325 New House Plans
Country Homes

Plan:
HPK2600136

Style:
COUNTRY

Square Footage:
2,373

Bonus Space:
776 SQ. FT.

Bedrooms:
4

Bathrooms:
3

Width:
76' - 10"

Depth:
53' - 4"

Foundation:
CRAWLSPACE, SLAB

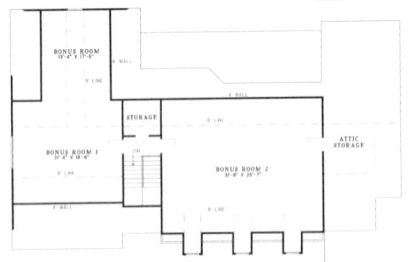

Plan:
HPK2600137

Style:
FARMHOUSE

First Floor:
1,066 SQ. FT.

Second Floor:
1,418 SQ. FT.

Total:
2,484 SQ. FT.

Bedrooms:
3

Bathrooms:
2 1/2

Width:
56' - 0"

Depth:
44' - 10"

Foundation:
CRAWLSPACE

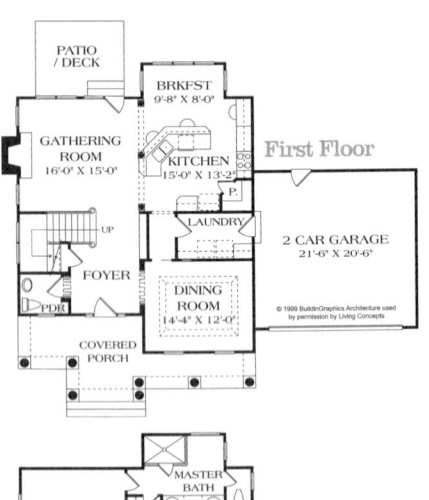

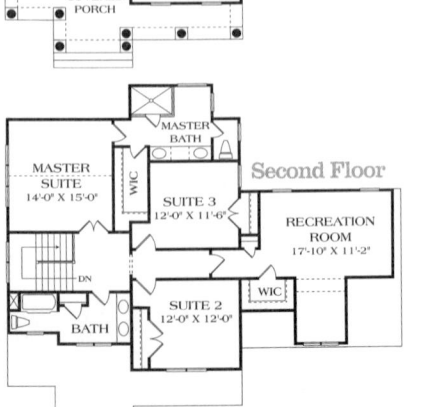

114   ORDER BLUEPRINTS 24 HOURS, 7 DAYS A WEEK, AT 1-800-521-6797 OR EPLANS.COM

Country Homes

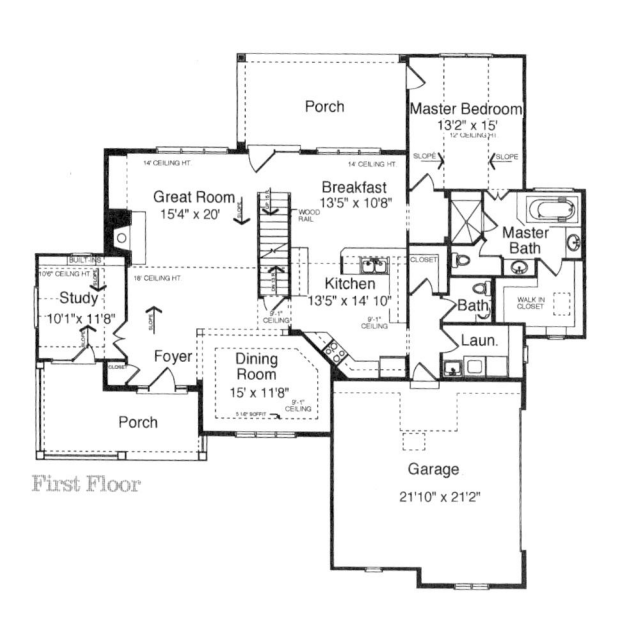

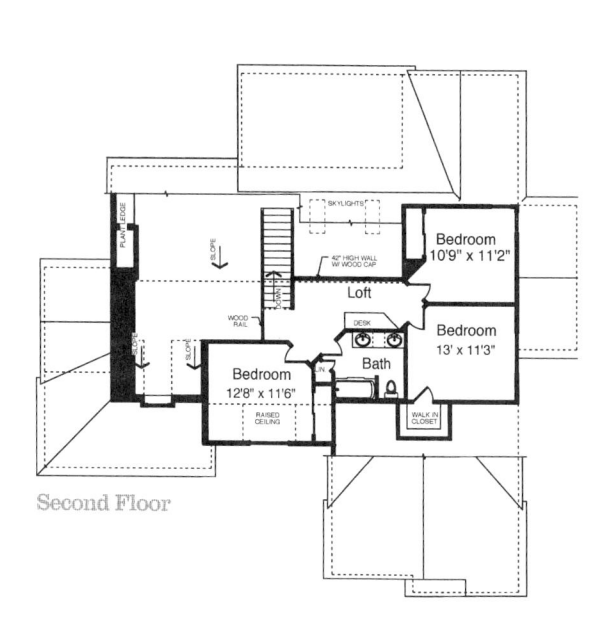

325
New House Plans

Plan:
HPK2600138

Style:
FRENCH COUNTRY

First Floor:
1,786 SQ. FT.

Second Floor:
722 SQ. FT.

Total:
2,508 SQ. FT.

Bedrooms:
4

Bathrooms:
2 1/2

Width:
64' - 2"

Depth:
60' - 10"

Foundation:
UNFINISHED BASEMENT

Stone, cedar shakes, siding, and a covered porch decorate the exterior of this French Country-inspired home. The interior boasts sloped ceilings above formal and informal spaces. A gas fireplace warms the great room. The private study accesses the front porch, making it ideal for a home office or business. On the opposite side of the plan, the master bedroom features a ceiling that slopes to 11 feet high and a bath with two vanities, a whirlpool tub, and separate shower enclosure. A staircase divides the great from from the kitchen and breakfast nook. Three additional bedrooms and shared full bath on the second floor complete this beautiful home.

First Floor

Second Floor

ORDER BLUEPRINTS 24 HOURS, 7 DAYS A WEEK, AT 1-800-521-6797 OR EPLANS.COM

115

325 New House Plans
Country Homes

Plan:
HPK2600139

Style:
FOLK VICTORIAN

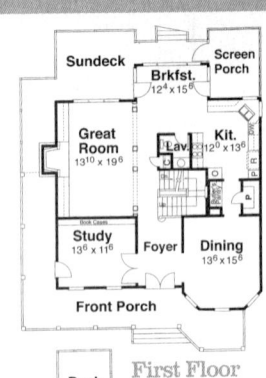

First Floor:
1,278 SQ. FT.

Second Floor:
1,284 SQ. FT.

Total:
2,562 SQ. FT.

Bedrooms:
4

Bathrooms:
2 1/2

Width:
42' - 0"

Depth:
55' - 0"

Foundation:
UNFINISHED WALKOUT BASEMENT

Plan:
HPK2600140

Style:
COTTAGE

Square Footage:
2,615

Bedrooms:
3

Bathrooms:
2 1/2

Width:
66' - 3"

Depth:
61' - 0"

Foundation:
WALKOUT BASEMENT

116 ORDER BLUEPRINTS 24 HOURS, 7 DAYS A WEEK, AT 1-800-521-6797 OR EPLANS.COM

Country Homes

325 New House Plans

Plan:
HPK2600141

Style:
COTTAGE

First Floor:
1,904 SQ. FT.

Second Floor:
819 SQ. FT.

Total:
2,723 SQ. FT.

Bedrooms:
4

Bathrooms:
4

Width:
39' - 8"

Depth:
78' - 8"

Foundation:
CRAWLSPACE

This well-mannered home establishes a good sense of formality at the front of the plan, greeting visitors with a brief foyer that opens to the dining room and study. Connecting the three rooms conveys the full width of the home; similarly, the foyer and main hallway reveal the home's attractive length, leading to the great room. The island kitchen and nook provide casual dining space for the family. Lastly, the master bedroom is located for comfort on the main floor. The upper floor contains two bedrooms, each with a dedicated bath. Spec the future room to suit the family's need for an entertainment space, office, exercise room, or storage; or take advantage of four dormer windows and turn the space into a fourth bedroom.

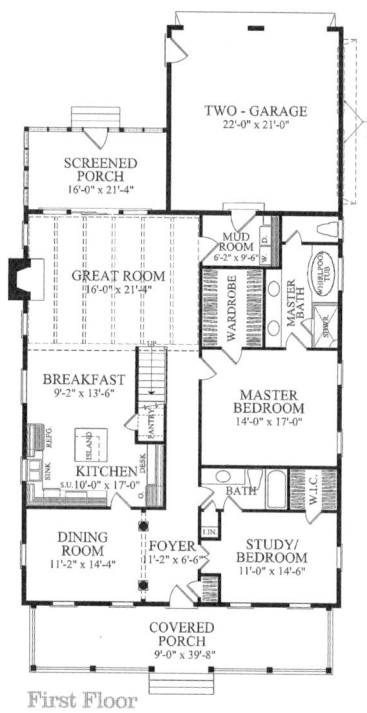

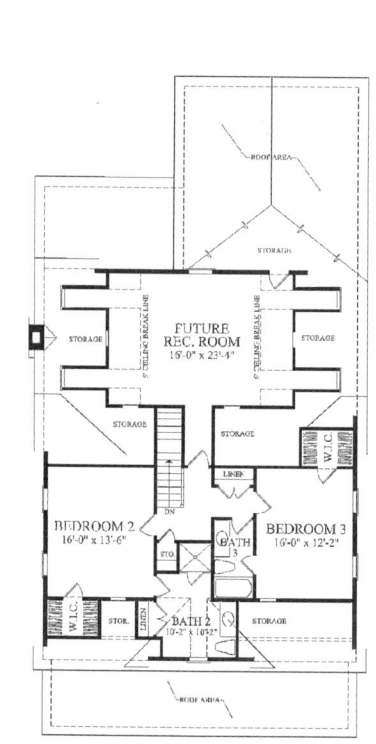

First Floor

Second Floor

ORDER BLUEPRINTS 24 HOURS, 7 DAYS A WEEK, AT 1-800-521-6797 OR EPLANS.COM

117

325 New House Plans
Country Homes

Plan:
HPK2600142

Style:
COUNTRY

First Floor:
1,524 SQ. FT.

Second Floor:
1,275 SQ. FT.

Total:
2,799 SQ. FT.

Bedrooms:
4

Bathrooms:
2 ½

Width:
63' - 0"

Depth:
42' - 2"

Foundation:
UNFINISHED BASEMENT

Brick and siding accent the covered porch, while wood trim adds color and dimension to the exterior of this two-story home. Standard 9-foot ceilings throughout the first floor, and amenities such as a gas fireplace, furniture alcoves, a study with built-ins, angled stairs with wood rails, and a large work area in both the kitchen and laundry room make this a wonderful family home. A second-floor master bedroom enjoys a sloped ceiling and a bath with whirlpool tub, double-bowl vanity, and shower enclosure. The second-floor balcony overlooks the staircase and leads to three additional bedrooms.

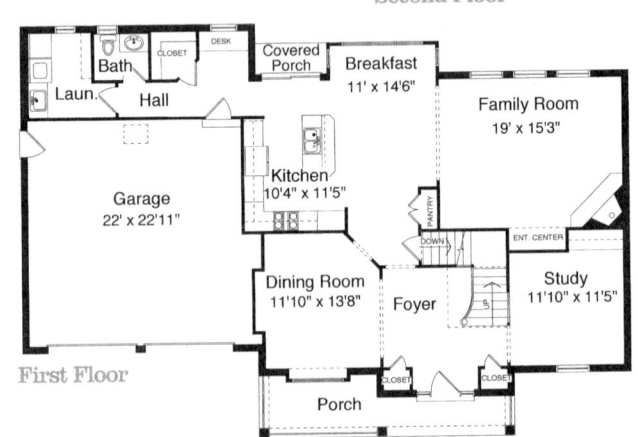

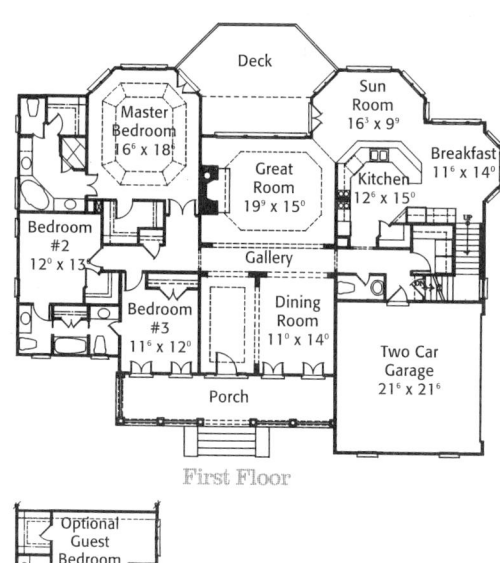

Country Homes

325 New House Plans

Plan:
HPK2600143

Style:
COTTAGE

Square Footage:
2,800

Bedrooms:
3

Bathrooms:
2 1/2

Width:
73' - 2"

Depth:
57' - 3"

Foundation:
WALKOUT BASEMENT

Plan:
HPK2600144

Style:
COTTAGE

First Floor:
2,465 SQ. FT.

Second Floor:
374 SQ. FT.

Total:
2,839 SQ. FT.

Bedrooms:
4

Bathrooms:
3 1/2

Width:
69' - 0"

Depth:
54' - 10"

Foundation:
WALKOUT BASEMENT

First Floor

Second Floor

ORDER BLUEPRINTS 24 HOURS, 7 DAYS A WEEK, AT 1-800-521-6797 OR EPLANS.COM

325 New House Plans

Country Homes

Plan:
HPK2600145

Style:
VICTORIAN ECLECTIC

Square Footage:
2,962

Basement:
2,268 SQ. FT.

Bedrooms:
3

Bathrooms:
2 ½

Width:
88' - 8"

Depth:
61' - 8"

The columned porch of this charming French Country house is only one of the spaces it offers for quiet reflection and relaxation with the family. Inside, a turret houses a formal den. Bayed spaces and lots of windows toward the rear of the home bring fill the rooms with light. At dinner time, the family can gather around the island snack bar for informal chatter with the chef, then withdraw to the double-sided fireplace for the remainder of the evening. Mom can retreat to her whirlpool tub in the master bath while the kids can enjoy the entertainment spaces in the finished basement.

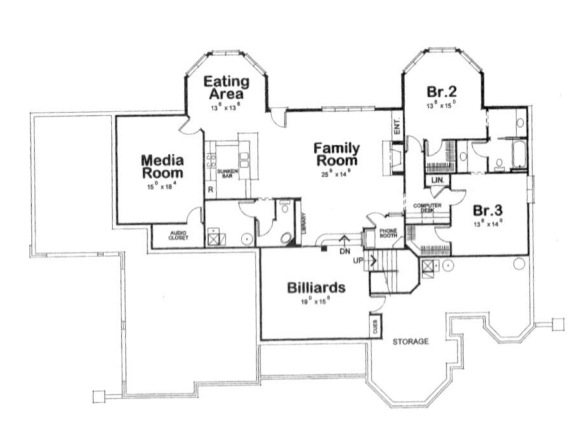

120　ORDER BLUEPRINTS 24 HOURS, 7 DAYS A WEEK, AT 1-800-521-6797 OR EPLANS.COM

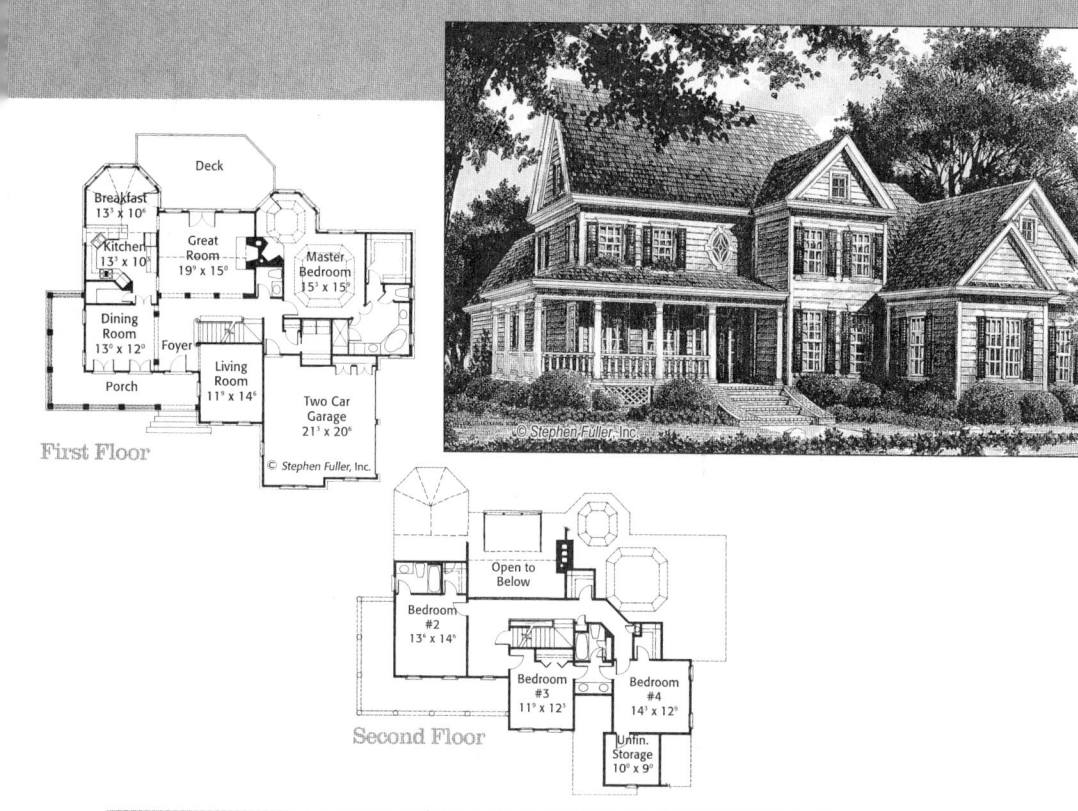

Country Homes

325 New House Plans

Plan:
HPK2600146

Style:
COTTAGE

First Floor:
1,935 SQ. FT.

Second Floor:
1,115 SQ. FT.

Total:
3,050 SQ. FT.

Bedrooms:
4

Bathrooms:
3 1/2

Width:
69' - 9"

Depth:
60' - 0"

Foundation:
WALKOUT BASEMENT

Plan:
HPK2600147

Style:
FARMHOUSE

First Floor:
2,260 SQ. FT.

Second Floor:
986 SQ. FT.

Total:
3,246 SQ. FT.

Bedrooms:
4

Bathrooms:
3 1/2

Width:
64' - 4"

Depth:
61' - 0"

Foundation:
CRAWLSPACE, UNFINISHED WALKOUT BASEMENT

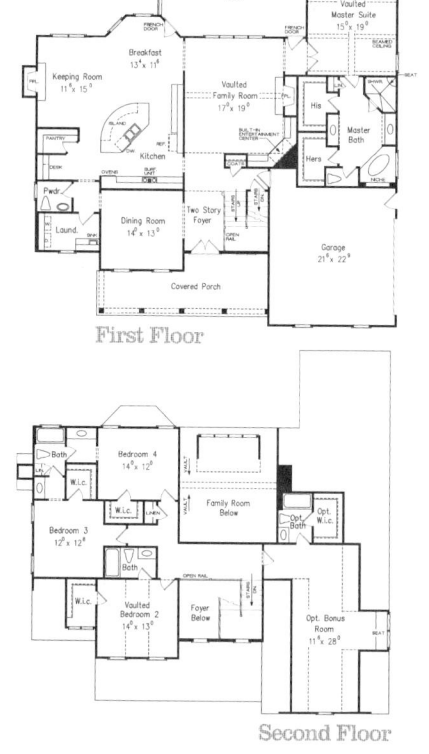

ORDER BLUEPRINTS 24 HOURS, 7 DAYS A WEEK, AT 1-800-521-6797 OR EPLANS.COM

325 New House Plans
Country Homes

Plan:
HPK2600148

Style:
FARMHOUSE

First Floor:
2,150 SQ. FT.

Second Floor:
975 SQ. FT.

Total:
3,125 SQ. FT.

Bedrooms:
5

Bathrooms:
4

Width:
53' - 0"

Depth:
86' - 0"

Foundation:
SLAB

Plan:
HPK2600149

Style:
COUNTRY

First Floor:
2,183 SQ. FT.

Second Floor:
1,108 SQ. FT.

Total:
3,291 SQ. FT.

Bedrooms:
4

Bathrooms:
3 1/2

Width:
86' - 0"

Depth:
65' - 0"

Foundation:
UNFINISHED BASEMENT

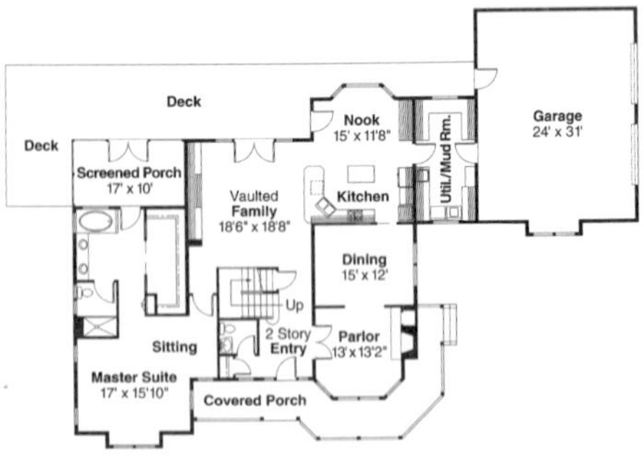

ORDER BLUEPRINTS 24 HOURS, 7 DAYS A WEEK, AT 1-800-521-6797 OR EPLANS.COM

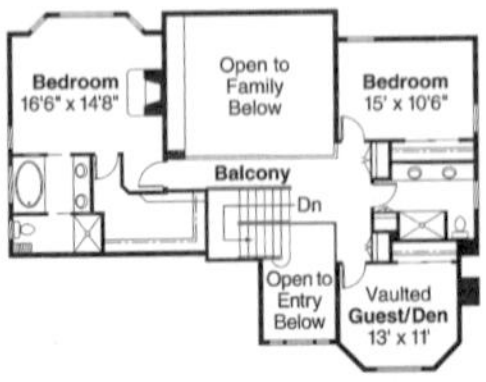

Country Homes

325
New House Plans

Plan:
HPK2600150

Style:
COUNTRY
First Floor:
2,314 SQ. FT.
Second Floor:
978 SQ. FT.
Total:
3,292 SQ. FT.
Bonus Space:
358 SQ. FT.
Bedrooms:
4
Bathrooms:
4
Width:
60' - 3"
Depth:
61' - 11"

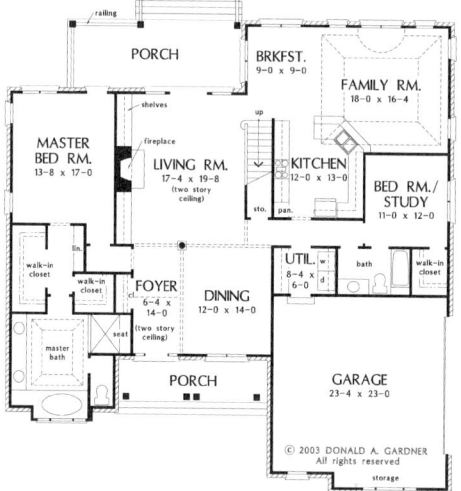

With a nod to the Colonial past, this country home uses gables and columns to make the house appear larger from the street. A box-bay window and three Palladian windows add dimension to the exterior, and porches take living outdoors. A natural traffic flow makes easy living obtainable. Using minimal walls, the open floor plan fills with natural light and creates a feeling of togetherness. The staircase helps showcase the two-story ceiling in the foyer. A full bath separates the secondary bedrooms, acting as a buffer to reduce noise. A dormer makes a nice reading or study alcove. The bonus room provides versatility.

First Floor

Second Floor

ORDER BLUEPRINTS 24 HOURS, 7 DAYS A WEEK, AT 1-800-521-6797 OR EPLANS.COM

325 New House Plans
Country Homes

Plan:
HPK2600151

Style:
COUNTRY

Main Level:
2,056 SQ. FT.

Lower Level:
1,242 SQ. FT.

Total:
3,298 SQ. FT.

Bedrooms:
3

Bathrooms:
3

Width:
54' - 0"

Depth:
74' - 0"

Foundation:
FINISHED WALKOUT BASEMENT

Lower Level

Main Level

Photo Courtesy of Living Concepts
This home, as shown in photographs, may differ from the actual blueprints. For more detailed information, please check the floor plans carefully.

Plan:
HPK2600152

Style:
FARMHOUSE

First Floor:
2,510 SQ. FT.

Second Floor:
825 SQ. FT.

Total:
3,335 SQ. FT.

Bedrooms:
3

Bathrooms:
3 1/2

Width:
76' - 0"

Depth:
64' - 0"

Foundation:
CRAWLSPACE

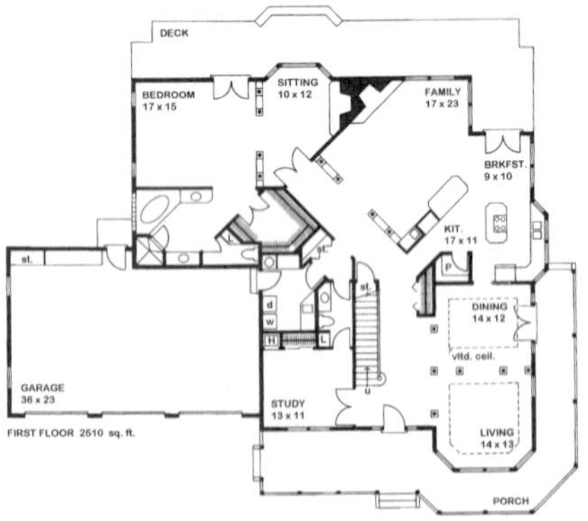

First Floor

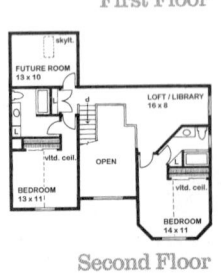

Second Floor

Country Homes

325
New House Plans

Plan:
HPK2600153

Style:
COUNTRY
First Floor:
2,113 SQ. FT.
Second Floor:
1,243 SQ. FT.
Total:
3,356 SQ. FT.
Bedrooms:
4
Bathrooms:
4
Width:
68' - 8"
Depth:
51' - 4"

© 2004 Donald A. Gardner, Inc.

First- and second-floor porches call back to the days of old, providing a modern twist to the Plantation style, but unlike the past, low-maintenance siding affords minimal upkeep. Using columns, dormers, and a prominent gable, the front elevation showcases architectural interest, creating striking curb appeal. A sweeping staircase makes a stunning focal point upon entering the foyer. With distinct room definition, the kitchen, breakfast nook, and great room remain open to each other. The first floor features 10-foot ceilings, with the great room's being coffered and the master bedroom's stepped. The upstairs includes a rec room with a cathedral ceiling and columns. One of two secondary bedrooms could be a second master or guest suite, and both access the porch through French doors. A bonus room awaits expansion.

Second Floor

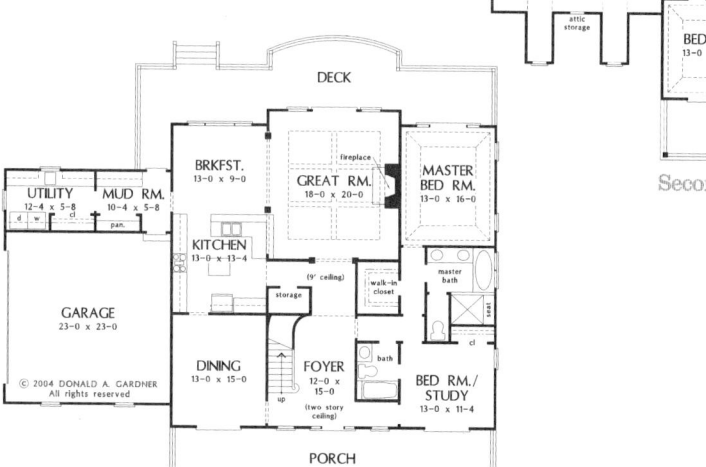

First Floor

ORDER BLUEPRINTS 24 HOURS, 7 DAYS A WEEK, AT 1-800-521-6797 OR EPLANS.COM

325 New House Plans

Country Homes

Plan:
HPK2600154

Style:
COTTAGE

First Floor:
2,360 SQ. FT.

Second Floor:
1,133 SQ. FT.

Total:
3,493 SQ. FT.

Bedrooms:
4

Bathrooms:
3 1/2

Width:
68' - 0"

Depth:
62' - 5"

Foundation:
WALKOUT BASEMENT

Plan:
HPK2600155

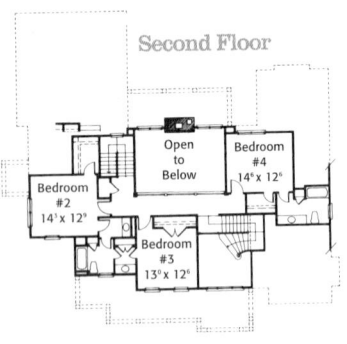

Style:
COTTAGE

First Floor:
2,452 SQ. FT.

Second Floor:
1,309 SQ. FT.

Total:
3,761 SQ. FT.

Bonus Space:
240 SQ. FT.

Bedrooms:
4

Bathrooms:
3 1/2 + 1/2

Width:
59' - 6"

Depth:
81' - 0"

Foundation:
WALKOUT BASEMENT

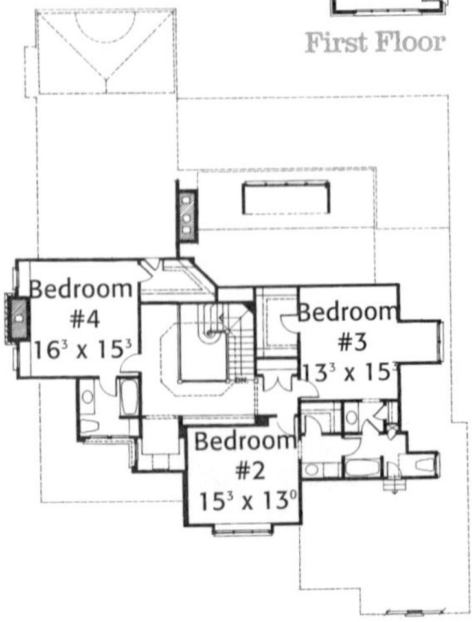

ORDER BLUEPRINTS 24 HOURS, 7 DAYS A WEEK, AT 1-800-521-6797 OR EPLANS.COM

Country Homes

325
New House Plans

Plan:
HPK2600156

Style:
FARMHOUSE

First Floor:
2,484 SQ. FT.

Second Floor:
1,336 SQ. FT.

Total:
3,820 SQ. FT.

Bedrooms:
4

Bathrooms:
3 1/2

Width:
65' - 6"

Depth:
108' - 6"

Foundation:
CRAWLSPACE, SLAB

A southern, traditional-style plan with wheelchair-accessible features, this home has something for everyone. Imagine welcoming friends and family on the full-length front porch with beautiful columns. Inside, the feeling of grandeur is evident with the spacious great room, while a computer center nearby keeps the space modern and convenient. A charming wraparound window seat in the breakfast room provides a place for conversation over coffee. The master suite features a personal exercise or hobby room as well as an opulent bath and two walk-in closets. Upstairs, discover the children's bedrooms, an office, and a home theater room.

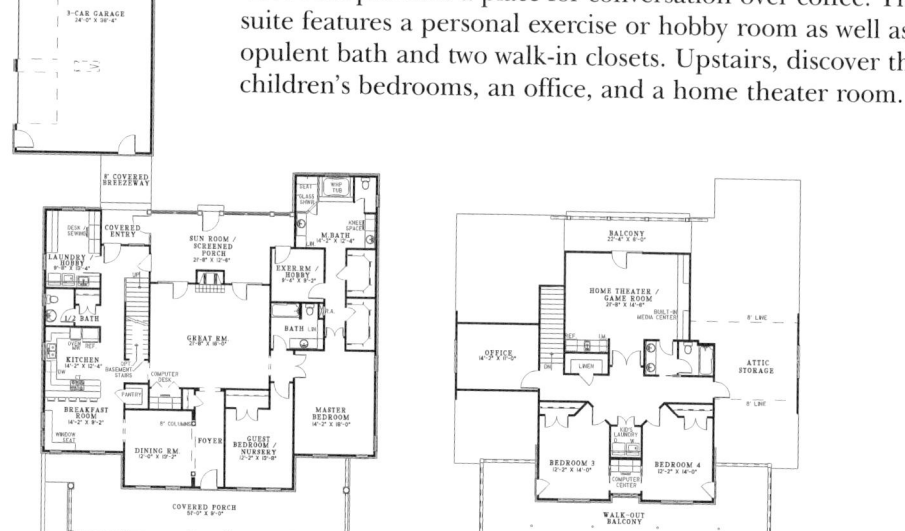

First Floor

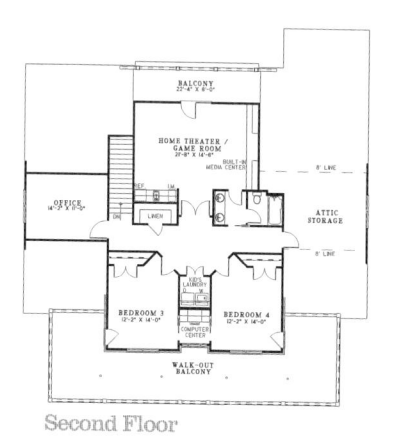

Second Floor

ORDER BLUEPRINTS 24 HOURS, 7 DAYS A WEEK, AT 1-800-521-6797 OR EPLANS.COM

325 New House Plans
Country Homes

Plan:
HPK2600157

Style:
FRENCH COUNTRY

First Floor:
2,158 SQ. FT.

Second Floor:
1,774 SQ. FT.

Total:
3,932 SQ. FT.

Bedrooms:
4

Bathrooms:
4

Width:
87' - 0"

Depth:
96' - 0"

Foundation:
CRAWLSPACE

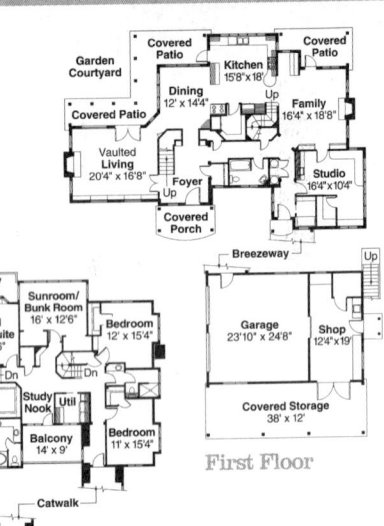

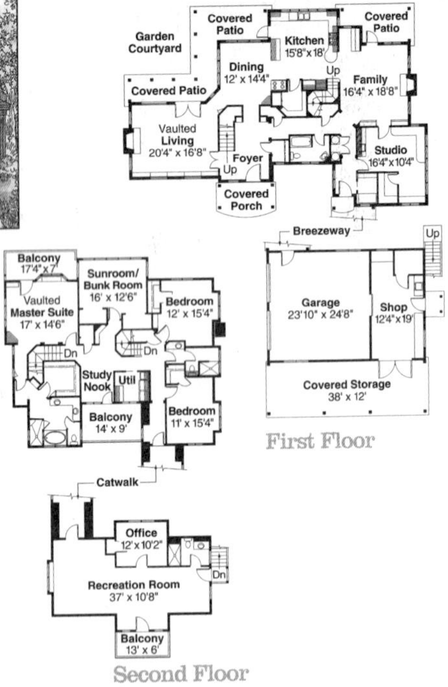

Plan:
HPK2600158

Style:
COUNTRY

First Floor:
3,409 SQ. FT.

Second Floor:
550 SQ. FT.

Total:
3,959 SQ. FT.

Bedrooms:
4

Bathrooms:
5 1/2

Width:
119' - 0"

Depth:
83' - 0"

Foundation:
CRAWLSPACE

128 ORDER BLUEPRINTS 24 HOURS, 7 DAYS A WEEK, AT 1-800-521-6797 OR EPLANS.COM

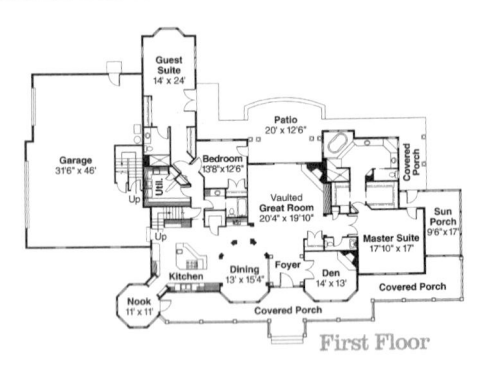

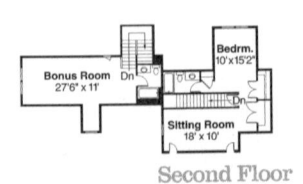

Country Homes
325 New House Plans

Plan:
HPK2600159

Style:
COTTAGE

First Floor:
2,332 SQ. FT.

Second Floor:
1,836 SQ. FT.

Total:
4,168 SQ. FT.

Bedrooms:
4

Bathrooms:
3 1/2

Width:
73' - 0"

Depth:
72' - 0"

Foundation:
WALKOUT BASEMENT

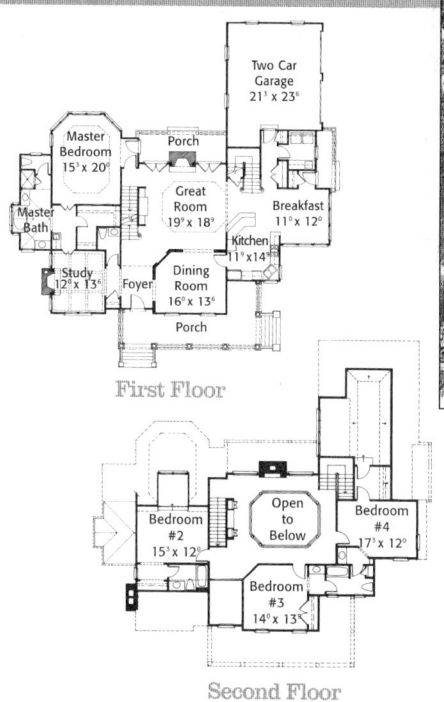

First Floor

Second Floor

Plan:
HPK2600160

Style:
COTTAGE

First Floor:
3,269 SQ. FT.

Second Floor:
1,612 SQ. FT.

Total:
4,881 SQ. FT.

Bonus Space:
739 SQ. FT.

Bedrooms:
4

Bathrooms:
4 1/2 + 1/2

Width:
96' - 3"

Depth:
73' - 8"

Foundation:
CRAWLSPACE

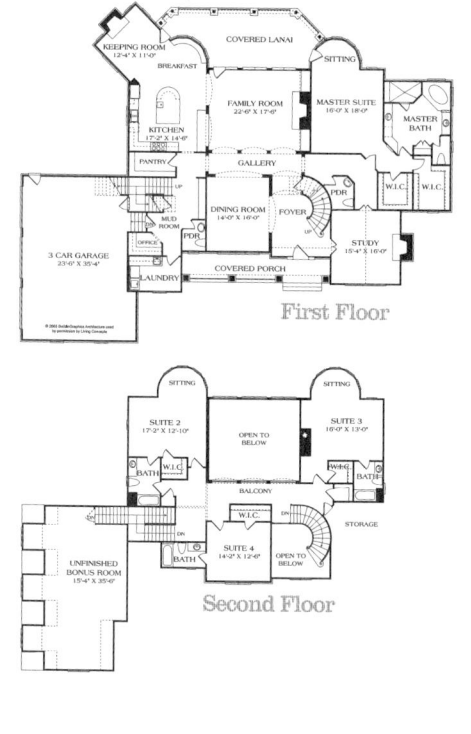

First Floor

Second Floor

ORDER BLUEPRINTS 24 HOURS, 7 DAYS A WEEK, AT 1-800-521-6797 OR EPLANS.COM

325 New House Plans

Country Homes

Plan:
HPK2600161

Style:
COTTAGE

Main Level:
2,962 SQ. FT.

Upper Level:
1,522 SQ. FT.

Lower Level:
2,105 SQ. FT.

Total:
6,589 SQ. FT.

Bedrooms:
5

Bathrooms:
4 1/2 + 2 HALF-BATHS

Width:
76' - 3"

Depth:
88' - 1"

Foundation:
FINISHED WALKOUT BASEMENT

A deceptively modest exterior reveals an extravagent hillside home of over 6,500 square feet. The basement level entices with a recreation room, an impressive wet bar, a billiards area, and space for a future media room. A fireplace here ensures year-round comfort. On the main level, access to the study from the master suite is an added bonus. The covered lanai and screened porch invite the possibility of outdoor gatherings or meals. On the upper level, three additional secondary bedrooms share two full baths. An elevator conveniently services all three levels.

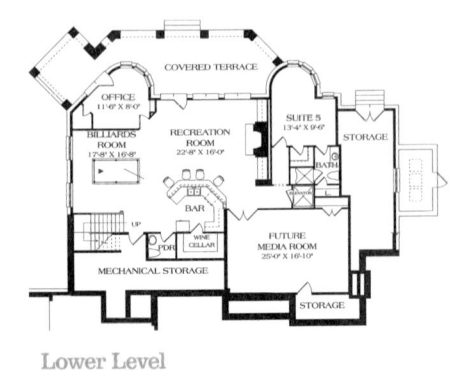

Lower Level

Main Level

Upper Level

130   ORDER BLUEPRINTS 24 HOURS, 7 DAYS A WEEK, AT 1-800-521-6797 OR EPLANS.COM

Colonial Homes

325 New House Plans

Plan:
HPK2600162

Style:
COLONIAL

First Floor:
755 SQ. FT.

Second Floor:
635 SQ. FT.

Total:
1,390 SQ. FT.

Bedrooms:
3

Bathrooms:
1 1/2

Width:
40' - 0"

Depth:
25' - 0"

Foundation:
CRAWLSPACE

Compact yet elegant, this home features a symmetrical front facade, a gabled roof, and wide cornices, for which the Greek Revival style is noted. The interior is well thought out with an ample front-to-back living room. A breakfast nook is incorporated into the kitchen, and a utility room and powder room are adjacent. Three spacious bedrooms occupy the second floor. The master bedroom has a dressing area and vanity and shares a compartmented bath with the other two bedrooms.

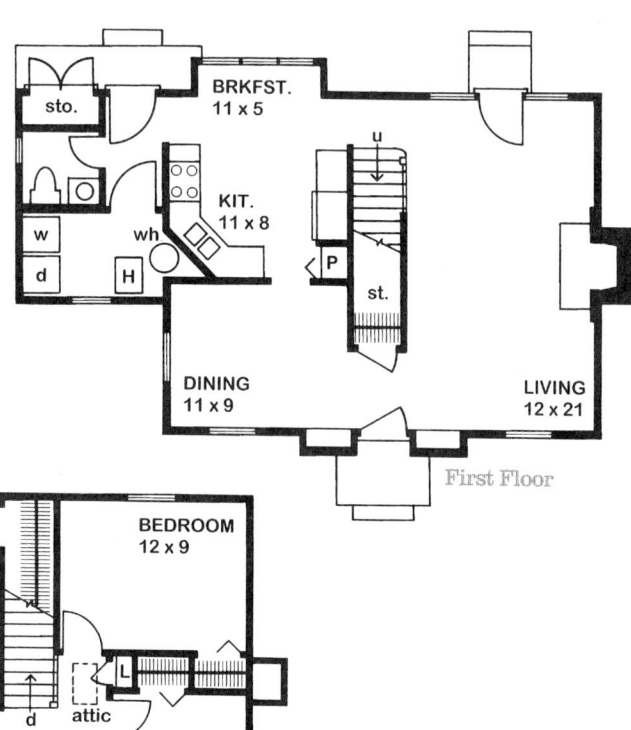

ORDER BLUEPRINTS 24 HOURS, 7 DAYS A WEEK, AT 1-800-521-6797 OR EPLANS.COM

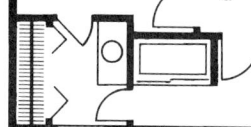

325 New House Plans
Colonial Homes

Plan:
HPK2600163

Style:
CAPE COD

First Floor:
1,188 SQ. FT.

Second Floor:
222 SQ. FT.

Total:
1,410 SQ. FT.

Bedrooms:
1

Bathrooms:
2

Width:
38' - 0"

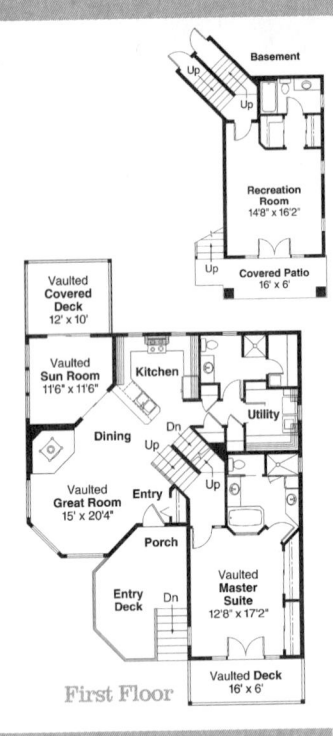

Depth:
60' - 0"

Foundation:
BASEMENT

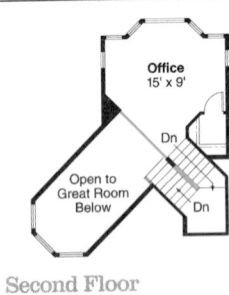

Plan:
HPK2600164

Style:
COLONIAL

First Floor:
925 SQ. FT.

Second Floor:
510 SQ. FT.

Total:
1,435 SQ. FT.

Bedrooms:
3

Bathrooms:
2

Width:
35' - 0"

Depth:
36' - 0"

Foundation:
CRAWLSPACE

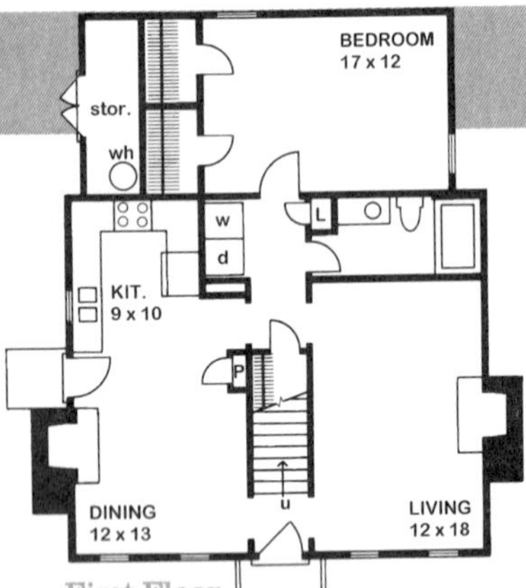

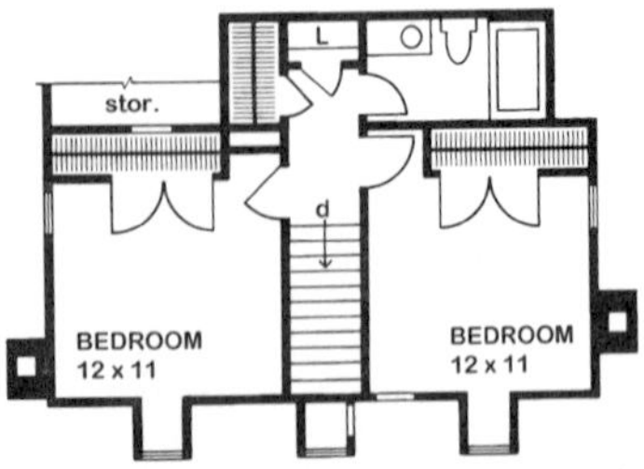

ORDER BLUEPRINTS 24 HOURS, 7 DAYS A WEEK, AT 1-800-521-6797 OR EPLANS.COM

Colonial Homes

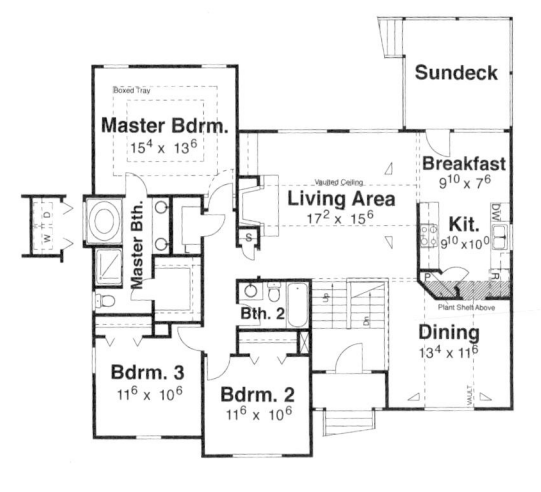

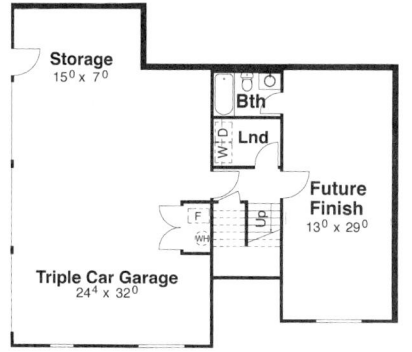

325 New House Plans

Plan:
HPK2600165

Style:
COLONIAL REVIVAL

Square Footage:
1,557

Bonus Space:
377 SQ. FT.

Bedrooms:
3

Bathrooms:
3

Width:
46' - 0"

Depth:
40' - 0"

Foundation:
UNFINISHED WALKOUT BASEMENT

This split-foyer plan has the charm of a bungalow with its stone-and-shake facade. The visual impact is impressive as you stand in the foyer looking into the living and dining rooms, both voluminous with modified cathedral ceilings. The master suite features all the amenities of a large plan with separate tub and shower and double vanities. The oversized linen closet can convert to a washer/dryer closet if the ground-level location is not used. The third bath on the ground level allows for a fourth bedroom/rec room to be finished as the family grows. The best feature of this small home is the triple side-entrance garage. As with all split foyers, it can also be built with a front entry garage.

ORDER BLUEPRINTS 24 HOURS, 7 DAYS A WEEK, AT 1-800-521-6797 OR EPLANS.COM

Colonial Homes

Plan:
HPK2600166

Style:
COLONIAL REVIVAL

First Floor:
879 SQ. FT.

Second Floor:
816 SQ. FT.

Total:
1,695 SQ. FT.

Bedrooms:
3

Bathrooms:
3

Width:
30' - 0"

Depth:
48' - 8"

Foundation:
UNFINISHED BASEMENT

This timeless two-story home is both affordable and elegant. The siding exterior is accented with classic details. Its front porch is accented with an arched entry. The layout of the home is both flexible and functional. With a spacious family room, a screened porch, and workshop, this design has something to please everyone. In addition to the abundant living areas on the main level, special details have been added such as a shower in the bath to allow for clean-up after entering from the garage workshop. The rear leads to the three bedrooms and large bonus area. Bedrooms 2 and 3 have walk-in closets and share a hall bath. The master suite boasts a 9-foot tray ceiling, luxurious bath, and sizeable walk-in closet. The lower level has 9-foot ceilings, while the upper level ceilings are 8 feet high.

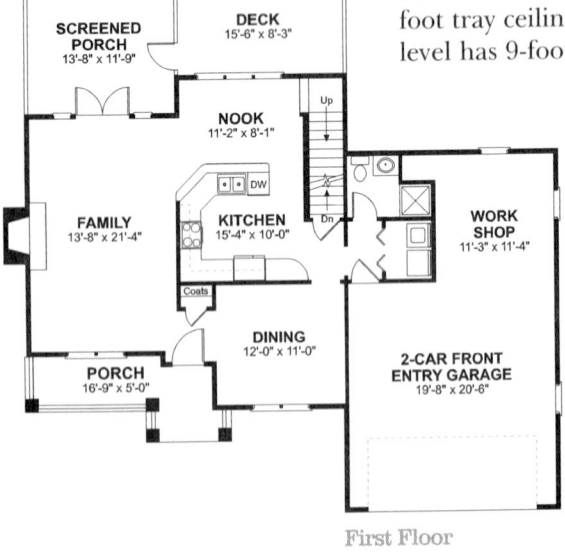

First Floor

Second Floor

Colonial Homes

325 New House Plans

Plan:
HPK2600167

Style:
NEOCLASSICAL

First Floor:
1,108 SQ. FT.

Second Floor:
677 SQ. FT.

Total:
1,785 SQ. FT.

Bedrooms:
3

Bathrooms:
2 ½

Width:
26' - 1"

Depth:
80' - 2"

Foundation:
SLAB

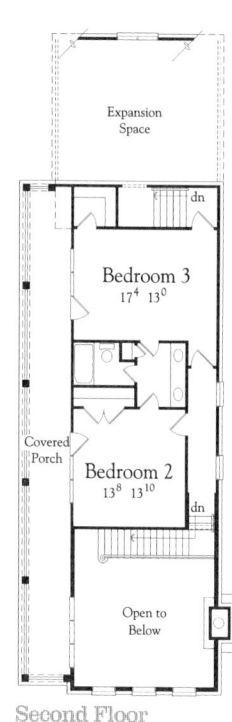

Like the famous "single houses" of Charleston, this lovely Colonial would be perfect for a narrow lot. The window-lined entry porch opens directly into the living room, where a two-story ceiling enhances the sense of spaciousness. The kitchen and dining area lie beyond the staircase, and the master bedroom occupies the far end of the main floor. Here, a wall of windows provides views to the side porch and garden. On the second floor, two family bedrooms share a compartmented bath. Both open onto a covered balcony that runs the length of the home.

ORDER BLUEPRINTS 24 HOURS, 7 DAYS A WEEK, AT 1-800-521-6797 OR EPLANS.COM

325 New House Plans

Colonial Homes

Plan:
HPK2600168

Style:
GEORGIAN

First Floor:
774 SQ. FT.

Second Floor:
754 SQ. FT.

Third Floor:
260 SQ. FT.

Total:
1,788 SQ. FT.

Bedrooms:
2

Bathrooms:
2 ½

Width:
20' - 0"

Depth:
40' - 0"

Foundation:
UNFINISHED BASEMENT

The luxury of detached housing, combined with the convenience and sophistication of city living, serves as the primary focus of this home. Provocative touches, such as a corner fireplace in the great room, a generous open floor plan, third-floor loft, and an expansive master suite, highlight the Neotraditional design. The warmth of the fireplace, windows across the rear (overlooking a courtyard), and angled rear entry are alluring touches. With an expansive rear patio and porch, emphasis is placed on a balance of indoor and outdoor living.

First Floor

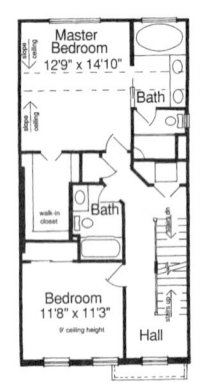

Second Floor

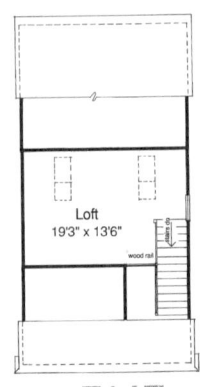

Third Floor

ORDER BLUEPRINTS 24 HOURS, 7 DAYS A WEEK, AT 1-800-521-6797 OR EPLANS.COM

Colonial Homes

325 New House Plans

Plan:
HPK2600169

Style:
COLONIAL

Square Footage:
1,800

Bedrooms:
3

Bathrooms:
3

Width:
63' - 4"

Depth:
53' - 0"

Foundation:
SLAB

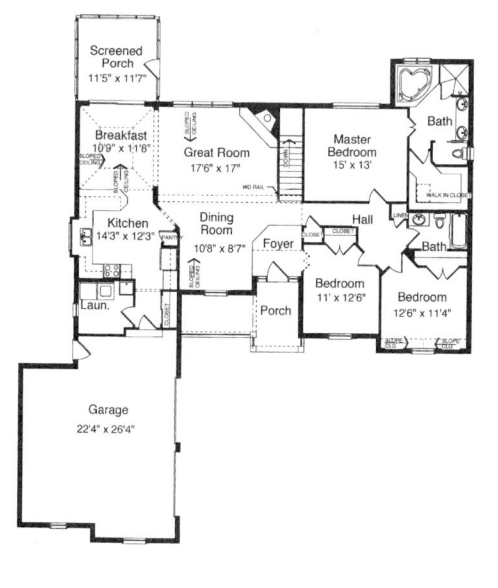

Plan:
HPK2600170

Style:
COLONIAL

Square Footage:
1,824

Bedrooms:
3

Bathrooms:
2

Width:
66' - 0"

Depth:
74' - 0"

Foundation:
UNFINISHED BASEMENT

ORDER BLUEPRINTS 24 HOURS, 7 DAYS A WEEK, AT 1-800-521-6797 OR EPLANS.COM

325 New House Plans

Colonial Homes

Plan:
HPK2600171

Style:
COLONIAL

First Floor:
1,215 SQ. FT.

Second Floor:
705 SQ. FT.

Total:
1,920 SQ. FT.

Bedrooms:
3

Bathrooms:
2

Width:
37' - 0"

Depth:
39' - 0"

Foundation:
CRAWLSPACE

First Floor
- DINING 14 x 10
- KIT. 15 x 10
- LIVING 14 x 22
- BEDROOM 14 x 13

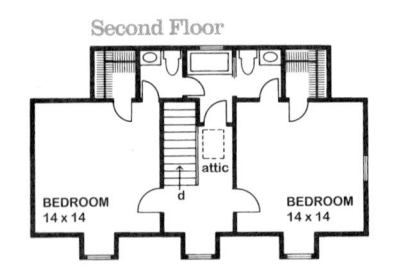

Second Floor
- BEDROOM 14 x 14
- BEDROOM 14 x 14
- attic

Plan:
HPK2600172

Style:
COLONIAL

First Floor:
1,140 SQ. FT.

Second Floor:
840 SQ. FT.

Total:
1,980 SQ. FT.

Bedrooms:
4

Bathrooms:
3

Width:
70' - 0"

Depth:
28' - 0"

Foundation:
UNFINISHED BASEMENT

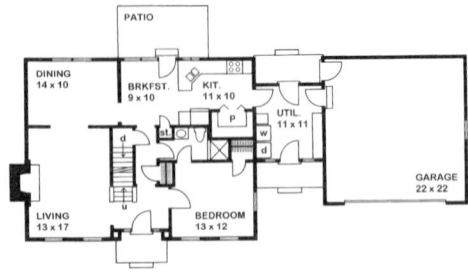

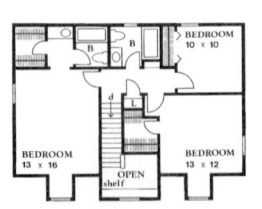

First Floor
- PATIO
- DINING 14 x 10
- BRKFST. 9 x 10
- KIT. 11 x 10
- UTIL. 11 x 11
- GARAGE 22 x 22
- LIVING 13 x 17
- BEDROOM 13 x 12

Second Floor
- BEDROOM 10 x 10
- BEDROOM 13 x 16
- BEDROOM 13 x 12
- OPEN shelf

138 ORDER BLUEPRINTS 24 HOURS, 7 DAYS A WEEK, AT 1-800-521-6797 OR EPLANS.COM

Colonial Homes

325
New House Plans

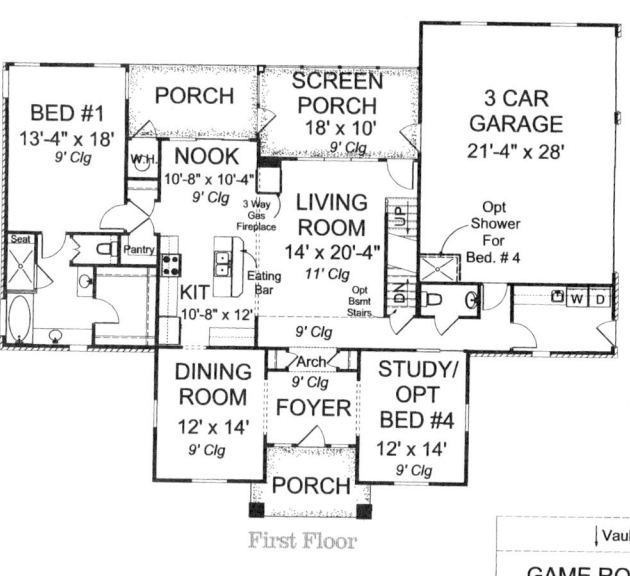

Plan:
HPK2600173

Style:
COLONIAL REVIVAL

First Floor:
1,467 SQ. FT.

Second Floor:
513 SQ. FT.

Total:
1,980 SQ. FT.

Bedrooms:
3

Bathrooms:
2 1/2

Width:
68' - 0"

Depth:
53' - 0"

This design expands upon the classic double-gabled farmhouse to make room for modern amenities like a three-car garage and a first-floor master suite. Traditional symmetry is maintained in the front rooms that flank the foyer; in this case, a formal dining room and a flexible space that could serve as a parlor, study, or even a bedroom. An arched opening gives way to a more contemporary open floor plan that includes a spacious gathering room with a three-way fireplace and a kitchen snack bar.

Choose from an open or a screened porch for outdoor meals. Upstairs, two generously sized bedrooms share a dual-sink bath, and a large game room over the garage provides kids with living space of their own.

ORDER BLUEPRINTS 24 HOURS, 7 DAYS A WEEK, AT 1-800-521-6797 OR EPLANS.COM

325 New House Plans
Colonial Homes

Plan:
HPK2600174

Style:
GEORGIAN

Square Footage:
2,004

Bedrooms:
3

Bathrooms:
2 ½

Width:
78' - 0"

Depth:
49' - 6"

Foundation:
SLAB

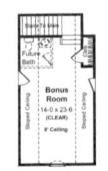

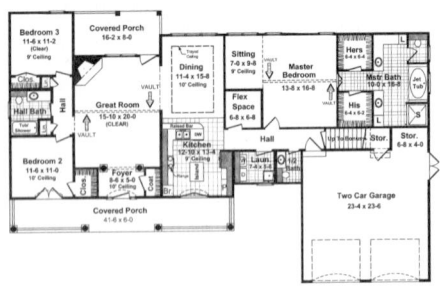

Plan:
HPK2600175

Style:
COLONIAL

First Floor:
1,512 SQ. FT.

Second Floor:
586 SQ. FT.

Total:
2,098 SQ. FT.

Bedrooms:
3

Bathrooms:
2 ½

Width:
47' - 0"

Depth:
32' - 0"

Foundation:
CRAWLSPACE

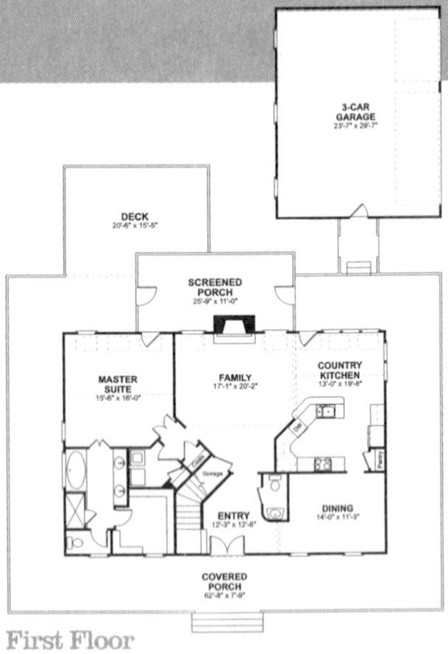

First Floor

Second Floor

Colonial Homes

325
New House Plans

Plan:
HPK2600176

Style:
COLONIAL

First Floor:
1,588 SQ. FT.

Second Floor:
537 SQ. FT.

Total:
2,125 SQ. FT.

Bedrooms:
3

Bathrooms:
2 ½

Width:
30' - 8"

Depth:
56' - 2"

Foundation:
CRAWLSPACE

©2006 William E Poole Designs, Inc.

A distinctive front-gable facade and rustic exterior materials bring a lot of country charm to this home. The interior provides expansive gathering spaces by only partially separating, by way of a dual-facing fireplace, the great room and dining room. Larger gatherings can incorporate the dine-in kitchen as well as the nook, which opens to the outdoors. The back of the plan holds two bedrooms and a shared bath. The second floor is reserved for the master suite. Lastly, an optional two-car garage can be accessed by way of a rear porch.

First Floor

Second Floor

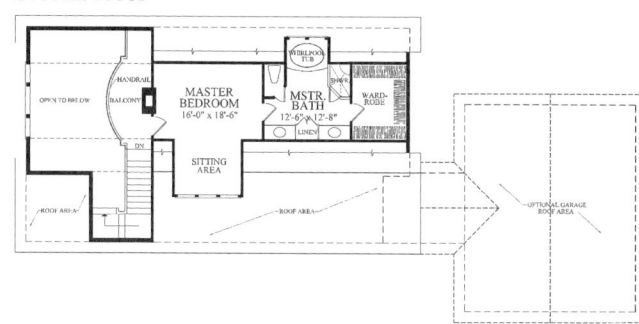

ORDER BLUEPRINTS 24 HOURS, 7 DAYS A WEEK, AT 1-800-521-6797 OR EPLANS.COM

325 New House Plans
Colonial Homes

Plan:
HPK2600177

Style:
COLONIAL REVIVAL

First Floor:
1,639 SQ. FT.

Second Floor:
532 SQ. FT.

Total:
2,171 SQ. FT.

Bedrooms:
3

Bathrooms:
2 ½

Width:
49' - 0"

Depth:
60' - 0"

This traditional-style home's exterior is highlighted by a multigabled roof and 18th-century style window panes. Elaborate gridwork on the garage entries complement this design. Two-by-four horizontal wood paneling is well enhanced by a brick facade. The foyer is graced with an abundance of light from the dormer, and has a square column leading to the dining room and an archway to the living room. On the main floor, the kitchen—with two pantries—is conveniently situated between the breakfast nook and server area, with the dining room located beyond. The nook also provides entry onto the home's rear porch. This house allows for the addition of a game room and basement. The upstairs bedrooms face the front and rear of the house, respectively, and are conjoined by a full bath.

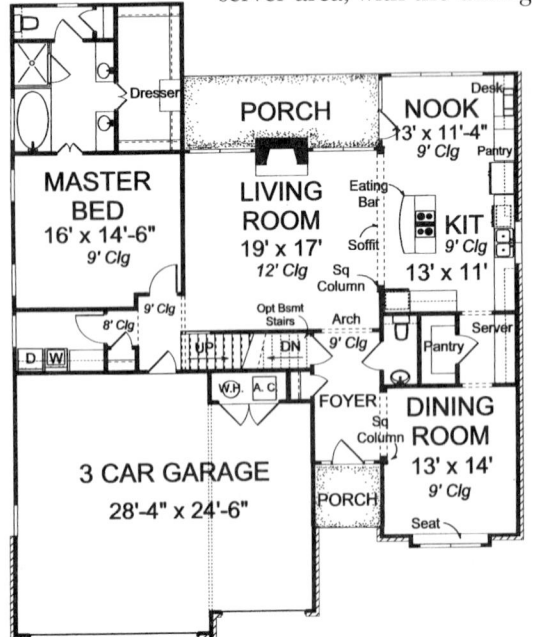

First Floor

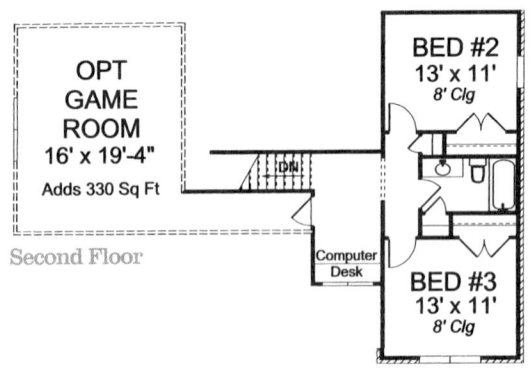

Second Floor

ORDER BLUEPRINTS 24 HOURS, 7 DAYS A WEEK, AT 1-800-521-6797 OR EPLANS.COM

Colonial Homes

325 New House Plans

Plan:
HPK2600178

Style:
FEDERAL - ADAMS

First Floor:
1,542 SQ. FT.

Second Floor:
635 SQ. FT.

Total:
2,177 SQ. FT.

Bonus Space:
348 SQ. FT.

Bedrooms:
3

Bathrooms:
2 ½

Width:
55' - 10"

Depth:
51' - 4"

© 2004 Donald A. Gardner, Inc.

A porch framed by two sets of bold columns, siding, and a brick chimney adorns the facade of this eye-catching home. Palladian windows allow natural light to illuminate the interior. The expansive great room is augmented by a cathedral ceiling, massive windows, and an outlet to the rear porch. Tucked away in a corner is the master bedroom, where you can enjoy a spectacular view while lying in bed or soaking in the luxurious angled bathtub. A full bath separates the secondary bedrooms, acting as a noise buffer. The kitchen conveniently accesses the dining room, great room, and rear porch, making it easier to serve alfresco meals. The utility room, powder room, plenty of storage space and built-in shelves, and a fireplace are just a few of the numerous amenities that accompany this family-efficient home. A bonus room above the two-car garage allows room to grow.

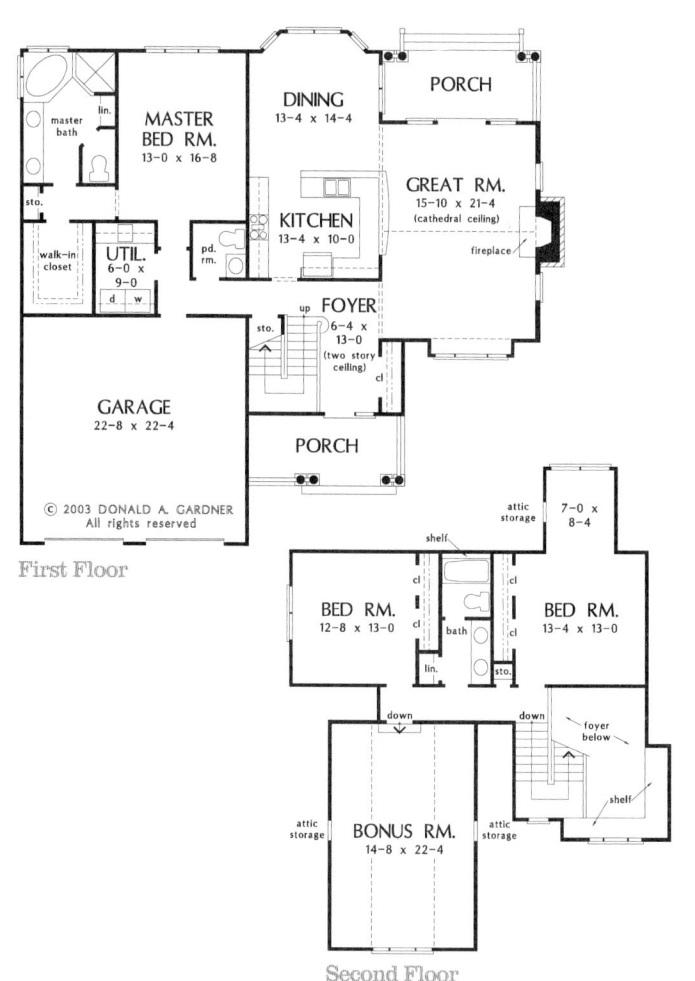

First Floor

Second Floor

ORDER BLUEPRINTS 24 HOURS, 7 DAYS A WEEK, AT 1-800-521-6797 OR EPLANS.COM

325 Colonial Homes
New House Plans

Plan:
HPK2600179

Style:
COLONIAL

First Floor:
1,305 SQ. FT.

Second Floor:
890 SQ. FT.

Total:
2,195 SQ. FT.

Bedrooms:
3

Bathrooms:
2 ½

Width:
74' - 0"

Depth:
30' - 0"

Foundation:
UNFINISHED BASEMENT

This house draws inspiration from the classic 18th-century stone farmhouses of Lancaster County, Pennsylvania. The home's narrow face belies its spacious layout, which even has a guest suite over the garage. The two-panel window shutters flanking the windows are designed to work just like those of the Colonial era, while distinctive windowpanes and exaggerated battens give the garage door the look of carriage-house doors.

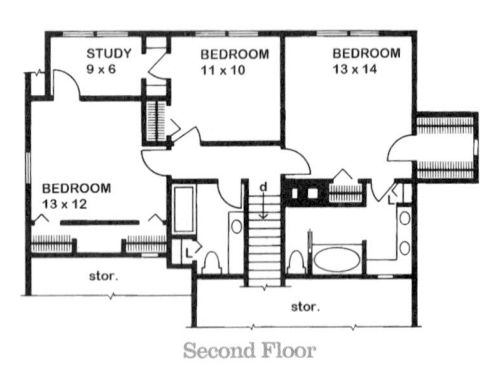

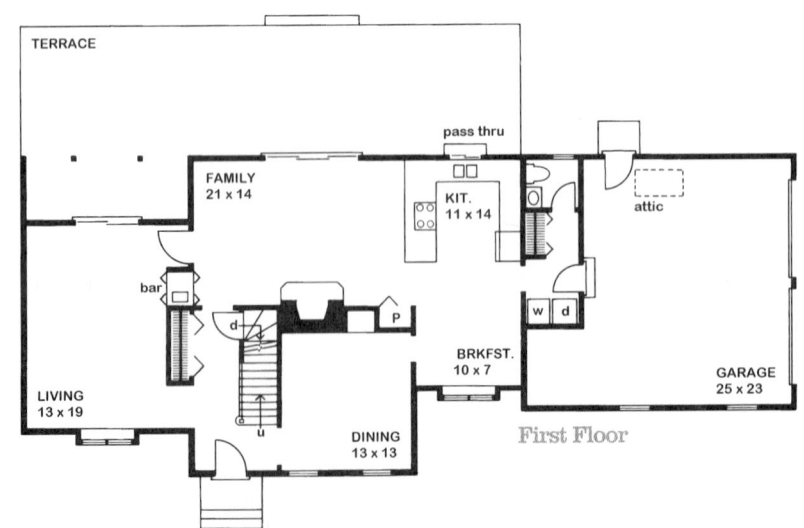

144 ORDER BLUEPRINTS 24 HOURS, 7 DAYS A WEEK, AT 1-800-521-6797 OR EPLANS.COM

Colonial Homes

325 New House Plans

Plan:
HPK2600180

Style:
COLONIAL

Square Footage:
2,256

Bonus Space:
862 SQ. FT.

Bedrooms:
3

Bathrooms:
2 1/2

Width:
61' - 4"

Depth:
66' - 8"

Foundation:
CRAWLSPACE, UNFINISHED BASEMENT

©2005 William E Poole Designs, Inc.

An arched portico beckons you up the front steps to explore the Seabrook Cottage. Inside, decorative columns, built-in cabinetry, and lofty ceilings are pleasantly surprising, yet not out of place in this gracious home. There is a corner for every function: family gathering spaces are clustered around a kitchen snack bar; the master suite enjoys the privacy of its own wing, and secondary bedrooms share the opposite wing with a full bath. The optional second floor provides an additional bedroom and bath and a spacious rec room.

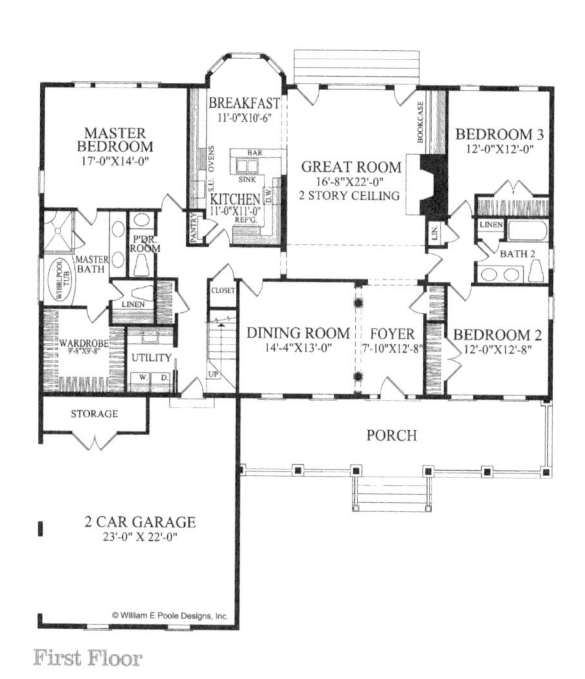

First Floor

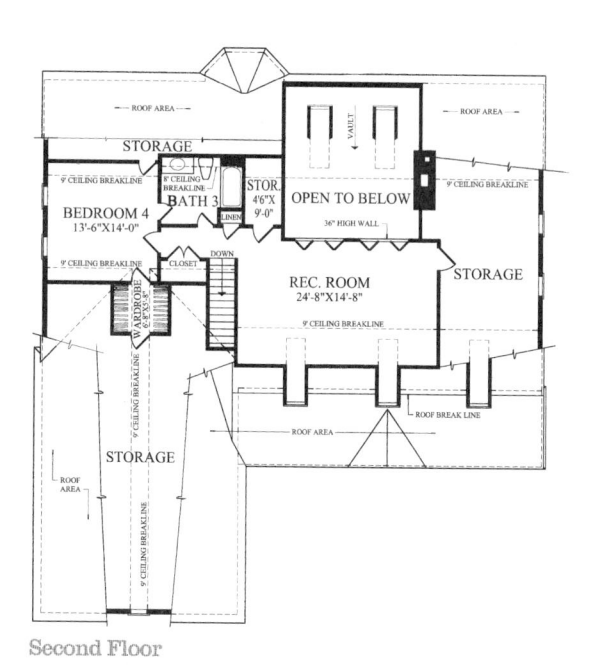

Second Floor

ORDER BLUEPRINTS 24 HOURS, 7 DAYS A WEEK, AT 1-800-521-6797 OR EPLANS.COM

325 New House Plans

Colonial Homes

Plan:
HPK2600181

Style:
COLONIAL
First Floor:
1,150 SQ. FT.
Second Floor:
1,125 SQ. FT.
Total:
2,275 SQ. FT.
Bedrooms:
4
Bathrooms:
2 ½
Width:
85' - 0"
Depth:
36' - 0"
Foundation:
UNFINISHED BASEMENT

Inspired by Colonial-era architecture, this two-story home has five bedrooms. Tall sash windows, a second-floor overhang, and a batten-board front door give this amenities-filled Colonial the style of an early 1700s New England original. A roomy country kitchen conveniently accesses a laundry room, a half bath, and an angled garage that resembles a carriage house.

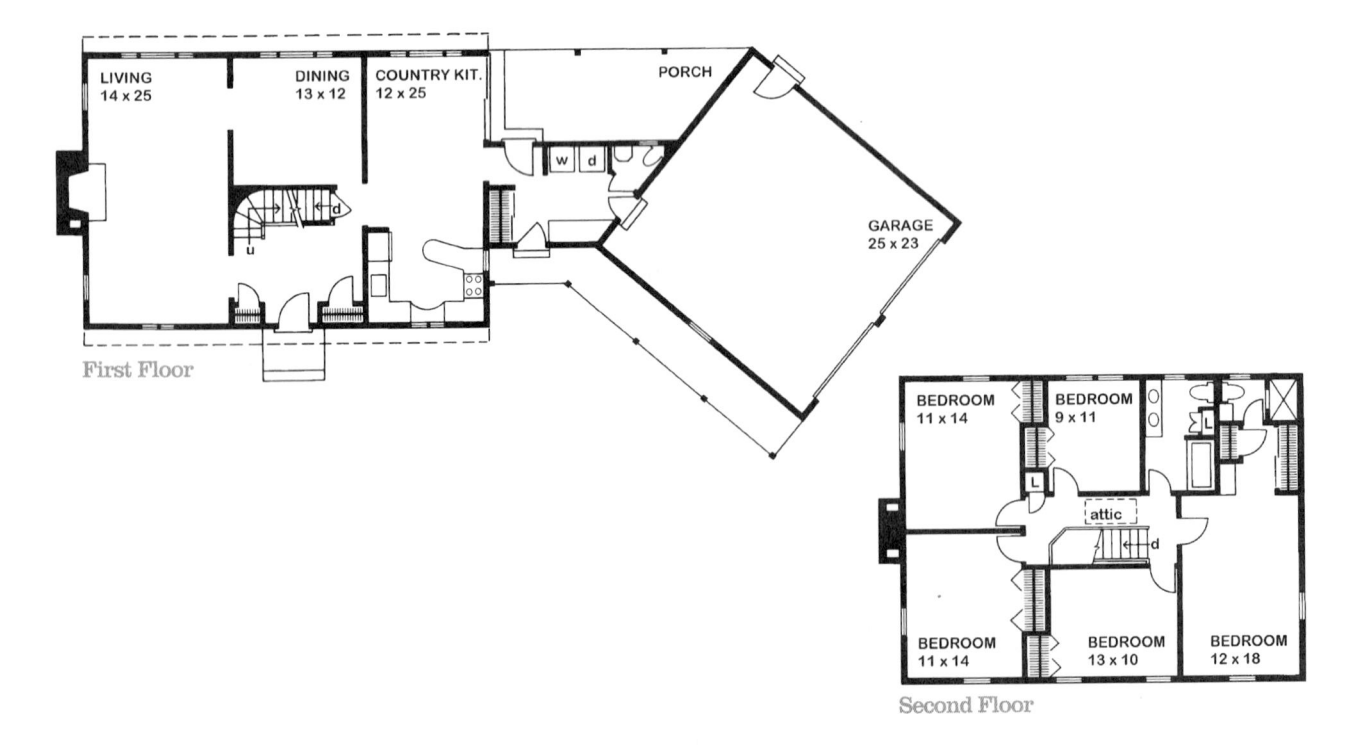

First Floor

Second Floor

146   ORDER BLUEPRINTS 24 HOURS, 7 DAYS A WEEK, AT 1-800-521-6797 OR EPLANS.COM

Colonial Homes

325 New House Plans

Plan:
HPK2600182

Style:
NEOCLASSICAL

First Floor:
1,606 SQ. FT.

Second Floor:
764 SQ. FT.

Total:
2,370 SQ. FT.

Bedrooms:
3

Bathrooms:
2 1/2

Width:
34' - 7"

Depth:
80' - 1"

Foundation:
SLAB

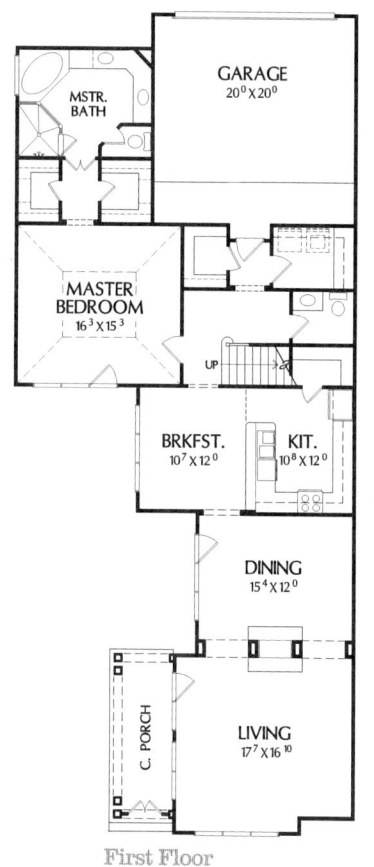

Early American stylings lend a timeless feel to this urban in-fill home. Enter at the first-floor covered porch, flanked by the courtyard, and step inside the spacious living room. A see-through fireplace opens to the adjacent dining room. The master suite sits at the rear of the first floor. Enhanced by a tray ceiling, His and Hers walk-in closets, a dual-sink vanity, a garden tub with separate shower, and a compartmented toilet—it is a homeowner's dream. Upstairs, two additional bedrooms share a full bath. Bedroom 2 boasts private access to a covered porch.

First Floor

Second Floor

325 New House Plans

Colonial Homes

Plan:
HPK2600183

Style:
COLONIAL

First Floor:
1,455 SQ. FT.

Second Floor:
985 SQ. FT.

Total:
2,440 SQ. FT.

Bedrooms:
3

Bathrooms:
2 1/2

Width:
70' - 0"

Depth:
43' - 0"

Foundation:
CRAWLSPACE

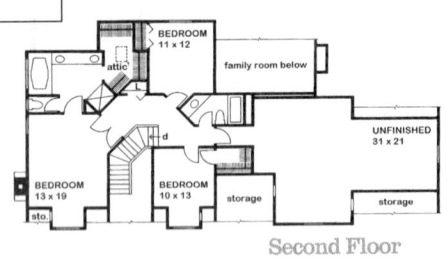

Plan:
HPK2600184

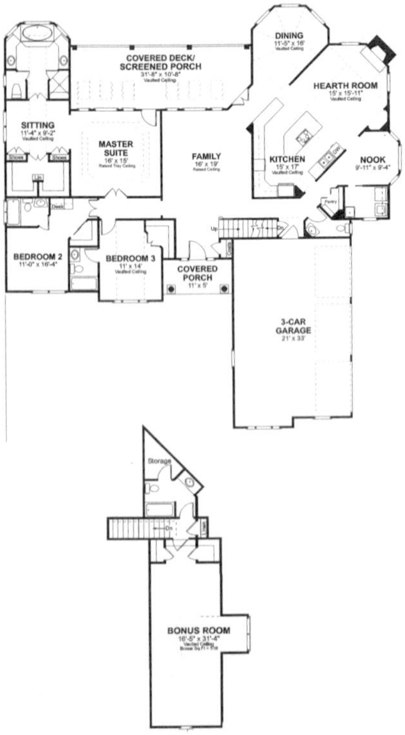

Style:
COLONIAL

Square Footage:
2,461

Bedrooms:
3

Bathrooms:
3 1/2

Width:
71' - 4"

Depth:
74' - 8"

Foundation:
UNFINISHED BASEMENT

148 ORDER BLUEPRINTS 24 HOURS, 7 DAYS A WEEK, AT 1-800-521-6797 OR EPLANS.COM

Colonial Homes

325 New House Plans

Plan: HPK2600185

Style:
COLONIAL

First Floor:
1,674 SQ. FT.

Second Floor:
808 SQ. FT.

Total:
2,482 SQ. FT.

Bonus Space:
409 SQ. FT.

Bedrooms:
4

Bathrooms:
2 1/2

Width:
70' - 10"

Depth:
50' - 6"

Foundation:
CRAWLSPACE, SLAB

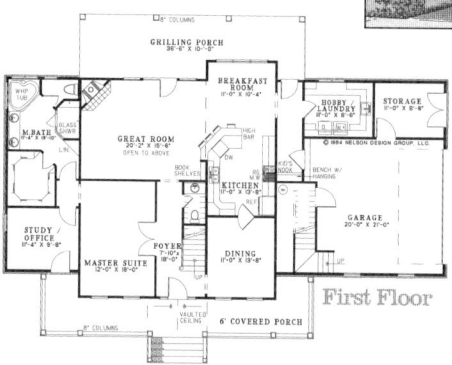

Plan: HPK2600186

Style:
COLONIAL

Square Footage:
2,501

Bedrooms:
4

Bathrooms:
3

Width:
84' - 0"

Depth:
54' - 0"

Foundation:
SLAB

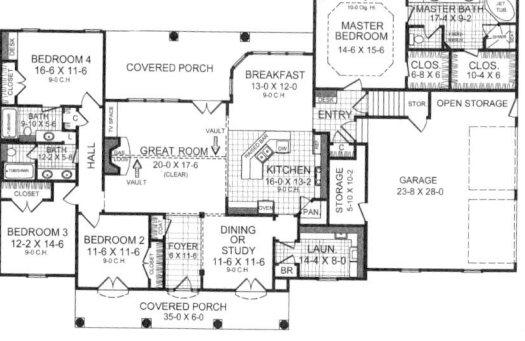

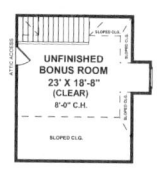

ORDER BLUEPRINTS 24 HOURS, 7 DAYS A WEEK, AT 1-800-521-6797 OR EPLANS.COM

149

325 Colonial Homes
New House Plans

Plan:
HPK2600187

Style:
GEORGIAN

First Floor:
1,487 SQ. FT.

Second Floor:
1,025 SQ. FT.

Total:
2,512 SQ. FT.

Bedrooms:
3

Bathrooms:
3

Width:
78' - 0"

Depth:
44' - 0"

Foundation:
UNFINISHED BASEMENT

Second Floor

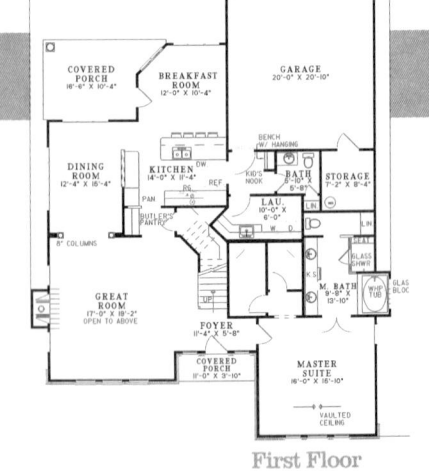

First Floor

Plan:
HPK2600188

Style:
CAPE COD

First Floor:
1,676 SQ. FT.

Second Floor:
869 SQ. FT.

Total:
2,545 SQ. FT.

Bedrooms:
3

Bathrooms:
2 1/2

Width:
49' - 8"

Depth:
60' - 2"

Foundation:
CRAWLSPACE

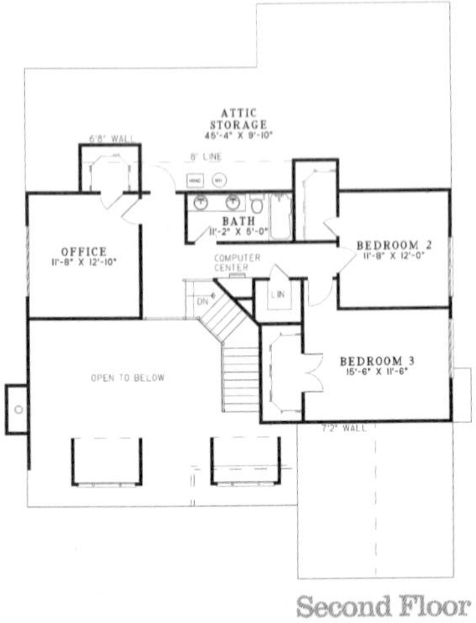

First Floor

Second Floor

150   ORDER BLUEPRINTS 24 HOURS, 7 DAYS A WEEK, AT 1-800-521-6797 OR EPLANS.COM

Colonial Homes

325
New House Plans

Plan:
HPK2600189

Style:
COLONIAL REVIVAL

Square Footage:
2,568

Bonus Space:
303 SQ. FT.

Bedrooms:
4

Bathrooms:
3

Width:
66' - 0"

Depth:
61' - 0"

Foundation:
CRAWLSPACE, SLAB, UNFINISHED WALKOUT BASEMENT

A double-gabled portico over an L-shaped, covered front porch, and shuttered, multi-paned windows create a cheerful facade to this country cottage. Across the threshold is a foyer with an 11-foot-high ceiling, and a formal dining room that opens up to the right. A long hallway connects the wings of the plan, and a vaulted family room with built-in cabinets, fireplace, and a window wall faces the rear property. Open to the right of the family room is the kitchen and breakfast area, with a door to the outside. A convenient corner pantry, perfect for storage of food items and table linens, is stowed in the nook. The opulent, vaulted master wing resides on the left of the plan, and includes an angled vanity counter and oversized tub, with generous walk-in closet. The split staircase leads to a full bath and additional closet space upstairs, plus a bonus room (ideal for an additional bedroom).

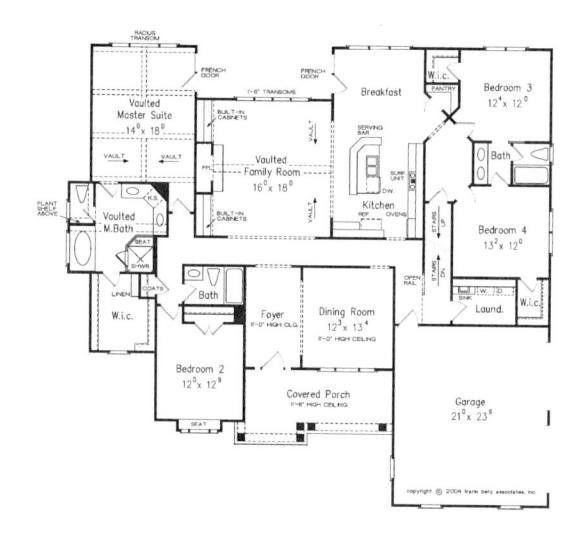

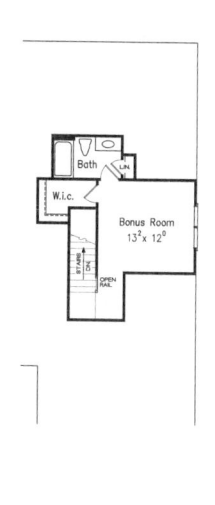

ORDER BLUEPRINTS 24 HOURS, 7 DAYS A WEEK, AT 1-800-521-6797 OR EPLANS.COM

151

325 New House Plans

Colonial Homes

Plan:
HPK2600190

Style:
COLONIAL
First Floor:
1,525 SQ. FT.
Second Floor:
1,055 SQ. FT.
Total:
2,580 SQ. FT.
Bedrooms:
3
Bathrooms:
2 ½
Width:
60' - 0"
Depth:
44' - 0"
Foundation:
CRAWLSPACE

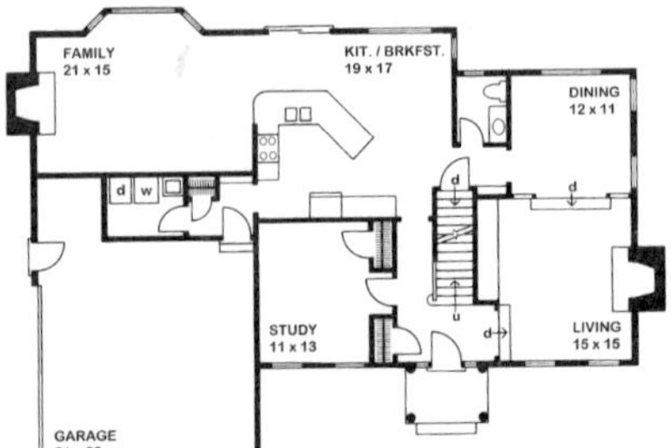

First Floor

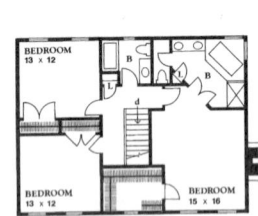

Second Floor

Plan:
HPK2600191

Style:
COLONIAL
First Floor:
1,884 SQ. FT.
Second Floor:
661 SQ. FT.
Total:
2,545 SQ. FT.

Bonus Space:
489 SQ. FT.
Bedrooms:
3
Bathrooms:
2 ½
Width:
71' - 4"

Depth:
62' - 2"
Foundation:
CRAWLSPACE

First Floor

Second Floor

ORDER BLUEPRINTS 24 HOURS, 7 DAYS A WEEK, AT 1-800-521-6797 OR EPLANS.COM

Colonial Homes

325 New House Plans

Plan:
HPK2600192

Style:
GEORGIAN

First Floor:
1,498 SQ. FT.

Second Floor:
1,275 SQ. FT.

Total:
2,773 SQ. FT.

Bedrooms:
4

Bathrooms:
2 1/2

Width:
63' - 0"

Depth:
41' - 2"

Foundation:
UNFINISHED BASEMENT

Brick quoins, limestone keys, wood trim, and a metal roof above the small porch decorate the solid brick exterior of this lovely home. Nine-foot ceiling heights are standard on the first floor, with 8-foot ceilings found on the second floor. The master bedroom enjoys a vaulted ceiling that reaches 9 1/2 feet in the center. A gas fireplace warms the family room, and turned stairs decorate the foyer. A private study has an alcove for built-ins, and provides a quiet space to relax. Entry from the garage introduces a spectacular work area, with large laundry room, half bath, walk-in closet, built-in desk, and large kitchen. The location of the sliding doors to the rear yard complement this efficient floor plan.

ORDER BLUEPRINTS 24 HOURS, 7 DAYS A WEEK, AT 1-800-521-6797 OR EPLANS.COM

325 New House Plans
Colonial Homes

Plan:
HPK2600193

Style:
COLONIAL

First Floor:
1,816 SQ. FT.

Second Floor:
968 SQ. FT.

Total:
2,784 SQ. FT.

Bedrooms:
4

Bathrooms:
3 1/2

Width:
54' - 6"

Depth:
52' - 5"

Foundation:
CRAWLSPACE

©2005 William E Poole Designs, Inc.

First Floor

Second Floor

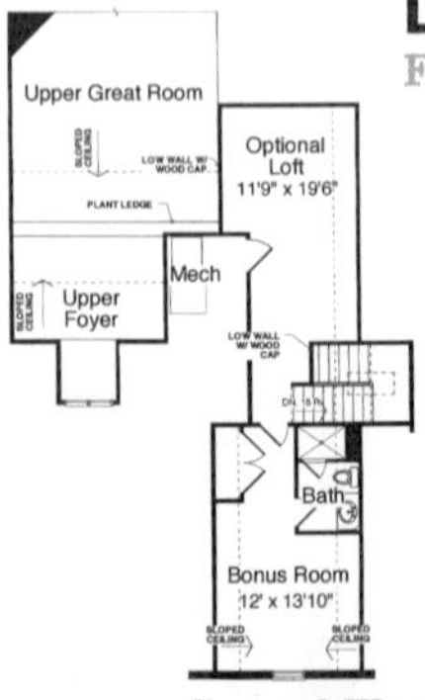

Plan:
HPK2600194

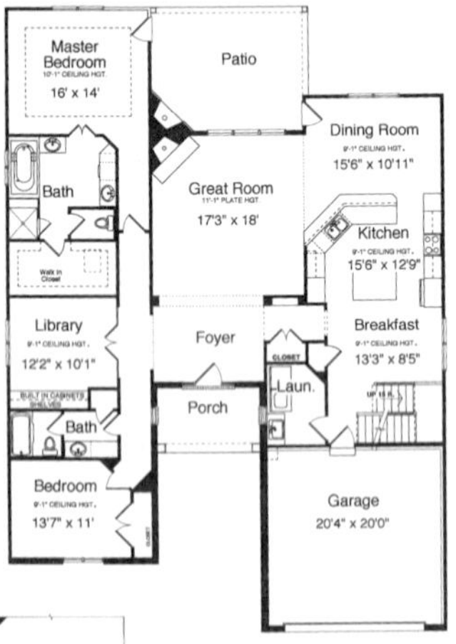

Style:
COLONIAL

First Floor:
2,221 SQ. FT.

Second Floor:
602 SQ. FT.

Total:
2,823 SQ. FT.

Bedrooms:
2

Bathrooms:
3

Width:
50' - 0"

Depth:
70' - 4"

Foundation:
SLAB, UNFINISHED BASEMENT

First Floor

Second Floor

154   ORDER BLUEPRINTS 24 HOURS, 7 DAYS A WEEK, AT 1-800-521-6797 OR EPLANS.COM

Colonial Homes

325
New House Plans

Plan:
HPK2600195

Style:
COLONIAL REVIVAL

First Floor:
1,522 SQ. FT.

Second Floor:
1,305 SQ. FT.

Total:
2,827 SQ. FT.

Bedrooms:
4

Bathrooms:
2 ½

Width:
63' - 0"

Depth:
41' - 2"

Foundation:
UNFINISHED BASEMENT

First Floor

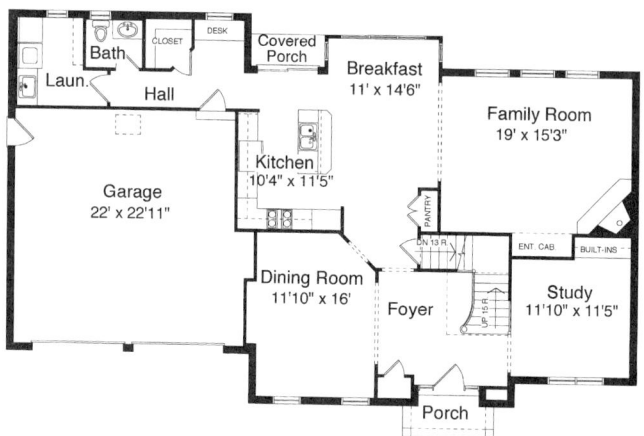

Second Floor

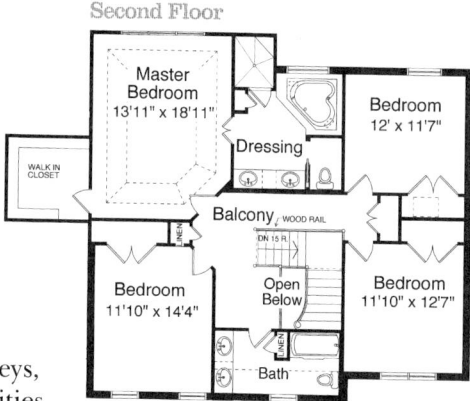

This lovely, two-level home is decorated by arches, limestone keys, shutters, and a metal roof atop the small porch. Interior amenities include a gas fireplace, furniture alcoves, a sizeable laundry room, built-in desk off the kitchen, and sliding doors conveniently located for outdoor access. An island with seating defines the kitchen, and a large breakfast area enjoys views to the rear yard from multiple windows. Angled stairs lead to a second-floor balcony, overlooking the staircase, and introduce the master bedroom suite with vaulted 9'6" height ceiling. The master bath enjoys a whirlpool tub, double bowl vanity and shower enclosure for the homeowner's comfort. Three additional bedrooms complete this wonderful home.

ORDER BLUEPRINTS 24 HOURS, 7 DAYS A WEEK, AT 1-800-521-6797 OR EPLANS.COM

325 New House Plans
Colonial Homes

Plan:
HPK2600196

Style:
GEORGIAN

First Floor:
1,442 SQ. FT.

Second Floor:
1,456 SQ. FT.

Total:
2,898 SQ. FT.

Bedrooms:
3

Bathrooms:
3

Width:
41' - 8"

Depth:
53' - 0"

Foundation:
FINISHED BASEMENT

Designed for a narrow lot, this stately two-story home offers views out the rear from two decks and a screened porch, as well as from the dining room and formal great room. The great room combines with the dining area and kitchen to create one large living space. The gourmet kitchen enjoys a clear view to the rear and includes a snack bar with seating and a walk-in pantry. Split stairs lead to a second-floor balcony, home office, and two bedrooms. The master bedroom suite enjoys a whirlpool tub, shower enclosure, double-bowl vanity, gas fireplace, and windows to the rear and side. Every part of this home is designed wtih an eye for function and aesthetics.

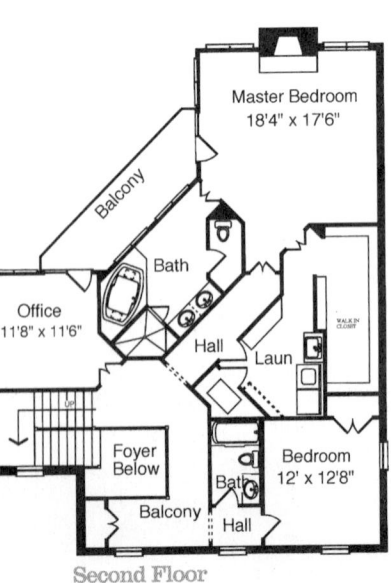

First Floor

Second Floor

Photo By: Exposures Unlimited, Ron and Donna Kolb
This home, as shown in photographs, may differ from the actual blueprints. For more detailed information, please check the floor plans carefully.

156 ORDER BLUEPRINTS 24 HOURS, 7 DAYS A WEEK, AT 1-800-521-6797 OR EPLANS.COM

Colonial Homes

325 New House Plans

Plan:
HPK2600197

Style:
FEDERAL - ADAMS

First Floor:
1,659 SQ. FT.

Second Floor:
1,290 SQ. FT.

Total:
2,949 SQ. FT.

Bonus Space:
463 SQ. FT.

Bedrooms:
4

Bathrooms:
3 1/2

Width:
43' - 4"

Depth:
82' - 0"

Foundation:
UNFINISHED WALKOUT BASEMENT

The stately brick facade evokes a timeless design. Once inside, formal living areas give way to the open floor plan, great for family interaction and entertaining. A side deck extends the living space outdoors. A rear staircase leads to a media room housed over the garage. A second stairwell accesses the remainder of the second floor, including the master suite and two family bedrooms separated by a Jack-and-Jill bath. Extra storage space in the garage is an added bonus.

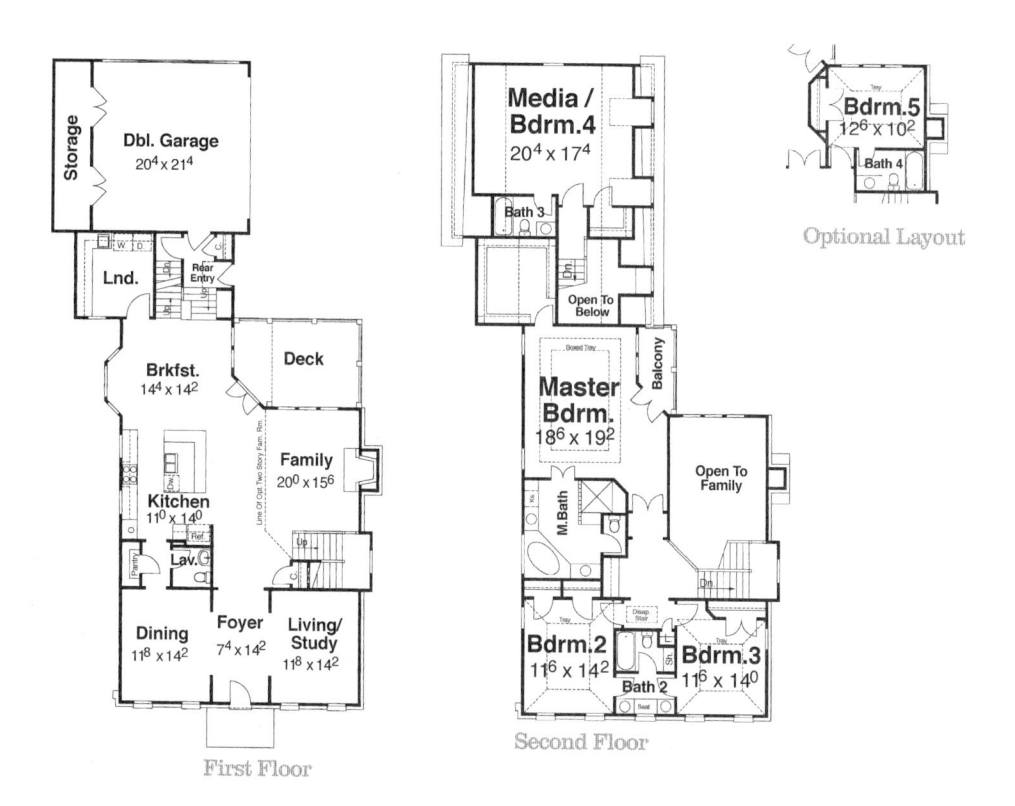

First Floor

Second Floor

Optional Layout

ORDER BLUEPRINTS 24 HOURS, 7 DAYS A WEEK, AT 1-800-521-6797 OR EPLANS.COM

157

325 New House Plans

Colonial Homes

Plan:
HPK2600198

Style:
GEORGIAN

First Floor:
1,659 SQ. FT.

Second Floor:
1,290 SQ. FT.

Total:
2,949 SQ. FT.

Bonus Space:
463 SQ. FT.

Bedrooms:
4

Bathrooms:
3 ½

Width:
43' - 4"

Depth:
82' - 0"

Foundation:
UNFINISHED WALKOUT BASEMENT

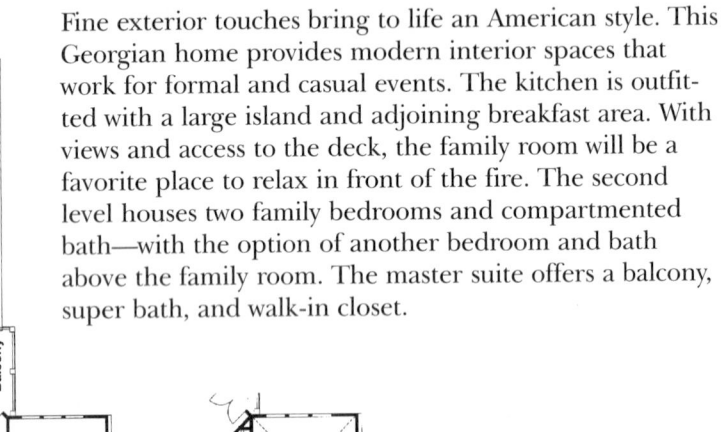

Fine exterior touches bring to life an American style. This Georgian home provides modern interior spaces that work for formal and casual events. The kitchen is outfitted with a large island and adjoining breakfast area. With views and access to the deck, the family room will be a favorite place to relax in front of the fire. The second level houses two family bedrooms and compartmented bath—with the option of another bedroom and bath above the family room. The master suite offers a balcony, super bath, and walk-in closet.

First Floor

Second Floor

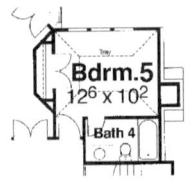

Optional Layout

Colonial Homes
325 New House Plans

Plan:
HPK2600199

Style:
GEORGIAN

First Floor:
2,473 SQ. FT.

Second Floor:
485 SQ. FT.

Total:
2,958 SQ. FT.

Bedrooms:
3

Bathrooms:
2

Width:
83' - 4"

Depth:
88' - 11"

Foundation:
SLAB

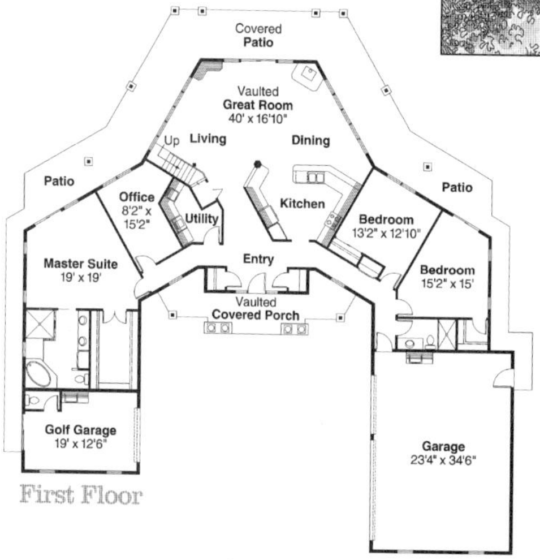

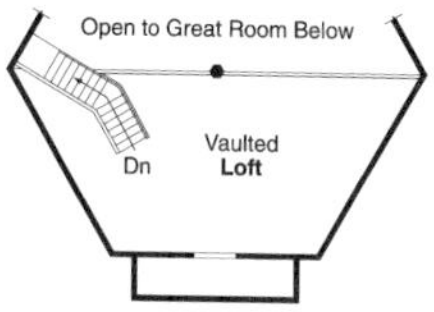

Plan:
HPK2600200

Style:
COLONIAL REVIVAL

First Floor:
1,936 SQ. FT.

Second Floor:
1,159 SQ. FT.

Total:
3,095 SQ. FT.

Bedrooms:
4

Bathrooms:
3 1/2

Width:
73' - 10"

Depth:
61' - 1"

Foundation:
CRAWLSPACE

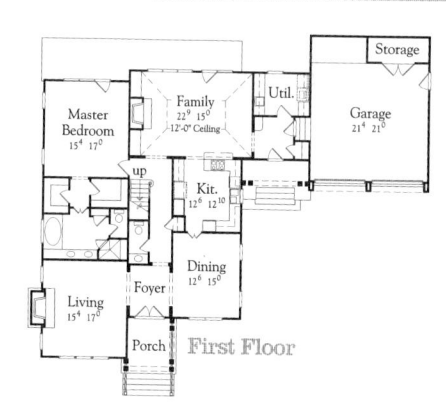

ORDER BLUEPRINTS 24 HOURS, 7 DAYS A WEEK, AT 1-800-521-6797 OR EPLANS.COM

325 New House Plans
Colonial Homes

Plan:
HPK2600201

Style:
COLONIAL

First Floor:
2,360 SQ. FT.

Second Floor:
800 SQ. FT.

Total:
3,160 SQ. FT.

Bedrooms:
3

Bathrooms:
3 ½

Width:
78' - 0"

Depth:
110' - 0"

Foundation:
UNFINISHED BASEMENT

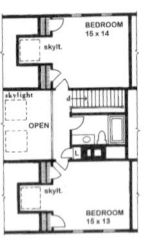

Second Floor

First Floor

Plan:
HPK2600202

Style:
GEORGIAN

First Floor:
1,785 SQ. FT.

Second Floor:
1,398 SQ. FT.

Total:
3,183 SQ. FT.

Bonus Space:
553 SQ. FT.

Bedrooms:
4

Bathrooms:
3

Width:
61' - 0"

Depth:
46' - 0"

Foundation:
CRAWLSPACE

First Floor

Second Floor

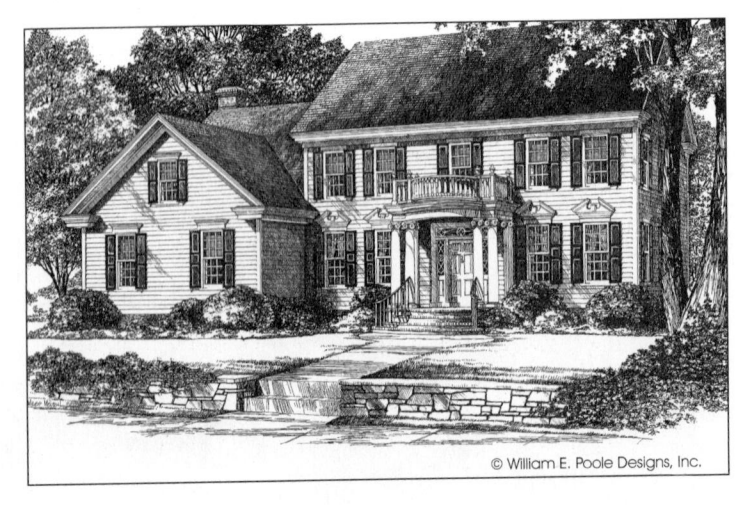

© William E. Poole Designs, Inc.

160 ORDER BLUEPRINTS 24 HOURS, 7 DAYS A WEEK, AT 1-800-521-6797 OR EPLANS.COM

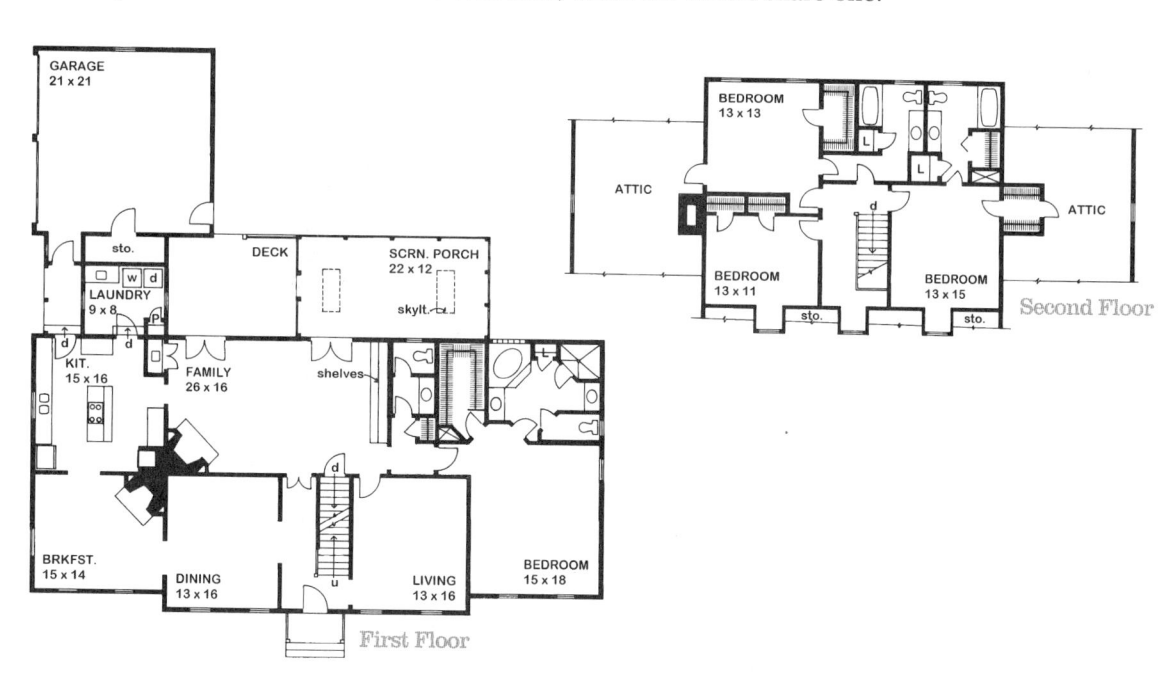

Colonial Homes

325 New House Plans

Plan:
HPK2600203

Style:
COLONIAL
First Floor:
2,255 SQ. FT.
Second Floor:
1,075 SQ. FT.
Total:
3,330 SQ. FT.
Bedrooms:
4
Bathrooms:
3 1/2
Width:
69' - 0"
Depth:
66' - 0"
Foundation:
UNFINISHED BASEMENT

This southern-style Colonial is influenced by the timeless appeal of Appalachian farmhouses. The compact exterior belies the fact that it is an expansive dwelling featuring generously sized rooms. In addition to formal living and dining rooms, a huge family room occupies the rear of the first floor. Nearby, the well-planned kitchen opens to a breakfast room that could be used as a private study. The impressive master bedroom has an opulent bath with every amenity. Three additional bedrooms with oversized closets are upstairs. One bedroom has its own bath, while the others share one.

ORDER BLUEPRINTS 24 HOURS, 7 DAYS A WEEK, AT 1-800-521-6797 OR EPLANS.COM

325 New House Plans
Colonial Homes

Plan:
HPK2600204

Style:
FEDERAL - ADAMS

First Floor:
2,562 SQ. FT.

Second Floor:
805 SQ. FT.

Total:
3,367 SQ. FT.

Bonus Space:
622 SQ. FT.

Bedrooms:
4

Bathrooms:
4

Width:
87' - 7"

Depth:
59' - 6"

© 2004 Donald A. Gardner, Inc.

Evoking stately manors of the past, this traditional plan would be at home in any neighborhood. Inside, the design balances formal and informal spaces. Decorative windows usher in natural light, while columns and built-in cabinetry enhance elegance. A formal dining room and study flank the lofty foyer; beyond, the gallery gives way to a soaring great room. The common spaces offer all the latest amenities to enhance family life, such as a vast island kitchen, walk-in pantry, and a utility/mudroom just inside the garage. A high-ceilinged screened porch will become a favorite place to enjoy the summer breezes. In a quiet corner of the first floor, the master suite offers all the necessary luxuries to help reduce the stress of everyday life. Children or guests will enjoy the privacy of the two upstairs bedrooms and baths, and the generous bonus space is large enough to accommodate several uses.

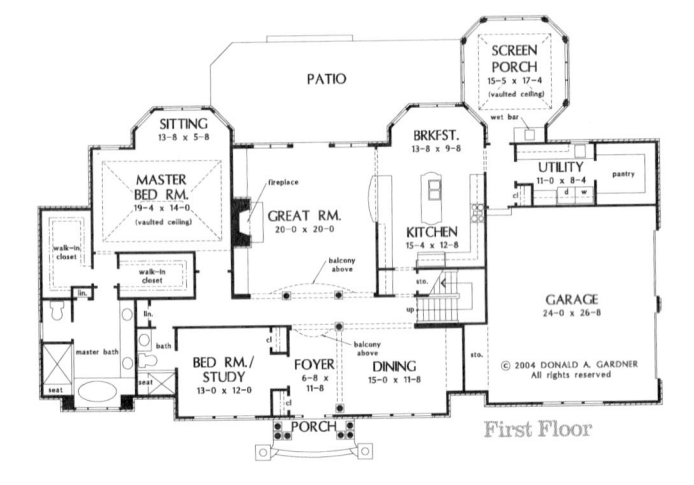

First Floor

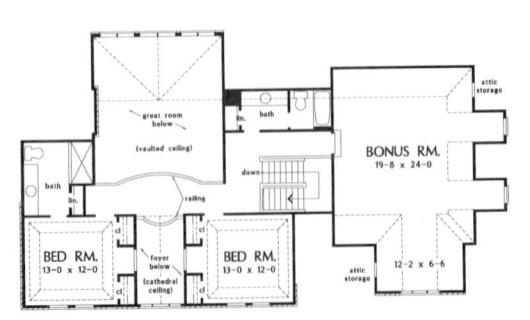

Second Floor

162 ORDER BLUEPRINTS 24 HOURS, 7 DAYS A WEEK, AT 1-800-521-6797 OR EPLANS.COM

Colonial Homes

325 New House Plans

Plan:
HPK2600205

Style:
COLONIAL

First Floor:
2,321 SQ. FT.

Second Floor:
1,060 SQ. FT.

Total:
3,381 SQ. FT.

Bonus Space:
340 SQ. FT.

Bedrooms:
4

Bathrooms:
3 1/2

Width:
64' - 0"

Depth:
55' - 0"

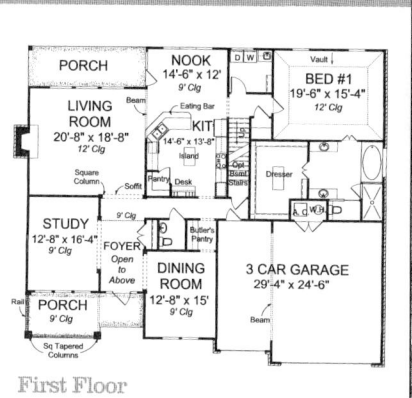

Plan:
HPK2600206

Style:
COLONIAL REVIVAL

First Floor:
3,132 SQ. FT.

Second Floor:
2,280 SQ. FT.

Total:
5,412 SQ. FT.

Bedrooms:
5

Bathrooms:
4 1/2

Width:
99' - 3"

Depth:
93' - 6"

Foundation:
UNFINISHED BASEMENT

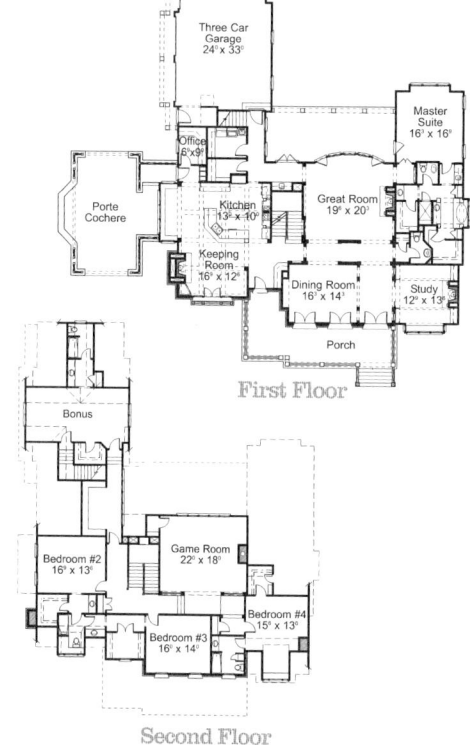

ORDER BLUEPRINTS 24 HOURS, 7 DAYS A WEEK, AT 1-800-521-6797 OR EPLANS.COM

325 Colonial Homes
New House Plans

Plan:
HPK2600207

Style:
COLONIAL REVIVAL

First Floor:
2,928 SQ. FT.

Second Floor:
2,456 SQ. FT.

Basement:
1,625 SQ. FT.

Total:
7,009 SQ. FT.

Bonus Space:
651 SQ. FT.

Bedrooms:
5

Bathrooms:
4 1/2 + 1/2

Width:
116' - 0"

Depth:
61' - 0"

Foundation:
FINISHED BASEMENT

This is a rambling estate-sized home with a distinctly Southern Colonial flavor. Arched openings to the right and left of the foyer lead into the living room and dining room, respectively. Sliding glass doors in the den, and French doors in the family room, open onto an elevated and partially covered deck—a great place to enjoy summer breezes while taking in the view. A large work island rimmed with an eating bar fills the center of the spacious kitchen, where a bayed garden window offers a panoramic view. A French door in the sunroom/nook opens onto another elevated deck. Five bedrooms, three bathrooms, and a deep bonus room are on the upper level. A backyard pool would fit in nicely by the ground-level patio, which is set one level lower than the main floor. The basement boasts a wine cellar and separate rooms for crafts, exercise, recreation, and storage.

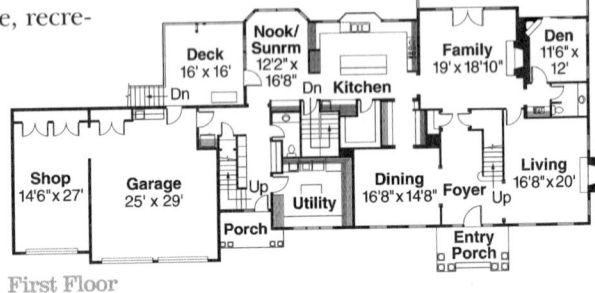

Basement

First Floor

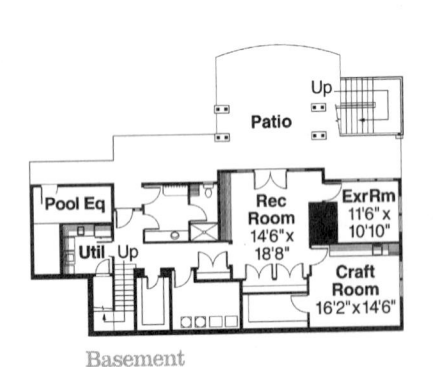

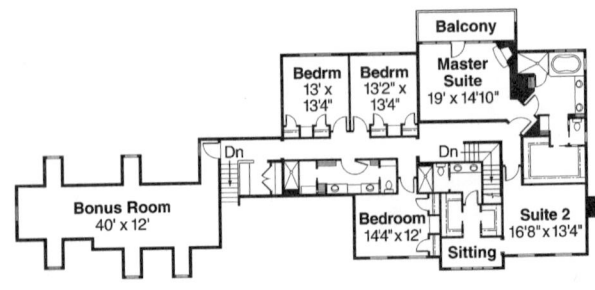

Second Floor

164   ORDER BLUEPRINTS 24 HOURS, 7 DAYS A WEEK, AT 1-800-521-6797 OR EPLANS.COM

Colonial Homes

325 New House Plans

Plan:
HPK2600208

Style:
COLONIAL

First Floor:
3,988 SQ. FT.

Second Floor:
3,165 SQ. FT.

Total:
7,153 SQ. FT.

Bedrooms:
5

Bathrooms:
5 1/2

Width:
68' - 3"

Depth:
71' - 3"

Foundation:
UNFINISHED BASEMENT

This home is an eclectic mix of warm New England coastal materials with the horizontal proportions of an Italianate villa. A fine, full-length porch with slender Adam-style twin columns mark the front of the home. The highlight of the porch is a beautiful fanlight entry leading to a classical center-stair hall. A see-through fireplace separates the family and breakfast rooms. Don't miss His and Hers walk-in closets in the grand master suite. The second floor houses four secondary bedrooms, each with a full bath and walk-in closet. The second-floor laundry room is a smart consideration.

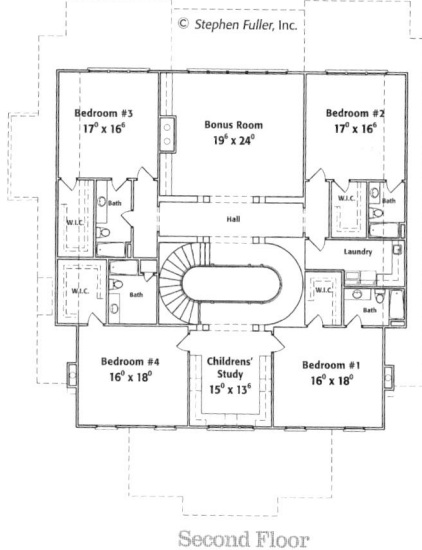

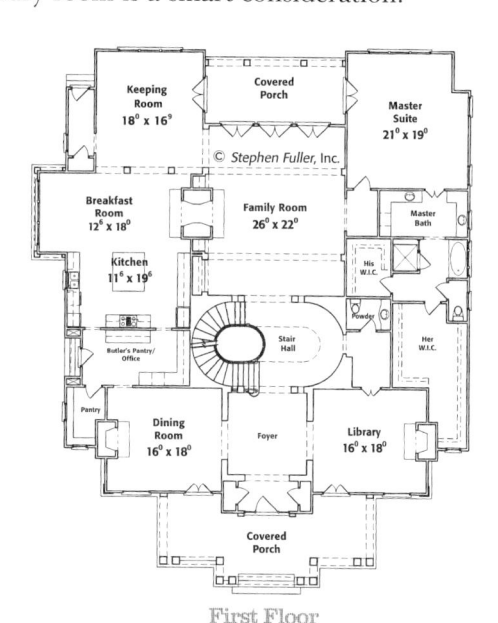

First Floor

Second Floor

ORDER BLUEPRINTS 24 HOURS, 7 DAYS A WEEK, AT 1-800-521-6797 OR EPLANS.COM

325 New House Plans
European & Mediterranean Homes

Plan:
HPK2600209

Style:
FRENCH COUNTRY

Square Footage:
1,400

Bonus Space:
297 SQ. FT.

Bedrooms:
3

Bathrooms:
2

Width:
50' - 0"

Depth:
42' - 8"

Foundation:
CRAWLSPACE

The compact, yet pleasant exterior houses a design that is perfect for homeowners at any stage of life. This home is well-suited for first-time home builders, empty-nesters, and those on the verge of starting a family. The second bedroom is great as a guest suite or child's room. The third bedroom is a possible home office. The U-shaped kitchen is both functional and efficient. The rear patio is ideal for outdoor meals.

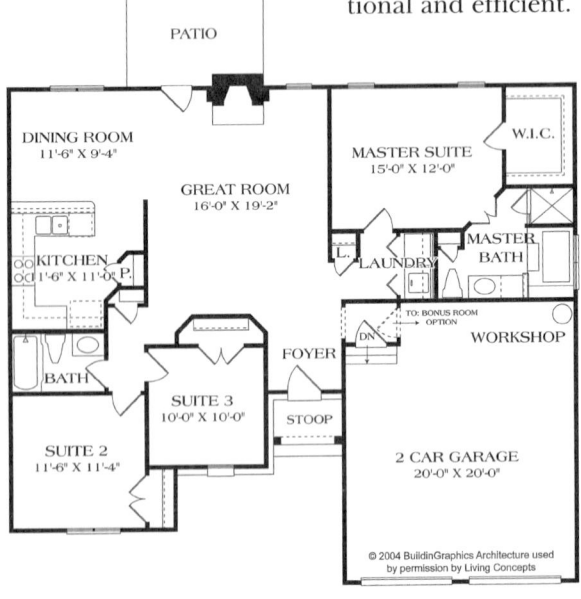

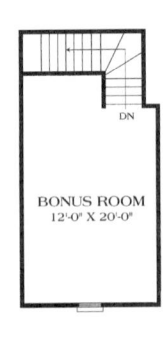

166   ORDER BLUEPRINTS 24 HOURS, 7 DAYS A WEEK, AT 1-800-521-6797 OR EPLANS.COM

European & Mediterranean Homes

325
New House Plans

Plan:
HPK2600210

Style:
EUROPEAN

Square Footage:
1,639

Bedrooms:
3

Bathrooms:
2

Width:
62' - 0"

Depth:
46' - 0"

Foundation:
SLAB

Plan:
HPK2600211

Style:
EUROPEAN

Square Footage:
1,654

Bedrooms:
3

Bathrooms:
2

Width:
64' - 0"

Depth:
39' - 0"

Foundation:
SLAB

ORDER BLUEPRINTS 24 HOURS, 7 DAYS A WEEK, AT 1-800-521-6797 OR EPLANS.COM

325 New House Plans
European & Mediterranean Homes

Plan:
HPK2600212

Style:
FRENCH COUNTRY

First Floor:
864 SQ. FT.

Second Floor:
895 SQ. FT.

Total:
1,759 SQ. FT.

Bonus Space:
242 SQ. FT.

Bedrooms:
3

Bathrooms:
2 1/2

Width:
45' - 0"

Depth:
37' - 0"

Foundation:
CRAWLSPACE

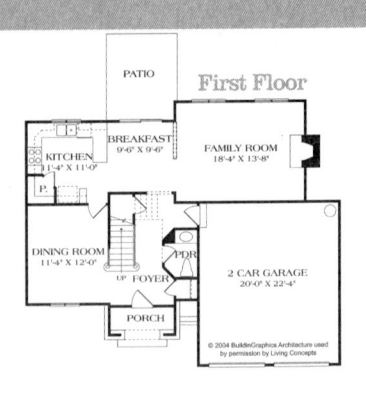

First Floor

Second Floor

Plan:
HPK2600213

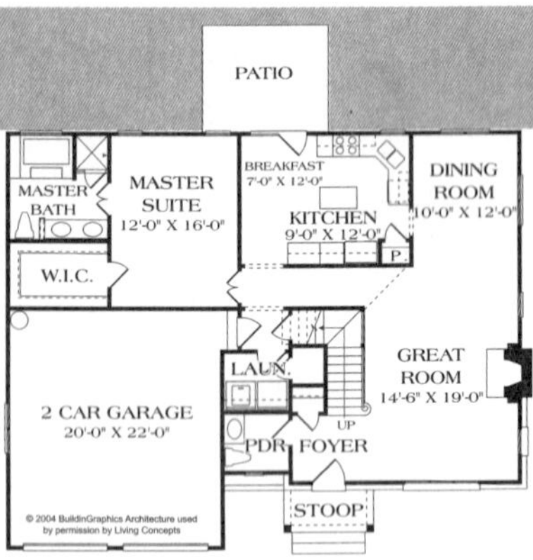

First Floor

Second Floor

Style:
FRENCH COUNTRY

First Floor:
1,272 SQ. FT.

Second Floor:
507 SQ. FT.

Total:
1,779 SQ. FT.

Bonus Space:
398 SQ. FT.

Bedrooms:
3

Bathrooms:
2 1/2

Width:
49' - 0"

Depth:
39' - 0"

Foundation:
CRAWLSPACE

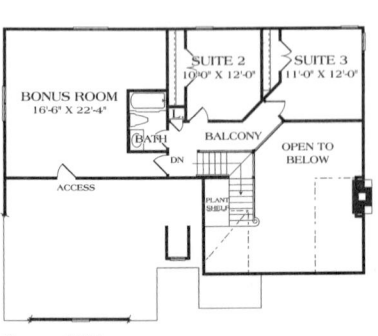

ORDER BLUEPRINTS 24 HOURS, 7 DAYS A WEEK, AT 1-800-521-6797 OR EPLANS.COM

European & Mediterranean Homes

325 New House Plans

Plan:
HPK2600214

Style:
FRENCH COUNTRY

Square Footage:
1,800

Bedrooms:
3

Bathrooms:
2

Width:
65' - 0"

Depth:
54' - 10"

Foundation:
SLAB

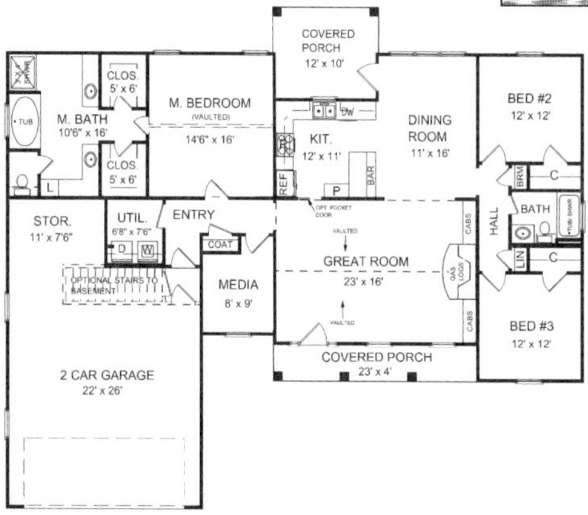

Plan:
HPK2600215

Style:
FRENCH COUNTRY

Square Footage:
1,960

Bedrooms:
3

Bathrooms:
2

Width:
65' - 0"

Depth:
55' - 4"

Foundation:
FINISHED WALKOUT BASEMENT

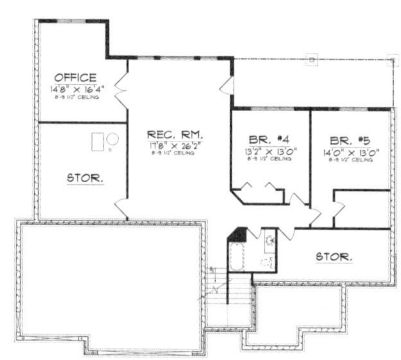

ORDER BLUEPRINTS 24 HOURS, 7 DAYS A WEEK, AT 1-800-521-6797 OR EPLANS.COM

325 New House Plans
European & Mediterranean Homes

Plan:
HPK2600216

Style:
EUROPEAN COTTAGE

First Floor:
1,518 SQ. FT.

Second Floor:
486 SQ. FT.

Square Footage:
2,004

Bedrooms:
3

Bathrooms:
2 1/2

Width:
59' - 0"

Depth:
57' - 9"

Foundation:
CRAWLSPACE, UNFINISHED WALKOUT BASEMENT

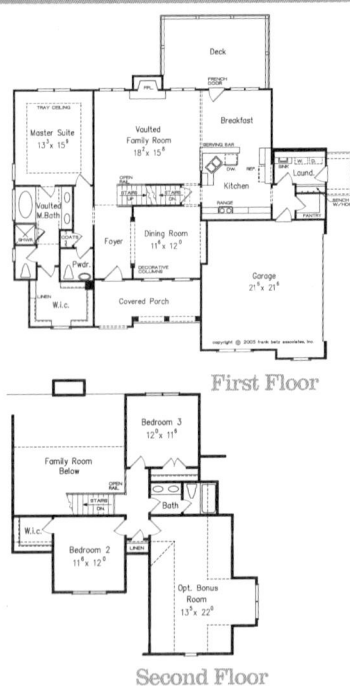

First Floor

Second Floor

Plan:
HPK2600217

Style:
FRENCH COUNTRY

Square Footage:
2,110

Bedrooms:
3

Bathrooms:
2

Width:
92' - 6"

Depth:
56' - 8"

Foundation:
UNFINISHED WALKOUT BASEMENT

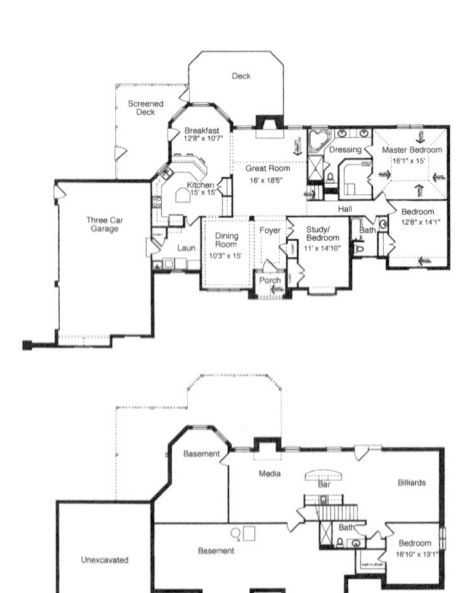

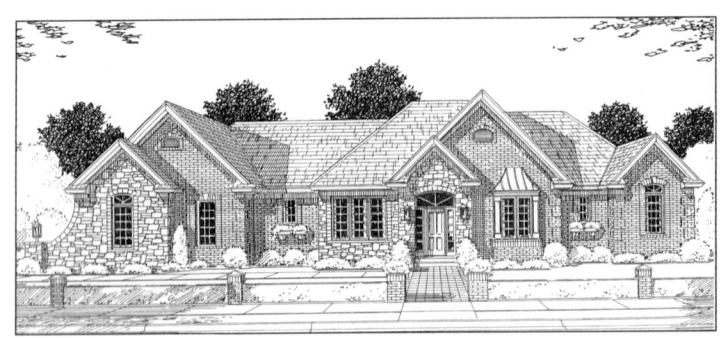

170   ORDER BLUEPRINTS 24 HOURS, 7 DAYS A WEEK, AT 1-800-521-6797 OR EPLANS.COM

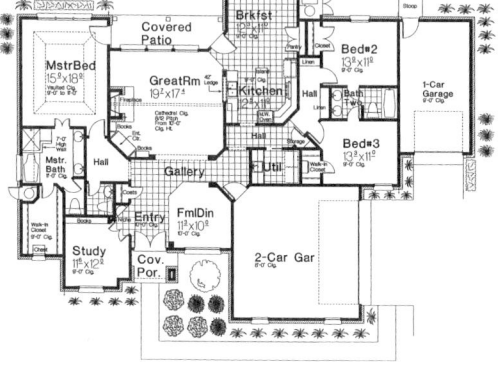

European & Mediterranean Homes

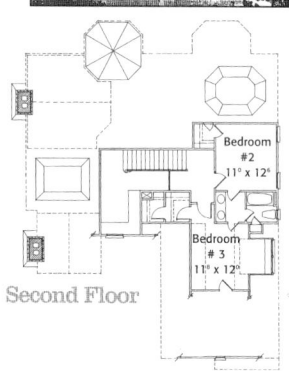

325 New House Plans

Plan:
HPK2600218

Style:
FRENCH COUNTRY

First Floor:
1,732 SQ. FT.

Second Floor:
504 SQ. FT.

Total:
2,236 SQ. FT.

Bedrooms:
3

Bathrooms:
2 1/2

Width:
47' - 3"

Depth:
63' - 6"

Foundation:
WALKOUT BASEMENT

Plan:
HPK2600219

Style:
FRENCH COUNTRY

Square Footage:
2,260

Bedrooms:
3

Bathrooms:
2 1/2

Width:
77' - 0"

Depth:
55' - 3"

Foundation:
SLAB

ORDER BLUEPRINTS 24 HOURS, 7 DAYS A WEEK, AT 1-800-521-6797 OR EPLANS.COM

325 New House Plans

European & Mediterranean Homes

Plan:
HPK2600220

Style:
COTTAGE

First Floor:
1,769 SQ. FT.

Second Floor:
555 SQ. FT.

Total:
2,324 SQ. FT.

Bonus Space:
287 SQ. FT.

Bedrooms:
3

Bathrooms:
2 ½

Width:
59' - 0"

Depth:
52' - 0"

Foundation:
CRAWLSPACE, SLAB, UNFINISHED WALKOUT BASEMENT

Come home to timeless style and a delight around every corner. From the foyer, a formal dining room lies to the right. On the left, a double-door entry leads to the sitting room of the opulent master suite with accomodating bath and oversized walk-in closet. Stairs on the right lead up to two bedrooms, a bonus room, and a full hall bath. Walk a little farther and the foyer opens to a vaulted family room with fireplace and gorgeous views of the deck and rear property. To the right, the room blends with a gourmet kitchen and breakfast nook with easy access to a powder room, laundry room, and the two-bay garage.

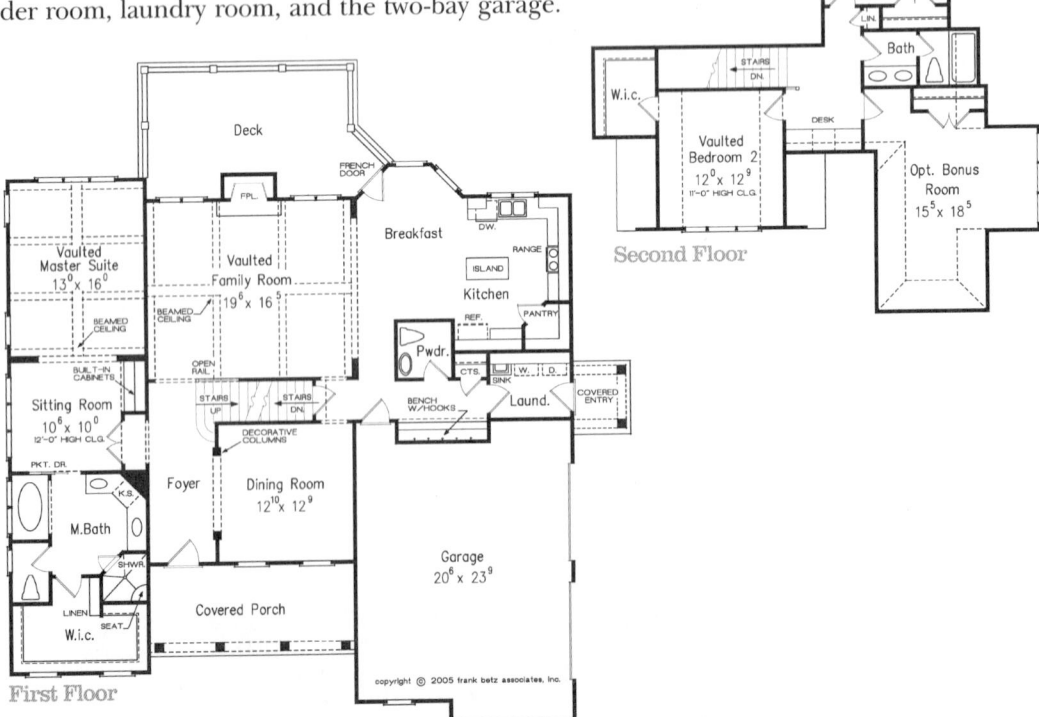

ORDER BLUEPRINTS 24 HOURS, 7 DAYS A WEEK, AT 1-800-521-6797 OR EPLANS.COM

European & Mediterranean Homes

325 New House Plans

Plan:
HPK2600221

Style:
BUNGALOW

First Floor:
1,215 SQ. FT.

Second Floor:
1,263 SQ. FT.

Total:
2,478 SQ. FT.

Bedrooms:
3

Bathrooms:
2 1/2

Width:
45' - 0"

Depth:
46' - 6"

Foundation:
CRAWLSPACE

First Floor

Second Floor

A massive stone entry on this two-story classic complements its cedar shingle siding and board-and-batten detailing. The open great room is at the heart of the living space. It features a corner media center, a warm hearth, and a wall of windows overlooking a covered patio. The kitchen serves the family gourmet and is graced by a walk-in pantry, a built-in desk, and a service door to the double garage. A convenient laundry room sits nearby. At the front of the home sits a half bath, a coat closet, and a vaulted home office with a window seat. The bedrooms are on the upper level—a master suite and two family bedrooms with a shared full bath. The master salon is vaulted. It adjoins a pampering bath with corner spa tub, glass enclosed shower, double sinks, and a walk-in closet. Bedroom 2 also sports a walk-in closet.

ORDER BLUEPRINTS 24 HOURS, 7 DAYS A WEEK, AT 1-800-521-6797 OR EPLANS.COM

325 New House Plans
European & Mediterranean Homes

Plan:
HPK2600222

Style:
FRENCH COUNTRY

First Floor:
1,603 SQ. FT.

Second Floor:
943 SQ. FT.

Total:
2,546 SQ. FT.

Bedrooms:
4

Bathrooms:
3 1/2

Width:
45' - 0"

Depth:
59' - 8"

Foundation:
CRAWLSPACE

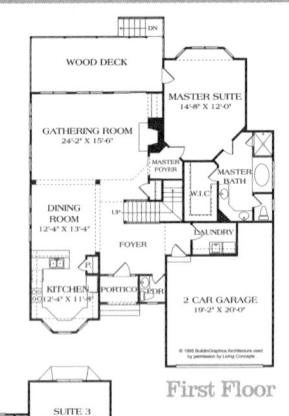

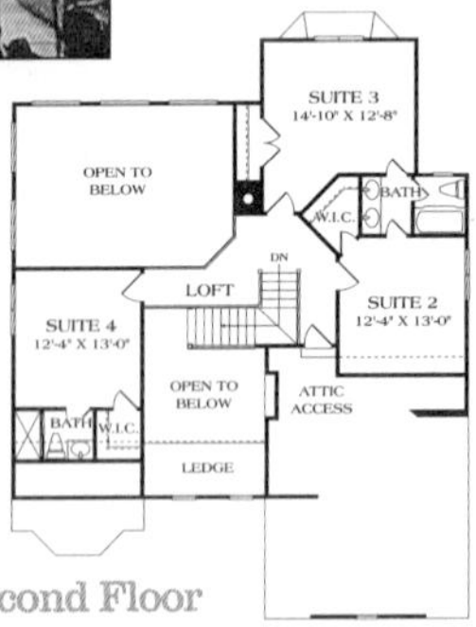

Photo Courtesy of Living Concepts
This home, as shown in photographs, may differ from the actual blueprints.
For more detailed information, please check the floor plans carefully.

First Floor

Second Floor

Plan:
HPK2600223

Style:
FRENCH COUNTRY

First Floor:
1,305 SQ. FT.

Second Floor:
1,461 SQ. FT.

Total:
2,766 SQ. FT.

Bonus Space:
274 SQ. FT.

Bedrooms:
4

Bathrooms:
2 1/2

Width:
57' - 4"

Depth:
45' - 4"

First Floor

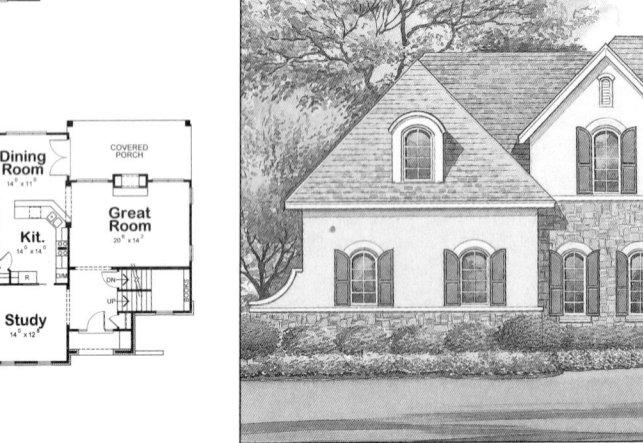

Second Floor

174 ORDER BLUEPRINTS 24 HOURS, 7 DAYS A WEEK, AT 1-800-521-6797 OR EPLANS.COM

European & Mediterranean Homes

325 New House Plans

Plan:
HPK2600224

Style:
EUROPEAN

First Floor:
2,218 SQ. FT.

Second Floor:
678 SQ. FT.

Total:
2,896 SQ. FT.

Bedrooms:
4

Bathrooms:
3

Width:
85' - 4"

Depth:
43' - 4"

© 2004 Donald A. Gardner, Inc.

A metal-topped portico joins an arched clerestory, creating a towering entrance. Twin dormers flank a prominent stone gable, while sidelights and a transom frame the front door. Inside, the floor plan is traditionally defined, yet the common rooms are open to each other. The foyer's capped by a cathedral ceiling and features a plant shelf. A vaulted ceiling adds volume to the great room. The fireplace can also be enjoyed from the kitchen and breakfast nook. French doors lead to outdoor entertaining, and built-in cabinetry provides architectural interest. A private staircase ascends to the large bonus room that's perfect for a home office. Versatility increases by the incorporation of a study/bedroom. Storage space lies near the utility room.

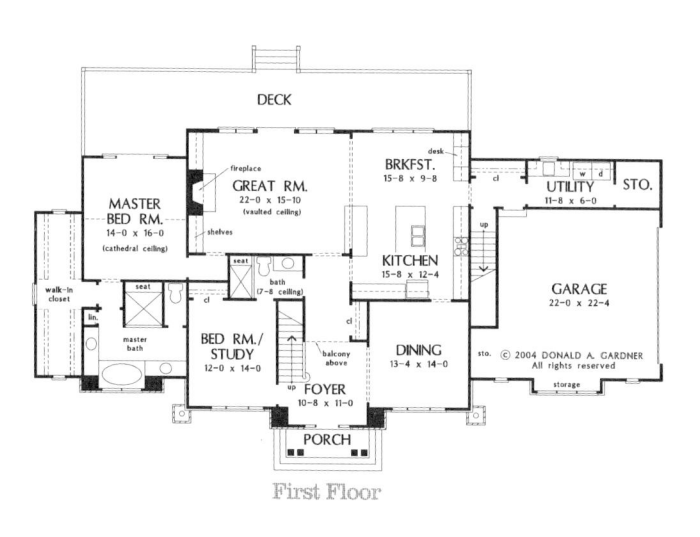

First Floor

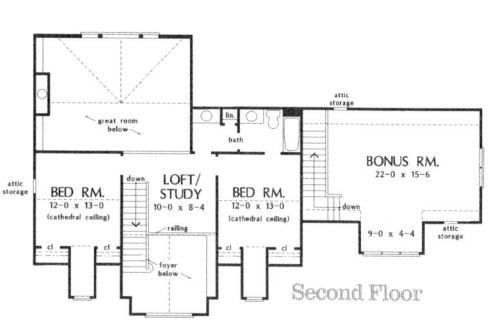

Second Floor

ORDER BLUEPRINTS 24 HOURS, 7 DAYS A WEEK, AT 1-800-521-6797 OR EPLANS.COM

325 New House Plans
European & Mediterranean Homes

Plan:
HPK2600225

Style:
FRENCH COUNTRY

First Floor:
1,915 SQ. FT.

Second Floor:
982 SQ. FT.

Total:
2,897 SQ. FT.

Bedrooms:
4

Bathrooms:
3 1/2

Width:
62' - 3"

Depth:
50' - 6"

Foundation:
WALKOUT BASEMENT

First Floor

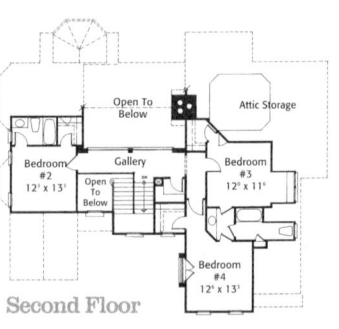

Second Floor

Plan:
HPK2600226

Style:
EUROPEAN COTTAGE

First Floor:
2,145 SQ. FT.

Second Floor:
754 SQ. FT.

Total:
2,899 SQ. FT.

Bonus Space:
385 SQ. FT.

Bedrooms:
4

Bathrooms:
3

Width:
62' - 4"

Depth:
64' - 0"

Foundation:
CRAWLSPACE, UNFINISHED WALKOUT BASEMENT

First Floor

Second Floor

176   ORDER BLUEPRINTS 24 HOURS, 7 DAYS A WEEK, AT 1-800-521-6797 OR EPLANS.COM

European & Mediterranean Homes

325 New House Plans

Plan:
HPK2600227

Style:
FRENCH COUNTRY

First Floor:
2,142 SQ. FT.

Second Floor:
779 SQ. FT.

Total:
2,921 SQ. FT.

Bonus Space:
393 SQ. FT.

Bedrooms:
3

Bathrooms:
3 1/2

Width:
57' - 0"

Depth:
81' - 0"

Foundation:
CRAWLSPACE

First Floor

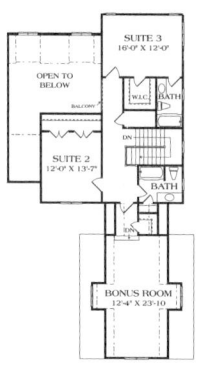

Second Floor

Plan:
HPK2600228

Style:
CHATEAUESQUE

Square Footage:
2,927

Bedrooms:
4

Bathrooms:
3 1/2

Width:
80' - 0"

Depth:
73' - 10"

Foundation:
SLAB

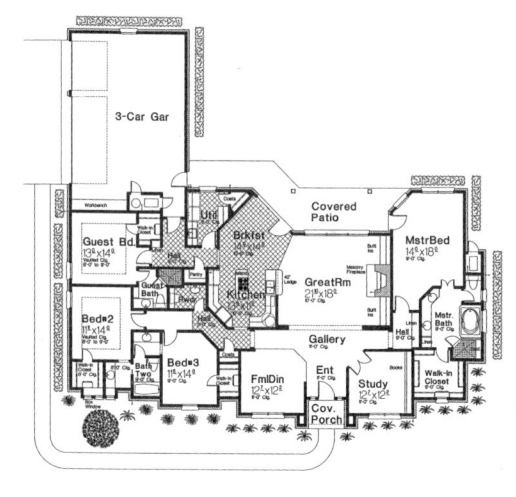

ORDER BLUEPRINTS 24 HOURS, 7 DAYS A WEEK, AT 1-800-521-6797 OR EPLANS.COM

325 New House Plans
European & Mediterranean Homes

Plan:
HPK2600229

Style:
MEDITERRANEAN

First Floor:
2,375 SQ. FT.

Second Floor:
604 SQ. FT.

Total:
2,979 SQ. FT.

Bedrooms:
3

Bathrooms:
3

Width:
77' - 1"

Depth:
85' - 8"

Foundation:
CRAWLSPACE

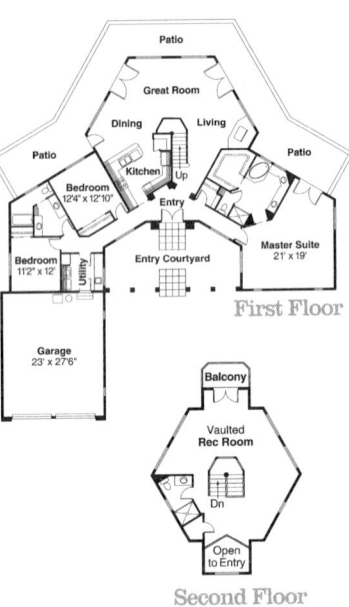

First Floor

Second Floor

Plan:
HPK2600230

Style:
EUROPEAN

Square Footage:
2,984

Bedrooms:
4

Bathrooms:
3

Width:
60' - 6"

Depth:
76' - 6"

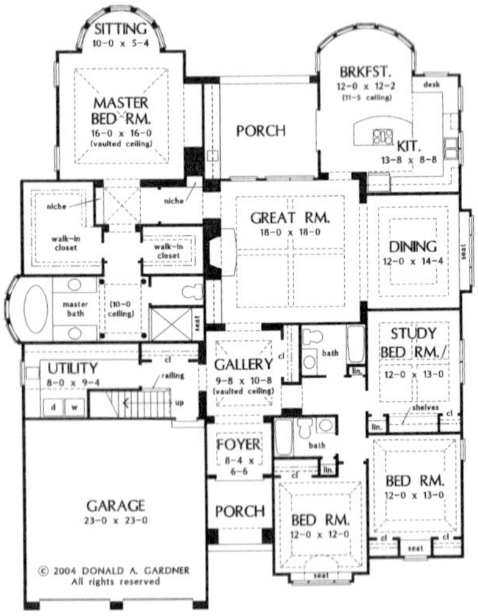

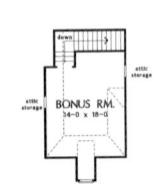

© 2004 Donald A. Gardner, Inc.

178   ORDER BLUEPRINTS 24 HOURS, 7 DAYS A WEEK, AT 1-800-521-6797 OR EPLANS.COM

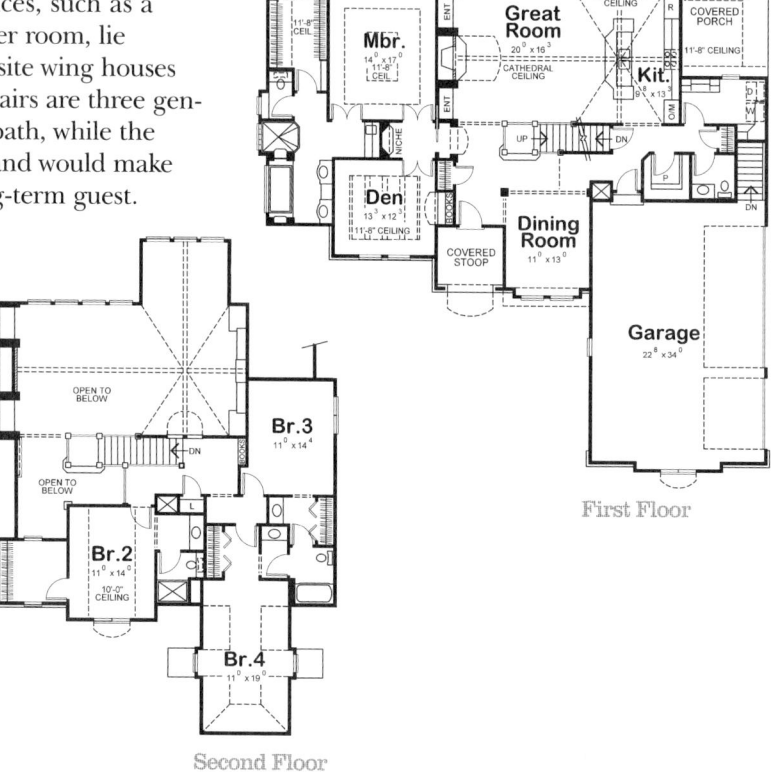

European & Mediterranean Homes

325 New House Plans

Plan:
HPK2600231

Style:
FRENCH COUNTRY

First Floor:
2,059 SQ. FT.

Second Floor:
1,021 SQ. FT.

Total:
3,080 SQ. FT.

Bedrooms:
4

Bathrooms:
3 1/2

Width:
67' - 0"

Depth:
69' - 0"

Make an impression on your neighborhood with this inviting European home. The floor plan offers outstanding design, with formal, family, and private spaces clearly delineated. Elegant built-ins and ceiling treatments lend a custom feel. The entrance hall showcases a columned dining area and stairway, then gives way to the family gathering space. Here, a spacious great room, open island kitchen, and sunny breakfast nook share a stunning cathedral ceiling and a fireplace large enough to cheer the whole area. In summer, a covered porch offers the opportunity to dine outdoors. Handy conveniences, such as a walk-in pantry, spacious laundry, and powder room, lie between the kitchen and garage. The opposite wing houses the luxe master suite and private den. Upstairs are three generous bedrooms. Two share a Jack-and-Jill bath, while the third has a private bath and walk-in closet and would make excellent quarters for an older child or long-term guest.

First Floor

Second Floor

ORDER BLUEPRINTS 24 HOURS, 7 DAYS A WEEK, AT 1-800-521-6797 OR EPLANS.COM

325 New House Plans
European & Mediterranean Homes

Plan:
HPK2600232

Style:
FRENCH COUNTRY

First Floor:
1,988 SQ. FT.

Second Floor:
1,136 SQ. FT.

Total:
3,124 SQ. FT.

Bonus Space:
499 SQ. FT.

Bedrooms:
4

Bathrooms:
3 1/2 + 1/2

Width:
68' - 0"

Depth:
62' - 8"

Life in this French Country cottage revolves around the grand fireplace. Beyond it, a wall of windows rises to the cathedral ceiling of the family room. To the left lies the master bedroom suite, with a luxury bath and generous walk-in closet. To the right, the kitchen wraps around an island snack bar. Upstairs, two bedrooms and a full bath flank a cozy loft overlooking the great room. Built-in bookshelves can accomodate the family library, or the space may be used as an additional bedroom.

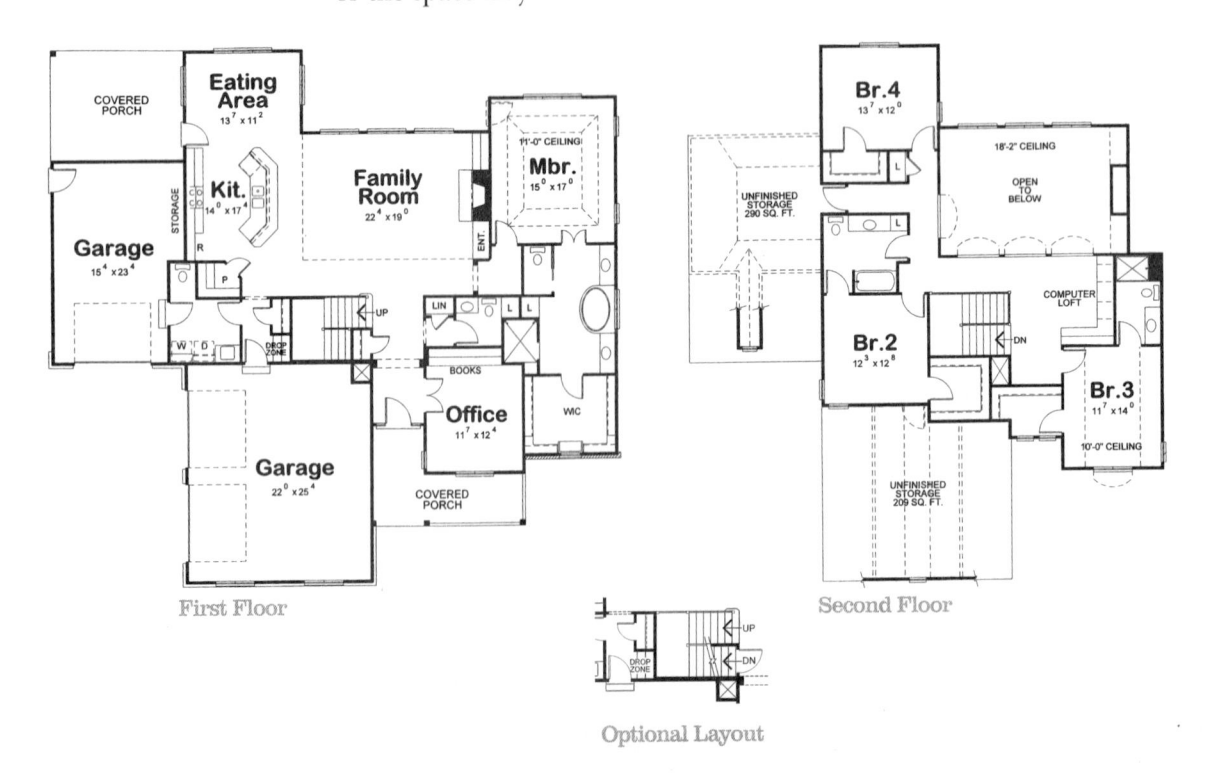

First Floor

Second Floor

Optional Layout

ORDER BLUEPRINTS 24 HOURS, 7 DAYS A WEEK, AT 1-800-521-6797 OR EPLANS.COM

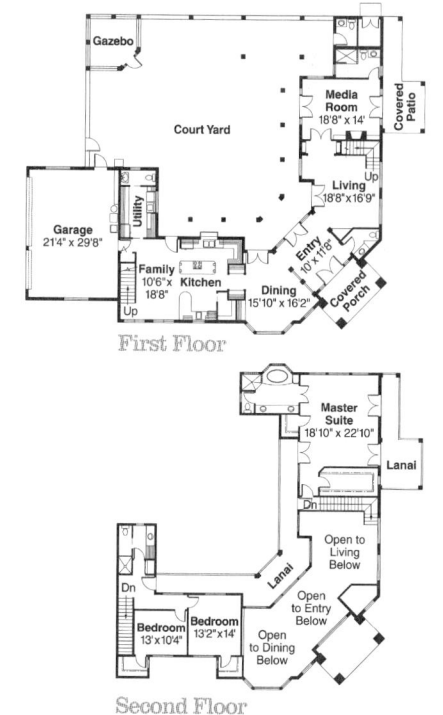

European & Mediterranean Homes

325 New House Plans

Plan:
HPK2600233

Style:
FRENCH COUNTRY

First Floor:
2,175 SQ. FT.

Second Floor:
1,150 SQ. FT.

Total:
3,325 SQ. FT.

Bedrooms:
3

Bathrooms:
2 1/2

Width:
73' - 9"

Depth:
56' - 6"

Foundation:
CRAWLSPACE

Plan:
HPK2600234

Style:
MEDITERRANEAN

First Floor:
2,022 SQ. FT.

Second Floor:
1,383 SQ. FT.

Total:
3,405 SQ. FT.

Bedrooms:
3

Bathrooms:
3 1/2 + 2 HALF-BATHS

Width:
95' - 5"

Depth:
75' - 11"

Foundation:
SLAB

ORDER BLUEPRINTS 24 HOURS, 7 DAYS A WEEK, AT 1-800-521-6797 OR EPLANS.COM

325 New House Plans
European & Mediterranean Homes

Plan:
HPK2600235

Style:
FRENCH COUNTRY

Square Footage:
3,423

Bedrooms:
4

Bathrooms:
3 1/2

Width:
112' - 0"

Depth:
76' - 6"

Foundation:
SLAB

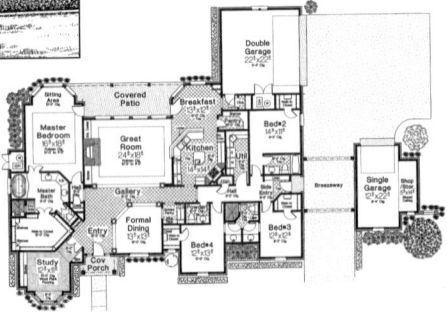

Plan:
HPK2600236

Style:
FRENCH COUNTRY

First Floor:
1,719 SQ. FT.

Second Floor:
1,735 SQ. FT.

Total:
3,454 SQ. FT.

Bedrooms:
4

Bathrooms:
3 1/2

Width:
56' - 0"

Depth:
57' - 8"

Foundation:
UNFINISHED BASEMENT

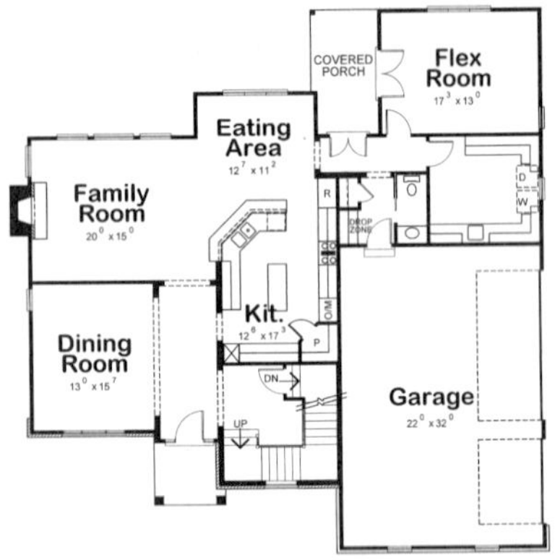

First Floor

Second Floor

182   ORDER BLUEPRINTS 24 HOURS, 7 DAYS A WEEK, AT 1-800-521-6797 OR EPLANS.COM

European & Mediterranean Homes

325 New House Plans

First Floor

Second Floor

Plan:
HPK2600237

Style:
CHATEAUESQUE
First Floor:
2,446 SQ. FT.
Second Floor:
1,013 SQ. FT.
Total:
3,459 SQ. FT.
Bonus Space:
187 SQ. FT.
Bedrooms:
5
Bathrooms:
4 1/2
Width:
73' - 0"
Depth:
68' - 0"
Foundation:
SLAB

Plan:
HPK2600238

Style:
EUROPEAN
First Floor:
2,550 SQ. FT.
Second Floor:
917 SQ. FT.
Total:
3,467 SQ. FT.
Bonus Space:
736 SQ. FT.
Bedrooms:
4
Bathrooms:
5
Width:
61' - 6"
Depth:
85' - 0"
Foundation:
CRAWLSPACE, SLAB, UNFINISHED WALKOUT BASEMENT

First Floor

Second Floor

ORDER BLUEPRINTS 24 HOURS, 7 DAYS A WEEK, AT 1-800-521-6797 OR EPLANS.COM

325 New House Plans

European & Mediterranean Homes

Plan:
HPK2600239

Style:
TUDOR

First Floor:
2,361 SQ. FT.

Second Floor:
1,177 SQ. FT.

Total:
3,538 SQ. FT.

Bonus Space:
465 SQ. FT.

Bedrooms:
4

Bathrooms:
4 ½

Width:
62' - 4"

Depth:
99' - 9"

Foundation:
CRAWLSPACE

Reminiscent of the cottages along the English countryside, the stone-and-stucco facade of this Tudor home is sure to impress. Inside, the open floor plan expands the living space. The dining and gathering rooms are defined only by columns. The island kitchen, breakfast area, and keeping room join to form a barrier-free space, enabling constant interaction between rooms. The master suite is well appointed with His and Hers walk-in closets and vanities and access to the covered terrace. The second floor houses three additional family bedrooms, each with a full bath.

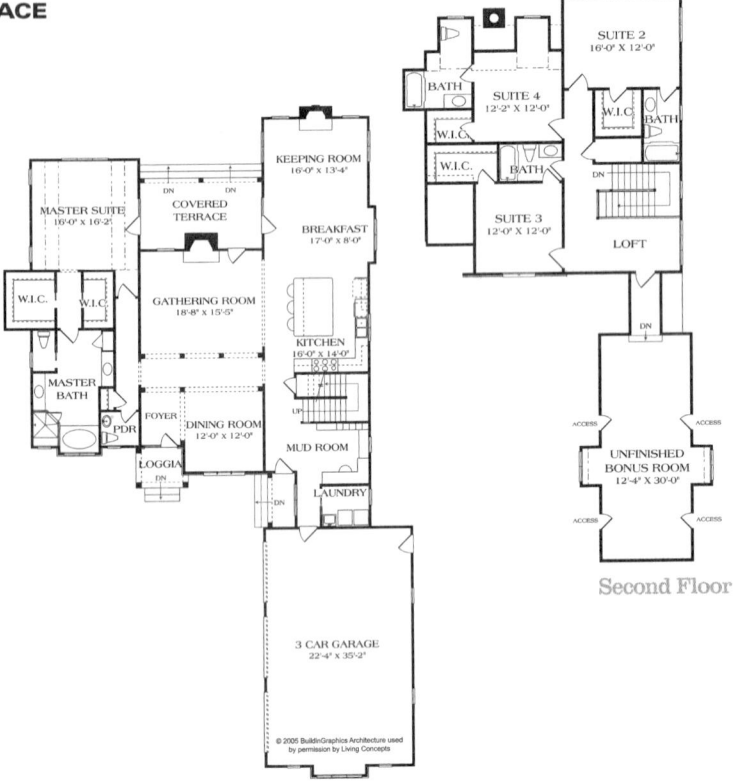

First Floor

Second Floor

ORDER BLUEPRINTS 24 HOURS, 7 DAYS A WEEK, AT 1-800-521-6797 OR EPLANS.COM

European & Mediterranean Homes

325 New House Plans

Plan:
HPK2600240

Style:
EUROPEAN COTTAGE

First Floor:
2,493 SQ. FT.

Second Floor:
1,065 SQ. FT.

Total:
3,558 SQ. FT.

Bonus Space:
277 SQ. FT.

Bedrooms:
4

Bathrooms:
3 1/2

Width:
76' - 0"

Depth:
68' - 0"

Foundation:
CRAWLSPACE

This design provides the ultimate in luxury for the homeowner. A spacious bedroom with an elegant tray ceiling opens through a columned portal to an exclusive retreat, where a fireplace can be enjoyed in privacy and quiet. At the other end of the suite, a large shower and soaking tub provide alternative ways to relax. If you ever feel like leaving this paradise, you'll find formal spaces defined by classic columns; casual living areas, such as a bayed breakfast nook and covered porch; and conveniences like a huge kitchen with a walk-in pantry and a laundry room big enough to catch the whole family's coats, shoes, and bags as they enter from the garage.

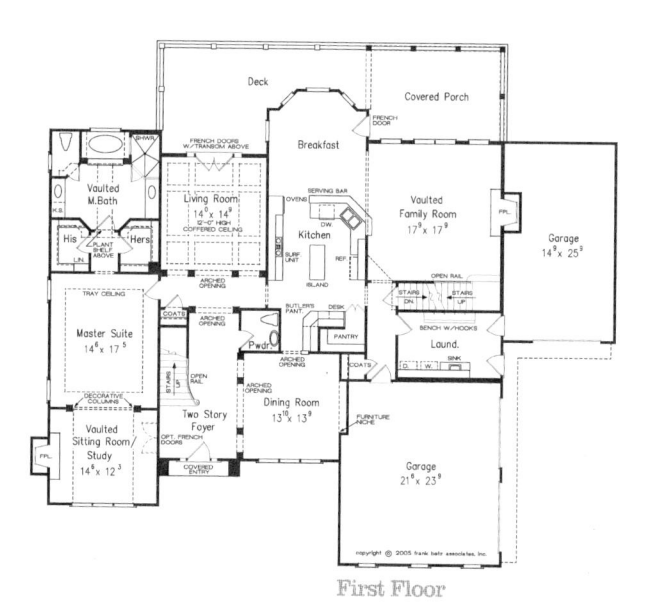

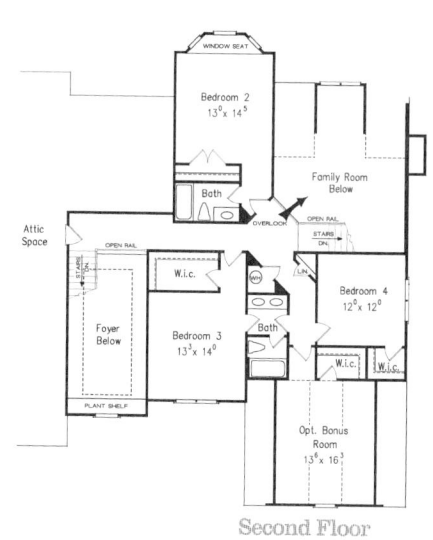

First Floor

Second Floor

ORDER BLUEPRINTS 24 HOURS, 7 DAYS A WEEK, AT 1-800-521-6797 OR EPLANS.COM

325 New House Plans

European & Mediterranean Homes

Plan:
HPK2600241

Style:
FRENCH COUNTRY

Main Level:
2,323 SQ. FT.

Lower Level:
1,615 SQ. FT.

Total:
3,938 SQ. FT.

Bedrooms:
4

Bathrooms:
3 1/2

Width:
90' - 0"

Depth:
80' - 8"

Foundation:
FINISHED WALKOUT BASEMENT

Perfect for hillside lots, this stucco-and-brick bilevel has appeal and room to spread out. The main level features a fine combined living area consisting of the great room, breakfast nook, and island kitchen. A formal dining room adds eating space for special occasions. Two bedrooms also grace this level: a master suite with deck access and Bedroom 2 at the opposite end of the house. A three-season porch off the nook leads to another deck. The lower level contains two additional bedrooms, a full bath, and a rec room with a two-sided fireplace. Note the two double garages.

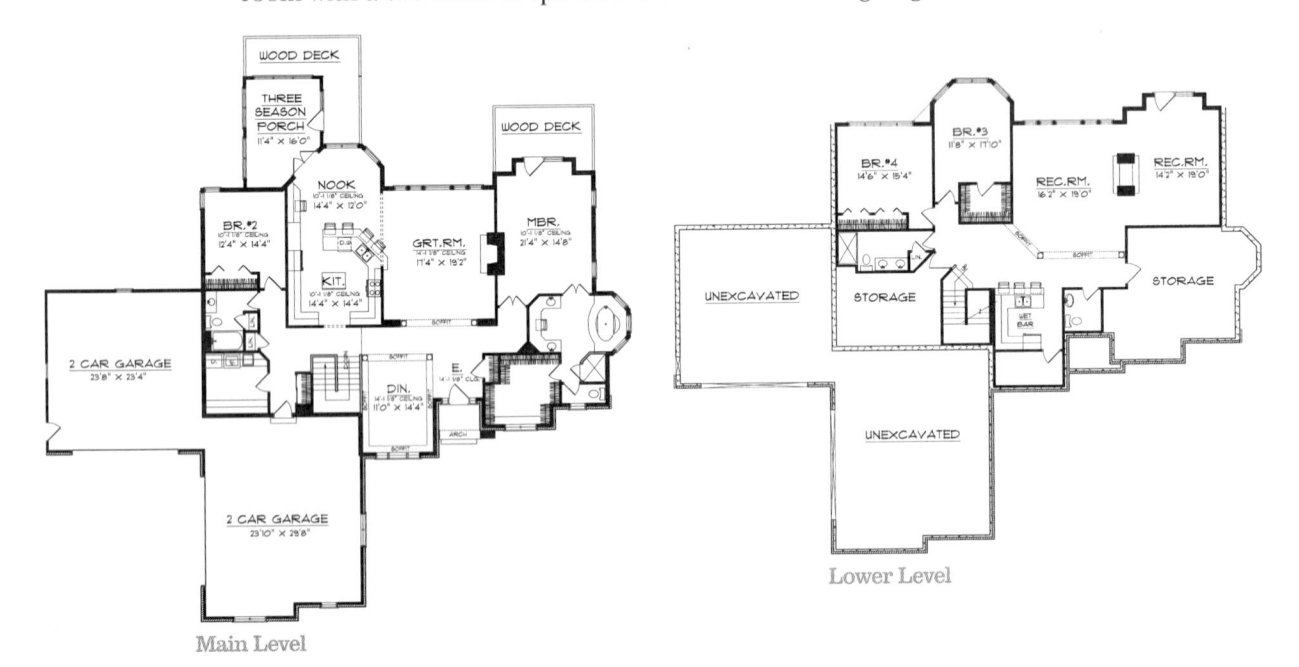

Main Level

Lower Level

186 ORDER BLUEPRINTS 24 HOURS, 7 DAYS A WEEK, AT 1-800-521-6797 OR EPLANS.COM

European & Mediterranean Homes

325 New House Plans

Plan:
HPK2600242

Style:
FRENCH COUNTRY

First Floor:
2,484 SQ. FT.

Second Floor:
1,615 SQ. FT.

Total:
4,099 SQ. FT.

Bonus Space:
572 SQ. FT.

Bedrooms:
4

Bathrooms:
4 1/2

Width:
71' - 8"

Depth:
74' - 3"

Foundation:
CRAWLSPACE

Plan:
HPK2600243

Style:
EUROPEAN

Square Footage:
4,190

Bedrooms:
3

Bathrooms:
3 1/2 + 1/2

Width:
113' - 4"

Depth:
88' - 0"

Foundation:
UNFINISHED BASEMENT

ORDER BLUEPRINTS 24 HOURS, 7 DAYS A WEEK, AT 1-800-521-6797 OR EPLANS.COM

325 New House Plans
European & Mediterranean Homes

Plan:
HPK2600244

Style:
FRENCH COUNTRY

First Floor:
2,405 SQ. FT.

Second Floor:
1,718 SQ. FT.

Total:
4,123 SQ. FT.

Bedrooms:
4

Bathrooms:
4 ½

Width:
59' - 10"

Depth:
81' - 11"

Foundation:
CRAWLSPACE

Experience luxury European style with this French Country home. At just over 4,100 square feet, spacious, amenity-filled rooms are the norm. A fireplace on the rear veranda adds ambiance to alfresco meals. The kitchen is highly efficient, aptly serving the breakfast area and the dining room. The butler's pantry is an added convenience. The master suite is a lavish, private retreat for the homeowner. Three additional secondary bedrooms reside upstairs, each with a full bath.

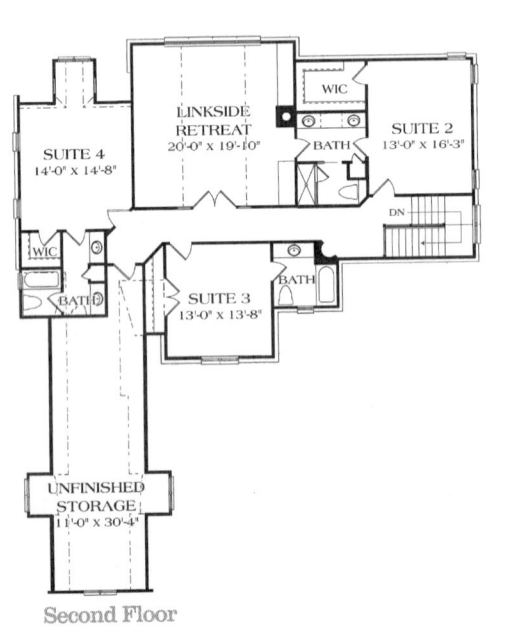

First Floor

Second Floor

Living Concepts
This home, as shown in photographs, may differ from the actual blueprints. For more detailed information, please check the floor plans carefully.

188 ORDER BLUEPRINTS 24 HOURS, 7 DAYS A WEEK, AT 1-800-521-6797 OR EPLANS.COM

European & Mediterranean Homes

325 New House Plans

Plan:
HPK2600245

Style:
FRENCH COUNTRY

First Floor:
2,526 SQ. FT.

Second Floor:
1,720 SQ. FT.

Total:
4,246 SQ. FT.

Bedrooms:
4

Bathrooms:
3 1/2

Width:
77' - 6"

Depth:
62' - 0"

Foundation:
CRAWLSPACE

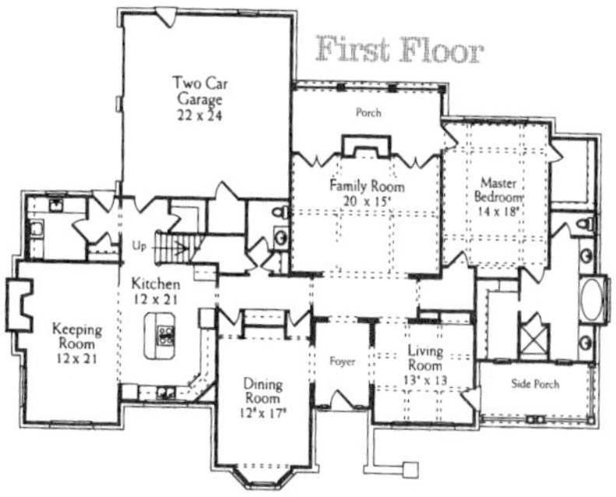

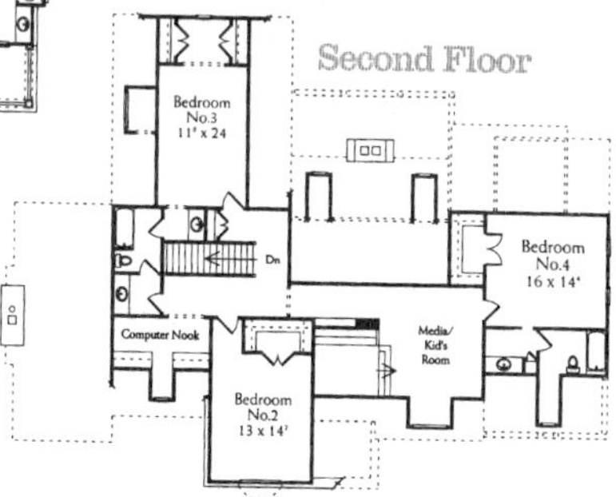

Plan:
HPK2600246

Style:
FRENCH COUNTRY

First Floor:
2,962 SQ. FT.

Second Floor:
1,307 SQ. FT.

Total:
4,269 SQ. FT.

Bonus Space:
200 SQ. FT.

Bedrooms:
4

Bathrooms:
4 1/2

Width:
88' - 8"

Depth:
62' - 0"

ORDER BLUEPRINTS 24 HOURS, 7 DAYS A WEEK, AT 1-800-521-6797 OR EPLANS.COM

325 New House Plans
European & Mediterranean Homes

Plan:
HPK2600247

Style:
FRENCH COUNTRY

First Floor:
2,763 SQ. FT.

Second Floor:
1,543 SQ. FT.

Total:
4,306 SQ. FT.

Bedrooms:
3

Bathrooms:
3 1/2

Width:
59' - 10"

Depth:
73' - 2"

Foundation:
CRAWLSPACE

First Floor

Second Floor

Plan:
HPK2600248

Style:
FRENCH COUNTRY

First Floor:
2,603 SQ. FT.

Second Floor:
1,881 SQ. FT.

Total:
4,484 SQ. FT.

Bedrooms:
4

Bathrooms:
4 1/2

Width:
71' - 2"

Depth:
88' - 4"

Foundation:
CRAWLSPACE

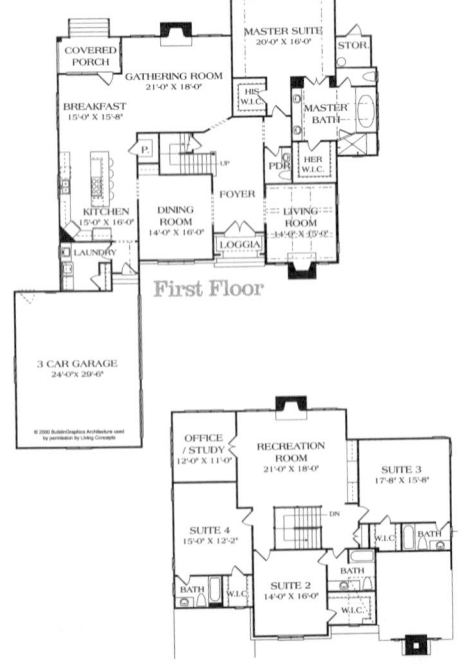

First Floor

Second Floor

ORDER BLUEPRINTS 24 HOURS, 7 DAYS A WEEK, AT 1-800-521-6797 OR EPLANS.COM

European & Mediterranean Homes

325 New House Plans

Plan:
HPK2600249

Style:
ITALIANATE

First Floor:
3,947 SQ. FT.

Second Floor:
545 SQ. FT.

Total:
4,492 SQ. FT.

Bedrooms:
4

Bathrooms:
4 ½

Width:
105' - 9"

Depth:
100' - 9"

Foundation:
SLAB

Repeating arches hint of a seaside resort in this fabulous Mediterranean manor. The triple arches of the facade are creatively repeated inside as pass-through points between the ultra-elegant kitchen and great room. An entire wall of glass pocket doors adds volumes of fresh-air living opportunities to this charming family space. Floor-to-ceiling glass panels also enhance the master suite, where they embrace a sitting nook and slide open to a private end of the veranda. A spa-style tub sits center stage in the master bath. Behind the curved wall is a walk-in shower with views to a private garden. The idyllic courtyard—with its stunning stone fireplace and gazebo-style, open-beamed canopy—has an arbor-like ambiance perfect for a cool drink and warm friends. A twilight glow highlights the indoor-outdoor connections of this home as the public and private rooms cast their personalities outside to the meandering veranda and glittering pool.

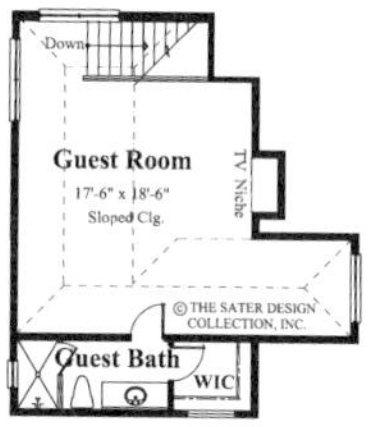

Second Floor

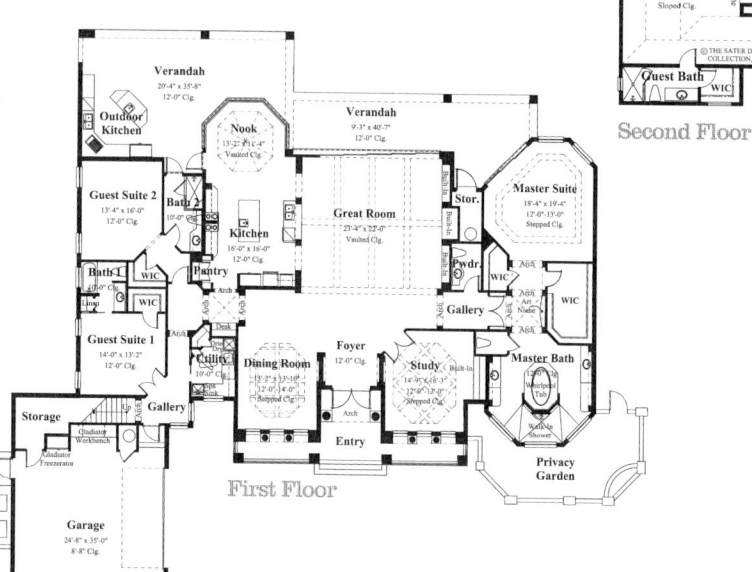

First Floor

ORDER BLUEPRINTS 24 HOURS, 7 DAYS A WEEK, AT 1-800-521-6797 OR EPLANS.COM

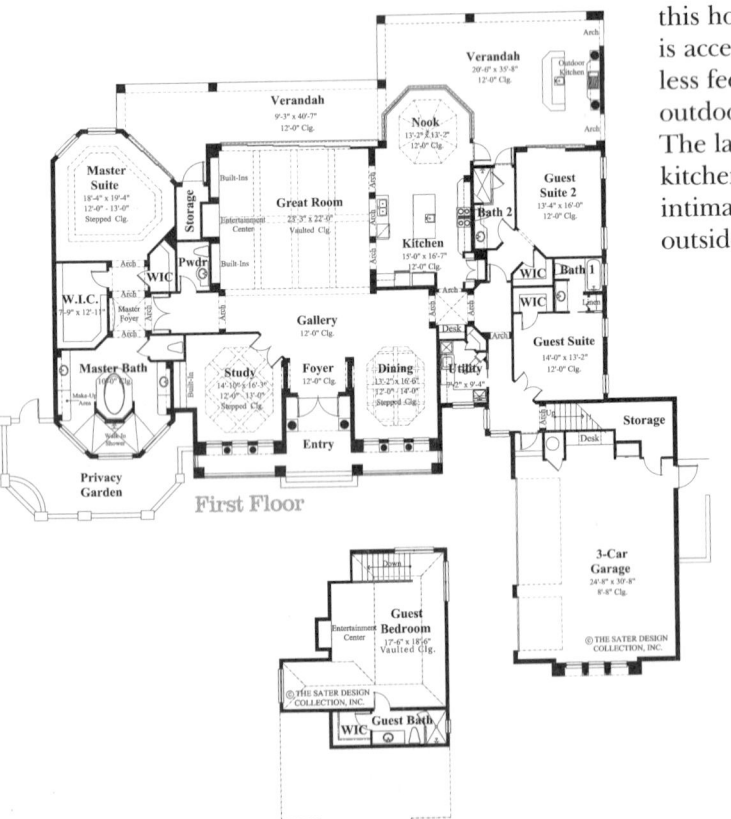

325 New House Plans
European & Mediterranean Homes

Plan:
HPK2600250

Style:
ITALIANATE

First Floor:
3,947 SQ. FT.

Second Floor:
545 SQ. FT.

Total:
4,492 SQ. FT.

Bedrooms:
4

Bathrooms:
4 1/2

Width:
105' - 9"

Depth:
100' - 9"

Foundation:
SLAB

The Mediterranean appeal is undeniable and this home is no exception. The stucco exterior is accentuated by a red tile roof lending a timeless feel. The open floor plan and expansive outdoor living space is ideal for entertaining. The large rear veranda features an outdoor kitchen, perfect for alfresco meals. For more intimate occasions, relax in the private garden outside of the master bath.

Photographer: Laurence Taylor
This home, as shown in photographs, may differ from the actual blueprints. For more detailed information, please check the floor plans carefully.

ORDER BLUEPRINTS 24 HOURS, 7 DAYS A WEEK, AT 1-800-521-6797 OR EPLANS.COM

European & Mediterranean Homes

325 New House Plans

Plan:
HPK2600251

Style:
MEDITERRANEAN

First Floor:
2,528 SQ. FT.

Second Floor:
2,045 SQ. FT.

Total:
4,573 SQ. FT.

Bedrooms:
4

Bathrooms:
4 1/2

Width:
90' - 0"

Depth:
56' - 0"

Foundation:
FINISHED BASEMENT

A vaulted, recessed portico creates a strong first impression of contemporary classicism that echoes throughout the home. The foyer is traditionally flanked by a formal dining room and living room, yet the plan is far from being stuffy with symmetry. The living room is slightly sunken and features a polygonal nook. This shape is repeated in the study and in the master bedroom upstairs. At the rear of the lower level lies the kitchen, where a gentle curving wall and island countertop lend a contemporary air. At one end of the kitchen, a butler's pantry leads to the dining room, and a short corridor gives access to the laundry room and three-car garage. At the other end of the kitchen, a breakfast nook and hearth-warmed family room enfold an outdoor patio. The grand staircase leads to three private bedroom suites plus the master suite, whose luxury bath promises the ultimate in indulgence.

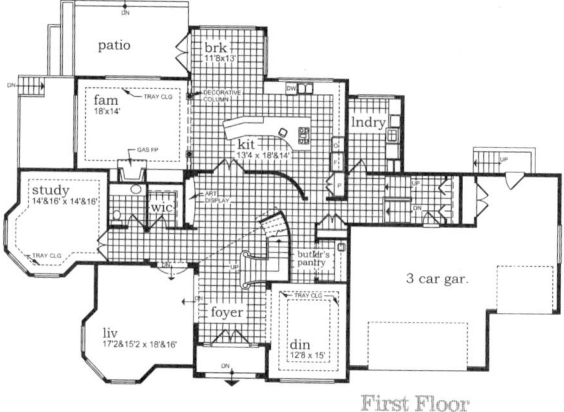

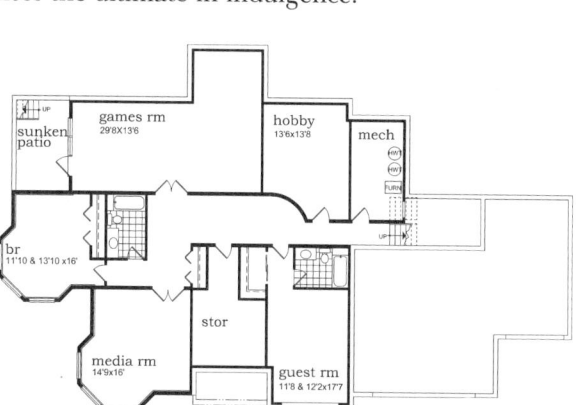

Photo by Steve Riley, Courtesy of Select Home Designs. This home, as shown in photographs, may differ from the actual blueprints. For more detailed information, please check the floor plans carefully.

First Floor

Second Floor

ORDER BLUEPRINTS 24 HOURS, 7 DAYS A WEEK, AT 1-800-521-6797 OR EPLANS.COM

325 New House Plans
European & Mediterranean Homes

Plan:
HPK2600252

Style:
FRENCH COUNTRY

First Floor:
3,397 SQ. FT.

Second Floor:
1,324 SQ. FT.

Total:
4,721 SQ. FT.

Bonus Space:
355 SQ. FT.

Bedrooms:
4

Bathrooms:
4

Width:
104' - 0"

Depth:
73' - 9"

The front entry, with two-story arched opening and brilliant window, is a preview of what you will find inside. The foyer is open to above and a sweeping staircase rises to the left. Round columns lead to the dining room on the left and den/study on the right. A great room with fireplace and built-ins flows directly into the hearth/breakfast room with fireplace. These rooms have access to a rear grilling porch and are open to the kitchen with island snack bar, desk, and butler's pantry. The master suite with fireplace, sitting area, and private bath is on the right side of the floor plan. This master bath is complete with a whirlpool tub, vaulted ceiling, and walk-in closet. The upper floor has three bedrooms in addition to a game room/home theater where family members can gather for fun or entertain guests.

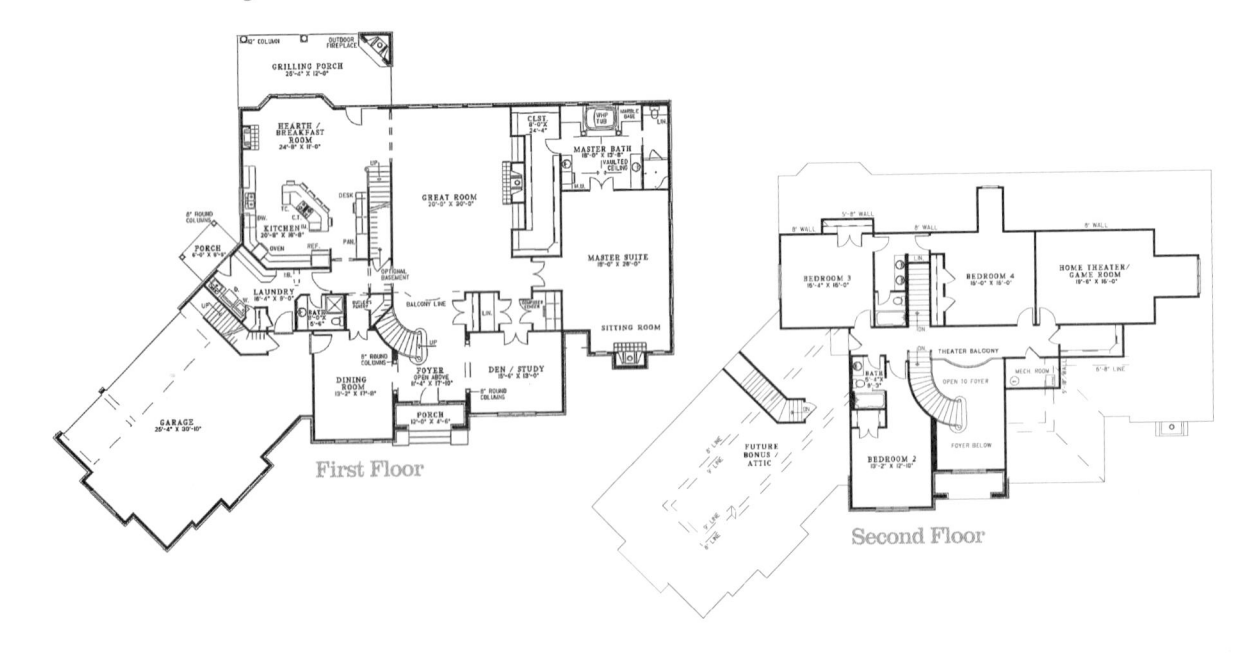

First Floor

Second Floor

European & Mediterranean Homes

325
New House Plans

Plan:
HPK2600253

Style:
SECOND EMPIRE

First Floor:
1,929 SQ. FT.

Second Floor:
1,925 SQ. FT.

Third Floor:
969 SQ. FT.

Total:
4,823 SQ. FT.

Bedrooms:
3

Bathrooms:
3 ½

Width:
35' - 0"

Depth:
72' - 6"

Foundation:
UNFINISHED WALKOUT BASEMENT

A first-floor master bedroom offers a quiet retreat with its private deck and see-through fireplace connecting to the circular master bath. The second floor offers a stunning great room and breakfast area with access to a rear viewing deck. A music room and study create charming spaces. A large island with seating defines the kitchen and a butler's pantry serves the formal dining room. The third-floor recreation room leads to a covered porch and rooftop terrace featuring an outdoor fireplace. An elevator allows easy access throughout the house.

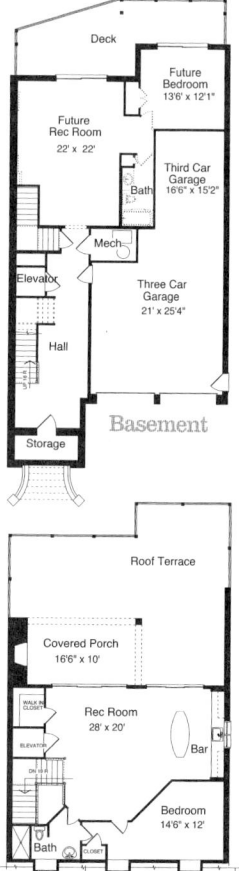

Photos by Ron Kolb, Exposures Unlimited; digital editing by Joseph Bove, Cincinnati Aerial Photography. This home, as shown in photographs, may differ from the actual blueprints. For more detailed information, please check the floor plans carefully.

ORDER BLUEPRINTS 24 HOURS, 7 DAYS A WEEK, AT 1-800-521-6797 OR EPLANS.COM

325 New House Plans
European & Mediterranean Homes

Plan:
HPK2600254

Style:
FRENCH COUNTRY

Main Level:
1,703 SQ. FT.

Upper Level:
1,958 SQ. FT.

Lower Level:
1,249 SQ. FT.

Total:
4,910 SQ. FT.

Bedrooms:
4

Bathrooms:
4 1/2

Width:
69' - 0"

Depth:
60' - 0"

Foundation:
FINISHED WALKOUT BASEMENT

The stone-and-shake facade of this hillside retreat lends it a rustic feel, but there is no compromising the luxury within. Elegantly arched openings lead from the foyer to the surrounding rooms: a formal dining room, a flex room, and the spacious family room. This room is entirely open to the breakfast room and kitchen, whose snack counter and planning area will make it the true hub of family activity. At the back of the home are several options for outdoor living: a covered porch and an open deck, which serves as the roof of the veranda below. The lower level features plenty of space for recreation and entertaining, including a small kitchen and bar, a media room, and a full bath for guest use. On the upper level, two family bedrooms share a compartmented bath and another enjoys its own bath. The deluxe master suite boasts a corner fireplace and a private balcony.

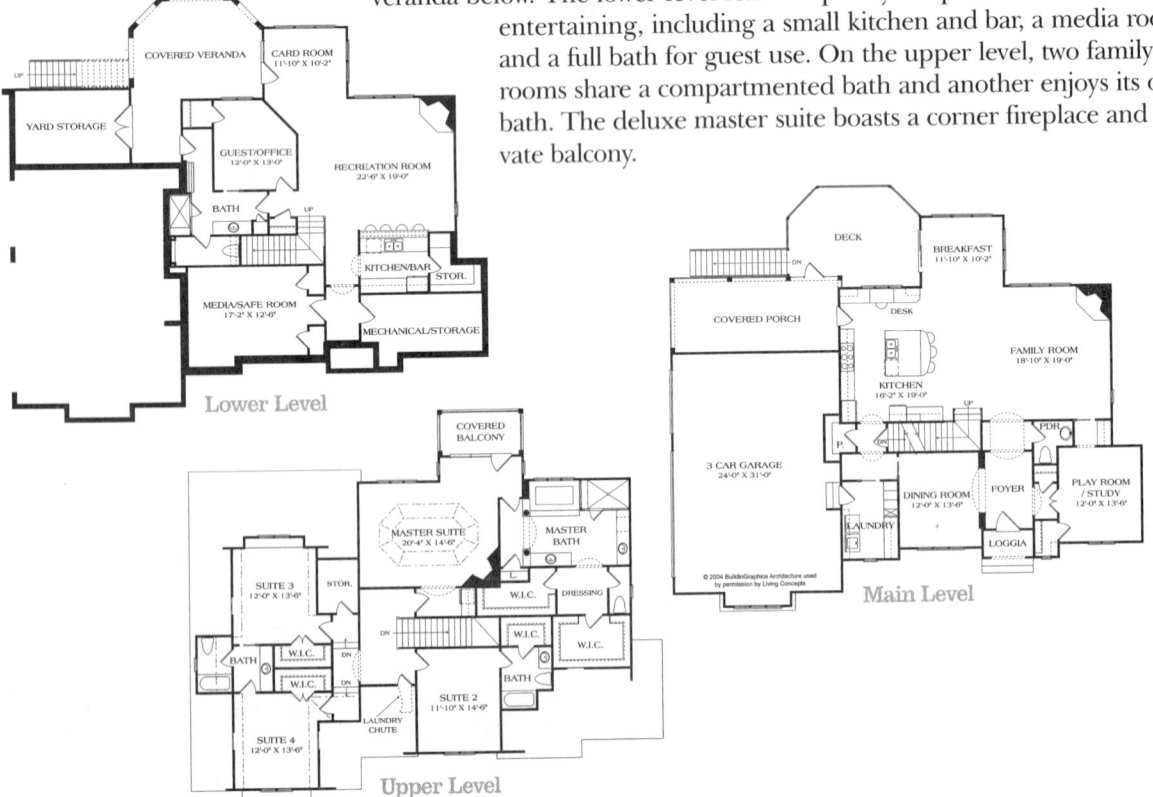

196   ORDER BLUEPRINTS 24 HOURS, 7 DAYS A WEEK, AT 1-800-521-6797 OR EPLANS.COM

European & Mediterranean Homes

325 New House Plans

Plan:
HPK2600255

Style:
FRENCH COUNTRY
First Floor:
3,265 SQ. FT.
Second Floor:
1,706 SQ. FT.
Total:
4,971 SQ. FT.
Bonus Space:
569 SQ. FT.
Bedrooms:
4
Bathrooms:
3 1/2
Width:
101' - 0"
Depth:
102' - 0"
Foundation:
CRAWLSPACE

First Floor

Second Floor

Plan:
HPK2600256

Style:
FRENCH COUNTRY
First Floor:
3,310 SQ. FT.
Second Floor:
1,881 SQ. FT.
Total:
5,191 SQ. FT.
Bonus Space:
929 SQ. FT.
Bedrooms:
5
Bathrooms:
4 1/2 + 1/2
Width:
111' - 6"
Depth:
71' - 0"
Foundation:
CRAWLSPACE

First Floor

Second Floor

ORDER BLUEPRINTS 24 HOURS, 7 DAYS A WEEK, AT 1-800-521-6797 OR EPLANS.COM

325 New House Plans
European & Mediterranean Homes

Plan:
HPK2600257

Style:
EUROPEAN

First Floor:
2,864 SQ. FT.

Second Floor:
2,329 SQ. FT.

Total:
5,193 SQ. FT.

Bedrooms:
4

Bathrooms:
4 1/2 + 1/2

Width:
64' - 6"

Depth:
87' - 6"

Foundation:
WALKOUT BASEMENT

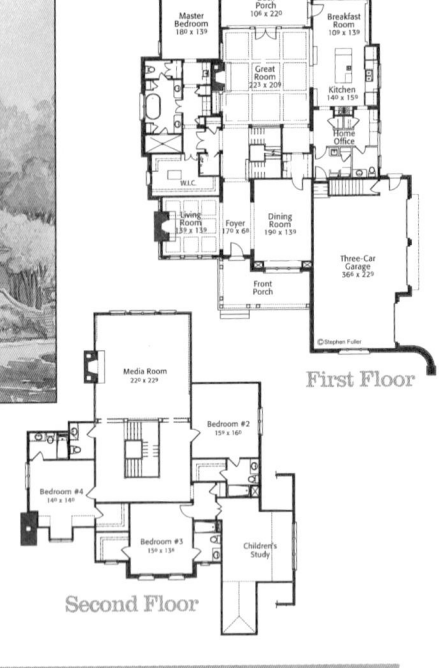

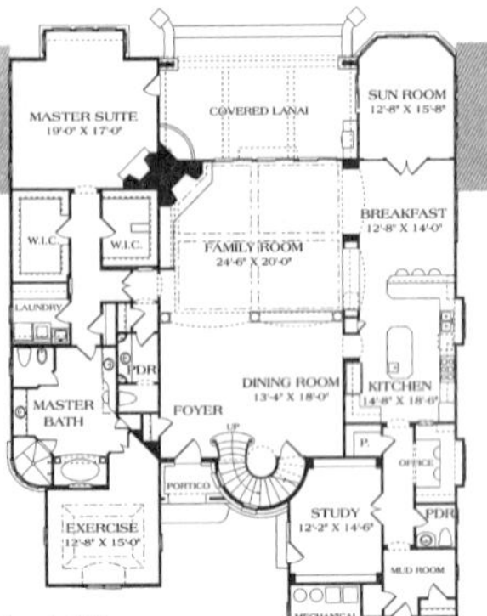

First Floor

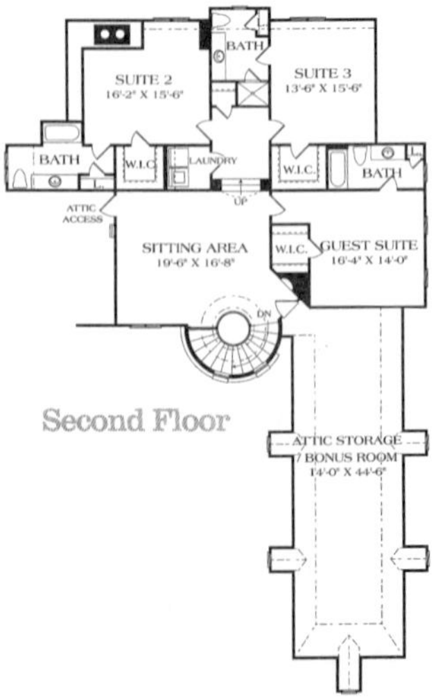

Second Floor

Plan:
HPK2600258

Style:
TUDOR

First Floor:
3,592 SQ. FT.

Second Floor:
1,653 SQ. FT.

Total:
5,245 SQ. FT.

Bonus Space:
804 SQ. FT.

Bedrooms:
4

Bathrooms:
4 1/2 + 1/2

Width:
60' - 0"

Depth:
111' - 2"

Foundation:
CRAWLSPACE

First Floor

Second Floor

European & Mediterranean Homes

325 New House Plans

Plan:
HPK2600001

Style:
MEDITERRANEAN

First Floor:
4,716 SQ. FT.

Second Floor:
619 SQ. FT.

Total:
5,335 SQ. FT.

Bedrooms:
4

Bathrooms:
5 1/2

Width:
95' - 0"

Depth:
134' - 6"

Foundation:
SLAB

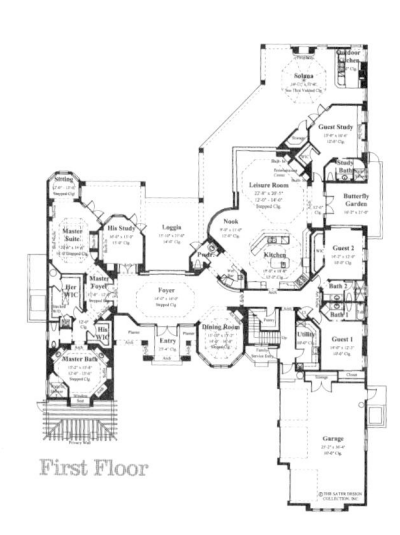

First Floor

Second Floor

Plan:
HPK2600259

Style:
ITALIANATE

First Floor:
5,290 SQ. FT.

Second Floor:
551 SQ. FT.

Total:
5,841 SQ. FT.

Bedrooms:
4

Bathrooms:
4 1/2

Width:
89' - 4"

Depth:
139' - 10"

Foundation:
SLAB

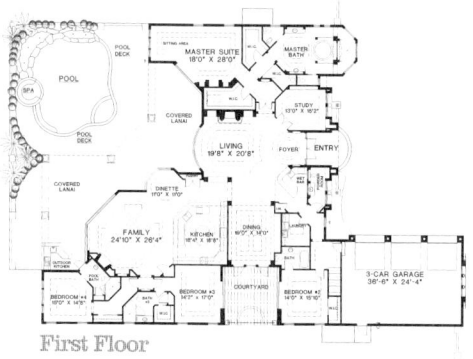

First Floor

Second Floor

ORDER BLUEPRINTS 24 HOURS, 7 DAYS A WEEK, AT 1-800-521-6797 OR EPLANS.COM

325 New House Plans

European & Mediterranean Homes

Plan:
HPK2600260

Style:
EUROPEAN

Main Level:
2,863 SQ. FT.

Upper Level:
1,522 SQ. FT.

Lower Level:
1,903 SQ. FT.

Total:
6,288 SQ. FT.

Bedrooms:
5

Bathrooms:
4 1/2 + 1/2

Width:
120' - 7"

Depth:
68' - 2"

Foundation:
FINISHED WALKOUT BASEMENT

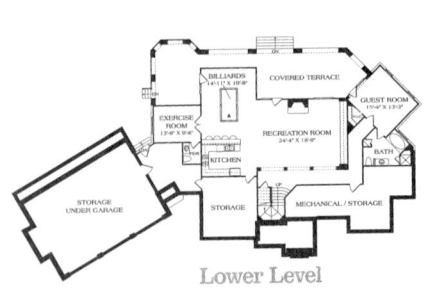

Lower Level

Upper Level

Main Level

Plan:
HPK2600261

Style:
FRENCH COUNTRY

First Floor:
3,763 SQ. FT.

Second Floor:
2,603 SQ. FT.

Total:
6,366 SQ. FT.

Bedrooms:
4

Bathrooms:
4 1/2 + 1/2

Width:
110' - 6"

Depth:
79' - 5"

Foundation:
CRAWLSPACE

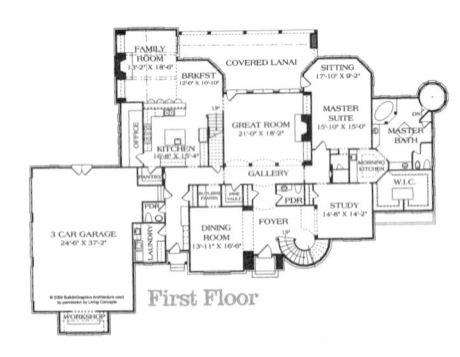

First Floor

Second Floor

Michael Lobiondo
This home, as shown in photographs, may differ from the actual blueprints. For more detailed information, please check the floor plans carefully.

ORDER BLUEPRINTS 24 HOURS, 7 DAYS A WEEK, AT 1-800-521-6797 OR EPLANS.COM

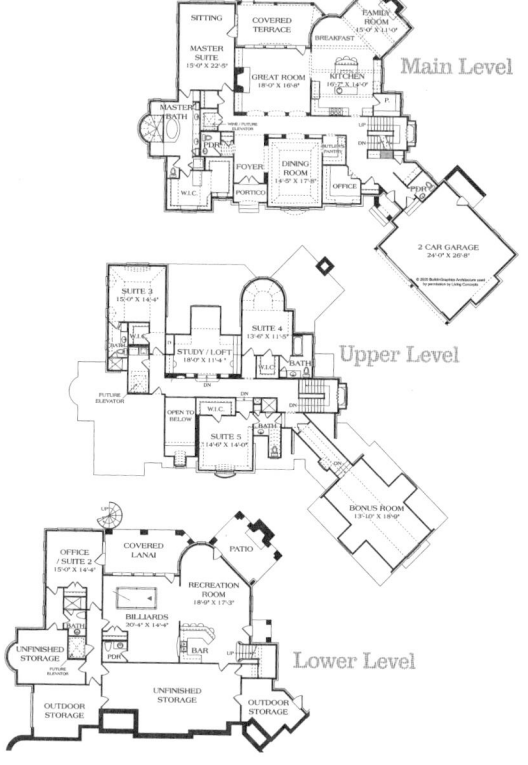

European & Mediterranean Homes

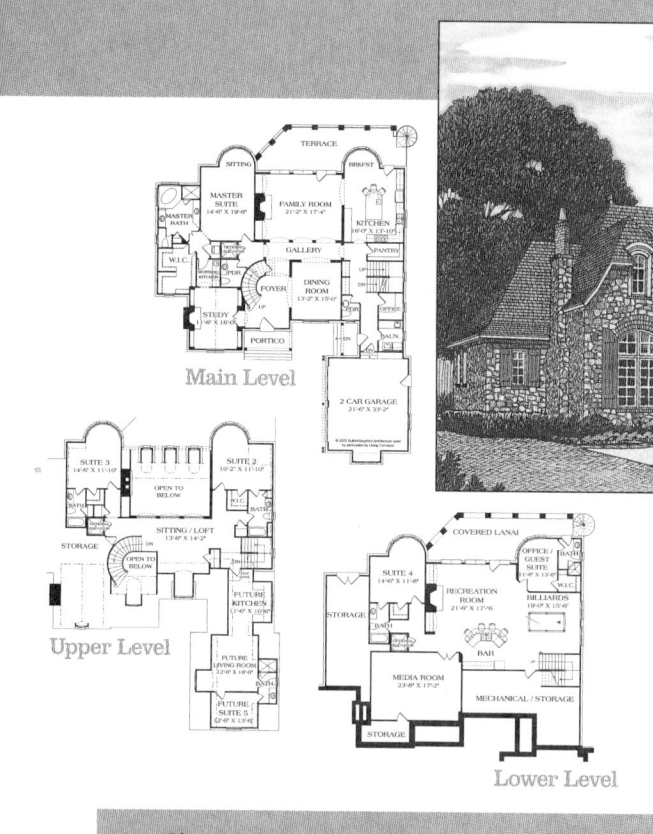

325 New House Plans

Plan:
HPK2600262

Style:
EUROPEAN

Main Level:
2,887 SQ. FT.

Upper Level:
1,384 SQ. FT.

Lower Level:
2,166 SQ. FT.

Total:
6,437 SQ. FT.

Bonus Space:
579 SQ. FT.

Bedrooms:
5

Bathrooms:
5 1/2 + 1/2

Width:
70' - 0"

Depth:
89' - 6"

Foundation:
FINISHED WALKOUT BASEMENT

Plan:
HPK2600263

Style:
FRENCH COUNTRY

Main Level:
3,040 SQ. FT.

Upper Level:
1,899 SQ. FT.

Lower Level:
1,526 SQ. FT.

Total:
6,465 SQ. FT.

Bonus Space:
542 SQ. FT.

Bedrooms:
5

Bathrooms:
5 1/2 + 2 HALF-BATHS

Width:
102' - 0"

Depth:
89' - 1"

Foundation:
FINISHED WALKOUT BASEMENT

ORDER BLUEPRINTS 24 HOURS, 7 DAYS A WEEK, AT 1-800-521-6797 OR EPLANS.COM

325 New House Plans
European & Mediterranean Homes

Plan:
HPK2600264

Style:
NORMAN

First Floor:
3,807 SQ. FT.

Second Floor:
2,698 SQ. FT.

Total:
6,505 SQ. FT.

Bedrooms:
5

Bathrooms:
5

Width:
66' - 0"

Depth:
73' - 6"

Foundation:
UNFINISHED BASEMENT

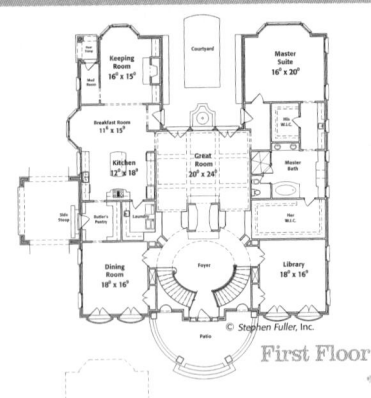

First Floor

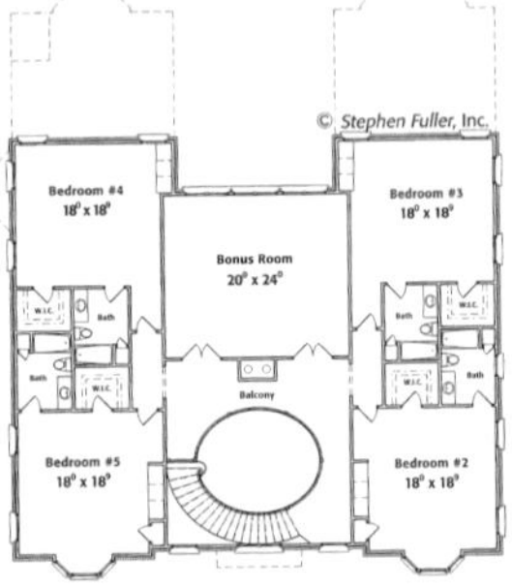

Second Floor

Plan:
HPK2600265

Lower Level

Main Level

Upper Level

Style:
FRENCH COUNTRY

Main Level:
3,230 SQ. FT.

Upper Level:
1,881 SQ. FT.

Lower Level:
1,847 SQ. FT.

Total:
6,598 SQ. FT.

Bonus Space:
869 SQ. FT.

Bedrooms:
5

Bathrooms:
6 1/2 + 1/2

Width:
113' - 8"

Depth:
84' - 6"

Foundation:
FINISHED WALKOUT BASEMENT

ORDER BLUEPRINTS 24 HOURS, 7 DAYS A WEEK, AT 1-800-521-6797 OR EPLANS.COM

European & Mediterranean Homes

325 New House Plans

Plan:
HPK2600266

Style:
FRENCH COUNTRY

Main Level:
2,822 SQ. FT.

Upper Level:
2,072 SQ. FT.

Lower Level:
2,522 SQ. FT.

Total:
7,416 SQ. FT.

Bonus Space:
1,134 SQ. FT.

Bedrooms:
5

Bathrooms:
5 1/2

Width:
102' - 8"

Depth:
101' - 11"

Foundation:
FINISHED WALKOUT BASEMENT

With a French Country appeal, this home will surely distinguish itself from others in the neighborhood. Equally impressive are smart amenities in unlikely places throughout the interior: Laundry facilities in the expansive walk-in closet of the master suite is just one example. A screened porch adjacent to the kitchen is ideal for alfresco meals. On the second floor, three additional family bedrooms feature private baths and share a second laundry room. A bonus room on this level offers a wealth of expansion opportunities. The basement level is entertainment central, complete with a recreation room, a billiards area, a wine cellar and wet bar, and an exercise room. Access to the covered terrace extends the party outdoors. A guest suite on this level is an added convenience. Elevator access is available on all three floors.

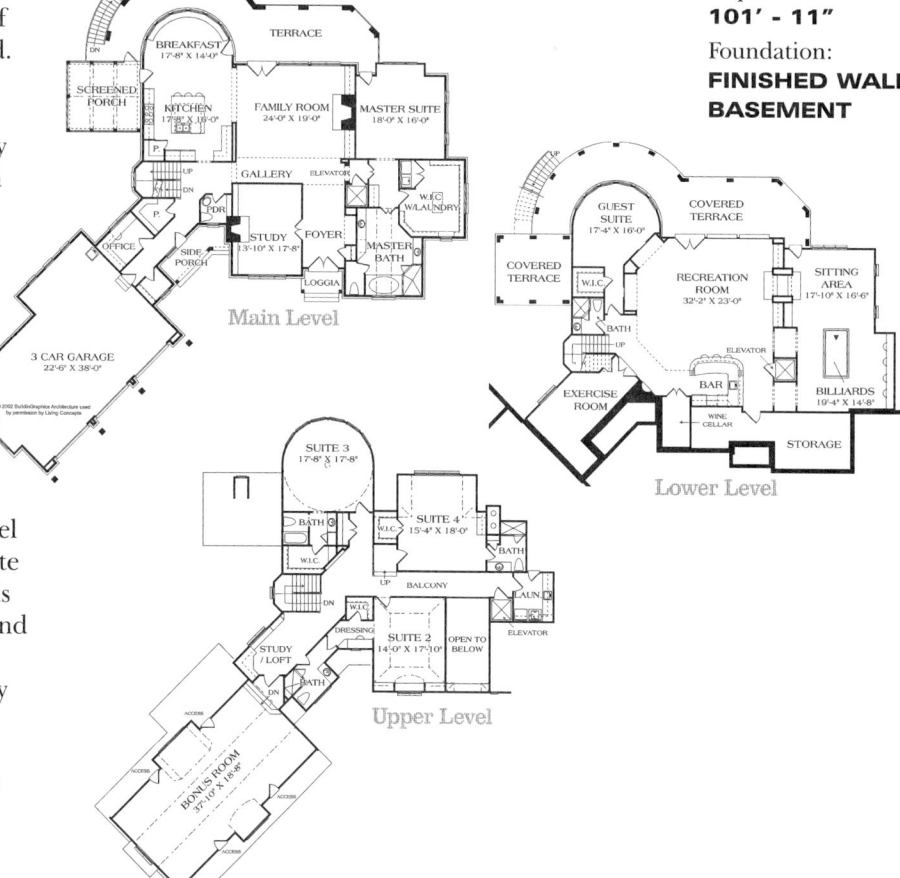

ORDER BLUEPRINTS 24 HOURS, 7 DAYS A WEEK, AT 1-800-521-6797 OR EPLANS.COM

325 New House Plans
European & Mediterranean Homes

Plan:
HPK2600267

Style:
CHATEAUESQUE

First Floor:
4,302 SQ. FT.

Second Floor:
2,402 SQ. FT.

Third Floor:
1,422 SQ. FT.

Total:
8,126 SQ. FT.

Bedrooms:
5

Bathrooms:
5 1/2 + 1/2

Width:
100' - 0"

Depth:
92' - 0"

Foundation:
CRAWLSPACE

Classic symmetry and elegant details combine to perfection in this fantastic manor house. A pair of double garages flank the entry courtyard, where an arcaded portico supports a second-story balcony. Inside, a reception hall with a corner bar is the perfect place to begin an evening of entertainment. Beyond, the grand salon promises a warm fire and a spectacular view. A formal dining room lies to the left, and the kitchen and family living areas beyond that. The right wing holds the master suite, which features a bath worthy of a spa resort. A dramatic stairway leads to a library that overlooks the salon; two pairs of bedrooms extend to either side. Another stair rises to the third-floor eagle's nest where a media room, a rec room, and a bar enjoy a cozy atmosphere under the eaves of this grand home.

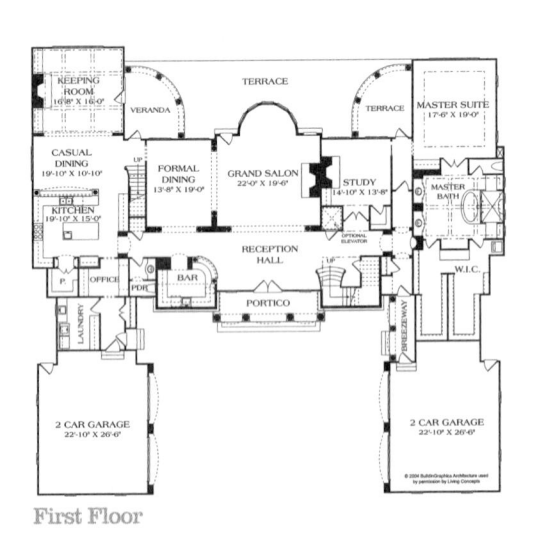

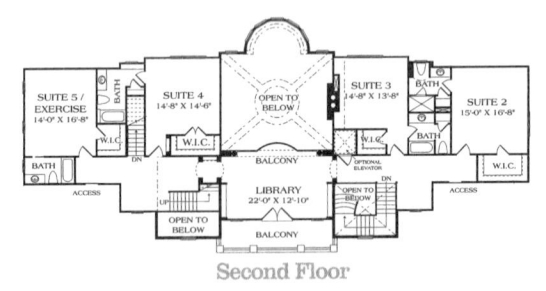

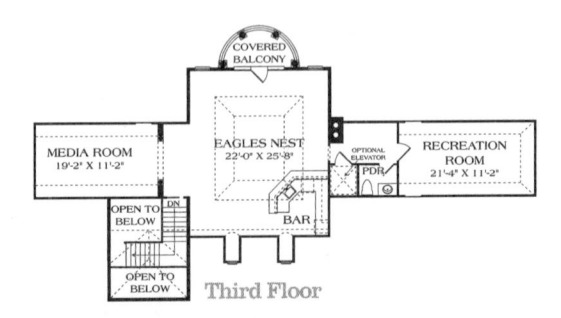

European & Mediterranean Homes

325 New House Plans

Plan:
HPK2600268

Style:
ITALIANATE

First Floor:
5,827 SQ. FT.

Second Floor:
2,492 SQ. FT.

Total:
8,319 SQ. FT.

Bonus Space:
357 SQ. FT.

Bedrooms:
5

Bathrooms:
5 1/2

Width:
129' - 8"

Depth:
124' - 10"

Foundation:
SLAB

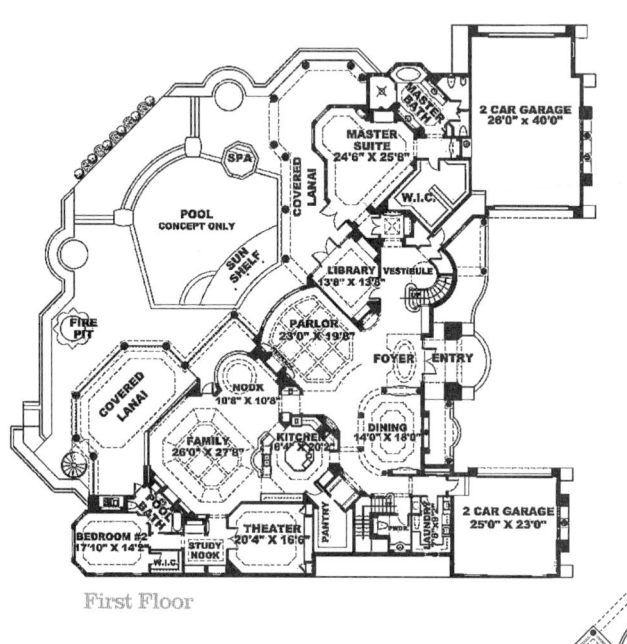

This home is second to none. Having received the 2005 Sand Dollar Award for Outstanding Architecture for Product Design, this Tuscan-style home was designed for a special lot with spectacular views. Many rooms for entertaining are designed to take advantage of comfort and luxury with convenient built-in cabinets, multiple fireplaces, decorative ceilings, and gorgeous window applications. Private spaces for the homeowner offer peace and tranquility. Find the quiet view in the library soothing and the master appointments relaxing. Amenities include the theater room, parlor, several covered lanais, bonus room, exercise room, and so much more.

First Floor

Second Floor

ORDER BLUEPRINTS 24 HOURS, 7 DAYS A WEEK, AT 1-800-521-6797 OR EPLANS.COM

325 New House Plans
European & Mediterranean Homes

Plan:
HPK2600269

Style:
FRENCH COUNTRY

Main Level:
3,904 SQ. FT.

Upper Level:
1,710 SQ. FT.

Lower Level:
3,006 SQ. FT.

Total:
8,620 SQ. FT.

Bonus Space:
723 SQ. FT.

Bedrooms:
5

Bathrooms:
6 1/2 + 1/2

Width:
93' - 0"

Depth:
117' - 11"

Foundation:
FINISHED WALKOUT BASEMENT

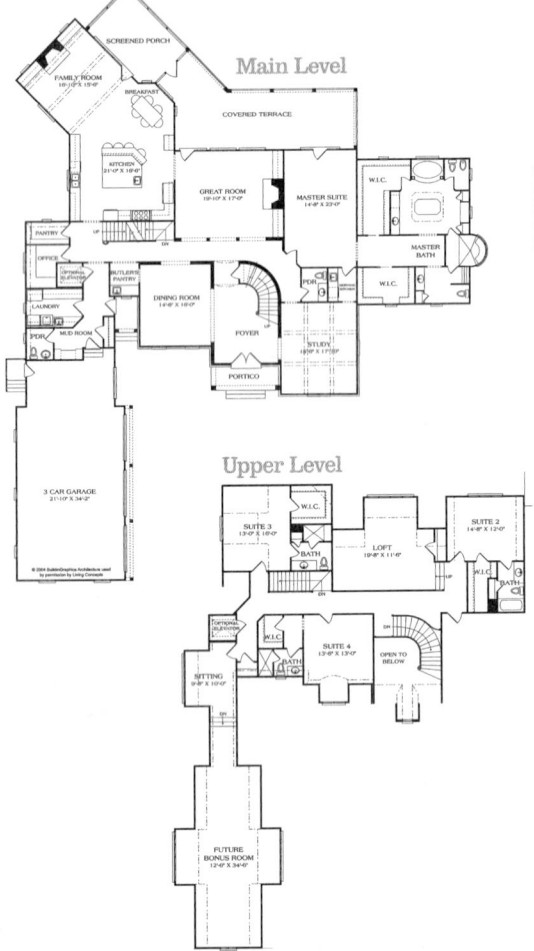

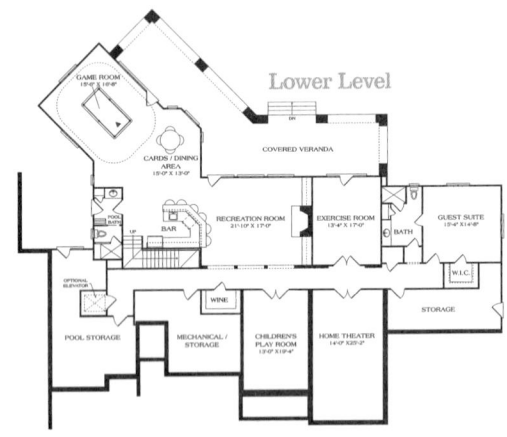

Behold the enormity of this European estate replete with high-end amenities. The lower level holds a wealth of entertainment possibilities plus the convenience of a 24-hour gym. On the main level, the master suite is well-appointed with His and Hers accomodations. The size and shape of the kitchen and the adjoining famiy room is efficient and functional. A covered terrace and screened porch encourage outdoor living. Fireplaces in the great and family rooms add appeal. On the upper level, three secondary bedrooms feature full baths. A sitting room with a wall of windows is a peaceful retreat. An optional elevator services all three levels.

European & Mediterranean Homes

325 New House Plans

Plan:
HPK2600270

Style:
CHATEAUESQUE

Main Level:
4,003 SQ. FT.

Upper Level:
2,654 SQ. FT.

Lower Level:
2,273 SQ. FT.

Total:
8,930 SQ. FT.

Bedrooms:
5

Bathrooms:
6 1/2 + 1/2

Width:
145' - 11"

Depth:
126' - 6"

Foundation:
FINISHED WALKOUT BASEMENT

This stone-faced chateau is just the thing for a lakeside or mountainside sloping lot. Valley views can be enjoyed from several spectacular vantage points on all three levels, and there is plenty of room for visitors. Fireplaces abound indoors and out, lighting up a formal dinner in the dining room, providing a focal point for a romantic evening in the master retreat, and keeping outdoors-lovers warm as an afternoon barbecue on the terrace lasts into the chilly night. In addition to the master suite, there are four bedroom suites on the second level, each with its own private bath. A wealth of amenities on the lower level makes this home a perfect getaway for recreation and relaxation.

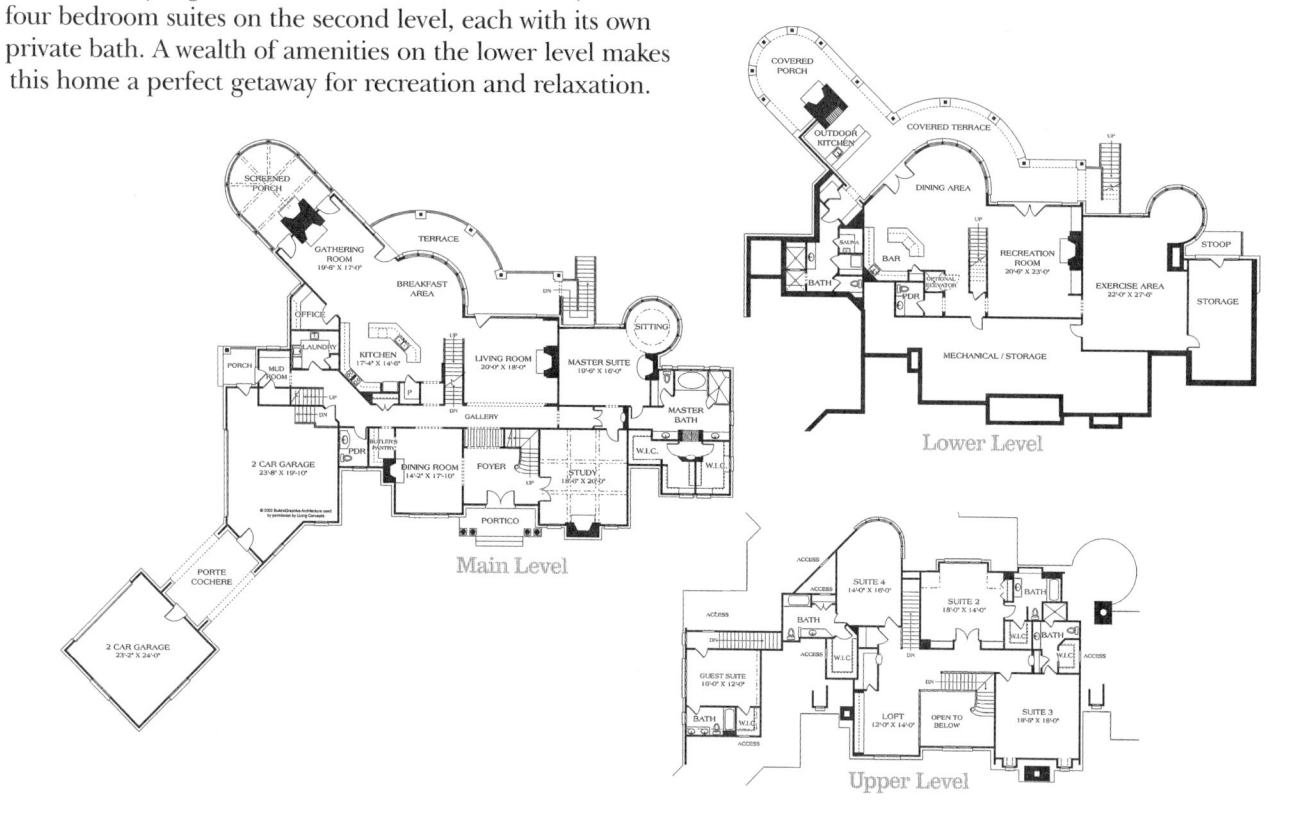

Photo By Carolina Photo Group.
This home, as shown in photographs, may differ from the actual blueprints. For more detailed information, please check the floor plans carefully.

ORDER BLUEPRINTS 24 HOURS, 7 DAYS A WEEK, AT 1-800-521-6797 OR EPLANS.COM

325 New House Plans
European & Mediterranean Homes

Plan:
HPK2600271

Style:
EUROPEAN

Main Level:
4,511 SQ. FT.

Upper Level:
2,295 SQ. FT.

Lower Level:
2,234 SQ. FT.

Total:
9,040 SQ. FT.

Bedrooms:
4

Bathrooms:
5 1/2 + 1/2

Width:
90' - 2"

Depth:
104' - 5"

Foundation:
FINISHED BASEMENT

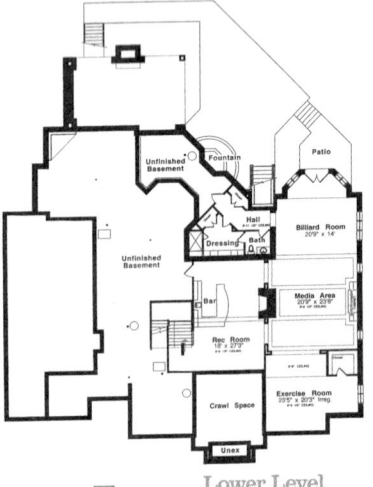

This European-inspired home showcases exterior architectural elements such as elliptical arches, a parapet, limestone trim, and a solid brick facade. Ceiling treatments on the interior range from a spectacular octagonal skylight in the foyer to a stunning celestial dome above the breakfast area to beamed ceilings in the great and hearth rooms. The master bedroom pampers the homeowner with a whirlpool tub, two-person shower, dual vanities, and a bayed sitting area overlooking the rear yard. The terrace and rear porch combine to create an amazing outdoor living space. The second floor houses three additional bedrooms, each with a private bath and walk-in closet. Entertaining in the basement becomes more fun with a bar, gas fireplace, media area, and billiards room. An exercise room makes it fun and easy for the homeowner to stay in shape.

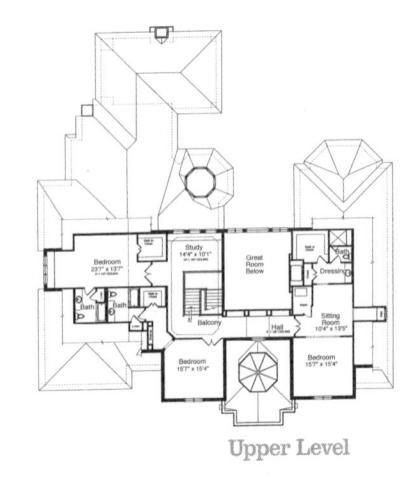

Lower Level

Main Level

Upper Level

Exposures Unlimited Ron and Donna Kolb
This home, as shown in photographs, may differ from the actual blueprints. For more detailed information, please check the floor plans carefully.

208 ORDER BLUEPRINTS 24 HOURS, 7 DAYS A WEEK, AT 1-800-521-6797 OR EPLANS.COM

European & Mediterranean Homes

325 New House Plans

Plan:
HPK2600272

Style:
EUROPEAN

Main Level:
4,232 SQ. FT.

Upper Level:
1,841 SQ. FT.

Lower Level:
3,962 SQ. FT.

Total:
10,035 SQ. FT.

Bedrooms:
4

Bathrooms:
5 1/2 + 1/2

Width:
108' - 4"

Depth:
82' - 4"

Foundation:
FINISHED WALKOUT BASEMENT

A spectacular brick exterior with limestone trim, decorative carvings, and various window styles creates an elegant European manor. A gas fireplace decorates the great room, while a wood-burning fireplace warms the hearth room. The master bedroom offers a quiet retreat for the homeowner, with a stepped ceiling and luxurious bath. The gourmet kitchen with island and walk-in pantry easily serves the breakfast and dining rooms. A wood-burning fireplace is the highlight of the covered porch, with access from the breakfast room, great room, and master suite. Split stairs lead to a second floor where three bedrooms, each with a walk-in closet and private bath, access a raised computer room. Let the good times roll in the lower level; there's a room for every activity.

Lower Level

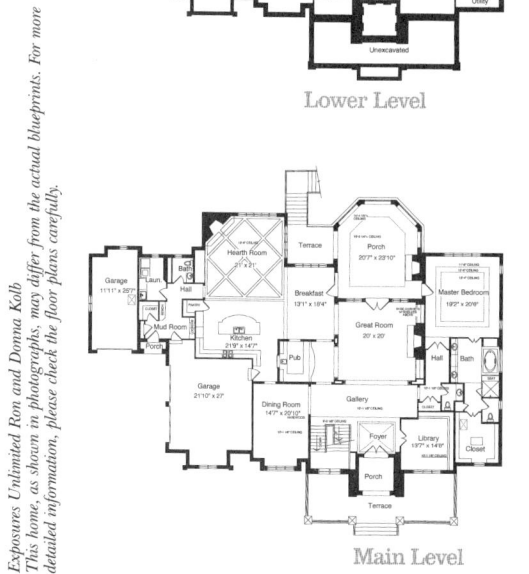

Main Level

Upper Level

Exposures Unlimited Ron and Donna Kolb
This home, as shown in photographs, may differ from the actual blueprints. For more detailed information, please check the floor plans carefully.

ORDER BLUEPRINTS 24 HOURS, 7 DAYS A WEEK, AT 1-800-521-6797 OR EPLANS.COM

209

325 New House Plans
European & Mediterranean Homes

Plan:
HPK2600273

Style:
EUROPEAN

Main Level:
5,418 SQ. FT.

Upper Level:
2,670 SQ. FT.

Lower Level:
3,396 SQ. FT.

Total:
11,484 SQ. FT.

Bedrooms:
5

Bathrooms:
5 1/2 + 1/2

Width:
130' - 0"

Depth:
84' - 6"

Foundation:
FINISHED BASEMENT

This home represents an Old World authentic European manor with timely and luxurious amenities. A cozy hearth room, first-floor pub, elaborate gourmet kitchen with two islands, sunken solarium, and formal dining room combined with outdoor living spaces to create the public area of the home. The spectacular master suite features a vaulted ceiling, extravagant dressing room with whirlpool tub and fireplace, and walk-in closets that extend beyond imagination. Dual stairs lead to three bedrooms on the second floor, each a secondary master suite. The finished basement impresses with a gameroom, wine grotto and wet bar, sixth fireplace, media area, and billiards room. A huge exercise room and additional bedroom make the lower level a complete living space.

Lower Level

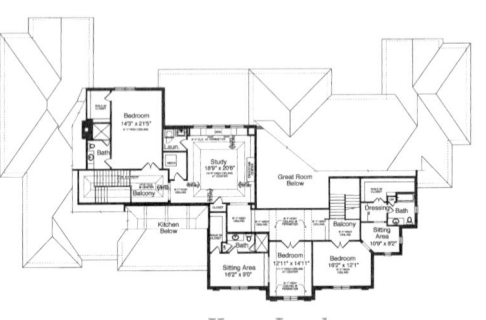

Upper Level

Main Level

Exposures Unlimited Ron and Donna Kolb
This home, as shown in photographs, may differ from the actual blueprints. For more detailed information, please check the floor plans carefully.

ORDER BLUEPRINTS 24 HOURS, 7 DAYS A WEEK, AT 1-800-521-6797 OR EPLANS.COM

New American Homes

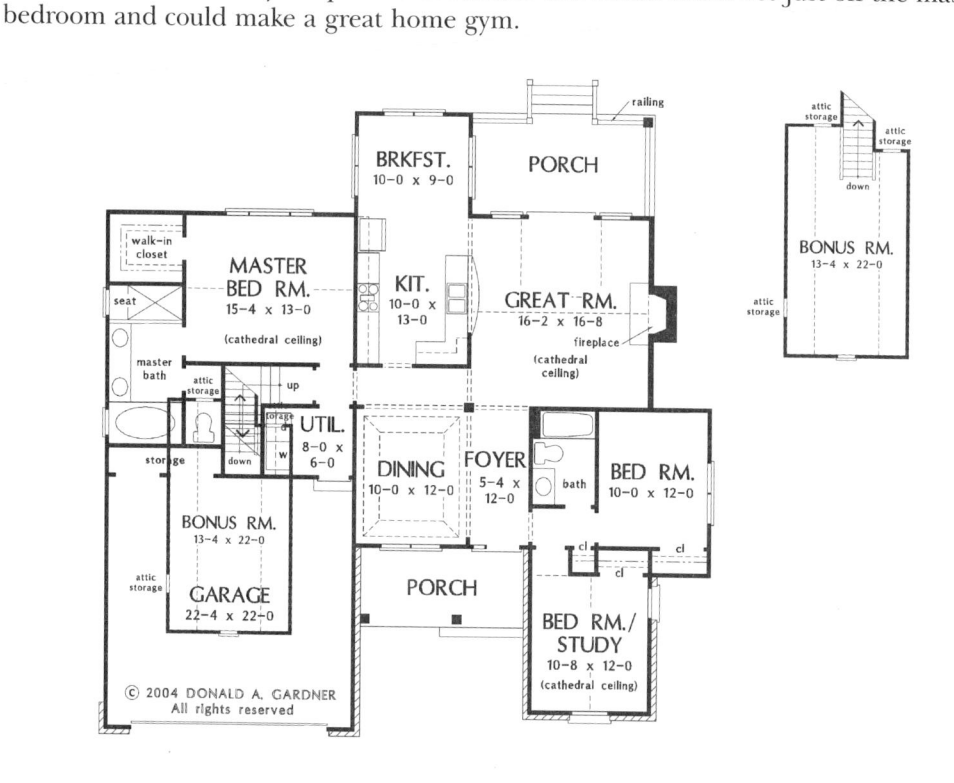

325 New House Plans

Plan:
HPK2600274

Style:
NEW AMERICAN

Square Footage:
1,640

Bedrooms:
3

Bathrooms:
2

Width:
55' - 10"

Depth:
55' - 6"

© 2004 Donald A. Gardner, Inc.

Low-maintenance siding and brick blend together beautifully. Keystones top curved transoms and the front-entry garage creates convenience. A column and tray ceiling distinguish the dining room, while a cathedral ceiling and fireplace enhance the great room. French doors lead to the rear porch. A breakfast bar acts as a serving counter to the great room. The master bedroom features a soaring cathedral ceiling and large walk-in closet. With a double vanity, shower with seat, garden tub, and private privy, the master bath is ready to spoil homeowners. The bonus room lies just off the master bedroom and could make a great home gym.

ORDER BLUEPRINTS 24 HOURS, 7 DAYS A WEEK, AT 1-800-521-6797 OR EPLANS.COM

325 New House Plans
New American Homes

Plan:
HPK2600275

Style:
NEW AMERICAN

First Floor:
1,024 SQ. FT.

Second Floor:
673 SQ. FT.

Total:
1,697 SQ. FT.

Bonus Space:
372 SQ. FT.

Bedrooms:
3

Bathrooms:
2

Width:
48' - 0"

Depth:
39' - 0"

Foundation:
UNFINISHED BASEMENT

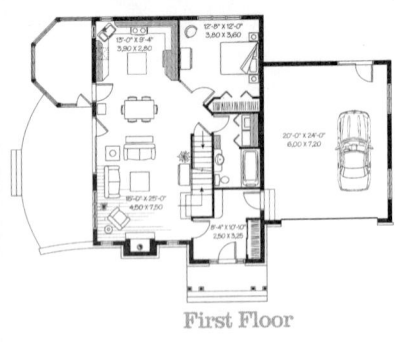

First Floor

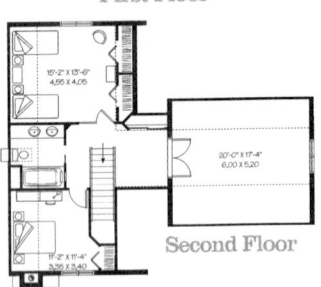

Second Floor

Plan:
HPK2600276

Style:
NEW AMERICAN

Square Footage:
1,711

Bedrooms:
3

Bathrooms:
2

Width:
61' - 0"

Depth:
50' - 0"

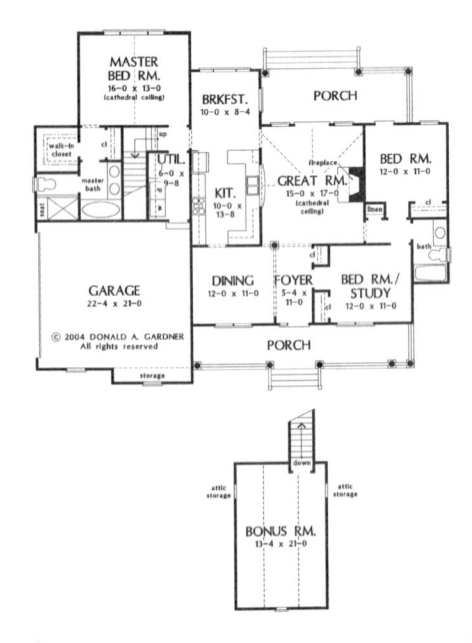

© 2004 Donald A. Gardner, Inc.

ORDER BLUEPRINTS 24 HOURS, 7 DAYS A WEEK, AT 1-800-521-6797 OR EPLANS.COM

New American Homes

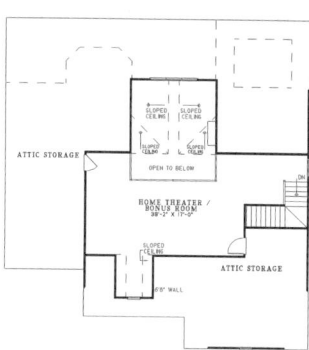

325 New House Plans

Plan:
HPK2600277

Style:
NEW AMERICAN

Square Footage:
1,723

Bonus Space:
557 SQ. FT.

Bedrooms:
3

Bathrooms:
2

Width:
52' - 6"

Depth:
55' - 6"

Foundation:
CRAWLSPACE, SLAB

Plan:
HPK2600278

Style:
NEW AMERICAN

First Floor:
881 SQ. FT.

Second Floor:
852 SQ. FT.

Total:
1,733 SQ. FT.

Bedrooms:
3

Bathrooms:
2 ½

Width:
36' - 0"

Depth:
42' - 0"

Foundation:
UNFINISHED BASEMENT

First Floor

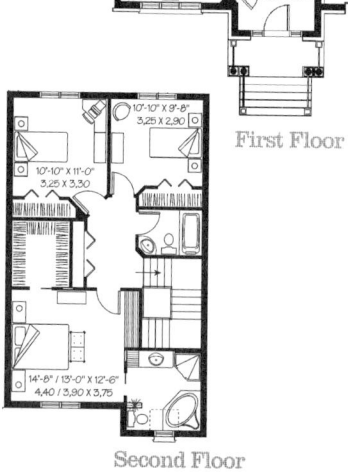

Second Floor

ORDER BLUEPRINTS 24 HOURS, 7 DAYS A WEEK, AT 1-800-521-6797 OR EPLANS.COM

213

325 New American Homes
New House Plans

Plan:
HPK2600279

Style:
NEW AMERICAN

Square Footage:
1,871

Bedrooms:
3

Bathrooms:
2

Width:
58' - 0"

Depth:
52' - 0"

Foundation:
UNFINISHED BASEMENT

Plan:
HPK2600280

Style:
NEW AMERICAN

Square Footage:
1,900

Bedrooms:
3

Bathrooms:
2

Width:
56' - 0"

Depth:
72' - 0"

Foundation:
CRAWLSPACE, SLAB

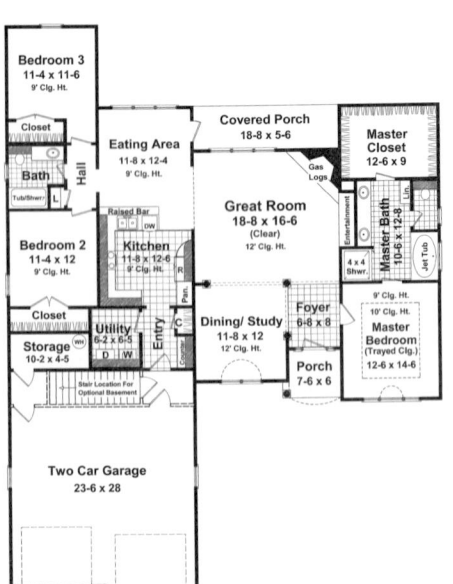

New American Homes

325
New House Plans

Plan:
HPK2600281

Style:
NEW AMERICAN

Square Footage:
1,938

Bedrooms:
2

Bathrooms:
2 ½

Width:
70' - 0"

Depth:
60' - 4"

Foundation:
UNFINISHED BASEMENT

A front arched window and an arched entryway with graceful columns make this split-level home truly elegant. The inside design will make social affairs easy and pleasant. From the main-level guest room with a private bath to the spacious great room with an extended-hearth fireplace, visitors will feel at home. The dining area is separated from the great room by soffits and corner columns. Family members will gravitate to the sunlit eating nook and spacious kitchen, which are connected by sliding doors to the screened porch. Also on the main level is the lavish master suite brimming with frills that will make you feel fully pampered.

ORDER BLUEPRINTS 24 HOURS, 7 DAYS A WEEK, AT 1-800-521-6797 OR EPLANS.COM

325 New House Plans
New American Homes

Plan:
HPK2600282

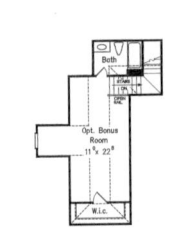

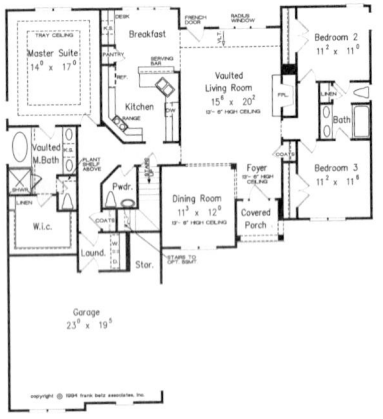

Style:
NEW AMERICAN

Square Footage:
1,949

Bonus Space:
398 SQ. FT.

Bedrooms:
3

Bathrooms:
2 1/2

Width:
56' - 0"

Depth:
65' - 0"

Foundation:
CRAWLSPACE, SLAB, UNFINISHED WALKOUT BASEMENT

Plan:
HPK2600283

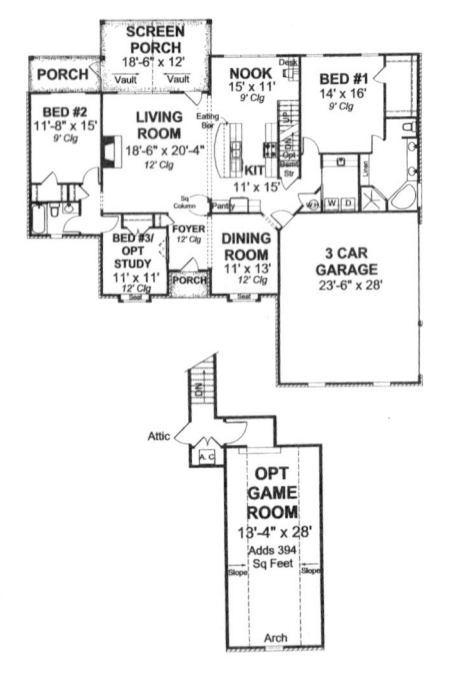

Style:
NEW AMERICAN

Square Footage:
1,985

Bonus Space:
394 SQ. FT.

Bedrooms:
3

Bathrooms:
2

Width:
66' - 0"

Depth:
61' - 0"

216 ORDER BLUEPRINTS 24 HOURS, 7 DAYS A WEEK, AT 1-800-521-6797 OR EPLANS.COM

New American Homes

325 New House Plans

Plan:
HPK2600284

Style:
NEW AMERICAN

Square Footage:
2,005

Bedrooms:
3

Bathrooms:
2 1/2

Width:
65' - 2"

Depth:
71' - 0"

Foundation:
CRAWLSPACE, SLAB

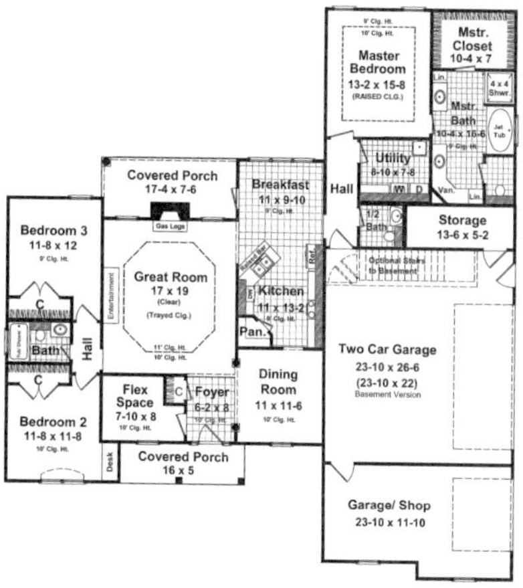

Plan:
HPK2600285

Style:
NEW AMERICAN

First Floor:
1,507 SQ. FT.

Second Floor:
523 SQ. FT.

Total:
2,030 SQ. FT.

Bedrooms:
3

Bathrooms:
2 1/2

Width:
42' - 5"

Depth:
63' - 2"

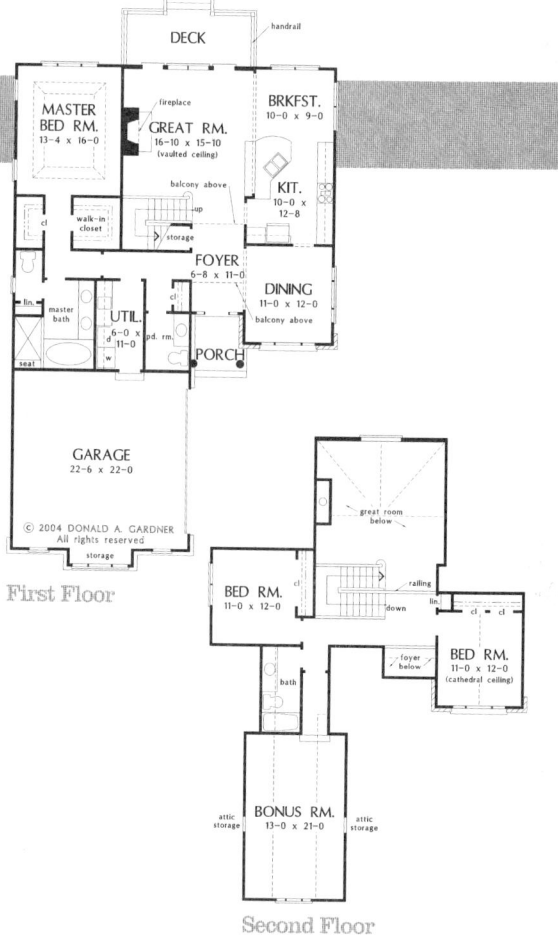

© 2004 Donald A. Gardner, Inc.

First Floor

Second Floor

ORDER BLUEPRINTS 24 HOURS, 7 DAYS A WEEK, AT 1-800-521-6797 OR EPLANS.COM

325 New House Plans

New American Homes

Plan:
HPK2600286

Style:
NEW AMERICAN

First Floor:
1,448 SQ. FT.

Second Floor:
619 SQ. FT.

Total:
2,067 SQ. FT.

Bonus Space:
195 SQ. FT.

Bedrooms:
3

Bathrooms:
2 1/2

Width:
64' - 0"

Depth:
48' - 0"

Foundation:
UNFINISHED BASEMENT

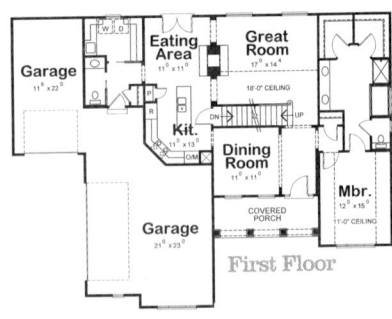

Plan:
HPK2600287

Style:
NEW AMERICAN

First Floor:
1,069 SQ. FT.

Second Floor:
1,000 SQ. FT.

Total:
2,069 SQ. FT.

Bedrooms:
4

Bathrooms:
2 1/2

Width:
46' - 5"

Depth:
47' - 4"

Foundation:
UNFINISHED BASEMENT

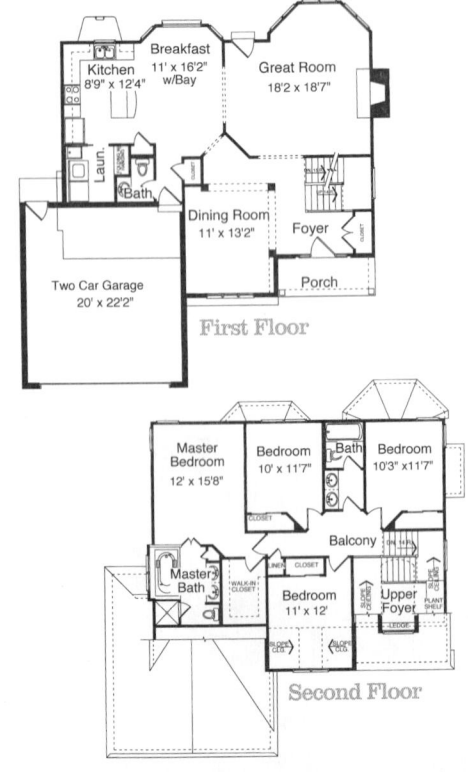

ORDER BLUEPRINTS 24 HOURS, 7 DAYS A WEEK, AT 1-800-521-6797 OR EPLANS.COM

New American Homes

325 New House Plans

Plan:
HPK2600288

Style:
NEW AMERICAN

Square Footage:
2,071

Bonus Space:
434 SQ. FT.

Bedrooms:
3

Bathrooms:
2 1/2

Width:
63' - 0"

Depth:
63' - 0"

Foundation:
CRAWLSPACE, UNFINISHED BASEMENT

Palladian windows and an arcaded front porch lend Georgian elegance to this one-story home. Inside, vaulted ceilings enhance the sense of spaciousness created by the generously sized rooms and walls of windows. Formal living and dining rooms delight homeowners who enjoy entertaining, although the living room could easily be furnished as a den or study for those who prefer a quieter lifestyle. The family room, breakfast nook, and kitchen come together at an informal snack counter, which is close enough to the fireplace to benefit from its cheer. The vaulted master bedroom and bath occupy the back corner of the home, while two secondary bedrooms share a split bath on the opposite side. A partially-screened deck with access from the breakfast nook and master suite spans the rear of the home.

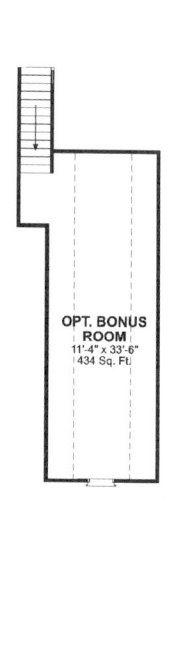

ORDER BLUEPRINTS 24 HOURS, 7 DAYS A WEEK, AT 1-800-521-6797 OR EPLANS.COM

325 New American Homes
New House Plans

Plan:
HPK2600289

Style:
NEW AMERICAN

Square Footage:
2,072

Bonus Space:
316 SQ. FT.

Bedrooms:
3

Bathrooms:
2

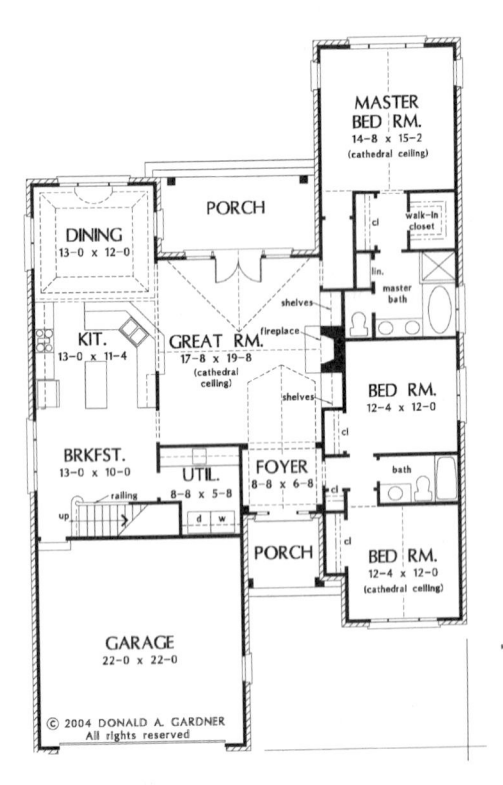

Width:
47' - 7"

Depth:
75' - 7"

© 2004 Donald A. Gardner, Inc.

This well-planned home provides big living on a small lot. The brick-and-siding exterior assures curb appeal, while the front-loading garage provides convenience with a space-saving design. Columns and a curved transom frame the entrance. Inside, the foyer reveals an expansive open floor plan that combines the great room, kitchen, and breakfast area. A formal dining room with tray ceiling, conveniently located off the kitchen, offers a wide view of the backyard. Every bedroom is located on the right side of the home, away from daily activity. The master suite includes one conventional and one walk-in closet, plus the most desired bath amenities. Off the foyer, two extra bedrooms—one with a palladian window—are buffered by a common bath. The bonus room above the garage can serve a number of uses: rec room, exercise room, or even a fourth bedroom.

New American Homes

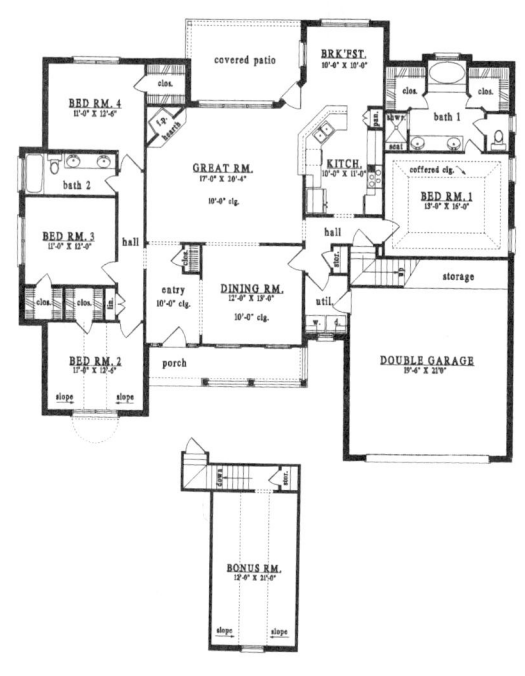

325 New House Plans

Plan:
HPK2600290

Style:
NEW AMERICAN

First Floor:
1,052 SQ. FT.

Second Floor:
1,033 SQ. FT.

Total:
2,085 SQ. FT.

Bonus Space:
276 SQ. FT.

Bedrooms:
3

Bathrooms:
2

Width:
46' - 0"

Depth:
34' - 6"

Foundation:
FINISHED BASEMENT

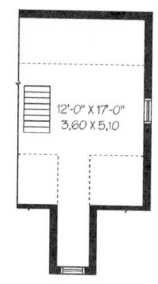

Plan:
HPK2600291

Style:
NEW AMERICAN

Square Footage:
2,196

Bonus Space:
266 SQ. FT.

Bedrooms:
4

Bathrooms:
2

Width:
64' - 6"

Depth:
55' - 4"

Foundation:
CRAWLSPACE, SLAB

ORDER BLUEPRINTS 24 HOURS, 7 DAYS A WEEK, AT 1-800-521-6797 OR EPLANS.COM

325 New House Plans
New American Homes

Plan:
HPK2600292

Style:
NEW AMERICAN

Square Footage:
2,200

Bonus Space:
400 SQ. FT.

Bedrooms:
3

Bathrooms:
3 1/2

Width:
78' - 0"

Depth:
58' - 6"

Foundation:
CRAWLSPACE, SLAB

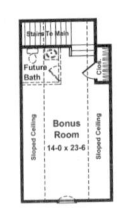

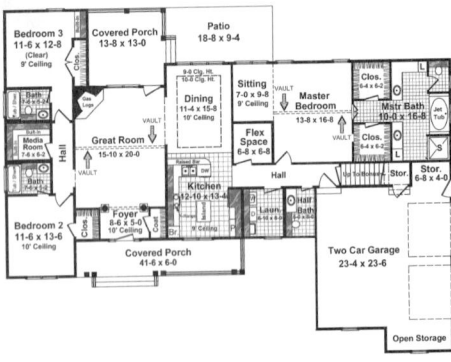

Plan:
HPK2600293

Style:
NEW AMERICAN

First Floor:
1,690 SQ. FT.

Second Floor:
544 SQ. FT.

Total:
2,234 SQ. FT.

Bonus Space:
254 SQ. FT.

Bedrooms:
3

Bathrooms:
2 1/2

Width:
55' - 0"

Depth:
48' - 0"

Foundation:
CRAWLSPACE, UNFINISHED WALKOUT BASEMENT

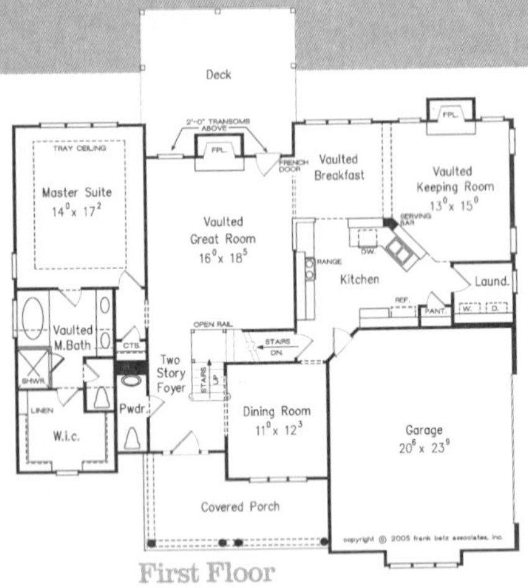

First Floor

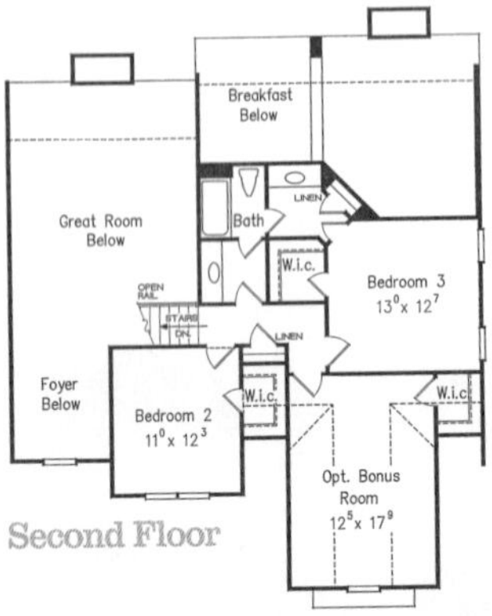

Second Floor

ORDER BLUEPRINTS 24 HOURS, 7 DAYS A WEEK, AT 1-800-521-6797 OR EPLANS.COM

New American Homes

325 New House Plans

Plan:
HPK2600294

Style:
NEW AMERICAN

Square Footage:
2,358

Bedrooms:
4

Bathrooms:
2

Width:
65' - 8"

Depth:
68' - 10"

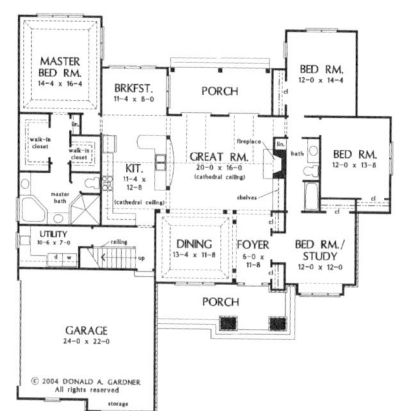

Plan:
HPK2600295

Style:
NEW AMERICAN

Square Footage:
2,360

Bedrooms:
3

Bathrooms:
3

Width:
62' - 8"

Depth:
96' - 0"

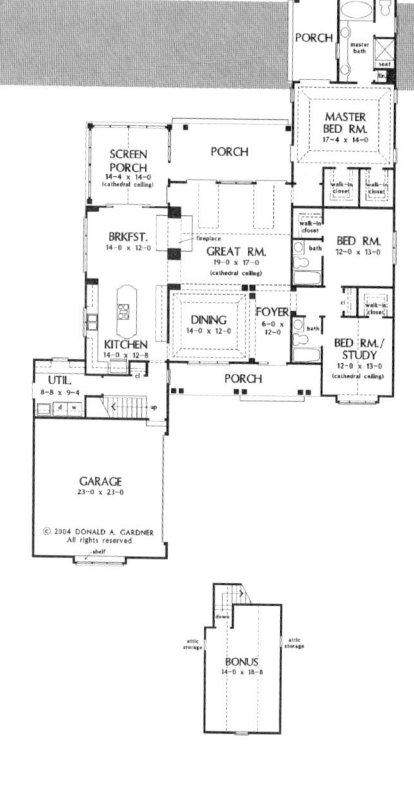

ORDER BLUEPRINTS 24 HOURS, 7 DAYS A WEEK, AT 1-800-521-6797 OR EPLANS.COM

325 New American Homes
New House Plans

Plan:
HPK2600296

Style:
NEW AMERICAN

Square Footage:
2,405

Bedrooms:
4

Bathrooms:
3

Width:
65' - 4"

Depth:
67' - 2"

Foundation:
CRAWLSPACE, SLAB

Tradition begins in this home. Enter through the foyer and notice the elegant columns that define the dining room—perfect for elegant dinner parties. The great room, complete with media center and fireplace, has beautiful French-door access to the rear porch for entertaining guests during the warm seasons. A cozy hearth room will become the favorite gathering room for the family with a computer center nearby. Upstairs, discover a bonus room that can be converted into a kids' playroom.

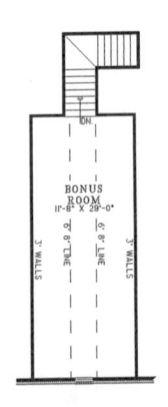

224 ORDER BLUEPRINTS 24 HOURS, 7 DAYS A WEEK, AT 1-800-521-6797 OR EPLANS.COM

New American Homes

325 New House Plans

Plan:
HPK2600297

Style:
NEW AMERICAN

Square Footage:
2,426

Bedrooms:
4

Bathrooms:
3

Width:
73' - 2"

Depth:
58' - 0"

© 2004 Donald A. Gardner, Inc.

Gable-topped stone walls join low-maintenance siding and charming twin dormers for exceptional curb appeal. Palladian windows and columns add architectural interest, while front and rear porches take living to the great outdoors. Positioning gives rooms definition, while the floorplan remains open. Decorative ceiling treatments and interior columns accentuate the gathering rooms, and built-in cabinetry flanks the fireplace, which peers into the kitchen. Common rooms divide the master suite from the secondary bedroom wing, promoting privacy and tranquility for each bedroom. The master suite includes dual walk-in closets and a well-appointed bath, and versatility is provided by a flexible study/bedroom and bonus room above the garage.

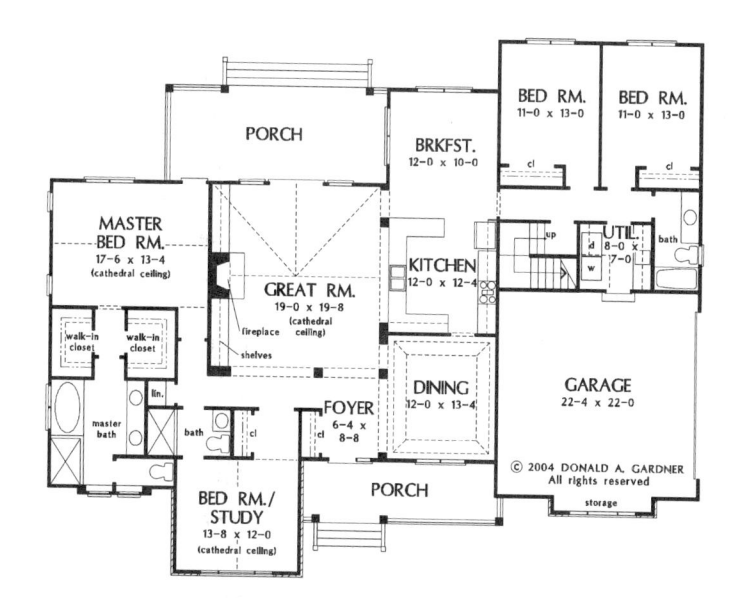

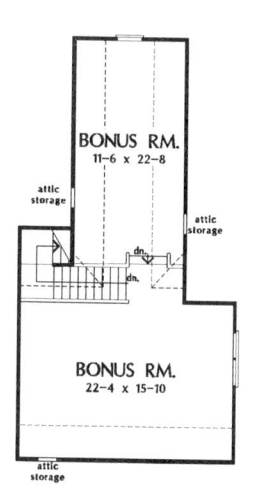

ORDER BLUEPRINTS 24 HOURS, 7 DAYS A WEEK, AT 1-800-521-6797 OR EPLANS.COM

325 New House Plans
New American Homes

Plan:
HPK2600298

Style:
NEW AMERICAN

First Floor:
1,595 SQ. FT.

Second Floor:
875 SQ. FT.

Total:
2,470 SQ. FT.

Bonus Space:
389 SQ. FT.

Bedrooms:
4

Bathrooms:
2 1/2

Width:
47' - 4"

Depth:
58' - 8"

Foundation:
CRAWLSPACE, SLAB

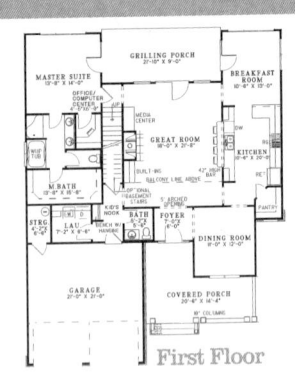

First Floor

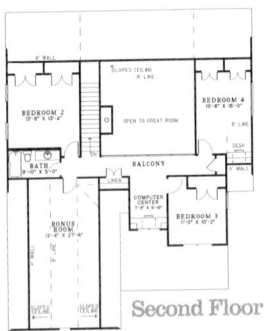

Second Floor

Plan:
HPK2600299

Style:
NEW AMERICAN

First Floor:
1,785 SQ. FT.

Second Floor:
710 SQ. FT.

Total:
2,495 SQ. FT.

Bedrooms:
4

Bathrooms:
2 1/2

Width:
57' - 6"

Depth:
50' - 6"

Foundation:
CRAWLSPACE, UNFINISHED BASEMENT

First Floor

Second Floor

ORDER BLUEPRINTS 24 HOURS, 7 DAYS A WEEK, AT 1-800-521-6797 OR EPLANS.COM

New American Homes

325 New House Plans

Plan:
HPK2600300

Style:
NEW AMERICAN

Square Footage:
2,570

Bedrooms:
3

Bathrooms:
2 ½

Width:
73' - 9"

Depth:
58' - 6"

Foundation:
WALKOUT BASEMENT

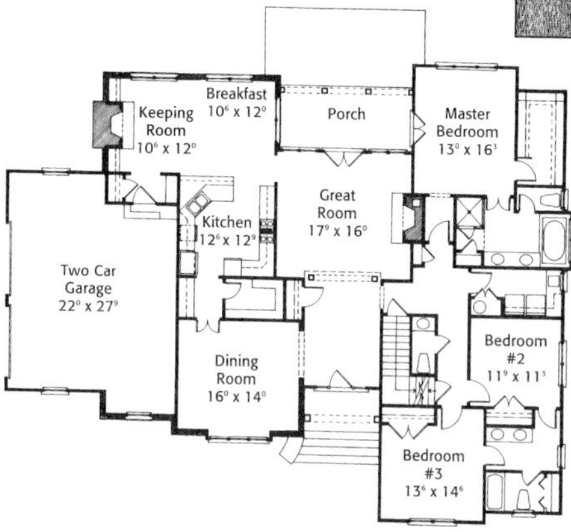

Plan:
HPK2600301

Style:
NEW AMERICAN

Square Footage:
2,600

Bonus Space:
311 SQ. FT.

Bedrooms:
3

Bathrooms:
2 ½

Width:
57' - 0"

Depth:
70' - 0"

Foundation:
CRAWLSPACE, SLAB, UNFINISHED WALKOUT BASEMENT

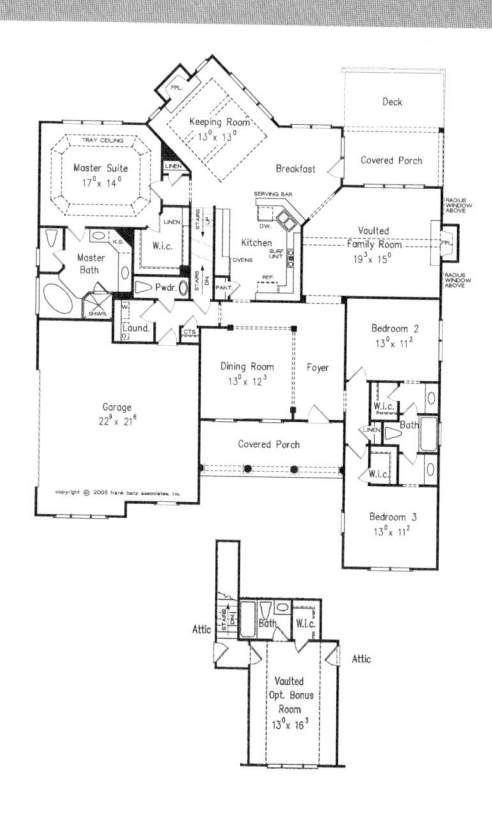

ORDER BLUEPRINTS 24 HOURS, 7 DAYS A WEEK, AT 1-800-521-6797 OR EPLANS.COM

325 New American Homes
New House Plans

Plan:
HPK2600302

Style:
NEW AMERICAN

Square Footage:
2,609

Bedrooms:
3

Bathrooms:
2

Width:
73' - 10"

Depth:
61' - 7"

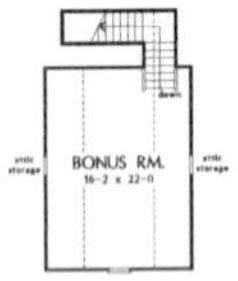

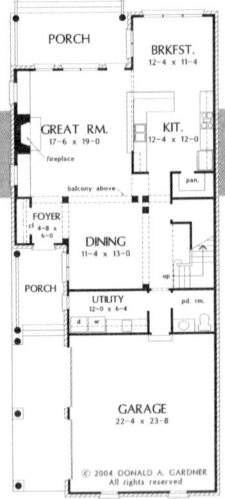

Plan:
HPK2600303

Style:
NEW AMERICAN

First Floor:
1,308 SQ. FT.

Second Floor:
1,321 SQ. FT.

Total:
2,629 SQ. FT.

Bedrooms:
3

Bathrooms:
2 ½

Width:
31' - 11"

Depth:
73' - 3"

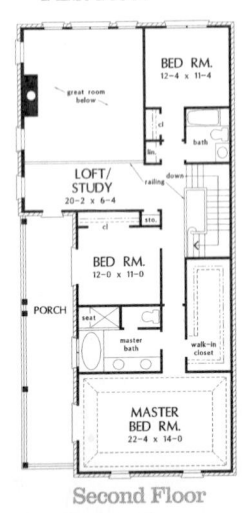

First Floor

Second Floor

228 ORDER BLUEPRINTS 24 HOURS, 7 DAYS A WEEK, AT 1-800-521-6797 OR EPLANS.COM

New American Homes

325 New House Plans

Plan:
HPK2600304

Style:
NEW AMERICAN

Square Footage:
2,699

Bonus Space:
418 SQ. FT.

Bedrooms:
4

Bathrooms:
3 1/2

Width:
42' - 0"

Depth:
75' - 4"

Foundation:
CRAWLSPACE, SLAB, UNFINISHED WALKOUT BASEMENT

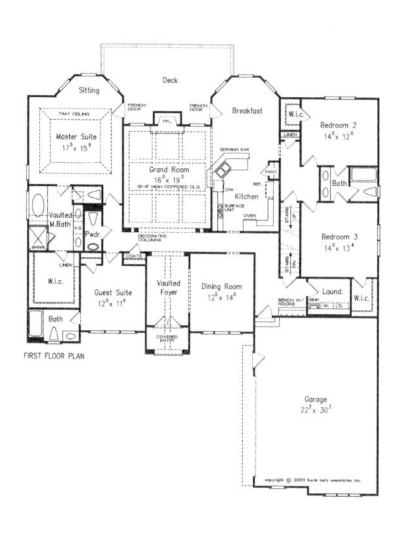

Plan:
HPK2600305

Style:
NEW AMERICAN

First Floor:
2,065 SQ. FT.

Second Floor:
652 SQ. FT.

Total:
2,717 SQ. FT.

Bonus Space:
636 SQ. FT.

Bedrooms:
4

Bathrooms:
4

Width:
65' - 2"

Depth:
52' - 8"

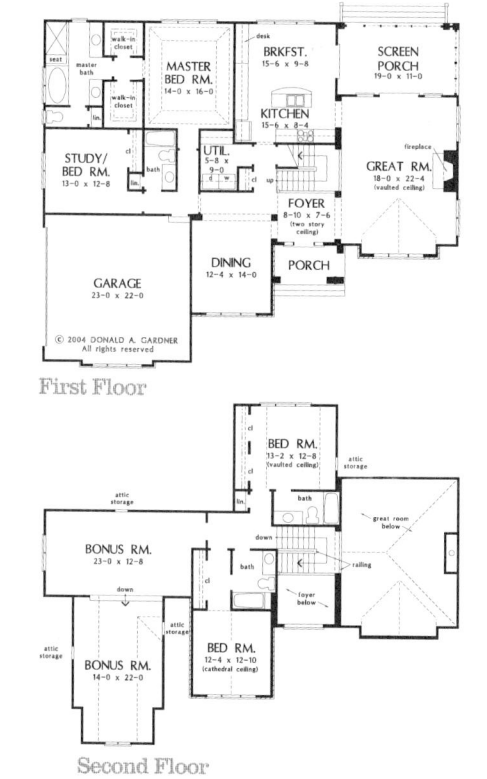

First Floor

Second Floor

ORDER BLUEPRINTS 24 HOURS, 7 DAYS A WEEK, AT 1-800-521-6797 OR EPLANS.COM

325 New House Plans

New American Homes

Plan:
HPK2600306

Style:
NEW AMERICAN

Square Footage:
2,764

Bedrooms:
3

Bathrooms:
2 ½

Width:
66' - 4"

Depth:
66' - 1"

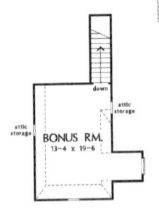

© 2004 Donald A. Gardner, Inc.

Plan:
HPK2600307

Style:
NEW AMERICAN

First Floor:
1,818 SQ. FT.

Second Floor:
994 SQ. FT.

Total:
2,812 SQ. FT.

Bedrooms:
4

Bathrooms:
3 ½

Width:
75' - 0"

Depth:
56' - 8"

Foundation:
UNFINISHED BASEMENT

First Floor

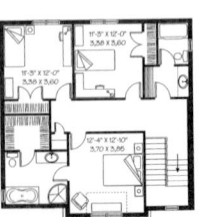

Second Floor

230   ORDER BLUEPRINTS 24 HOURS, 7 DAYS A WEEK, AT 1-800-521-6797 OR EPLANS.COM

New American Homes

325 New House Plans

Plan:
HPK2600308

Style:
NEW AMERICAN
First Floor:
1,895 SQ. FT.
Second Floor:
963 SQ. FT.
Total:
2,858 SQ. FT.
Bonus Space:
352 SQ. FT.
Bedrooms:
5
Bathrooms:
4
Width:
54' - 0"
Depth:
70' - 4"
Foundation:
CRAWLSPACE, UNFINISHED WALKOUT BASEMENT

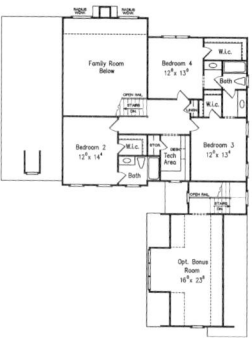

First Floor

Second Floor

Plan:
HPK2600309

Style:
NEW AMERICAN
First Floor:
1,483 SQ. FT.
Second Floor:
1,413 SQ. FT.
Total:
2,896 SQ. FT.
Bedrooms:
4
Bathrooms:
2 1/2
Width:
58' - 6"
Depth:
41' - 6"
Foundation:
UNFINISHED WALKOUT BASEMENT

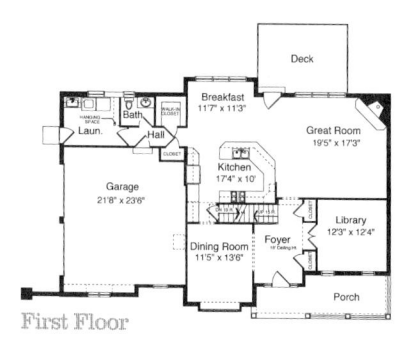

First Floor

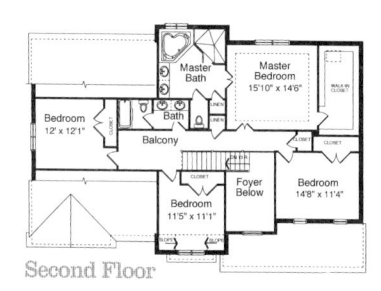

Second Floor

ORDER BLUEPRINTS 24 HOURS, 7 DAYS A WEEK, AT 1-800-521-6797 OR EPLANS.COM

325 New House Plans
New American Homes

Plan:
HPK2600310

Style:
NEW AMERICAN

Square Footage:
2,934

Bedrooms:
4

Bathrooms:
3

Width:
85' - 4"

Depth:
57' - 8"

© 2004 Donald A. Gardner, Inc.

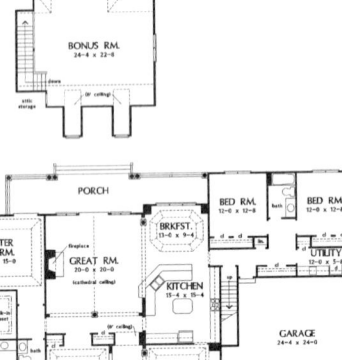

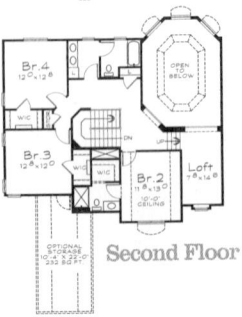

Plan:
HPK2600311

Style:
NEW AMERICAN

First Floor:
1,872 SQ. FT.

Second Floor:
1,127 SQ. FT.

Total:
2,999 SQ. FT.

Bonus Space:
232 SQ. FT.

Bedrooms:
4

Bathrooms:
3 1/2

Width:
60' - 0"

Depth:
60' - 0"

First Floor

Second Floor

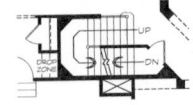

Optional Layout

232   ORDER BLUEPRINTS 24 HOURS, 7 DAYS A WEEK, AT 1-800-521-6797 OR EPLANS.COM

New American Homes

325 New House Plans

Plan:
HPK2600312

Style:
NEW AMERICAN

First Floor:
1,526 SQ. FT.

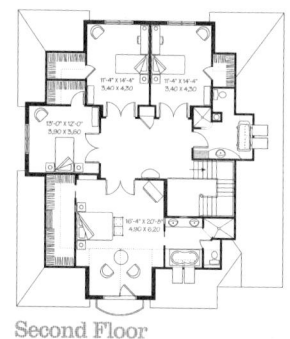

Second Floor:
1,600 SQ. FT.

Total:
3,126 SQ. FT.

Bedrooms:
4

Bathrooms:
2 1/2

Width:
46' - 0"

Depth:
50' - 0"

Foundation:
UNFINISHED BASEMENT

First Floor

Second Floor

Plan:
HPK2600313

Style:
NEW AMERICAN

First Floor:
2,056 SQ. FT.

Second Floor:
1,111 SQ. FT.

Total:
3,167 SQ. FT.

Bedrooms:
4

Bathrooms:
3 1/2

Width:
69' - 8"

Depth:
51' - 6"

Foundation:
CRAWLSPACE

First Floor

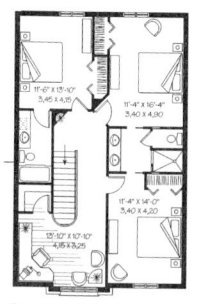

Second Floor

ORDER BLUEPRINTS 24 HOURS, 7 DAYS A WEEK, AT 1-800-521-6797 OR EPLANS.COM

325 New House Plans
New American Homes

Plan:
HPK2600314

Style:
NEW AMERICAN

First Floor:
2,480 SQ. FT.

Second Floor:
780 SQ. FT.

Total:
3,260 SQ. FT.

Bonus Space:
981 SQ. FT.

Bedrooms:
3

Bathrooms:
2 1/2

Width:
79' - 0"

Depth:
62' - 0"

Foundation:
CRAWLSPACE

Classic keystone arches and lintels run harmonious counterpoint to a rustic background of stone veneer and shake-textured siding. This home can comfortably house a large family. Linked gathering spaces are naturally bright and delightfully spacious. Daylight washes into the two-story foyer through sidelights and a transom. An arch on the right leads into the den, and a wider arch on the left feeds into the dining room. A niche in its rear corner could house a bubbling fountain or a treasured family heirloom. A transverse hallway opens to the vaulted family room on the other side. Windows fill most of the family room's rear wall, offering views of the patio and landscape beyond. Above the gas fireplace is another niche. Just past the stairs, the room flows into a sunny, bayed nook. It's an energizing space to start the day. Counters wrap around three sides of a large kitchen with a generously sized work island. A roomy pantry nestles under the stairs.

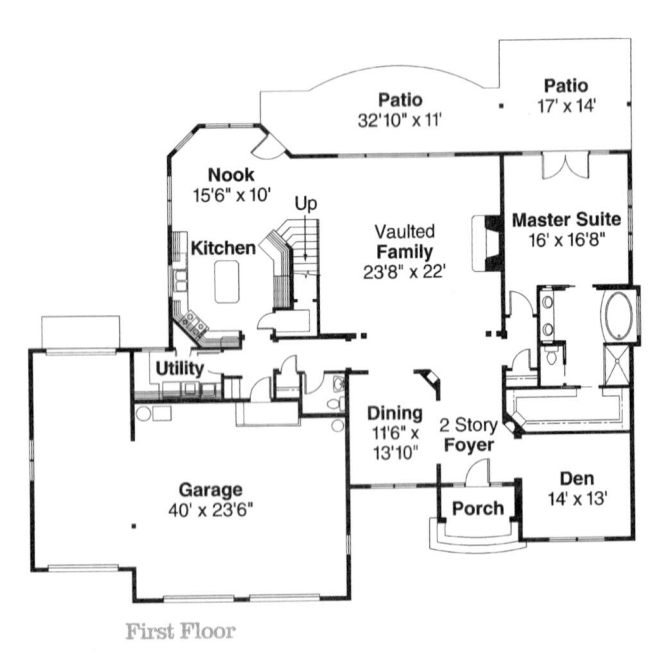

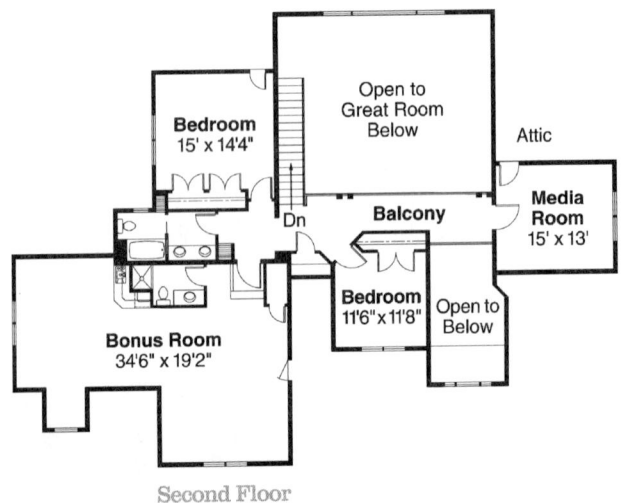

First Floor

Second Floor

234 ORDER BLUEPRINTS 24 HOURS, 7 DAYS A WEEK, AT 1-800-521-6797 OR EPLANS.COM

New American Homes

325 New House Plans

Plan:
HPK2600315

Style:
NEW AMERICAN

First Floor:
2,108 SQ. FT.

Second Floor:
1,319 SQ. FT.

Total:
3,427 SQ. FT.

Bonus Space:
340 SQ. FT.

Bedrooms:
4

Bathrooms:
3 1/2

Width:
55' - 0"

Depth:
78' - 0"

Foundation:
CRAWLSPACE, UNFINISHED WALKOUT BASEMENT

Within these brick walls lies a superior floor plan, excellent for an active family. Note the separate entry next to the garage, which leads directly into a mudroom and adjacent laundry room. A spacious kitchen offers all that the family chef could want: central island, wall ovens, huge walk-in pantry, and easy access to both the formal dining room and a sunny breakfast nook. Beyond the nook, a keeping room shares a two-sided fireplace with the vaulted family room, and a French door opens to a screened porch. The family room features built-in cabinets flanking the fireplace and a wall of windows looking out over the rear deck. The master suite opens discreetly from a small foyer at the end of the central hall. Upstairs, a bridge leading to a private bedroom suite offers a close-up of the family room's beamed ceiling. Two additional bedrooms share a compartmented bath, and a loft with built-in desk and optional bonus room provide even more space.

ORDER BLUEPRINTS 24 HOURS, 7 DAYS A WEEK, AT 1-800-521-6797 OR EPLANS.COM

325 New American Homes
New House Plans

Plan:
HPK2600316

Style:
NEW AMERICAN

First Floor:
2,468 SQ. FT.

Second Floor:
981 SQ. FT.

Total:
3,449 SQ. FT.

Bedrooms:
4

Bathrooms:
4

Width:
58' - 7"

Depth:
79' - 6"

© 2004 Donald A. Gardner, Inc.

Pillars, arches, and banding lend a subtle sophistication to the brick exterior. A Palladian window tops a triple window, which is capped by a metal roof, while a patio and porches— including a screened one—extend living to the outdoors. Opening to the dining room and study/bedroom, the foyer leads to a gallery, which features an art niche. Columns, built-in cabinetry, and ceiling treatments enhance the open floor plan, while a butler's pantry, home office, and spacious laundry room provide convenience. Upstairs, a generous loft separates the secondary bedrooms and provides enough room for a recreation area or second-floor study, and a versatile bonus room adds more flex space. The balcony visually connects both floors.

First Floor

Second Floor

ORDER BLUEPRINTS 24 HOURS, 7 DAYS A WEEK, AT 1-800-521-6797 OR EPLANS.COM

New American Homes

325 New House Plans

Plan:
HPK2600317

Style:
NEW AMERICAN

First Floor:
2,379 SQ. FT.

Second Floor:
1,149 SQ. FT.

Total:
3,528 SQ. FT.

Bedrooms:
4

Bathrooms:
3 1/2

Width:
73' - 3"

Depth:
48' - 0"

Foundation:
WALKOUT BASEMENT

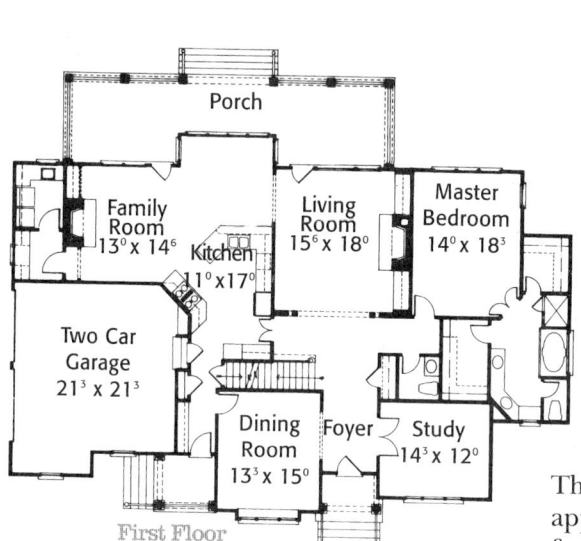

© Stephen Fuller, Inc.

First Floor
- Porch
- Family Room 13⁰ x 14⁶
- Kitchen 11⁰ x 17⁰
- Living Room 15⁶ x 18⁰
- Master Bedroom 14⁰ x 18³
- Two Car Garage 21³ x 21³
- Dining Room 13³ x 15⁰
- Foyer
- Study 14³ x 12⁰

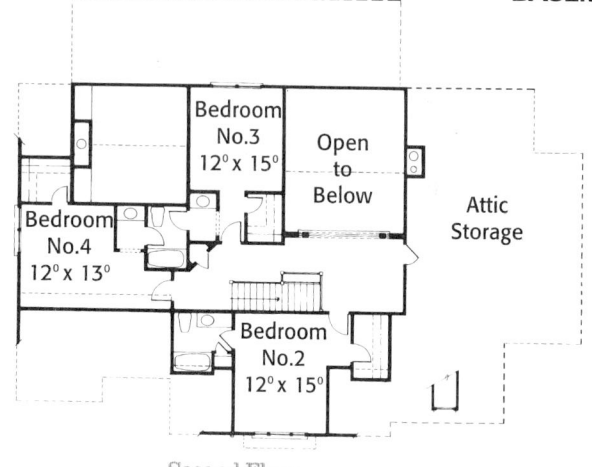

Second Floor
- Bedroom No.3 12⁰ x 15⁰
- Open to Below
- Attic Storage
- Bedroom No.4 12⁰ x 13⁰
- Bedroom No.2 12⁰ x 15⁰

This cozy cottage has tremendous curb appeal beginning with the steeply pitched front gable. Inside, the foyer is flanked by the dining room and a private study. The two-story great room sits at the center of the home and offers an abundance of natural light. The keeping room features a vaulted ceiling and decorative nooks above the fireplace. Tucked away behind the keeping room are the laundry room and a small office. Interestingly, this home offers separate entrances for family and guests.

ORDER BLUEPRINTS 24 HOURS, 7 DAYS A WEEK, AT 1-800-521-6797 OR EPLANS.COM

325 NEW AMERICAN Homes
New House Plans

Plan:
HPK2600318

Style:
NEW AMERICAN

First Floor:
1,838 SQ. FT.

Second Floor:
1,772 SQ. FT.

Total:
3,610 SQ. FT.

Bedrooms:
4

Bathrooms:
3 ½

Width:
65' - 8"

Depth:
52' - 8"

Foundation:
UNFINISHED WALKOUT BASEMENT

Brick and stone, multiple gables, and a two-story tower decorate the exterior of this beautiful home. The sunken great room boasts a gas fireplace, twin doors to the deck, and a corner entertainment cabinet. Well-conceived, upgraded amenities elevate this home to the highest level of comfort and convenience. A second-floor balcony overlooks the foyer. The master bedroom suite with raised ceiling, whirlpool tub, shower enclosure, commode room, and large walk-in closet pamper the homeowner. Three additional bedrooms each enjoy private access to a bath, and spacious closets. A finished basement completes this spectacular home.

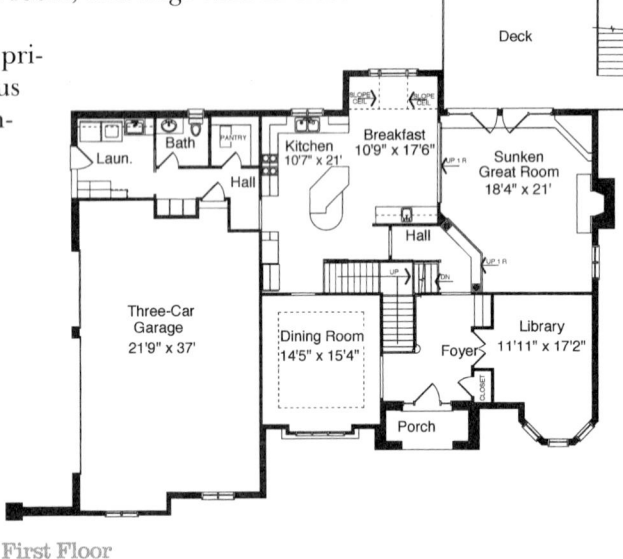

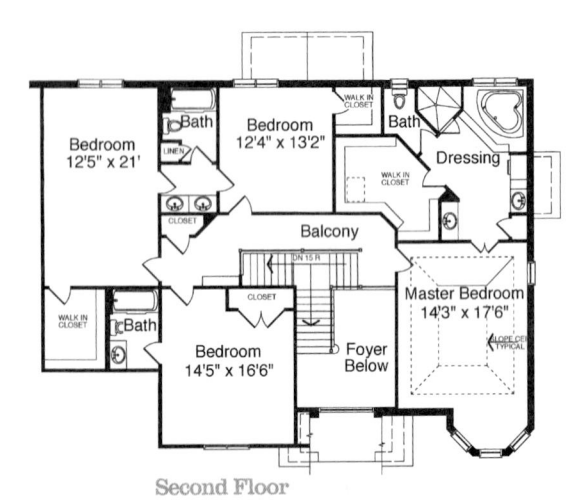

First Floor

Second Floor

New American Homes

325 New House Plans

Plan:
HPK2600319

Style:
NEW AMERICAN

First Floor:
2,483 SQ. FT.

Second Floor:
1,694 SQ. FT.

Total:
4,177 SQ. FT.

Bonus Space:
779 SQ. FT.

Bedrooms:
4

Bathrooms:
4 ½

Width:
89' - 4"

Depth:
62' - 5"

Foundation:
UNFINISHED BASEMENT

The simplicity of country living meets luxury in this modern design. A wealth of windows adds natural light to the open floor plan. Formal living spaces are undefined, lending a casual, welcoming feel. The first floor master suite enjoys privacy and convenient access to the nearby study. On the second level, three secondary bedrooms each boast a private, full bath. A spacious three-car garage completes this plan.

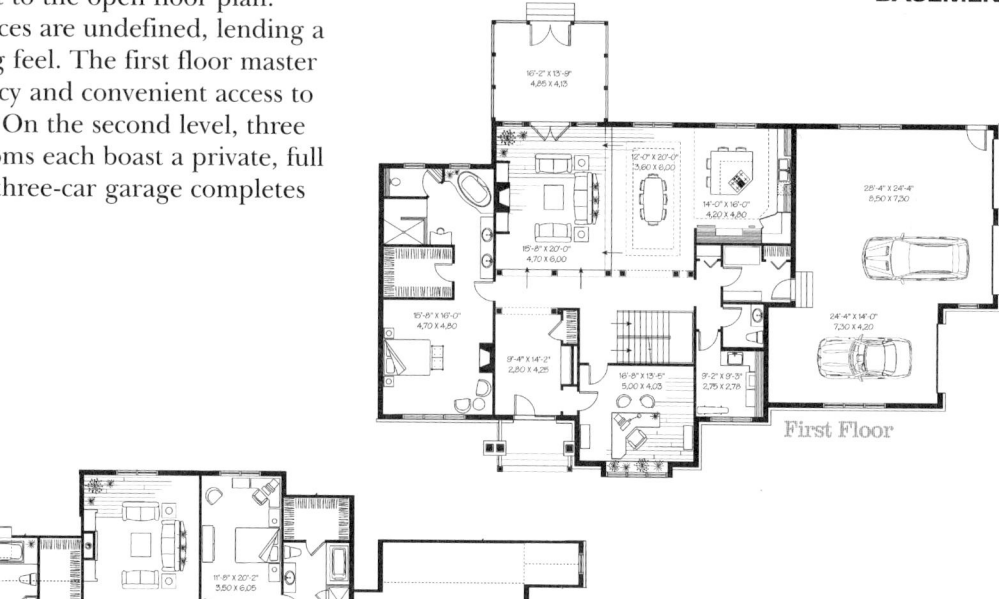

First Floor

Second Floor

ORDER BLUEPRINTS 24 HOURS, 7 DAYS A WEEK, AT 1-800-521-6797 OR EPLANS.COM

325 New American Homes
New House Plans

Plan:
HPK2600320

Style:
NEW AMERICAN

First Floor:
1,720 SQ. FT.

Second Floor:
1,740 SQ. FT.

Third Floor:
1,611 SQ. FT.

Total:
5,071 SQ. FT.

Bedrooms:
2

Bathrooms:
2 1/2 + 1/2

Width:
45' - 0"

Depth:
60' - 0"

Foundation:
UNFINISHED WALKOUT BASEMENT

This stunning three-story home combines eclectic European style with modern amenities, all in a footprint small enough for an urban lot. The first floor is designed for recreation; a deluxe media room with tiered seating lies across from a billiard or exercise room, with a built-in wine rack tucked into the vestibule between. Guests will enjoy ultimate privacy in the bedroom suite on this level. The upper floors are accessible by two stairways and an elevator, a priceless amenity for elderly or wheelchair-bound family members. On the second floor, a formal dining room is graced by a detailed ceiling, and the library sports a wall of custom built-ins. The kitchen features an oversized island, walk-in pantry, and an arched pass-through to the great room, which opens to a wide porch. Upstairs, the posh master suite includes a spa tub and oversized walk-in shower. A partially-covered terrace and pub with wet bar provide myriad opporunities to relax and enjoy views of the city.

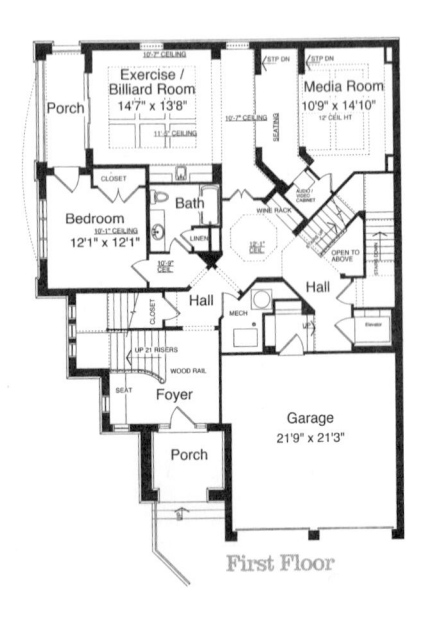

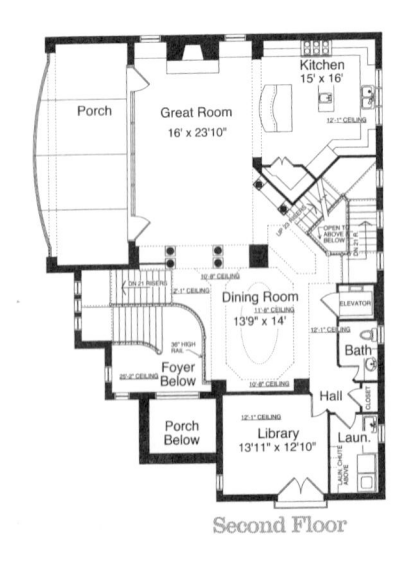

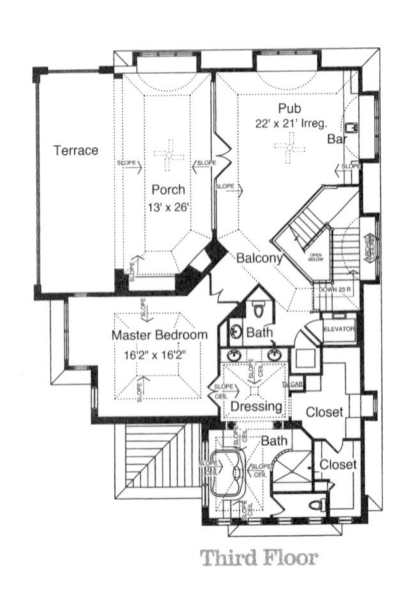

First Floor

Second Floor

Third Floor

ORDER BLUEPRINTS 24 HOURS, 7 DAYS A WEEK, AT 1-800-521-6797 OR EPLANS.COM

New American Homes

325 New House Plans

Plan:
HPK2600321

Style:
NEW AMERICAN

First Floor:
2,864 SQ. FT.

Second Floor:
2,284 SQ. FT.

Total:
5,148 SQ. FT.

Bedrooms:
5

Bathrooms:
5 ½ + ½

Width:
71' - 2"

Depth:
67' - 0"

Foundation:
CRAWLSPACE

Traditional elegance characterizes this home both inside and out, while the most up-to-date conveniences make it a joy to inhabit. A wide-open foyer offers the options of heading right into a sophisticated study or left into a formal dining room. Or, pass through the foyer to the arcaded gallery and into the family room, where three sets of French doors offer an invitation to the rear patio. At one end of the gallery lies a spacious guest suite; at the other is the gourmet kitchen, which serves as the hub of the casual living areas. A walk-in pantry and hobby room off the kitchen, along with a toy closet and a mudroom at the rear entrance, provide plenty of hiding places for household clutter. An upstairs laundry room is an additional convenience with its proximity to the master suite and three family bedrooms, each with its own private bath.

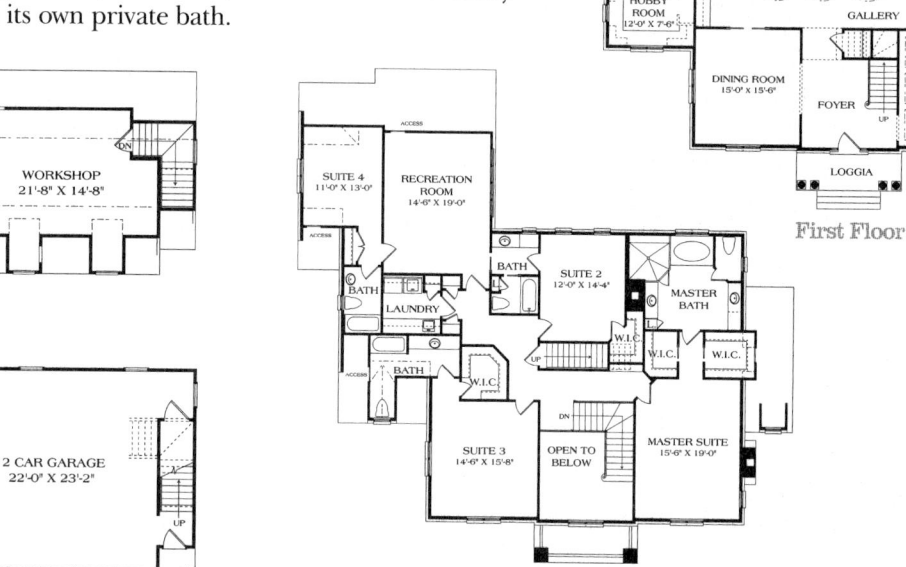

First Floor

Second Floor

ORDER BLUEPRINTS 24 HOURS, 7 DAYS A WEEK, AT 1-800-521-6797 OR EPLANS.COM

325 New American Homes
New House Plans

Plan:
HPK2600322

Style:
NEW AMERICAN

Main Level:
2,694 SQ. FT.

Upper Level:
1,041 SQ. FT.

Lower Level:
1,556 SQ. FT.

Total:
5,291 SQ. FT.

Bonus Space:
389 SQ. FT.

Bedrooms:
4

Bathrooms:
3 1/2

Width:
74' - 4"

Depth:
82' - 6"

Foundation:
FINISHED BASEMENT

Imagine the fantastic parties that could be hosted in this home, where every space flows into the next. Whether a formal feast in the columned dining room or a casual gathering for drinks and nibbles, the gourmet kitchen can handle it. Guests may congregate for music or games in the large room at the front of the home, spilling out through the French door onto the veranda. Or, move aside the furniture in the gathering room and turn it into a dance floor! A rear deck and an adjacent sunroom beckon guests in need of fresh air or a quieter spot. When the party's over, retreat to the master suite for a soak in the garden tub.

ORDER BLUEPRINTS 24 HOURS, 7 DAYS A WEEK, AT 1-800-521-6797 OR EPLANS.COM

New American Homes

325 New House Plans

Plan:
HPK2600323

Style:
NEW AMERICAN

Main Level:
1,450 SQ. FT.

Second Level:
1,450 SQ. FT.

Third Level:
730 SQ. FT.

Lower Level:
1,676 SQ. FT.

Total:
5,306 SQ. FT.

Bedrooms:
3

Bathrooms:
3 1/2 + 2 HALF-BATHS

Width:
38' - 0"

Depth:
82' - 0"

Foundation:
FINISHED WALKOUT BASEMENT

Beyond the understated entryway, a grand spiral staircase lifts the eyes up to the domed rotunda three floors above. Take the long way up or ride the built-in elevator from floor to floor. The master suite resides on the entry level, joined by a library, lounge, and conveniently located laundry room. Upstairs, an open great room, dining room, and kitchen find abundant space beneath an 11-foot ceiling. Outdoor living is offered at each level, but the third-floor terrace and media center are the home's main entertaining spaces. An outdoor fireplace allows year-round enjoyment.

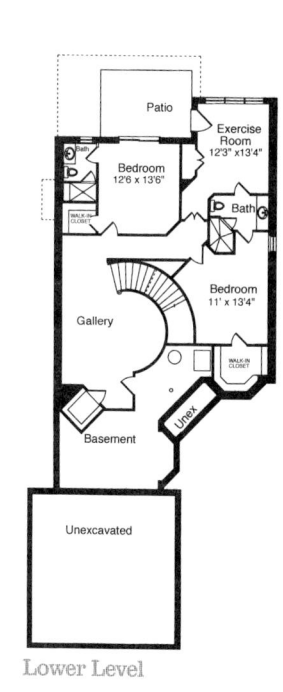

Lower Level

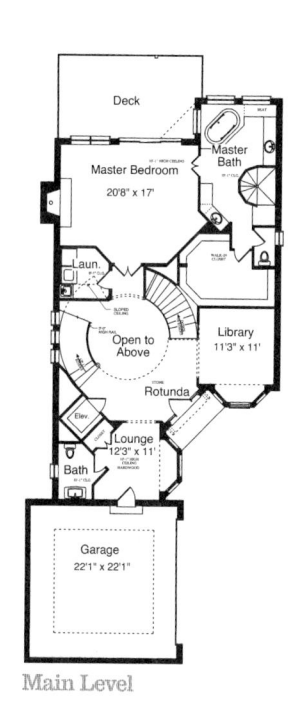

Main Level

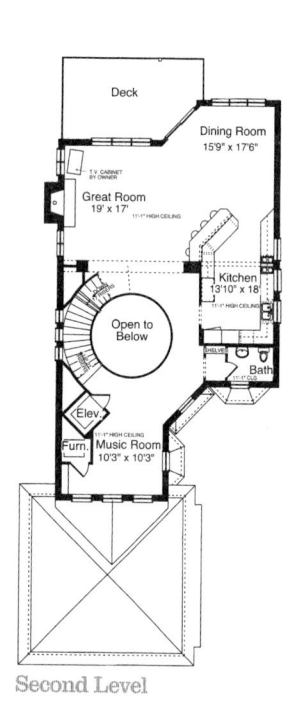

Second Level

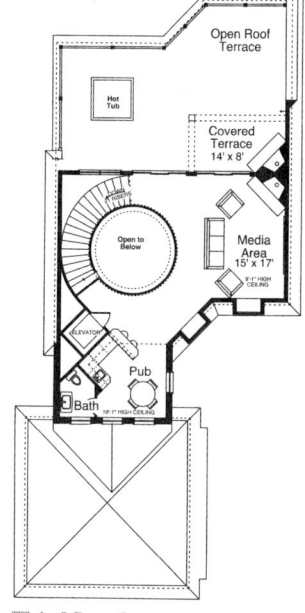

Third Level

ORDER BLUEPRINTS 24 HOURS, 7 DAYS A WEEK, AT 1-800-521-6797 OR EPLANS.COM

325 New American Homes
New House Plans

Plan:
HPK2600324

Style:
NEW AMERICAN

Main Level:
1,945 SQ. FT.

Second Level:
1,945 SQ. FT.

Third Level:
1,250 SQ. FT.

Lower Level:
1,010 SQ. FT.

Total:
6,150 SQ. FT.

Bedrooms:
3

Bathrooms:
2 1/2 + 2 HALF-BATHS

Width:
34' - 0"

Depth:
75' - 0"

Foundation:
FINISHED BASEMENT

For a night of relaxation or to host a celebration, turn to this versatile urban design. The top floor features a wide-open layout and adjoining outdoor spaces that facilitate large social events. The second floor is a responsive living space for comfortable family gatherings. A rounded dining counter provides a casual alternative to the formal dining area. At the front of the plan, two libraries and a comfortable great room provide quieter space. Luxurious sleeping quarters fill the first level. The master suite includes a generously proportioned divided walk-in closet and private access to the rear deck.

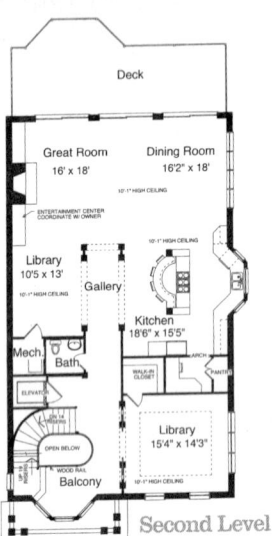

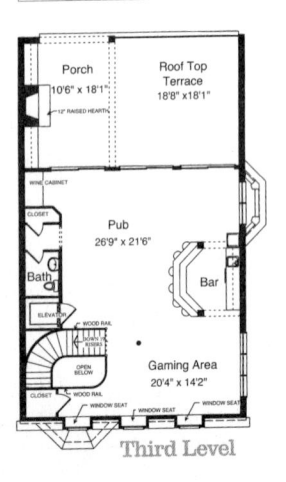

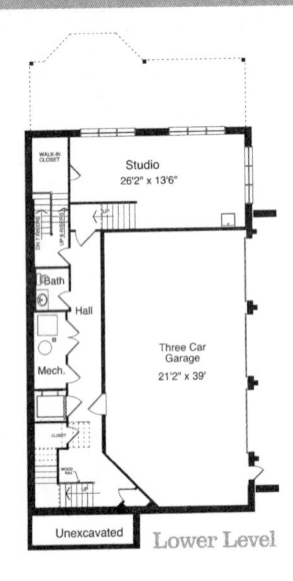

244 ORDER BLUEPRINTS 24 HOURS, 7 DAYS A WEEK, AT 1-800-521-6797 OR EPLANS.COM

New American Homes

325 New House Plans

Plan:
HPK2600325

The cottage-like exterior of this four-story home is decorated with a balcony, gables, and a scallop trim. The foyer features a beautiful curved staircase and a 20-foot ceiling. The master bedroom suite showcases a see-through fireplace and a master bath with spacious walk-in closet. The main level has open living and entertaining space. The gourmet kitchen features an oven cabinet, pantry, and island with sink and seating. The dining room is topped with a raised ceiling, and the great room and library boast backyard views and deck access. Each level has its own rear deck, but the top level offers a fourth bedroom, large entertainment area, and rooftop terrace with covered porch. An elevator offers easy access between floors.

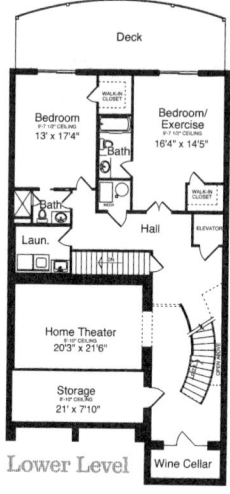

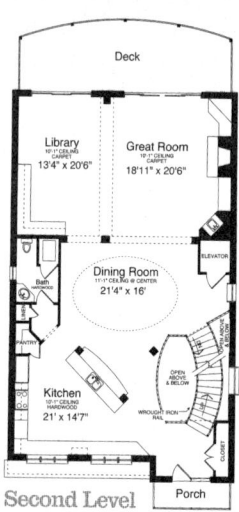

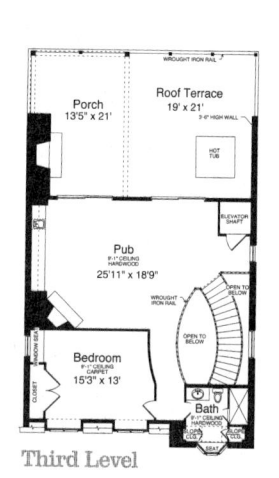

Style:
NEW AMERICAN
Main Level:
1,454 SQ. FT.
Second Level:
1,968 SQ. FT.
Third Level:
1,056 SQ. FT.
Lower Level:
2,024 SQ. FT.
Total:
6,502 SQ. FT.
Bedrooms:
4
Bathrooms:
4 1/2
Width:
34' - 0"
Depth:
74' - 0"
Foundation:
UNFINISHED BASEMENT

Lower Level

Second Level

Main Level

Third Level

Photos by Ron Kolb, Exposures Unlimited; digital editing by Joseph Bave, Cincinnati Aerial Photography. This home, as shown in photographs, may differ from the actual blueprints. For more detailed information, please check the floor plans carefully.

ORDER BLUEPRINTS 24 HOURS, 7 DAYS A WEEK, AT 1-800-521-6797 OR EPLANS.COM

House Plans— Super Sized

Hanley Wood has compiled the best-selling and most popular home plans into the most extensive home plan resources available. Now delivering more of everything you want—more plans, more styles and more choices—your dream home is right around the corner.

If you are looking to build a new home, look to Hanley Wood first. Pick up a copy today!

NEW!

325 New Home Plans for 06/07

The 5th volume in the popular "New Home Plans" series offers all new plans for 2006 and 2007. Every plan is guaranteed to be fresh and exciting, and updated with the most popular trends in residential architecture.

$10.95 U.S.
ISBN-10: 1-931131-65-1
ISBN-13: 978-1-931131-65-0
256 pages (32 full-color)

NEW!

The New Encyclopedia of Home Plans

Already in its 3rd edition, this best-selling volume offers over 600 house plans ranging from 1,000 to 6,300 sq. feet.

$14.95 U.S.
ISBN-10: 1-931131-48-1
528 full-color pages

1001 All Time Best Selling Home Plans

The largest compendium available, with complete blueprints for every style of home—from Tudor to Southwestern, Contemporary to Victorian, this book has it all.

$12.95 U.S.
ISBN-10: 1-881955-67-2
704 pages (32 full-color)

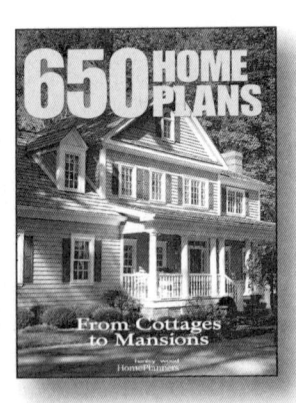

650 Home Plans

Tons of illustrations highlight 650 different plans covering all housing styles, from cottages to mansions.

$8.95 U.S.
ISBN-10: 1-931131-04-X
464 pages (16 full-color)

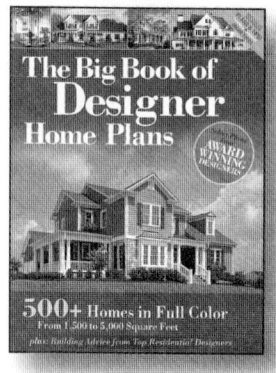

With over 2,500 home plans, finding the right new home to fit

- Your style
- Your budget
- Your life

Has never been easier.

New! Big Book of Designer Home Plans

This fabulous compilation profiles ten top designers and reveals dozens of their most popular home plans.

$12.95 U.S.
ISBN-10: 1-931131-68-6
ISBN-13: 978-1-931131-68-1
464 pages

The Big Book of Home Plans

Offering 500+ home designs in every style, plus expert tips to help readers make smart, cost-saving decisions and learn how to create the perfect garden.

$12.95 U.S.
ISBN-10: 1-931131-36-8
464 full-color pages

Hanley Wood Books
One Thomas Circle, NW | Suite 600 | Washington, DC 20005
877.447.5450 | www.hanleywoodbooks.com

hanley▲wood
SELECTION, CONVENIENCE, SERVICE!

With more than 50 years of experience in the industry and millions of blueprints sold, Hanley Wood is a trusted source of high-quality, high-value pre-drawn home plans.

Using pre-drawn home plans is a **reliable, cost-effective way** to build your dream home, and our vast selection of plans is second-to-none. The nation's finest designers craft these plans that builders know they can trust. Meanwhile, our friendly, knowledgeable customer service representatives can help you every step of the way.

WHAT YOU'LL GET WITH YOUR ORDER

The contents of each designer's blueprint package is unique, but all contain detailed, high-quality working drawings. You can expect to find the following standard elements in most sets of plans:

1. FRONT PERSPECTIVE
This artist's sketch of the exterior of the house gives you an idea of how the house will look when built and landscaped.

2. FOUNDATION AND BASEMENT PLANS
This sheet shows the foundation layout including concrete walls, footings, pads, posts, beams, bearing walls, and foundation notes. If the home features a basement, the first-floor framing details may also be included on this plan. If your plan features slab construction rather than a basement, the plan shows footings and details for a monolithic slab. This page, or another in the set, may include a sample plot plan for locating your house on a building site. Additional sheets focus on foundation cross-sections and other details.

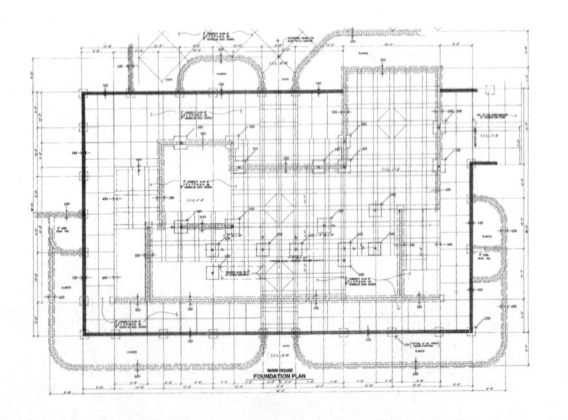

3. DETAILED FLOOR PLANS
These plans show the layout of each floor of the house. Rooms and interior spaces are carefully dimensioned, doors and windows located, and keys are given for cross-section details provided elsewhere in the plans.

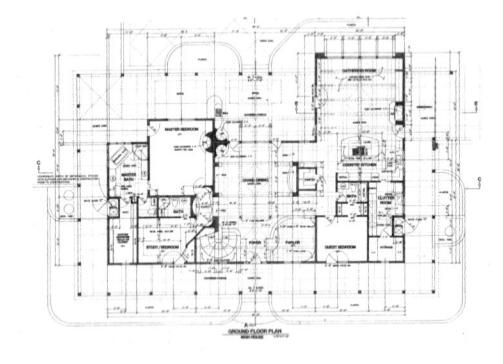

4. HOUSE AND DETAIL CROSS-SECTIONS
Large-scale views show sections or cutaways of the foundation, interior walls, exterior walls, floors, stairways, and roof details. Additional cross-sections may show important changes in floor, ceiling, or roof heights, or the relationship of one level to another. These sections show exactly how the various parts of the house fit together and are extremely valuable during construction. Additional sheets may include enlarged wall, floor, and roof construction details.

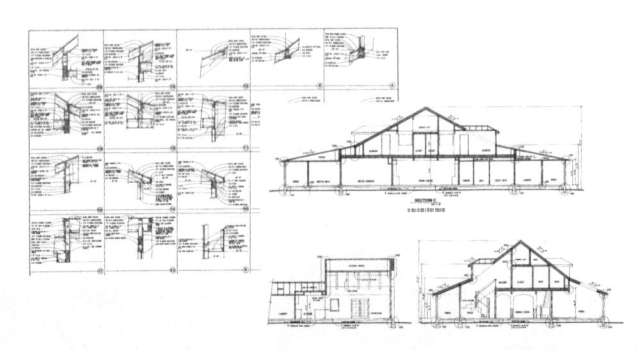

248   ORDER BLUEPRINTS 24 HOURS, 7 DAYS A WEEK, AT 1-800-521-6797 OR EPLANS.COM

5. ROOF AND FLOOR STRUCTURAL SUPPORTS

The roof and floor framing plans provide detail for these crucial elements of your home. Each includes floor joist, ceiling joist, rafter and roof joist size, spacing, direction, span, and specifications. Beam and window headers, along with necessary details for framing connections, stairways, skylights, or dormers are also included.

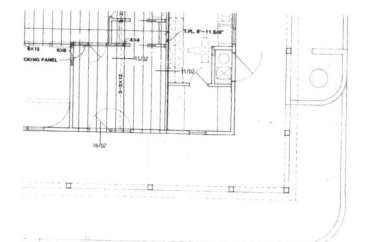

6. ELECTRICAL PLAN

The electrical plan offers a detailed outline of all wiring for your home, with notes for all lighting, outlets, switches, and circuits. A layout is provided for each level, as well as basements, garages, or other structures.

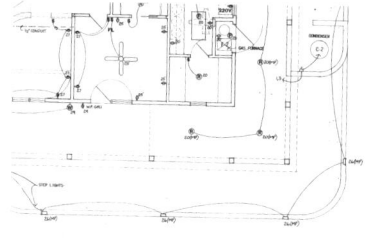

7. EXTERIOR ELEVATIONS

In addition to the front exterior, your blueprint set will include drawings of the rear and sides of your house as well. These drawings give notes on exterior materials and finishes. Particular attention is given to cornice detail, brick and stone accents, or other finish items that make your home unique.

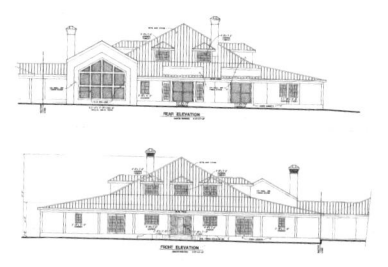

BEFORE YOU CALL

You are making a terrific decision to use a pre-drawn house plan—it is one you can make with confidence, knowing that your blueprints are crafted by national-award-winning certified residential designers and architects, and trusted by builders.

Once you've selected the plan you want—or even if you have questions along the way—our experienced customer service representatives are available 24 hours a day, seven days a week to help you navigate the home-building process. To help them provide you with even better service, please consider the following questions before you call:

■ Have you chosen or purchased your lot?
If so, please review the building setback requirements of your local building authority before you call. You don't need to have a lot before ordering plans, but if you own land already, please have the width and depth dimensions handy when you call.

■ Have you chosen a builder?
Involving your builder in the plan selection and evaluation process may be beneficial. Luckily, builders know they can have confidence with pre-drawn plans because they've been designed for livability, functionality, and typically are builder-proven at successful home sites across the country.

■ Do you need a construction loan?
Construction loans are unique because they involve determining the value of something that is not yet constructed. Several lenders offer convenient contstruction-to-permanent loans. It is important to choose a good lending partner—one who will help guide you through the application and appraisal process. Most will even help you evaluate your contractor to ensure reliability and credit worthiness. Our partnership with IndyMac Bank, a nationwide leader in construction loans, can help you save on your loan, if needed.

■ How many sets of plans do you need?
Building a home can typically require a number of sets of blueprints—one for yourself, two or three for the builder and subcontractors, two for the local building department, and one or more for your lender. For this reason, we offer 5- and 8-set plan packages, but your best value is the Reproducible Plan Package. Reproducible plans are accompanied by a license to make modifications and typically up to 12 duplicates of the plan so you have enough copies of the plan for everyone involved in the financing and construction of your home.

■ Do you want to make any changes to the plan?
We understand that it is difficult to find blueprints for a home that will meet all of your needs. That is why Hanley Wood is glad to offer plan Customization Services. We will work with you to design the modifications you'd like to see and to adjust your blueprint plans accordingly—anything from changing the foundation; adding square footage, redesigning baths, kitchens, or bedrooms; or most other modifications. This simple, cost-effective service saves you from hiring an outside architect to make alterations. Modifications may only be made to Reproducible Plan Packages that include the license to modify.

■ Do you have to make any changes to meet local building codes?
While all of our plans are drawn to meet national building codes at the time they were created, many areas required that plans be stamped by a local engineer to certify that they meet local building codes. Building codes are updated frequently and can vary by state, county, city, or municipality. Contact your local building inspection department, office of planning and zoning, or department of permits to determine how your local codes will affect your construction project. The best way to assure that you can make changes to your plan, if necessary, is to purchase a Reproducible Plan Package.

■ Has everyone—from family members to contractors—been involved in selecting the plan?
Building a new home is an exciting process, and using pre-drawn plans is a great way to realize your dreams. Make sure that everyone involved has had an opportunity to review the plan you've selected. While Hanley Wood is the only plans provider with an exchange policy, it's best to be sure all parties agree on your selection before you buy.

CALL TOLL-FREE 1-800-521-6797

Source Key
HPK26

DREAM HOME SOLUTIONS

CUSTOMIZE YOUR PLAN – HANLEY WOOD CUSTOMIZATION SERVICES

Creating custom home plans has never been easier and more directly accessible. Using state-of-the-art technology and top-performing architectural expertise, Hanley Wood delivers on a long-standing customer commitment to provide world-class home-plans and customization services. Our valued customers—professional home builders and individual home owners—appreciate the convenience and accessibility of this interactive, consultative service.

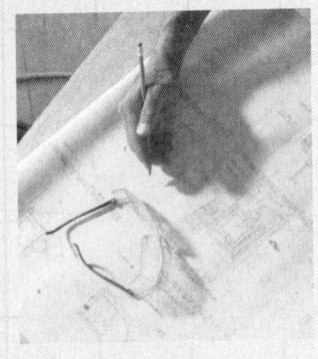

With the Hanley Wood Customization Service you can:
- Save valuable time by avoiding drawn-out and frequently repetitive face-to-face design meetings
- Communicate design and home-plan changes faster and more efficiently
- Speed-up project turn-around time
- Build on a budget without sacrificing quality
- Transform master home plans to suit your design needs and unique personal style

All of our design options and prices are impressively affordable. A detailed quote is available for a $50 consultation fee. Plan modification is an interactive service. Our skilled team of designers will guide you through the customization process from start to finish making recommendations, offering ideas, and determining the feasibility of your changes. This level of service is offered to ensure the final modified plan meets your expectations. If you use our service the $50 fee will be applied to the cost of the modifications.

You may purchase the customization consultation before or after purchasing a plan. In either case, it is necessary to purchase the Reproducible Plan Package and complete the accompanying license to modify the plan before we can begin customization.

Customization Consultation $50

TOOLS TO WORK WITH YOUR BUILDER

Two Reverse Options For Your Convenience – Mirror and Right-Reading Reverse (as available)
Mirror reverse plans simply flip the design 180 degrees—keep in mind, the text will also be flipped. For a minimal fee you can have one or all of your plans shipped mirror reverse, although we recommend having at least one regular set handy. Right-reading reverse plans show the design flipped 180 degrees but the text reads normally. When you choose this option, we ship each set of purchased blueprints in this format.

Mirror Reverse Fee (indicate the number of sets when ordering)....$55
Right Reading Reverse Fee (all sets are reversed).................$175

A Shopping List Exclusively for Your Home – Materials List
A customized Materials List helps you plan and estimate the cost of your new home, outlining the quantity, type, and size of materials needed to build your house (with the exception of mechanical system items). Included are framing lumber, windows and doors, kitchen and bath cabinetry, rough and finished hardware, and much more.

Materials List...$85 each
Additional Materials Lists (at original time of purchase only)..$20 each

Plan Your Home-Building Process – Specification Outline
Work with your builder on this step-by-step chronicle of 166 stages or items crucial to the building process. It provides a comprehensive review of the construction process and helps you choose materials.
Specification Outline..$10 each

Get Accurate Cost Estimates for Your Home – Quote One® Cost Reports
The Summary Cost Report, the first element in the Quote One® package, breaks down the cost of your home into various categories based on building materials, labor, and installation, and includes three grades of construction: Budget, Standard, and Custom. Make even more informed decisions about your project with the second element of our package, the Material Cost Report. The material and installation cost is shown for each of more than 1,000 line items provided in the standard-grade Materials List, which is included with this tool. Additional space is included for estimates from contractors and subcontractors, such as for mechanical materials, which are not included in our packages.

Quote One® Summary Cost Report...............................$35
Quote One® Detailed Material Cost Report.....................$140*
*Detailed material cost report includes the Materials List

Learn the Basics of Building – Electrical, Plumbing, Mechanical, Construction Detail Sheets
If you want to know more about building techniques—and deal more confidently with your subcontractors—we offer four useful detail sheets. These sheets provide non-plan-specific general information, but are excellent tools that will add to your understanding of Plumbing Details, Electrical Details, Construction Details, and Mechanical Details.

Electrical Detail Sheet..$14.95
Plumbing Detail Sheet...$14.95
Mechanical Detail Sheet.......................................$14.95
Construction Detail Sheet.....................................$14.95

SUPER VALUE SETS:
Buy any 2: $26.95; Buy any 3: $34.95; Buy All 4: $39.95

Best Value

ORDER BLUEPRINTS 24 HOURS, 7 DAYS A WEEK, AT 1-800-521-6797 OR EPLANS.COM

DREAM HOME SOLUTIONS

MAKE YOUR HOME TECH-READY – HOME AUTOMATION UPGRADE

Building a new home provides a unique opportunity to wire it with a plan for future needs. A Home Automation-Ready (HA-Ready) home contains the wiring substructure of tomorrow's connected home. It means that every room—from the front porch to the backyard, and from the attic to the basement—is wired for security, lighting, telecommunications, climate control, home computer networking, whole-house audio, home theater, shade control, video surveillance, entry access control, and yes, video gaming electronic solutions.

Along with the conveniences HA-Ready homes provide, they also have a higher resale value. The Consumer Electronics Association (CEA), in conjunction with the Custom Electronic Design and Installation Association (CEDIA), have developed a TechHome™ Rating system that quantifies the value of HA-Ready homes. The rating system is gaining widespread recognition in the real estate industry.

Developed by CEDIA-certified installers, our Home Automation Upgrade package includes everything you need to work with an installer during the construction of your home. It provides a short explanation of the various subsystems, a wiring floor plan for each level of your home, a detailed materials list with estimated costs, and a list of CEDIA-certified installers in your local area.
Home Automation Upgrade $250

GET YOUR HOME PLANS PAID FOR!

IndyMac Bank, in partnership with Hanley Wood, will reimburse you up to $1,000 toward the cost of your home plans simply by financing the construction of your new home with IndyMac Bank Home Construction Lending.

IndyMac's construction and permanent loan is a one-time close loan, meaning that one application—and one set of closing fees—provides all the financing you need.

Apply today at www.indymacbank.com, call toll free at 1-800-847-6138, or ask a Hanley Wood customer service representative for details.

DESIGN YOUR HOME – INTERIOR AND EXTERIOR FINISHING TOUCHES

Be Your Own Interior Designer! – Home Furniture Planner
Effectively plan the space in your home using our Hands-On Home Furniture Planner. It's fun and easy—no more moving heavy pieces of furniture to see how the room will go together. The kit includes reusable peel-and-stick furniture templates that fit on a 12"x18" laminated layout board—enough space to lay out every room in your house.
Home Furniture Planning Kit $15.95

Enjoy the Outdoors! – Deck Plans
Many of our homes have a corresponding deck plan, sold separately, which includes a Deck Plan Frontal Sheet, Deck Framing and Floor Plans, Deck Elevations, and a Deck Materials List. A Standard Deck Details Package, also available, provides all the how-to information necessary for building any deck. Get both the Deck Plan and the Standard Deck Details Package for one low price in our Complete Deck Building Package. See the price tier chart below and call for deck plan availability.
Deck Details (only) $14.95
Deck Building Package . . . . Plan price + $14.95

Create a Professionally Designed Landscape – Landscape Plans
Many of our homes have a front-yard Landscape Plan that is complementary in design to the house plan. These comprehensive Landscape Blueprint Packages include a Frontal Sheet, Plan View, Regionalized Plant & Materials List, a sheet on Planting and Maintaining Your Landscape, Zone Maps, and a Plant Size and Description Guide. Each set of blueprints is a full 18" x 24" with clear, complete instructions in easy-to-read type. Our Landscape Plans are available with a Plant & Materials List adapted by horticultural experts to eight regions of the country. Please specify your region when ordering your plan—see region map below. Call for more information about landscape plan availability and applicable regions.

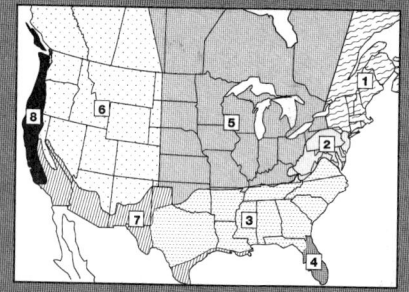

LANDSCAPE & DECK PRICE SCHEDULE

PRICE TIERS	1-SET STUDY PACKAGE	5-SET BUILDING PACKAGE	8-SET BUILDING PACKAGE	1-SET REPRODUCIBLE*
P1	$25	$55	$95	$145
P2	$45	$75	$115	$165
P3	$75	$105	$145	$195
P4	$105	$135	$175	$225
P5	$175	$205	$305	$405
P6	$215	$245	$345	$445

PRICES SUBJECT TO CHANGE   * REQUIRES A FAX NUMBER

ORDER BLUEPRINTS 24 HOURS, 7 DAYS A WEEK, AT 1-800-521-6797 OR EPLANS.COM

BEFORE YOU ORDER

TERMS & CONDITIONS

OUR 90-DAY EXCHANGE POLICY

Hanley Wood is committed to ensuring your satisfaction with your blueprint order, which is why we offer a 90-day exchange policy. With the exception of Reproducible Plan Package orders, we will exchange your entire first order for an equal or greater number of blueprints from our plan collection within 90 days of the original order. The entire content of your original order must be returned before an exchange will be processed. Please call our customer service department at 1-888-690-1116 for your return authorization number and shipping instructions. If the returned blueprints look used, redlined, or copied, we will not honor your exchange. Fees for exchanging your blueprints are as follows: 20% of the amount of the original order, plus the difference in cost if exchanging for a design in a higher price bracket or less the difference in cost if exchanging for a design in a lower price bracket. (Because they can be copied, Reproducible blueprints are not exchangeable or refundable.) Please call for current postage and handling prices. Shipping and handling charges are not refundable.

ARCHITECTURAL AND ENGINEERING SEALS

Some cities and states now require that a licensed architect or engineer review and "seal" a blueprint, or officially approve it, prior to construction. Prior to application for a building permit or the start of actual construction, we strongly advise that you consult your local building official who can tell you if such a review is required.

LOCAL BUILDING CODES AND ZONING REQUIREMENTS

Each plan was designed to meet or exceed the requirements of a nationally recognized model building code in effect at the time and place the plan was drawn. Typically plans designed after the year 2000 conform to the International Residential Building Code (IRC 2000 or 2003). The IRC is comprised of portions of the three major codes below. Plans drawn before 2000 conform to one of the three recognized building codes in effect at the time: Building Officials and Code Administrators (BOCA) International, Inc.; the Southern Building Code Congress International, (SBCCI) Inc.; the International Conference of Building Officials (ICBO); or the Council of American Building Officials (CABO).

Because of the great differences in geography and climate throughout the United States and Canada, each state, county, and municipality has its own building codes, zone requirements, ordinances, and building regulations. Your plan may need to be modified to comply with local requirements. In addition, you may need to obtain permits or inspections from local governments before and in the course of construction. We authorize the use of the blueprints on the express condition that you consult a local licensed architect or engineer of your choice prior to beginning construction and strictly comply with all local building codes, zoning requirements, and other applicable laws, regulations, ordinances, and requirements. Notice: Plans for homes to be built in Nevada must be redrawn by a Nevada-registered professional. Consult your local building official for more information on this subject.

TERMS AND CONDITIONS

These designs are protected under the terms of United States Copyright Law and may not be copied or reproduced in any way, by any means, unless you have purchased a Reproducible Plan Package and signed the accompanying license to modify and copy the plan, which clearly indicates your right to modify, copy, or reproduce. We authorize the use of your chosen design as an aid in the construction of ONE (1) single- or multifamily home only. You may not use this design to build a second dwelling or multiple dwellings without purchasing another blueprint or blueprints or paying additional design fees. Multi-use fees vary by designer—please call one of experienced sales representatives for a quote.

DISCLAIMER

The designers we work with have put substantial care and effort into the creation of their blueprints. However, because we cannot provide on-site consultation, supervision, and control over actual construction, and because of the great variance in local building requirements, building practices, and soil, seismic, weather, and other conditions, WE MAKE NO WARRANTY OF ANY KIND, EXPRESS OR IMPLIED, WITH RESPECT TO THE CONTENT OR USE OF THE BLUEPRINTS, INCLUDING BUT NOT LIMITED TO ANY WARRANTY OF MERCHANTABILITY OR OF FITNESS FOR A PARTICULAR PURPOSE. ITEMS, PRICES, TERMS, AND CONDITIONS ARE SUBJECT TO CHANGE WITHOUT NOTICE.

CALL TOLL-FREE 1-800-521-6797 OR VISIT EPLANS.COM

BEFORE YOU ORDER

IMPORTANT COPYRIGHT NOTICE
From the Council of Publishing Home Designers

Blueprints for residential construction (or working drawings, as they are often called in the industry) are copyrighted intellectual property, protected under the terms of the United States Copyright Law and, therefore, cannot be copied legally for use in building. The following are some guidelines to help you get what you need to build your home, without violating copyright law:

1. HOME PLANS ARE COPYRIGHTED
Just like books, movies, and songs, home plans receive protection under the federal copyright laws. The copyright laws prevent anyone, other than the copyright owner, from reproducing, modifying, or reusing the plans or design without permission of the copyright owner.

2. DO NOT COPY DESIGNS OR FLOOR PLANS FROM ANY PUBLICATION, ELECTRONIC MEDIA, OR EXISTING HOME
It is illegal to copy, change, or redraw home designs found in a plan book, CDROM or on the Internet. The right to modify plans is one of the exclusive rights of copyright. It is also illegal to copy or redraw a constructed home that is protected by copyright, even if you have never seen the plans for the home. If you find a plan or home that you like, you must purchase a set of plans from an authorized source. The plans may not be lent, given away, or sold by the purchaser.

3. DO NOT USE PLANS TO BUILD MORE THAN ONE HOUSE
The original purchaser of house plans is typically licensed to build a single home from the plans. Building more than one home from the plans without permission is an infringement of the home designer's copyright. The purchase of a multiple-set package of plans is for the construction of a single home only. The purchase of additional sets of plans does not grant the right to construct more than one home.

4. HOUSE PLANS IN THE FORM OF BLUEPRINTS OR BLACKLINES CANNOT BE COPIED OR REPRODUCED
Plans, blueprints, or blacklines, unless they are reproducibles, cannot be copied or reproduced without prior written consent of the copyright owner. Copy shops and blueprinters are prohibited from making copies of these plans without the copyright release letter you receive with reproducible plans.

5. HOUSE PLANS IN THE FORM OF BLUEPRINTS OR BLACKLINES CANNOT BE REDRAWN
Plans cannot be modified or redrawn without first obtaining the copyright owner's permission. With your purchase of plans, you are licensed to make non-structural changes by "red-lining" the purchased plans. If you need to make structural changes or need to redraw the plans for any reason, you must purchase a reproducible set of plans (see topic 6) which includes a license to modify the plans. Blueprints do not come with a license to make structural changes or to redraw the plans. You may not reuse or sell the modified design.

6. REPRODUCIBILE HOME PLANS
Reproducible plans (for example sepias, mylars, CAD files, electronic files, and vellums) come with a license to make modifications to the plans. Once modified, the plans can be taken to a local copy shop or blueprinter to make up to 10 or 12 copies of the plans to use in the construction of a single home. Only one home can be constructed from any single purchased set of reproducible plans either in original form or as modified. The license to modify and copy must be completed and returned before the plan will be shipped.

7. MODIFIED DESIGNS CANNOT BE REUSED
Even if you are licensed to make modifications to a copyrighted design, the modified design is not free from the original designer's copyright. The sale or reuse of the modified design is prohibited. Also, be aware that any modification to plans relieves the original designer from liability for design defects and voids all warranties expressed or implied.

8. WHO IS RESPONSIBLE FOR COPYRIGHT INFRINGEMENT?
Any party who participates in a copyright violation may be responsible including the purchaser, designers, architects, engineers, drafters, homeowners, builders, contractors, sub-contractors, copy shops, blueprinters, developers, and real estate agencies. It does not matter whether or not the individual knows that a violation is being committed. Ignorance of the law is not a valid defense.

9. PLEASE RESPECT HOME DESIGN COPYRIGHTS
In the event of any suspected violation of a copyright, or if there is any uncertainty about the plans purchased, the publisher, architect, designer, or the Council of Publishing Home Designers (www.cphd.org) should be contacted before proceeding. Awards are sometimes offered for information about home design copyright infringement.

10. PENALTIES FOR INFRINGEMENT
Penalties for violating a copyright may be severe. The responsible parties are required to pay actual damages caused by the infringement (which may be substantial), plus any profits made by the infringer commissions to include all profits from the sale of any home built from an infringing design. The copyright law also allows for the recovery of statutory damages, which may be as high as $150,000 for each infringement. Finally, the infringer may be required to pay legal fees which often exceed the damages.

PLAN #	PRICE TIER	PAGE	MATERIALS LIST	QUOTE ONE®	DECK	DECK PRICE	LANDSCAPE	LANDSCAPE PRICE	REGIONS
HPK2600002	SQ1	8							
HPK2600003	A3	12	Y						
HPK2600004	C1	13							
HPK2600005	C1	14	Y						
HPK2600006	A4	15							
HPK2600007	SQ5	16							
HPK2600008	C3	17							
HPK2600009	C1	18	Y						
HPK2600010	C1	19	Y						
HPK2600011	C4	20							
HPK2600012	C4	21							
HPK2600013	C2	22	Y						
HPK2600014	L1	23							
HPK2600015	L1	24							
HPK2600016	L1	25							
HPK2600017	SQ1	26	Y						
HPK2600018	L1	27							
HPK2600019	SQ7	28							
HPK2600020	L3	29							
HPK2600021	SQ1	30	Y						
HPK2600022	SQ7	31							
HPK2600023	SQ1	32	Y						
HPK2600024	A2	33	Y						
HPK2600025	A2	33	Y						
HPK2600026	A4	34							
HPK2600027	A2	34							
HPK2600028	A3	35	Y						
HPK2600029	A3	35	Y						
HPK2600030	A3	36							
HPK2600031	A3	36	Y						
HPK2600032	A3	37							
HPK2600033	A3	37	Y						
HPK2600034	C1	38	Y						
HPK2600035	A3	39							
HPK2600036	C1	40	Y						
HPK2600037	A4	41	Y						
HPK2600038	A4	42							
HPK2600039	A4	43							
HPK2600040	A3	44	Y						
HPK2600041	A3	44	Y						
HPK2600042	C1	45	Y						
HPK2600043	A3	46							
HPK2600044	A4	47							
HPK2600045	C1	48	Y						
HPK2600046	A3	48							
HPK2600047	A3	49	Y						
HPK2600048	A3	49	Y						
HPK2600049	A3	50							
HPK2600050	A4	51	Y						
HPK2600051	A3	52							
HPK2600052	A4	53	Y						
HPK2600053	A4	54	Y						
HPK2600054	A4	55							
HPK2600055	C1	56							
HPK2600056	A4	57	Y						

PLAN #	PRICE TIER	PAGE	MATERIALS LIST	QUOTE ONE®	DECK	DECK PRICE	LANDSCAPE	LANDSCAPE PRICE	REGIONS
HPK2600057	C1	58							
HPK2600058	A4	59	Y						
HPK2600059	A4	60							
HPK2600060	C1	61							
HPK2600061	A4	61							
HPK2600062	C1	62	Y						
HPK2600063	A4	63							
HPK2600064	A4	64							
HPK2600065	A4	65							
HPK2600066	A4	65							
HPK2600067	C1	66							
HPK2600068	C1	67							
HPK2600069	C1	68	Y						
HPK2600070	C1	69							
HPK2600071	A4	70							
HPK2600072	C1	71	Y						
HPK2600073	C1	71							
HPK2600074	C1	72							
HPK2600075	C1	72							
HPK2600076	A4	73	Y						
HPK2600077	C1	74							
HPK2600078	C1	74							
HPK2600079	C1	75	Y						
HPK2600080	C1	75							
HPK2600081	C1	76	Y						
HPK2600082	C1	76	Y						
HPK2600083	C3	77							
HPK2600084	C3	77							
HPK2600085	L1	78	Y						
HPK2600086	L1	78	Y						
HPK2600087	L2	79							
HPK2600088	L3	79							
HPK2600089	L3	80							
HPK2600090	L4	81							
HPK2600091	L4	82							
HPK2600092	L4	83							
HPK2600093	A2	84							
HPK2600094	A3	85	Y						
HPK2600095	A2	85							
HPK2600096	A4	86	Y						
HPK2600097	A3	87	Y						
HPK2600098	A4	87	Y						
HPK2600099	A3	88	Y						
HPK2600100	A4	89	Y						
HPK2600101	C2	90	Y						
HPK2600102	A3	90	Y						
HPK2600103	A3	91	Y						
HPK2600104	A3	92	Y						
HPK2600105	A3	92	Y						
HPK2600106	A4	93	Y						
HPK2600107	A3	94	Y						
HPK2600108	C2	94							
HPK2600109	A4	95							
HPK2600110	A4	96	Y						
HPK2600111	A4	97	Y						

ORDER BLUEPRINTS 24 HOURS, 7 DAYS A WEEK, AT 1-800-521-6797 OR EPLANS.COM

PLAN #	PRICE TIER	PAGE	MATERIALS LIST	QUOTE ONE®	DECK	DECK PRICE	LANDSCAPE	LANDSCAPE PRICE	REGIONS
HPK2600112	A4	98	Y						
HPK2600113	A4	99	Y						
HPK2600114	A4	99	Y						
HPK2600115	A4	100	Y						
HPK2600116	C1	100							
HPK2600117	A4	101							
HPK2600118	C1	102	Y						
HPK2600119	A4	103	Y						
HPK2600120	A4	103	Y						
HPK2600121	A4	104	Y						
HPK2600122	A4	104	Y						
HPK2600123	C2	105							
HPK2600124	C1	106	Y						
HPK2600125	A4	107	Y						
HPK2600126	C1	107	Y						
HPK2600127	C1	108							
HPK2600128	C1	109							
HPK2600129	C1	110							
HPK2600130	C1	111	Y						
HPK2600131	A4	111	Y						
HPK2600132	C4	112							
HPK2600133	C1	112	Y						
HPK2600134	A4	113							
HPK2600135	C1	113	Y						
HPK2600136	A4	114	Y						
HPK2600137	C1	114							
HPK2600138	C1	115							
HPK2600139	C1	116							
HPK2600140	C4	116							
HPK2600141	C2	117							
HPK2600142	C1	118	Y						
HPK2600143	C4	119							
HPK2600144	C4	119							
HPK2600145	L1	120							
HPK2600146	C4	121							
HPK2600147	C4	121							
HPK2600148	C2	122	Y						
HPK2600149	C2	122	Y						
HPK2600150	C3	123	Y						
HPK2600151	C3	124							
HPK2600152	C2	124	Y						
HPK2600153	C3	125	Y						
HPK2600154	C4	126							
HPK2600155	C4	126							
HPK2600156	C3	127	Y						
HPK2600157	C4	128							
HPK2600158	C3	128							
HPK2600159	L1	129							
HPK2600160	L2	129							
HPK2600161	L4	130							
HPK2600162	A2	131	Y						
HPK2600163	A3	132							
HPK2600164	A2	132	Y						
HPK2600165	A3	133							
HPK2600166	A3	134							

PLAN #	PRICE TIER	PAGE	MATERIALS LIST	QUOTE ONE®	DECK	DECK PRICE	LANDSCAPE	LANDSCAPE PRICE	REGIONS
HPK2600167	C1	135							
HPK2600168	A3	136							
HPK2600169	A3	137	Y						
HPK2600170	A3	137	Y						
HPK2600171	A3	138	Y						
HPK2600172	A3	138	Y						
HPK2600173	A3	139							
HPK2600174	A4	140	Y						
HPK2600175	A4	140							
HPK2600176	C2	141							
HPK2600177	A4	142	Y						
HPK2600178	C1	143	Y						
HPK2600179	A4	144	Y						
HPK2600180	C3	145							
HPK2600181	A4	146	Y						
HPK2600182	C2	147							
HPK2600183	A4	148	Y						
HPK2600184	A4	148							
HPK2600185	A4	149	Y						
HPK2600186	C1	149	Y						
HPK2600187	C1	150	Y						
HPK2600188	C1	150	Y						
HPK2600189	C2	151							
HPK2600190	C1	152	Y						
HPK2600191	C3	152							
HPK2600192	C1	153	Y						
HPK2600193	C2	154							
HPK2600194	C1	154	Y						
HPK2600195	C1	155	Y						
HPK2600196	C1	156							
HPK2600197	C2	157							
HPK2600198	C2	158							
HPK2600199	C1	159							
HPK2600200	C4	159							
HPK2600201	C2	160	Y						
HPK2600202	C4	160							
HPK2600203	C2	161	Y						
HPK2600204	C3	162	Y						
HPK2600205	C2	163							
HPK2600206	L2	163							
HPK2600207	L3	164							
HPK2600208	SQ1	165							
HPK2600209	A4	166							
HPK2600210	A3	167	Y						
HPK2600211	A3	167	Y						
HPK2600212	A4	168							
HPK2600213	A4	168							
HPK2600214	A3	169	Y						
HPK2600215	C2	169							
HPK2600216	C2	170							
HPK2600217	A4	170	Y						
HPK2600218	C4	171							
HPK2600219	C2	171							
HPK2600220	C3	172							
HPK2600221	A4	173	Y						

ORDER BLUEPRINTS 24 HOURS, 7 DAYS A WEEK, AT 1-800-521-6797 OR EPLANS.COM

PLAN #	PRICE TIER	PAGE	MATERIALS LIST	QUOTE ONE®	DECK	DECK PRICE	LANDSCAPE	LANDSCAPE PRICE	REGIONS
HPK2600222	C2	174							
HPK2600223	C1	174							
HPK2600224	C2	175	Y						
HPK2600225	C4	176							
HPK2600226	C4	176							
HPK2600227	C2	177							
HPK2600228	C3	177							
HPK2600229	C1	178	Y						
HPK2600230	C2	178	Y						
HPK2600231	C2	179							
HPK2600232	C2	180							
HPK2600233	C4	181							
HPK2600234	C2	181							
HPK2600235	C4	182							
HPK2600236	C2	182							
HPK2600237	C4	183							
HPK2600238	L2	183							
HPK2600239	C4	184							
HPK2600240	L1	185							
HPK2600241	C3	186							
HPK2600242	L1	187							
HPK2600243	L1	187							
HPK2600244	L1	188							
HPK2600245	L1	189							
HPK2600246	C4	189							
HPK2600247	L1	190							
HPK2600248	L1	190							
HPK2600249	SQ7	191							
HPK2600250	SQ5	192							
HPK2600251	C4	193							
HPK2600252	SQ7	194							
HPK2600253	C4	195							
HPK2600254	L2	196							
HPK2600255	L2	197							
HPK2600256	L3	197							
HPK2600257	L2	198							
HPK2600258	L3	198							
HPK2600001	SQ7	199							
HPK2600259	L2	199							
HPK2600260	L4	200	Y						
HPK2600261	L4	200							
HPK2600262	L4	201							
HPK2600263	L4	201							
HPK2600264	SQ1	202							
HPK2600265	L4	202							
HPK2600266	L4	203							
HPK2600267	L4	204							
HPK2600268	SQ1	205							
HPK2600269	L4	206							
HPK2600270	L4	207							
HPK2600271	L4	208							
HPK2600272	L4	209							
HPK2600273	L4	210							
HPK2600274	A4	211	Y						
HPK2600275	C1	212	Y						

PLAN #	PRICE TIER	PAGE	MATERIALS LIST	QUOTE ONE®	DECK	DECK PRICE	LANDSCAPE	LANDSCAPE PRICE	REGIONS
HPK2600276	A4	212	Y						
HPK2600277	A3	213	Y						
HPK2600278	C1	213	Y						
HPK2600279	C1	214	Y						
HPK2600280	A3	214	Y						
HPK2600281	A3	215							
HPK2600282	C2	216							
HPK2600283	A3	216							
HPK2600284	A4	217	Y						
HPK2600285	C1	217	Y						
HPK2600286	A4	218							
HPK2600287	A4	218	Y						
HPK2600288	A4	219							
HPK2600289	C1	220							
HPK2600290	C2	221	Y						
HPK2600291	A4	221							
HPK2600292	A4	222	Y						
HPK2600293	C2	222							
HPK2600294	C1	223	Y						
HPK2600295	C1	223	Y						
HPK2600296	A4	224	Y						
HPK2600297	C1	225	Y						
HPK2600298	C1	226	Y						
HPK2600299	A4	226	Y						
HPK2600300	C4	227							
HPK2600301	C3	227							
HPK2600302	C2	228	Y						
HPK2600303	C2	228	Y						
HPK2600304	C4	229							
HPK2600305	C2	229	Y						
HPK2600306	C2	230	Y						
HPK2600307	C3	230	Y						
HPK2600308	C3	231							
HPK2600309	C1	231	Y						
HPK2600310	C1	232							
HPK2600311	C1	232							
HPK2600312	C4	233	Y						
HPK2600313	C4	233	Y						
HPK2600314	C2	234							
HPK2600315	L1	235	Y						
HPK2600316	C3	236	Y						
HPK2600317	C4	237							
HPK2600318	C3	238	Y						
HPK2600319	L2	239	Y						
HPK2600320	L1	240							
HPK2600321	L3	241							
HPK2600322	L3	242							
HPK2600323	L1	243							
HPK2600324	L2	244							
HPK2600325	L2	245							

ORDER BLUEPRINTS 24 HOURS, 7 DAYS A WEEK, AT 1-800-521-6797 OR EPLANS.COM